John Rose Greene Hassard

Life of the Most Reverend John Hughes, D.D.

first archbishop of New York - with extracts from his private correspondence

John Rose Greene Hassard

Life of the Most Reverend John Hughes, D.D.
first archbishop of New York - with extracts from his private correspondence

ISBN/EAN: 9783741173172

Manufactured in Europe, USA, Canada, Australia, Japa

Cover: Foto ©Lupo / pixelio.de

Manufactured and distributed by brebook publishing software
(www.brebook.com)

John Rose Greene Hassard

Life of the Most Reverend John Hughes, D.D.

LIFE

OF

THE MOST REVEREND

JOHN HUGHES, D. D.,

FIRST ARCHBISHOP OF NEW YORK.

WITH

EXTRACTS FROM HIS PRIVATE CORRESPONDENCE.

BY
JOHN R. G. HASSARD.

NEW YORK:
D. APPLETON AND COMPANY,
443 & 445 BROADWAY.
1866.

PREFACE.

In writing this book, I have tried to use the archbishop's own language, as I have found it in his private letters, whenever it could be made to tell his history or illustrate his character. I believe that a man's correspondence almost always gives a better picture of his mind than the most elaborate biographical analysis; and that whatever may occasionally be sacrificed of completeness by following the plan which I have chosen, is counterbalanced by the unimpeachable accuracy of the portrait.

I have described pretty fully the public controversies and labors of Archbishop Hughes, because his life was essentially a public one, and his polemical discussions were, for long periods, almost the whole sum of his daily occupation. Few men ever lived who were so nearly the same in the closet and in the busy world. I have not forgotten, however, that personal traits are what the readers of a biography look for with the greatest interest, and I have told all that I could learn of the archbishop's private habits and peculiarities. My information on these subjects has been derived from his surviving relatives and the friends with whom he lived on terms of closest intimacy. Most of the other particulars, both of his public and his domestic history, I have gathered from his private papers, to which I have been allowed access through the kindness of the Very Rev. William Starrs, vicar-general of the diocese of New York, and the Rev. Francis McNeirny, secretary and chaplain both to Dr. Hughes and to his successor Dr. McCloskey. Of the privilege thus granted me I have availed myself to the fullest extent, and such value as my book may have is mainly derived from this source.

It affords me pleasure to express my deep gratitude to the reverend gentlemen above mentioned for their invaluable assistance. It would be too long a task to make acknowledgments in this place to all who have aided me, but I cannot forbear to mention my indebtedness to the Most Rev. Archbishops McCloskey and Purcell; the Right Rev. Bishop Bayley (who has laid me under obligations which I can hardly overstate); the Rev. Mr. Preston, chancellor of the diocese of New York; the Very Rev. Thomas Heyden, of Bedford, Pennsylvania; the Rev. Dr. McCaffrey, president of Mount St. Mary's College; the Honorable Joseph R. Chandler, and Mr. M. A. Frenaye, of Philadelphia; the late Peter A. Hargous, of New York; and especially Mr. Michael Hughes, the archbishop's brother, and his sisters Mrs. William Rodrigue, and Mother Angela, of the Sisters of Charity.

FORDHAM HEIGHTS, September 25th, 1865.

CONTENTS.

CHAPTER I. 1797–1816.

Ancestry—Parentage—Birth—School days—Lessons in gardening—Early feelings about the disabilities of the Irish Catholics—The family resolve to emigrate . . . . Page 9

CHAPTER II. 1816–1820.

Arrival in America—The family at Chambersburg—John works for a gardener in Baltimore—At Emmitsburg—Received at Mount St. Mary's College . 19

CHAPTER III.

Sketch of Mr. Dubois—Foundation of Mount St. Mary's College—Sketch of Mr. Bruté 26

CHAPTER IV. 1820–1826.

College Life—First published Controversy; Letter to Mr. Bruté—Newspaper Poetry 33

CHAPTER V. 1825–1827.

Ordination as Deacon—Letter from Father Hurley—Journey with Bishop Conwell—"The Cuckoo Sermon"—Answer to Nine Objections—Ordained Priest—At St. Augustine's Church—At Bedford—Called to Philadelphia—Troubles of St. Mary's Church 46

CHAPTER VI. 1827–1829.

Intimate relations with Mr. Bruté—Reply to Dr. Bedell—Letters to Mr. Heyden—Establishment of a Tract Society—Andrew Dunn—Converts at St. Joseph's—Death of Mr. Lynch—Letter to Thomas Heyden, Sr. . . . 72

CHAPTER VII. 1829–1830.

St. John's Orphan Asylum—Catholic Emancipation—Controversy with Dr. Delancey—Mr. Hughes recommended for Bishop—Letters to his sister and Mr. Purcell—Rev. F. P. Kenrick appointed Bishop of Philadelphia—Miscellaneous Correspondence—Letters to *The Protestant* . . 89

CHAPTER VIII. 1830-1832.

Journey with Bishop Kenrick—More trouble at St. Mary's—Foundation of St. John's church—Death of Mr. Hughes's mother—Letters to Ellen Hughes and Mr. Purcell—Article on the will of Stephen Girard—Dedication of the new church and removal from St. Joseph's—Mr. Hughes at the synod—Fourth of July celebration at St. John's—Letters to Ellen Hughes . Page 110

CHAPTER IX. 1832-1835.

First Controversy with Breckinridge—Establishment of *The Catholic Herald*—Review of Bishop Onderdonk on the Rule of Faith—Father Hughes's position in Philadelphia—Nominated Bishop of Cincinnati—Letters to Sister Angela, Mr. Bruté, and Bishop Purcell—Letters to Rev. Henry M. Mason on Infallibility 134

CHAPTER X. 1835.

Oral Discussion with Breckinridge—Death of Mr. Mayne—Proposal to publish a Catholic Annual—Affairs of St. John's—Contemplated visit to Mexico. 153

CHAPTER XI. 1835-1838.

Project for translating Bishop Kenrick to Pittsburg—Mr. Hughes nominated his successor in Philadelphia—Correspondence with Bishops Kenrick, England, and Purcell—Death of Mr. Hughes's father—Letter on the use of the Bible as a school-book—Mr. Hughes appointed coadjutor to the Bishop of New York—Letter from Bishop Dubois—Letter to Bishop Purcell—Letter from Bishop England—Consecration 166

CHAPTER XII. 1838-1839.

Condition of the diocese—Health of Bishop Dubois—Foundation of a seminary at Lafargeville—Trouble with the trustees of the Cathedral—Their final overthrow—Bishop Hughes appointed administrator—Foundation of St. John's college 186

CHAPTER XIII. 1839-1840.

Voyage to Europe—Letter from Rome—Letter to the Leopoldine Society—Interview with O'Connell—Letters from Dublin 206

CHAPTER XIV. 1840-1842.

The School question—Injudicious efforts of the Catholics to obtain a portion of the school fund—The Bishop enters the lists—Petition to the Board of Aldermen—Debate before the Common Council—Memorial to the Legislature—The Secretary of State proposes a plan of school reform—The Bishop supports it—The question postponed—Candidates for the Legislature pledged to oppose any change—The Bishop advises the Catholics to nominate an independent ticket—Mr. Maclay's school-bill passed—The Bishop's house attacked by a mob—Establishment of Catholic schools—St. John's College opened, 223

CHAPTER XV. 1841-1844.

The Church Debt Association—First diocesan synod—Controversy with David Hale—Difficulty with the trustees of St. Louis' church, Buffalo—Rules for the administration of churches without trustees—Visitation of the diocese—Visit to Europe for the purpose of raising money—Odd mistake of an English officer—Incident at Liverpool—The *Emprunt Catholique de New York*—Lectures in New York—Bishop McCloskey appointed coadjutor . . Page 254

CHAPTER XVI. 1844-1846.

The Native American movement—Riots in Philadelphia—Excitement in New York—The Bishop ready to fight for his churches—Letters to Mayor Harper and Colonel Stone—Third voyage to Europe—Reflections on the state of society abroad—Visit to his birthplace—Sisters of Mercy and Jesuits brought to New York—The diocese divided—The Bishop refuses a diplomatic mission to Mexico—Intimacy with statesmen 273

CHAPTER XVII. 1846.

Division of the Sisterhood of Charity—Correspondence with the Very Rev. Mr. Deluol 289

CHAPTER XVIII. 1847-1850.

Young Ireland—The Irish insurrection of 1848—The Bishop's speech at Vauxhall Garden—Letter to Mr. Emmet—Letters against Mr. McGee—The temporal power of the Pope 303

CHAPTER XIX. 1847-1848.

Sermon before Congress—Letters to Kirwan—Multitude of calls upon the Bishop's time—Letters of religious advice—Government of the clergy—Characteristics of his preaching—Personal appearance—Manners—Pride in his humble origin—His friends—Social qualities—Failing health—Daily occupations—Disorderly habits—Fondness for children—Kindness of heart—Generosity—Ignorance of money affairs—Income—Residence . . 316

CHAPTER XX. 1850-1852.

Dr. Hughes appointed an Archbishop—Visit to Rome—Project for making him a Cardinal—Letter on Toleration—Letter about Kossuth—Lecture on the Catholic Chapter in the History of the United States—Letter from Clement C. Biddle—Catholicism and the American people—The Auxiliary Church Building Association—Settlement of the affairs of St. Peter's church, and end of the trustee system 337

CHAPTER XXI. 1853-1855.

Arrival of a Papal Nuncio in the United States—Project of a permanent nunciature at Washington—Voyage to Cuba—Letter on the Madiai case—Controversy with Gen. Cass—Letters of Philo Veritas—First provincial council of New York—Visit to Rome—Definition of the dogma of the Immaculate Conception—Controversy with Senator Brooks—Letters to Terence Donnelly and Cassius M. Clay on political alliances 356

CHAPTER XXII. 1855-1858.

Visit to Newfoundland—Lectures in Baltimore and Pittsburg—Essay on the Catholic Press—Attack upon the Archbishop in the *Times*—Report to the Propaganda on his administration of the diocese—Curious scene at the Tabernacle—Letter on the death of an old friend—Letter on the consecration of two bishops—Alleged rivalship between the sees of New York and Baltimore—Primacy of honor conferred upon Baltimore at the request of Archbishop Hughes—Letter to Bishop McNally . . . Page 380

CHAPTER XXIII. 1858–1859.

The Archbishop talks about resigning—Applies for a coadjutor—Foundation of the American College in Rome—Letter on Ecclesiastical Education—The new St. Patrick's Cathedral begun—The Atlantic Telegraph—Death of Archbishop Walsh—Miscellaneous letters 398

CHAPTER XXIV. 1859–1860.

Letters on the Roman question—Provincial council—Address to the Pope—Pastoral letter on the Pope's temporal power—Its reception in Rome—Trip to Florida—Apostasy of Dr. Forbes—Proposed mass meeting to express sympathy with the Holy Father—Letter to Bishop Dupanloup—Collection for the Pope—The Archbishop and the City Inspector—Sermon at Chapel Hill University, North Carolina—Letters to the Rev. Bernard Smith . . 415

CHAPTER XXV. 1861.

Sentiments on the slavery question—Review of Brownson on Emancipation—Letter to Mr. Seward—Letters to Southern bishops—Advice to the Government on the conduct of the war—Interview with a Southern lady—Letter from President Lincoln 434

CHAPTER XXVI. 1861–1862.

The Archbishop accepts from the Government a special mission to Europe—Letters to Cardinal Barnabo—Correspondence with Mr. Seward—Arrival in Paris—Interview with the Emperor and Empress—Embarrassment of the American minister—Goes to Rome—Letters to Mr. Seward—Letters to his sisters—Canonization of the martyrs of Japan—Visit to Ireland—Sermon at the laying of the corner-stone of the Irish University—Speeches in Dublin—Enthusiastic reception—Address from Irish Nationalists—Letters to the Mayor of Cork, the Archbishop of Dublin, and the Bishop of Clogher—Return home—Visit to Mr. Seward—Promotion suggested to the Holy See . . . 443

CHAPTER XXVII. 1862–1863.

Sermon on the war—Displeasure of the Archbishop's Southern friends—Controversy with *The Catholic Mirror*—Letters to Father Smith—New seminary at Troy—Declining health—Daily life—Meeting for the relief of Ireland—Last sermon—Death of Archbishop Kenrick—Draft riot in New York—The Archbishop's speech to the mob—Last sickness—Death—Funeral—Conclusion 487

LIFE
OF
ARCHBISHOP HUGHES.

CHAPTER I.

1797–1816.

Ancestry—Parentage—Birth—School days—Lessons in gardening—Early feelings about the disabilities of the Irish Catholics—The family resolve to emigrate.

THE ancestors of John Hughes, for at least three or four generations back, were small farmers in the province of Ulster, in the north of Ireland. They seem to have held a respectable position in the world, but nothing more. The subject of this book was the first of his family who rose to eminence.

It is not easy to determine of what race the Hugheses came. Their name is the Anglicized form both of the Welsh Ap Hugh and of the Milesian O'Haodha, O'h'Aodha, or O'Haedha (*Aodh* being the equivalent of Hugh), pronounced in Munster O'Hay, in Connaught O'Hee, and in Ulster O'Hugh. The Welsh Ap Hughs who came into Ireland about the 17th century very soon changed their name to Hughes; the Milesian O'Haodhas, in order to avoid the persecution to which the Irish Catholics were subjected by their English conquerors, shortly afterward did the same. Some of the Welsh families, being Protestants, became rich and powerful, and still hold an honorable place among the landed gentry of the kingdom. The Milesians were Catholics, and consequently never rose above the middle ranks of life. Except in a few special cases, it is impossible to distinguish the collateral branches of these Welsh families from the descendants of the old Irish septs. The difference of faith is our only guide; but we could not trust this guide unless we could be sure that no Welsh Hughes had ever become a Catholic, and no Irish Hughes ever turned Protestant.

The Milesian O'Haodhas, or O'Hughs, were very numerous in Ulster before their Welsh namesakes began to come into Ireland. The patent-rolls of King James I. contain frequent mention of O'Hughs in that province, who are described as "yeomen." Inasmuch as the ancestors of John Hughes, so far as they can be traced, were Catholics and natives of Ulster, it is fair to presume that he descended from this genuine Irish stock. In the following letter to the late Dr. John O'Donovan, a learned antiquary of Dublin, he tells what little he knew about his own origin:

NEW YORK, *April* 10, 1860.

DEAR SIR:

I received your letter and pamphlet on Irish antiquities some time ago. I was much delighted with both. And now I would beg leave to call your attention to a subject in regard to which I have but faint traditional knowledge. It is in reference to the origin of my family.

What I know, or what I have heard, would amount to this: that my family, on the father's side, derived its origin from the sept of the Hugheses, in the county of Armagh; on the mother's side it would be from the sept of the McKennas in the barony of Truagh, in the county Monaghan. The tradition to me has been that my grandfather and one brother of his left county Armagh when young men. The one settled in Truagh in the county Monaghan, where he married a McKenna; and the other settled near Athlone, but of him, or of his descendants, I have not been able to learn any thing.

My father was born in the townland of Cavan-Moutray, in the

county Monaghan. He had four sisters and one brother, all of whom were respectably married and had families. My father's only brother took an equal share in a rented farm in the townland of Annaloghan, in the county Tyrone, where I was born.

I think it would be difficult, even with all your superior knowledge, to thread out the origin or history of such a family as mine. Still, if such a thing is possible, I know no one in Ireland, or out of it, besides yourself, that can accomplish it.

Several years ago I wrote to a relative of mine inquiring in regard to this subject. He did not know much more than myself. But there is our family tombstone, under which I remember, when a child, to have witnessed the interment of a sister and brother. In the cemetery where the tombstone stands, a Protestant church is now erected on the site of the former Catholic church, in the parish of Errigal Truagh. He sent me a crude sketch of what might be construed into a coat of arms of our family, as taken from the tombstone. I attached no importance to it at the time; but as well as I recollect, it represented a three-masted rude vessel without sails, three stars, and a half-moon in the crescent. This combination seemed to me a very unclassical symbol of heraldry; but this was all that was sent. Unfortunately, even this has been lost or mislaid.

Many years ago, in one of those contests which it has been my duty to enter into, I had occasion to refer to my family and birthplace. This was at a time when a quasi-Orange party called Native Americans were springing up in the country, and when I was held forth by them as the head conspirator against the rights of Protestants and the liberties of the United States. On that occasion I had to write much, or at least enough to repel their assaults. It is quite probable that I fell into a great blunder, by intimating the possibility that the sept of the Hugheses had been among the rascals from Wales who accompanied Strongbow at the first British invasion of Ireland.* This impression had been fixed upon my mind by

---

* "My early ancestors were from Wales, and very possibly shared with Strongbow and his companions in the plunder which rewarded the first successful invaders of lovely but unfortunate Ireland. Of course, from the time of their conversion from paganism, they were Catholics. You, sir, who must be acquainted with the melancholy annals of religious intolerance in Ireland, may remember that, when a traitor to his country, and for what I know to his creed also, McMahon, Prince of Monaghan, wished to make his peace with the Irish

what, at the time, I supposed to be historical authority. I thought it was stated so in Curry's *Review of the Civil Wars of Ireland*. I have since looked over that work, and cannot find any thing to bear me out. I am now inclined to think that the statement, or at least the ground on which my speculation was founded, was in a little work of poetry (or rather in one of its notes) called *The Emerald Isle*, said to have been written by Counsellor Phillips, in which it was stated that when Queen Elizabeth was extending her sway over the whole island, and when it was necessary for chieftains to make their peace with Her Majesty's government by some overt act of treason to their country, the prince or chieftain of Monaghan, named McMahon, stipulated with the agents of government that in case his own possessions might be spared he would root out the sept of the Hugheses. The fact that under such circumstances the Hugheses deserved to be rooted out, would prove that they loved their country and would not betray it. This is the only thing in their annals of which I could be particularly proud—if it is indeed true.

I have not been able to claim that the Hugheses were of Milesian origin. I cannot trace their name Hughes in the original language or early history of the country. McHugh appears to me quite another name—a translation from the original language of the Irish people.

* * * * * * *

Writing to the Bishop of Clogher on the same subject, he says:

My ambition would be to have the name traced up to something like a Milesian origin. Dr. O'Donovan lays down a test of distinction between the Irish and the Welsh Hugheses, turning on the fact, as alleged by him, that the Welsh of that name are not Catholics, whilst the real, original Hugheses were Catholics and nothing else. This does not appear to me a certain indication; for it is

government of Queen Elizabeth, the traitor's work which he ventured to accomplish was 'to root out the whole sept of the Hugheses.' He did not, however, succeed in destroying them, although he 'rooted them out;' proving, as a moral for future times, that persecution cannot always accomplish what it proposes."— *Letter to Mayor Harper of New York, 1844.*

very well known that the Welsh and the English, during centuries before Protestantism of any kind had been introduced, were in the habit of selling dependents—sometimes their own children—as slaves, into Ireland; and one of your own national councils, just before the advent of Strongbow, passed a decree for their emancipation. This occurred in purely Catholic times.

Toward the close of the eighteenth century, Patrick Hughes, the father of the archbishop, removed from Monaghan to Tyrone, and with his brother Michael rented a small farm at Annaloghan, one mile from the little market town of Augher on the Blackwater. This spot is near the boundary between Tyrone on the north and Monaghan and Armagh on the south, and only four or five miles from Cavan-Moutray, where Patrick Hughes was born. He married Margaret McKenna, the daughter of a family which, like his own, was not rich, but generally respected;* and had by her seven children: first, Michael; second, Patrick; third, John; fourth, Mary; fifth, Peter; sixth, Ellen; and seventh, Margaret. Of these, Mary and Peter died in childhood, and Patrick in 1855; Michael, Ellen, and Margaret are still living.

Patrick Hughes was a plain, well-to-do man; steady, upright, industrious, somewhat better educated than men of his class usually were at that day, fond of reading, fearing God, loving his Church, and strict in performing all the obligations of his religion. He held carefully aloof from the lawless factions which distracted Ireland so fearfully during the early part of the present century; and his reputation as a quiet, peaceable man, who minded his own business, seems on one occasion to have been the means of saving his son John's life. The archbishop relates that when he was about fifteen years of age, he fell into the hands of a band of Orangemen. "Five bayonets," he says, "were pointed at

* There seems to have been a strong affinity between the McKennas and the Hugheses. The archbishop's father and grandfather, and one of his first cousins, each married a McKenna.

my breast; but when I told my name, the men let me go, saying, 'All right; we know his father.'"

The wife of Patrick Hughes was devout, patient, and sweet-tempered; and, by the testimony of all who knew her, displayed, in the humble station of a farmer's wife, a good share of that refinement which is sometimes thought to come only from gentle blood. When she gave an alms, she loved to give it through the hands of her little children. Both parents took the greatest pains to train their young family in piety, the love of truth, and a firm faith in the Catholic Church. They did not allow them to associate much with other children, because the neighbors of their own rank were nearly all Protestants; and it was partly for this reason that Mr. Hughes, when he began to thrive and to find his little farm too small for his stock, took a lease of another at Dernaved, where there was Catholic society. Dernaved, or the "upper farm," as it was called, was about three miles from Annaloghan, and only a mile and a half from Cavan-Moutray. It was a rough place, where there was much hard work to be done, with little hope of quick returns; but to be among people of his own faith, and to look down, as he could from a part of this farm, upon the spot where he was born, were considerations which, in his mind, outweighed this objection. A part of the family accordingly removed to the upper farm, while a part remained in the homestead at Annaloghan. The father, we may suppose, went from the one to the other as his presence was called for. Like many other Irish farmers at that day, he gave up a large part of his land to the cultivation of flax, and devoted the winters to the domestic manufacture of linen. A number of women were employed in spinning and weaving, and the children assisted in this as well as the labors of the farm and household.

John, the subject of this book, was born at Annaloghan on the feast of St. John the Baptist, June 24, 1797. When he was confirmed he took the name of Joseph, in addition to that of John, and in after-life he often signed himself John

J. Hughes. From his earliest childhood he showed an inclination toward the Church, which his parents were glad to encourage. As soon as he was old enough, he was sent, with his elder brothers, to a day school at Augher, and was thence in due course of time transferred to a grammar school at Auchnacloy, two or three miles from his home. At this period of his life he is described as a hard student and a favorite with his masters, but for all that a jolly playfellow, and a leader in all boyish sports. Whatever he did, was done in earnest. He acquired a very good rudimentary English education, but probably learned nothing of Greek, and very little, if any thing, of Latin.

In the mean time things at home had fared ill. Large sums of money were sunk in the upper farm; there fell a bad year for the linen trade; perhaps, too, short crops, or some other of the many misfortunes to which farmers are subject, contributed to bring distress into the household. Mr. Hughes became seriously embarrassed, and unable to bear the cost of John's schooling any longer. It was not unusual in Ireland for neighbors to make up a purse for the support of poor candidates for the priesthood; but father and son were both too proud to accept such aid as this, and after an anxious family council John was taken away from school, to bear a part with his father and brothers in the work of the farm. He was not required to give up his whole time to manual labor. Mr. Hughes felt that to bid him wholly put aside his books, after he had made so much progress in them, would be little less than cruel; and probably he cherished the hope that better times would come, and he might yet live to see his son standing at the altar. So the lad was permitted to study at home as much as he could, and expected to perform only light duties about the place; to take care of his father's horses, or perhaps to work in the fields for a few hours at a time during the busiest seasons.

When he left school, John was nearly eighteen years of age. He did not accept his new life very cheerfully, and the whole of the first day at home he passed in tears. "Many a time," said he in later life to one of his friends, "have I thrown down my rake in the meadow, and kneeling behind a hay-rick, begged of God and the Blessed Virgin to let me become a priest." If not cheerful, he was at least obedient, and probably did as well at the plough as any man can do at a business which he does not love. It was easy to see, however, that he would never make a farmer; and his father casting about for some other calling to put him to, placed him, without knowing it, once more in the way of becoming a priest.

Near Dernaved is Favor Royal, the seat of the great county family of the Moutrays. Mr. Moutray's head gardener was an acquaintance of the Hugheses, and at the father's request he consented to teach John horticulture, reckoning the young man's labor an equivalent for the trouble of instructing him. John little suspected that his knowledge of this pursuit was to open for him in a distant country the door to that ecclesiastical career upon which he had set his heart.

He was living at this time at Dernaved, and besides his daily work at Favor Royal he used still to do light tasks about the farm. One would suppose that little time was left him for study, but he stole from the night a few hours for his books, reviewed all that he had learned at school, and taught himself much more. He had little or no love of learning for its own sake. He was a man of action rather than a man of study, and probably under no circumstances would he have become a profound scholar. But a certain amount of scholarship was a necessary qualification for the priesthood; and having made up his mind to be a priest in spite of all obstacles, he shrank from no labor which brought him nearer to his object. The pertinacity which distinguished him as a man was already a marked feature in his character.

The better times for which Patrick Hughes had looked were slow in coming. He was now passing the middle period of life, without a prospect of improving his condition, or of giving a proper education to his younger children. He began to turn his thoughts toward the usual resource of his countrymen in such circumstances—emigration to America. Other causes besides poverty impelled him to this step. He was a man of a proud and independent spirit, and he chafed under the restrictions which the laws of England still imposed upon the members of his faith. He reflected that in the political scale a Catholic farmer ranked below a Protestant beggar. The evil, perhaps, was no worse now than it had been for years, but it seemed harder to bear when the weight of poverty was added to it. A circumstance connected with the burial of his little daughter Mary must have increased the bitterness of his feelings with respect to the disabilities of Catholics. Fifty years afterward the archbishop shed tears when he told how the funeral procession halted at the gate of the graveyard, while the priest, whom the penal laws forbade to enter, blessed a handful of earth, and gave it to a layman to throw upon the coffin after it had been lowered into the grave. We may well suppose that to none of the family was the idea of emigration more agreeable than to John. Young as he was, he had thought deeply on the wrongs of the Catholics, and like his father he was not one to submit tamely to what he considered an injustice. In an unpublished letter to the editor of the Dublin *Freeman's Journal* (Dec. 11, 1861) he speaks of his early impressions on this subject as follows:

At the age of fifteen or sixteen, kind, but perhaps mistaken friends, made me acquainted with the state of affairs connected, not so much with my nativity, as with my baptism by a Roman Catholic priest.* Being of a pensive and reflective character of mind, the consequences of that baptism became painful. Of course, neither then nor now could I regret it in view of the civil degrada-

---

* As he elsewhere says: "The rights of my birth had been washed out by the rites of my baptism."

tion which, by the laws at that period, had been but too cunningly provided for the intruders into this world if they should incur the rite of religion to which I had been subjected. . . . I had been told of the circumstances that would attend my life if I should remain under the hereditary degradation of my ancestors. I could not, then or now, exchange my religious privileges and hopes as a Catholic for all the power, all the honors, all the glory (as it is sometimes called), or all the wealth of the British empire. They told me, when I was a boy, that for five days I was on a social and civil equality with the most favored subjects of the British empire. These five days would be the inverval between my birth and my baptism. The early information of this fact might have been withheld; but at all events it left a sting in my memory which it has cost me much to remove.

So, no doubt to the great joy of at least one member of his family, Patrick Hughes, accompanied by his second son, set sail for America in 1816, on a tour of observation. John, having learned in the course of a year all that Mr. Moutray's gardener could teach him, was again at home, and divided with Michael the care of the farms during his father's absence.

CHAPTER II.

1816–1820.

Arrival in America—The family at Chambersburg—John works for a gardener in Baltimore—At Emmitsburg—Received at Mount St. Mary's College.

PATRICK HUGHES travelled over various parts of the United States, and, like many of his countrymen of that day, directed his attention especially to Pennsylvania. A few months were enough to strengthen his favorable impressions of the country. He passed a little while at Bedford, Pennsylvania, and afterward removed to Chambersburg, the capital of Franklin County, in the same State. He had not money enough to buy or stock a farm, but Chambersburg was a thriving place, and he need never want for work. He hired a house, and wrote to his wife and children to settle matters with their landlord and join him as soon as possible. In the mean time Michael and John had not been idle. The crops were in a promising state; but the landlord refused either to make any allowance for them and the improvements on the estate, or to forego the rent for the year that the lease had yet to run; his rule, he said, was "to get all he could out of a good tenant." Under these circumstances the mother resolved to remain with Michael and the two daughters for another year; but John was sent out to his father in charge of one of their neighbors, a tradesman named Dixon. This was in 1817, when he was twenty years old. "I was afloat," he writes, "on the ocean, looking for a home and a country in which no stigma of inferiority would be impressed on my brow, simply because I professed one creed or another."

He landed about midsummer at Baltimore, where his brother Patrick had obtained work. After a short visit to his father, he returned to that city, and entered the service of a gardener who had a plantation or nursery on the eastern shore of Maryland. It was now the busy season of the year, and the young man, whose first anxiety was to lay up enough money to enable him to continue his studies, resolved to do his best, in the hope of keeping his situation through the winter. "Through the summer and fall," said he many years afterward, "I worked with all my might; and I think the hardest blow I ever received in my life was being discharged by my employer at the approach of winter, with the simple announcement that 'he did not need my services any longer.'" Heavy of heart and empty of pocket, he went back to Chambersburg, and there for a year or more we find him laboring with his father, working in stone quarries, mending roads, digging in gardens—turning his hand, in fact, to almost any honest employment of which he was capable. In August, 1818, his mother and the rest of the family arrived from Ireland, and for a while the household was once more united at Chambersburg. Patrick in the course of time obtained a farm at Youngstown, Pennsylvania. Old Mr. Hughes never grew rich, though upon the whole he was prosperous. He kept a few horses and carts, occasionally took contracts, bought a few rods of ground in the village, built one or two small houses, and after some years became the owner of a house and plot of land on the outskirts of the town, to which, from its fancied resemblance to his home in Ireland, he gave the name of "the new Trough." In the midst of his prosperity his heart still turned toward his native land, and at one time he seriously contemplated another voyage across the Atlantic. "One thing," he wrote to one of his children, "yet sustains my old heart; it is the hope of seeing all our dear friends in old

Trough. The new Trough is an enchanting cage to look at, but an old bird cannot be petted." His hope was never realized. He lived long enough to see his son a priest, and died in 1837, at the age of seventy-seven, leaving to his children a little property in land. His wife died in 1831, aged sixty-four.

John, at the age of twenty-one, is described as a sedate, well-dressed, respectable-looking young man, self-possessed, of pleasing conversation and manners, quiet and reserved before strangers, but gay and witty with those that knew him; although a person who would strike you as one above his station, and destined to make his mark in the world. He could tell a good story, and sing a good song. On Sundays he used to sing in the village choir. Neither he nor the rest of the family ever looked upon Chambersburg as his home. He was there waiting, so to speak, for God to admit him into the ranks of the ministry.

Some thirty miles from Chambersburg, and a little way from the village of Emmitsburg,* is Mount St. Mary's Catholic college and theological seminary. John Hughes heard that poor students were sometimes admitted to this institution without pay, on the condition of making themselves useful in teaching the lower classes and performing such other duties as they may be fit for. He had no friend to introduce or recommend him, but we may be certain that he lost no time in asking for admission. His first application was unsuccessful; there was no vacancy. Nevertheless he was not discouraged. Every now and then he would ride over from Chambersburg on horseback, and try again. At last, in the latter part of 1818, or the beginning of the following year, that he might be ready to seize the first opening, and slip into the college before another should get before him, he set out for Emmitsburg in quest of work near the village. Naturally, the first house that he entered was the tavern.

---

* Emmitsburg is situated in Frederick County, Maryland, a mile or two from the Pennsylvania boundary, and about fifty miles from Baltimore.

A countryman, seeing that he was a stranger, drew him into conversation. It turned out that both came from the same part of Ireland, and any one who knows Irishmen will understand that almost as a matter of course John Hughes, as soon as this appeared, received an offer of his new acquaintance's services. Nor was it an empty offer. The man at once obtained employment for John in digging a mill-race, and ever after took great credit to himself for having "got Archbishop Hughes his first job of work in Emmitsburg." The mill-race done, John worked at a stone bridge over a little stream on the road from Emmitsburg to Tancytown, handling the pickaxe and shovel, lifting stone, and waiting on the masons. Humble as these occupations were, there was a certain dignity and refinement in his manners which gained for him a social consideration not generally accorded to a day-laborer. He boarded in the family of an Irish schoolmaster named Mullon, and associated chiefly with his host, with respectable Catholic tradesmen and other persons of the middle class, and with the parish priest, Mr. Cooper—the same gentleman to whose liberality Mrs. Seton was so deeply indebted in the foundation of the sisterhood of charity in the United States.*

* Samuel Cooper was a Virginian, and a Protestant by birth. He chose the sea for his profession, visited various parts of the world, and falling sick at Paris turned his attention for the first time to religion. The result of much reading and thought, and consultation with clergymen of his own creed, was his embracing the Catholic faith in Philadelphia in 1807. Being a man of fortune and well known in fashionable circles, his conversion produced no little sensation. The next year he entered St. Mary's Seminary at Baltimore with the intention of preparing himself for the priesthood; and becoming acquainted there with Mrs. Seton, then at the threshold of her great undertaking, he gave her eight thousand dollars, with which she founded the first house of her order at Emmitsburg. Ordained in the summer of 1818, he was pastor of Emmitsburg for about nine months, and afterward removed to South Carolina. He made a pilgrimage to the Holy Land, on his return from which he was employed in different situations in the dioceses of Baltimore and Philadelphia until 1832, when he went to France, and settled permanently at Bordeaux. He was there the instrument of converting many prominent persons, and enjoyed the friendship of Cardinal Cheverus, who died in his arms. By his liberality towards re-

In November, 1819, he went again to the college, and begged the president, the Rev. Mr. Dubois, to receive him in any capacity in which he could be useful. Mr. Dubois replied that he could not take him; the college was poor, and every situation in and about it was occupied—"except," he added, "the garden; we have a vacant place there."

"I am not a professed gardener," replied John Hughes; "but I know something of gardening. I can do all that you require, at least until you find some one better qualified to take the place."

The result, to use the archbishop's own words, was "a regular contract between us, in which neither was required to acknowledge any obligation to the other." John was to superintend the garden, and receive in return his board, lodging, and private instruction, until he should be qualified to take charge of a class and enter the seminary on the regular footing. So, on the 10th of November, he took leave of his friends in the village, and with all his worldly store trudged up the mountain side to that little "nursery of the American Church," upon which his hopes had rested ever since he landed in the United States. In the toilsome path by which he had been led to this spot, how plainly do we not see the hand of God! Had not pecuniary losses compelled his father to take him away from school, he might have lived and died a parish priest in Ireland. He would have been distinguished, it is true, but distinction supposes opportunity as well as talent, and Ireland afforded no field for the full display of his peculiar powers. And again, had not necessity compelled him, much against his inclination, to dig, water, and weed at Favor Royal, though we cannot doubt that he would have found some way of getting into the priesthood— for he generally did whatever he determined to do—he might not have got admission to Mount St. Mary's College; he

ligious and charitable enterprises, Mr. Cooper reduced himself almost to a state of indigence. He died in December, 1843.—*Life of Mrs. Seton, by Rev. Charles I. White, D.D.*

might never have known either Mr. Dubois or his associate Father Bruté—both of whom exerted a happy influence upon his early career; and so the whole current of his life might have been changed.

Mr. Dubois was proud of his garden, and though it was almost winter when John Hughes first took charge of it, there is no doubt that it gave him enough to do. It was his duty to superintend rather than to work. His force of laborers consisted chiefly of two negroes, Timothy and Peter, well-known characters, who are still remembered by old students of the Mountain. John himself had to handle the spade on occasion; for Mount St. Mary's was a place where everybody worked at times, from the president down to the little school-boys. The various departments of the farm, grounds, and household were placed under the charge of the professors and elder students, all of whom accustomed themselves to hard labor, partly for health's sake, and partly for economy. John's predecessor in the garden was a French gentleman of high birth, a refugee from St. Domingo, who taught French in the college. There was nothing in John's position derogatory to the dignity of a candidate for orders, nothing that could lessen the respect with which his pupils would afterward be required to treat him. On a certain occasion, however, his honest labor was made a reproach to him. After he had become a regular student of the college, he one day met a workman employed about the place intoxicated. He rebuked him, when the man straightened himself up, and exclaimed, with a drunken attempt at dignity, "Who are you, I should like to know! You are nobody but John Hughes. Don't I remember when you used to work with your two hands, as I do?"

He spent about nine months employed in the garden, studying hard all the while under a private teacher, and taking his Latin grammar in his hand when he went to direct the labors out of doors. One day Mr. Dubois found him in the garden at dinner-time, poring over his book, instead of taking his meal. Struck by the young man's industry, he put a few questions to him, and was astonished at the rapid progress he had made in his studies. He saw too—for he was an excellent judge of character—that this was no commonplace person, and he resolved to relieve him of the greater part of his out-of-door duties. Accordingly, about the beginning of the fall term in 1820, we find John Hughes admitted as a regular student of the college. Before we trace his career further, it will be well for us to know something of the remarkable men under whom he was now to prepare himself for the priesthood, and the remarkable place in which he was to pass six quiet and happy years.

CHAPTER III.

Sketch of Mr. Dubois—Foundation of Mount St. Mary's College—Sketch of Mr. Bruté.

JOHN DUBOIS * was born in Paris, August 24, 1764, and educated at the college of Louis le Grand and the Oratorian Seminary of St. Magloire. Among his fellow-students at the former of these schools were Camille Desmoulins and Robespierre; at the latter, Cardinal Cheverus and the famous Jesuit preacher MacCarthy. Ordained priest in 1787, he officiated in Paris until the constitutional oaths were tendered to the clergy, when he fled from France in disguise, and landed at Norfolk, Virginia, in 1791. Letters of commendation from Lafayette introduced him to the Lees, the Randolphs, the Beverlys, James Monroe, and Patrick Henry, the last named of whom occasionally gave him lessons in the English language. While he was qualifying himself to take charge of a congregation, he earned a support by teaching French, in the mean time officiating occasionally in various places, and now and then saying mass in the capitol at Richmond. For a long time he was pastor of all western Maryland and Virginia, and indeed the only priest between Baltimore and St. Louis. Elegant and refined in his manners, and preserving at all times the digni-

* The following sketch is taken chiefly from Dr. McCaffrey's beautiful *Discourse on the Rt. Rev. John Dubois, D.D.*, *pronounced in St. Mary's Church, Emmitsburg*, Jan. 24, 1843. I am also indebted to the most Rev. John B. Purcell, D.D., Archbishop of Cincinnati, for some interesting verbal communications.

fied bearing of a Christian priest and gentleman, he was yet the friend and confidant of the rude countrymen who composed most of his flock, and who looked to him for advice and comfort in their worldly difficulties as well as the affairs of their souls. He was a stern enemy of every sort of extravagance and affectation. No labors seemed too arduous for his iron constitution and his indomitable courage. To give the consolations of religion to the sick and dying, he would journey almost any distance in the worst of weather, and over the worst of roads. One evening, while president of the college, he was called to visit a sick person some twenty-five miles away. The journey, performed on horseback, occupied the whole night. He reached home as the bell was ringing for morning meditation. Instead of taking the rest which he required, he went at once to the little church where the students of theology were assembled, and proceeded, according to his custom, to propose the subject of meditation and suggest some appropriate reflections. He had overrated his strength, and for a moment he fainted. Still he would not retire, but lying down on the church steps, he breathed the morning air until he revived enough to go on with the exercises.

The indomitable spirit of which this incident is an example, the sanguine temperament which caused him to overlook difficulties, the personal magnetism which gave him an influence over other men's thoughts, and the firm faith which assured him of God's help in every work undertaken for God's glory, were qualities which especially fitted him for the arduous enterprise to which, after fourteen years' pastorship in Maryland and Virginia, he resolved to devote himself. About two miles from the village of Emmitsburg, at the foot of a bold and picturesque spur of the Blue Ridge, was a rude chapel where at stated intervals Mr. Dubois used to gather together a little congregation. Here he resolved to establish an ecclesiastical preparatory seminary, and probably he hoped to connect with it at some future time a regular school of theology. A foreigner, without money, without credit, without help of any kind, and surrounded by a congregation almost as poor as himself, it is no wonder that people, when they heard his plan, called him a madman. In 1808 he took possession of a log-house near the foot of the mountain and opened his school. His pupils boarded with the farmers of the neighborhood, and assembled for class in a small brick building a little distance from the mountain; but soon a more commodious log structure was erected for them on the slope of the hill, and they were all gathered together under one roof. A few rods above the school, and about half way up the mountain, stood the plain little church, where the young Levites met on Sundays and feast days with the Catholics of the surrounding country. In rearing this humble house of God and the rough huts for his pupils, in clearing the dense wood, draining the morasses, and terracing the steep hill-side, this polished and dignified clergyman worked with his own hands, plied the spade and the axe, and shared in the roughest drudgery. In 1809, having joined the society of St. Sulpitius, he obtained a transfer to Emmitsburg of the Sulpitian preparatory seminary founded by Mr. Nagot at Pigeon Hill, near Abbotstown, Pennsylvania, in 1806, and made his school a branch of the theological seminary of St. Mary founded by the same society at Baltimore in 1791.* At first he proposed to receive none but candidates for the priesthood; but this restriction was soon laid aside; the number of pupils increased rapidly, and before long it became necessary to put up new buildings. A garden was marked out; a farm was begun; the sterile soil was brought to yield full harvests; and the students learned, by way of recreation, to plant and till the earth, to assist in gathering the crops, and to cut and haul wood for their winter fires. High up the mountain they built a little rustic oratory, and thither they repaired for solitary meditation, or sometimes to celebrate together the divine praises. Far remov-

* This connection did not prove happy, and was dissolved in 1824.

ed from the temptations of cities, Mount St. Mary's became the home of the virtues, and the blessing of God rested on it.

It would hardly be too much to say that the most signal favor which God ever showed this institution was in sending to it, in 1812, as Mr. Dubois' assistant, a priest of some thirty-three years, like himself a Frenchman, whose capacity for affairs released it from a maze of pecuniary difficulties, whose learning gave it a wide celebrity, and whose touching and extraordinary piety will keep his memory green for many a generation yet to come. Simon William Gabriel Bruté * was born of a good family at Rennes, in Brittany, March 20, 1779. His youth was passed amid the most turbulent scenes of the French Revolution, of which he left many curious reminiscences. When a boy of fourteen he was often sent by his family to attend the revolutionary tribunals at Rennes, and bring back information in regard to the trials of priests, which grown people were afraid to witness lest they should be suspected by the mob. He studied medicine under the most celebrated professors in Paris, and passed through his course with great credit; but he never practised physic, having resolved to devote himself to a higher calling. After four years of hard study at the seminary of St. Sulpitius, he was ordained priest in 1808, and two years later came to the United States in company with Mr. Flaget, the bishop elect of Bardstown, Kentucky. For nearly two years he taught philosophy in the seminary at Baltimore, and then came to Emmitsburg. The course of study at the college, after his arrival, was greatly enlarged, and in many other respects he quickly made the value of his services apparent. Mr. Dubois, in his eagerness to supply the American church with an educated and virtuous clergy, had freely opened his school to almost every lad who gave promise of a vocation. He had no head for money; he did not understand accounts; he was ready to believe and to trust all men; his

* *Memoirs of the Rt. Rev. Simon Wm. Gabriel Bruté, D.D., &c.*, by the Rt. Rev. James Roosevelt Bayley, D.D., Bishop of Newark. New York, 1861.

property was all bought on credit; and, however poor himself, he never could resist the impulse to give liberally to praiseworthy enterprises.* It is not surprising, then, that he soon became overwhelmed with financial difficulties; but the methodical habits and administrative talents of Mr. Bruté relieved him. Besides teaching Latin, French, and natural philosophy at the college, Father Bruté took charge of the congregation of Emmitsburg, and was chaplain at St. Joseph's, the mother-house of the Sisters of Charity, about a mile from the Mountain. In 1815 he visited France, and in 1816 and 1817 he was President of St. Mary's College in Baltimore; but at the beginning of the next year he returned to Mr. Dubois. The mountain seminary was now thoroughly organized. Classes of philosophy and theology were opened under the immediate direction of Father Bruté, and the seminarians were appointed prefects and tutors over the boys in the college. A system like this has its defects; but it enabled Mr. Dubois to train for the sanctuary many a worthy young man who could pay for his education in no other way. It taught the young ecclesiastics the art, so important for them to know, of ruling and instructing others; nor was there danger that while learning to govern they would forget how to obey, for Mr. Dubois, though kind and even affectionate to his pupils, was a strict disciplinarian, or, as one said who knew and loved him well, " a perfect little Bonaparte." " Under such a system, however," says Bishop Bayley, " it is of the greatest importance that the superior of the seminary should be much more than a mere professor of theology. He should be one fitted to keep before those under his charge the living image of a faithful priest, and capable of forming them to such habits of ecclesiastical virtue as would protect them against the distracting influences of their present duties, as well as the more worldly influences to which they will be exposed in after life. Such a superior, in the true sense of the word, was Father Bruté. He under-

---

* Sketch of Mount St. Mary's College, by an Alumnus, in *The United States Catholic Magazine*, vol. v., 1846.

stood fully all the responsibility which rested upon him, and never did any one, in his situation, discharge it more faithfully." A spiritual man, who kept his thoughts on heaven, and taught all the sacerdotal virtues by displaying them in his own person; who lost no opportunity of suggesting to his pupils some pious thought, or reminding them how they might sanctify every little action by doing it for God's glory, he has well been called " the angel guardian of the Mount." In the cause of religion, he seemed insensible to fatigue. "After a journey of fifty miles, performed on foot in a single day, book in hand, praying and reading by turns, and scarcely stopping to take the simple refection that nature required, he would meet his friends in the evening with a freshness of spirits and gaiety of conversation which could not be surpassed."* "If he had five dollars in his pocket," said one of his pupils, "it went to the first person who asked for it." He gave away even the clothes off his back, and was repeatedly known to take off his linen to bestow it upon the poor negroes whom he used to visit. "As a professor of theology, he excelled chiefly in two things—a vast erudition, which left nothing unexplored, and a singular power of generalizing, which enabled him to grasp his whole subject and handle it with ease, by bringing all its details under a few grand principles. In exhibiting and supporting these principles, he put forth all his strength. After adducing the evidence, which his extensive reading readily furnished, elucidating it by his luminous explanations, and applying the logical tests with cautious judgment and impartial rigor, his excursive mind brought in a rich and almost gorgeous profusion of analogies and illustrations from every part of the wide domains of human knowledge." † He enriched the college with a valuable library, and by means of his correspondence with the most eminent churchmen throughout the country, and his habit of making voluminous notes of what he read

* *Discourse on the Rt. Rev. Simon Gabriel Bruté, D. D.*, by the Rev. John McCaffrey, D.D., Pres. of Mount St. Mary's College, 1839.
† Ibid.

and of the prominent events in which he had a share, he brought together a store of manuscript materials for the future historian of the American church, such as few others would have had the ability or the patience to collect.* He was, in fine, a remarkable example of a man of retired and studious tastes, whom a sense of duty and a zeal for the Church drew away from his books and sent out into the world as a missionary and a teacher; a man who seemed to know so little about money, when only his own wants were to be provided for, that he would begin a journey of a hundred miles on foot, forgetting to carry even the means to buy his dinner; and who yet managed successfully the affairs of an institution burdened with debt, and several times in danger of dissolution. Bishops, priests, and scholars looked to him for advice and assistance, and he always gave freely to the utmost of his power. He wrote constantly for the Catholic periodicals, aided Mr. Duponceau in his works on the Indian languages, and contributed facts, suggestions, arguments, references, etc., to many a learned treatise or well-known controversy, in which his share was never suspected by the world.

Such were the two men under whom John Hughes resumed his studies; and we shall see that the intercourse which he now established with them continued to the end of their lives. Of the one, he was destined to be the assistant and the successor in the bishopric of New York; of the other, he was to the last a frequent correspondent and a devoted friend.†

---

* It is a matter of regret that a great part of these papers have perished. Some of them are now in the library of the Archbishop of New York.

† He was present in 1858, at the semi-centennial celebration of Mount St. Mary's College, when a sermon in commemoration of these two saintly men was preached by the Rev. Mr. Hitselberger. Bishop Dubois had then been dead sixteen years, and Bishop Bruté nineteen; but Archbishop Hughes was as much affected as if he had just lost them. "He came to me as we left the church," said Father Hitselberger, "and tried to speak, but he could not. He grasped my hand, and burst into tears."

CHAPTER IV.

1820–1826.

College Life—First published Controversy ; Letter to Mr. Bruté—Newspaper Poetry.

WHEN Mr. Hughes was taken from the garden and accepted as a student, he was twenty-three years old. The college and seminary at that time consisted of two rows of log buildings. There were about sixty boys in the collegiate or academical course,* and five or six young men studying theology. Mr. Hughes was placed in one of the lower Latin classes, though at the same time he continued to receive lessons in private. He was also required to exercise an occasional supervision over the garden. The first duty to which he was assigned in connection with the boys was that of prefect of the study-room. This study-room was a large hall in which the pupils assembled during the hours set apart for the preparation of their lessons, and the business of the prefect was to make them keep order and mind their books. It was not always a pleasant task. The students universally respected Mr. Hughes, but like all boys they loved to tease their tutors; and it must have been a sore trial to him, who prized so highly every hour of study, to have his candle charged with gunpowder while he was absorbed in Sallust, or be made the victim of the numberless other practical jokes in which school-boys delight. He was too good-tempered,

---

* The "college" was then little more than a high-school. It was not incorporated, with power to confer degrees, until 1830.

or too shrewd, to show his annoyance at such times; and the quickness with which he occasionally turned the laugh against his persecutors soon taught them that Mr. Hughes was not a good butt for their jokes.*

Before long he was appointed tutor in arithmetic, and a clergyman who was one of his pupils tells me that he would often leave class for a moment to give directions to the workmen in the garden, or raise the sashes of his hot-beds. He taught also at various times grammar, the common English branches, and perhaps the rudiments of Latin; but the truth is, he was not more than respectably proficient in the classics or in polite letters, and gave no evidence of superior scholarship until he became a student of theology; it was in that science that he first showed his strength. It would be strange indeed if his academic course had been a very brilliant one. Not only was he a student and teacher and gardener all at once, not only had he to learn the lessons of boyhood after he became a man, but by severe industry he had to crowd into three years the studies which are usually spread over five or six. Still he acquitted himself well, and Mr. Dubois took occasion publicly to commend him for his rapid progress.

It was during his academic course that he began to develop that fondness for controversy which afterward distinguished him. Whenever in the course of his reading he lighted upon a fact, an argument, or an illustration which seemed to bear upon the points of religious dispute, he treasured it up for future use. The first of his published essays with which I am acquainted appeared while he was at college

* The feast of St. Patrick was a day of special grief to all the Irish prefects; the boys thought of nothing but how to trick them. While Mr. Hughes was prefect of the study-room, they made ready for this feast a stuffed figure of the conventional Paddy, hid it behind the desks, and at an appointed signal drew it up into full view by means of a cord passing over one of the rafters. The boy who held the cord and led the sport was a son of Judge S——. Mr. Hughes showed no surprise at the appearance of the figure, but exclaimed, "O tempora! O mores! the son of a judge turned hangman!" He was not tormented much thereafter, and S——, till he left college, never lost the *sobriquet* of "Jack Ketch."

in the *Franklin Repository*, a weekly paper printed at Chambersburg. It was a reply to a certain Fourth of July speech, delivered before a military company at Chambersburg, in which the orator took occasion to speak ill of the Catholic Church, and Mr. Hughes was requested, by one of his friends who heard it, to write an answer. "He made the answer so sharp," says this friend, "that I had trouble to persuade the editor to print it."

It is probably to this "controversy" that Mr. Hughes alludes in the following note, which I find carefully preserved among the papers of Bishop Bruté:

MR. HUGHES TO MR. BRUTÉ.

[NO DATE.]

REVEREND AND DEAR FRIEND:

I am much obliged to you for your opinion, of which I know that charity was the motive. To all that relates to edification, I must lament that your remarks are too true. I confess that my example is not such as might be expected from a person in my situation, and that my younger brothers may have been scandalized in many instances by my presence as well as absence. To all this, truth compels me to plead guilty. But I assure you, as I know my own heart, that I did not make the search of my controversy a *pretext* for visiting my parents; that that visit did not enter my mind until after I had obtained permission to go to Waynesburg. When I had obtained that permission of the person who held the place of superior in Mr. Dubois' absence, I felt authorized to do as I have done, for the same reason that a refusal of that permission would have been received with the same docility as if it came from Mr. Dubois himself. I know that the subject of the controversy would appear too trifling to Mr. Dubois, because he was not interested in it; but it had cost me some labor, and *I had tried all the other means* that he could suggest to ascertain its fate. It was an imperfection to have gone any further; but being so far, I thought it a good opportunity to add a little comfort to the declining and almost solitary old age of my parents, and the more so as I was not conscious of violating thereby any precept of either God or man. After all, if I had been obliged with your kind opinions before my departure, I should not have gone further than Waynesburg, notwithstanding Mr. Hickey's permission. And if Mr. Dubois blame me on his return, I must submit to the reprimand, but I hope that God will forgive the imperfection of my conduct in this particular. I do acknowledge myself thankful to you for the charitable admonition you have given me, as it may be of service to me on future occasions; but I respectfully beg leave to disclaim the primary motive which circumstances led you to charge me with.

JOHN HUGHES.

There was a literary society at the college under the direction of the Rev. Mr. Hickey, mentioned in the foregoing letter, each member of which in turn was required to write an essay and read it in public. The first time that Mr. Hughes was called upon to perform this duty, he was overcome by timidity. His voice trembled, his hand shook, and the paper fell from his grasp. "That's pride, sir," exclaimed Mr. Hickey, "nothing but pride! Put it under your feet. Pick up your essay, and go on!" These words aroused a different sort of pride, which restored his courage. He never was similarly affected afterward.

The hard study to which he submitted would have ruined a less vigorous constitution. God had given him a robust frame, and his early habits no doubt prepared him to endure severe mental fatigue without much injury. The way of life, too, at Mount St. Mary's—the frequent manual labor, the climbing up and down the rugged mountain, the long walks lasting sometimes an entire holiday, the pure bracing atmosphere—all these things were well fitted to counteract the bad effects of close application to books. With his friends—Mayne, who died a priest in Florida; McCaffrey, now president of the college; Purcell, now Archbishop of Cincinnati—he would ramble about the beautiful region which lies at the foot of the mountain, explore the romantic valleys of the Blue Ridge, or climb to the hill-tops from which the eye looks down upon the undulating fields of Pennsylvania, or, casting itself across the narrow Maryland belt, meets the wooded heights which skirt the waters of the Potomac. Sometimes he would prolong his excursions to Chambersburg; where honest Patrick Hughes took pride in presenting his son to the parish priest;* and the devout mother, as she sat beside him in the village church and listened to the eloquent words of the good pastor, wondered whether her John would ever preach so well, and fancied that she already saw him standing in the pulpit in surplice and stole, or lifting up his hands in the holy sacrifice of the mass. So, having comforted the old couple by his presence for a day, John would go back to his books with fresh energy.

One day the woods caught fire on the mountain above the college, and the buildings were in imminent danger of destruction. The students were all sent up to check the progress of the flames. John Hughes showed such remarkable presence of mind and readiness of invention, that by tacit consent he was chosen foreman of the work. By great exertion a belt was cleared near the top of the mountain, where there was a rude wagon-track between the college and the blazing woods. Some dry wood was kindled on the further side of this clearing, for the purpose of "making fire fight fire." As the flames rose, and the heated air between the two fires began to ascend, a current setting in from the cooler atmosphere beyond drove the opposing flames together. Guards were stationed all along the cleared belt, to give the alarm in case any of the sparks flew across it. It was nine o'clock at night before the danger was beaten off. As a memento of his hard day's work, John Hughes carried away a big hole burned in the back of his best black coat. He was too poor to buy another, and old students remember to have seen him, long afterward, with a huge patch in a conspicuous place between his shoulders.

* The Rev. Thomas Heyden, afterward one of John Hughes's most intimate friends. "I preached one Sunday when he was there," says this excellent priest, "and the good old man, his father, introduced him to me. I was much taken with him. But this was not our first meeting. I had seen him when I visited Emmitsburg, and conceived a strong interest in him."

It must have been about 1823 that he began his course of theology, and thus came more immediately under the direction of Father Bruté. We can imagine the pleasure he must have experienced in this closer association with one who had already become more his friend than his preceptor. We can fancy, too, the feeling of triumph which thrilled him when he first put on the cassock, and the exultation with which he was greeted when he next visited Chambersburg.

He had now to preach occasionally before his fellow-students, for it was a rule of the house that every seminarian should once in a while write and deliver a sermon. He was never overtaken by fright, as he had been in the literary society, though in his early attempts he was often embarrassed. His first sermon convinced all who heard it that he would become an orator. His gestures and manner were indeed constrained, but he delivered his thoughts with a great deal of feeling, and was even affected to tears. About this time he was appointed prefect of the college—an officer whose duty it is to enforce discipline and look after the general behavior of the boys. He used to tell with no little spirit how, in the course of a few days, Mr. Dubois quietly turned him out of office for boxing the ears of an ill-conditioned fellow who had given him a world of trouble.

The college, in the mean time, had prospered; so that Mr. Dubois, after great exertion, erected a large building of stone, into which he prepared to remove in the summer of 1824. But on the night before the 7th of June, it caught fire and was entirely destroyed. As he watched the progress of the flames, Mr. Dubois calmly pointed out certain defects in the building, which he proposed to remedy in the next one.* He was sixty years old, but he began at once to repeat the labor which had just been brought to nothing. The students and professors fell to work, clearing away the ruins and preparing the ground; and during the vacation that summer, several of them offered to go about the country collect-

---

* Dr. McCaffrey, *Discourse*, etc.

ing money for the new enterprise. Among these was Mr. Hughes. He set out in July, visited all the region around Chambersburg, and after a month returned to Mr. Dubois with about four hundred dollars. He used to tell how, in the course of this begging tour, he entered a tavern in a certain village, and asked contributions from a number of persons assembled there. One of them thereupon began to declaim against Popery, and Mr. Hughes straightway plunged into controversy with him. The discussion waxed warm; the company became interested, and after our seminarian had silenced his adversary, nearly every one present made a liberal gift to the college. The people about Emmitsburg, stimulated by pity for Mr. Dubois in his misfortune, were especially generous, and the new college was finished in 1826.

In the mean time Mr. Hughes had been seeking relief from his theological studies in the cultivation of his knack of verse-making, and, with one of his fellow-students, had contributed frequently to a weekly paper of Gettysburg, called the *Adams Centinel*.* For more than a year, almost every number of the paper contained verses by one or the other of the two friends, Mr. Hughes using the *nom de plume* of Leander, his associate that of Æmilius. They would often walk to Gettysburg—a distance of twelve miles—to carry their manuscripts, or to behold themselves in the glory of print. On such occasions they used to dine with the editor, and no doubt enjoy, with the pardonable complacency of young authors, his compliments to their poetical talent. It must be admitted that Mr. Hughes never showed the true poetic fire, though his verses had a melodious flow and a pleasant flavor. I think, however, that no one will be sorry to read a few of these metrical recreations, if it is only to contrast them with the writings of a very different sort by

* The *Sentinel* is still published by the same gentleman—Mr. Robert Goodloe Harper—who printed Mr. Hughes's contributions. I am much indebted to him for his courtesy and assistance in identifying these pieces.

which their author is now remembered. They are not without interest, too, because they indicate to a certain degree some of the belles-lettres writers with whom he was at this time most familiar. It is a curious fact, that out of seventeen pieces, only one is distinctly religious in its character.

TO THE HOME OF MY FATHERS.

Does Freedom yet breathe in the bard's rustic number?
   Can his harp, by the Genius of Liberty strung,
Be mute, while the land where his forefathers slumber
   Is bleeding in bondage, and bleeding unsung?

. . . . .

Is no Washington near thee, thou captive of ages,
   To marshal thy brave ones and lead them to war?
Is no Franklin arrayed in the list of thy sages?
   In that of thy heroes, no young Bolivar?

Thy sons must forsake thee, if worth bids them cherish
   A hope on the records of glory to shine.
Does not Wellington reign? Had not Emmet to perish?
   The laurel is England's—the cypress is thine.

But weep not, poor Erin; though Emmet is wanting,
   His spirit still lives in the hearts of thy brave;
There are bosoms behind, as devotedly panting
   For the breath of the free—or the boon of the grave.

And hope tells my heart that a day will be given,
   When the chain shall be loosed and their sorrows redressed;
When thou shalt go forth in the pride of thy even,
   As free as the zephyrs that sport on thy breast.

Oh, then shall thy harp, which has slumbered in sadness,
   Feel the pulse of fair freedom that erst made it thrill;
Then the Bard shall awake it in accents of gladness,
   And sweep its wild chords on thy ever-green hill.

And oh, when the last scene of nature is closing,
   When this spirit of mine shall burst forth and be free,
How calm could I rest, on thy bosom reposing,
   Thou home of my fathers! Green Isle of the Sea!

A poetical address to his friend "Æmilius" closes with the following stanzas, which, in the light of subsequent events, are rather curious:

> And ah! when the minstrel, too proud or too humble
> To sue for a place on the legends of fame,
> Shall sleep in the tomb, like his fathers to crumble,
> Divulge not, Æmilius, divulge not his name.
>
> But if in the twilight perchance thou shouldst wander
> To where he shall slumber, unhonored, unknown,
> Be the dirge thou wilt sing o'er the grave of Leander,
> "Here resteth a heart which was part of my own!"

His constitutional fondness for dealing a blow at every sort of falsehood, appears even in his poetry. In November, 1825, he published some polemical Spenserian stanzas called *Lines occasioned by reading one of Lord Byron's sombre Effusions entitled "Epitaph on a New Foundland Dog,"* in which he seems to think the Dog has as good a Right to be admitted into Heaven as his Master, "*that degraded Mass of animated Dust.*"

From an "Ode to Death" I select the following:

> King conquers king, and slave his fellow-slave;
>   But slave and king shall fall
>   In thy sepulchral hall;
> Whilst thou, grim monarch, shalt triumphant wave
> Thy iron sceptre o'er their equal grave,
>   Dread conqueror of all!
>
> Those fools who fight for lords and thrones,
>   To thee at length shall yield
>   The helmet, lance, and shield,
> When princely pride shall ask their dying groans,
> Or wish the tribute of their valiant bones,
>   To whiten on a field.
>
> .   .   .   .   .
>
> Yet be not proud in thy resistless sway,
>   Thou scourge of human crime
>   In every land and clime;

For on the confines of eternal day
Thou too shalt fall, an angel's easy prey,
Upon the tomb of Time.

Those acquainted with the political sentiments of the archbishop in the prime and evening of his life will hardly be prepared for the piece which follows:

THE SLAVE.

Hard is the lot of him who's doomed to toil,
Without one slender hope to soothe his pain,
Whose sweat and labor are a master's spoil,
Whose sad reward a master's proud disdain.
Wipe from thy code, Columbia, wipe the stain;
Be free as air, but yet be kind as free,
And chase foul bondage from thy Southern plain:
If such the right of man, by heaven's decree,
Oh then let Afric's sons feel what it is—to be.

In hot meridian day of late, I hied
To court the covert of a spreading oak;
I sat beneath—and thence in pity eyed
The negro moiling at his daily yoke.
And still he plied the dull, desponding stroke,
Beneath the scorching of the noon-tide sun,
Sullen and silent, or if words he spoke,
I could not hear; but ever and anon
I heard the lash—which even brutes are fain to shun.

The ruthless driver soon was forced to yield:
Though strong of sinew, still he could not bear
The tyrant labors of the parching field,
But sought the shade to breathe a cooler air;
Whilst, less inhuman, but alas! less fair,
The drudging slave began to pour his song
Upon the heedless wind, and breathe despair.
He sung the negroes' foul, unpitied wrong,
Sad and ironical—late he felt the thong.

"Hail Columbia, happy land!
Where freedom waves her golden wand,
Where equal justice reigns.

But ah! Columbia great and free
Has not a boon for mine and me,
  But slavery and chains.
Oh! once I had a soothing joy,
  The hope of other years,
That free Columbia would destroy
  The source of these my tears.
    But pining, declining,
  I still drag to the grave,
    Doomed to sigh till I die,
  Free Columbia's slave.

"Hail Columbia, happy land!
Whose sons, a free, a heaven-born band,
  Will free us soon with blows.
If freeman's freest blood were shed,
Could it be purer or more red
  Than this of mine that flows?
'Twas freeman's whip that brought this gore
  That trickles down my breast;
But soon my bleeding will be o'er,
  My grave will yield me rest.
    I will, then, until then
  Abide my hard and hopeless lot;
    But there's room in the tomb
  For freemen too to rot.

"Hail Columbia, happy land!
Where those who show a fairer hand
  Enjoy sweet liberty.
But from the moment of my birth,
I slave along Columbia's earth,
  Nor freedom smiles on me.
Long have I pined through years of woe
  Adown life's bleeding track,
And still my tears, my blood must flow,
  Because my hand is black.
    Still boiling, still toiling,
  Beneath the burning heats of noon,
    I, poor slave, court the grave;
  O Columbia, grant the boon!

"Hail Columbia, hap—"

He ceased the song, and heaved another sigh
In silent, cheerless mood—for ah! the while
The driver's hated steps were drawing nigh;
Nor song of woe, nor words dare then beguile
The goaded sorrows of a thing so vile.
Yet such the plaintive song that caught my ear,
That cold humanity may blush to smile,
When dove-eyed mercy softly leans to hear,
And pity turns aside to shed another tear.

FOURTH OF JULY, 1826.

JUBILEE OF AMERICAN FREEDOM.

. . . . .

Great Lord of creation! we owe it to thee,
That our country is kingless, our people are free.
Oh, grant a like boon to that ill-fated Isle,
Where the ruled are as brave as their rulers are vile;
Where genius illumines, and minds are sincere,
Where hearts beat in bosoms that never felt fear.
Yes, children of freemen! your fathers could tell
How the Irishman fought, till he conquered or fell;
How the hero stood still when the heartless were flying;
How Arnold betrayed while Montgomery was dying.
Poor Erin, thy sons shall have fame in our story;
Their sickles were mixed in our harvest of glory.
Columbia invites thee to rise and be free,
Till she call thee her sister, thou gem of the sea.
But hark! O, that song, swelling higher and higher!
'Tis the voice of Columbia, attuned to the lyre;
'Tis her thanksgiving anthem—and millions combine
In the chorus of love around Liberty's shrine.

"Peace to the patriot, setting in glory;
  His eye hath grown dim, and his locks have grown hoary.
  He balanced no sceptre—he cushioned no throne;
  He was wise for his country, his country alone.

"Peace to the ashes of heroes that sleep
  In the battle-field grave, or the cells of the deep;
  Their deeds be the theme of both story and art,
  But their names are inscribed in the book of my heart.

"The holy inheritance their blood hath won
Shall descend in succession from father to son,
Till the trumpet-tongued angel check time in his flight,
And the dawn of eternity burst on my sight.

"Peace to my sons, and my rosy-crowned daughters,
My mountains, my oceans, my cities, my waters;
And peace to the stranger whom tyrants oppressed;
Let him come to my bosom and slumber at rest.

Chorus.—"It is Liberty's jubilee—swell the loud chorus;
Half an age hath gone by—there are whole ones before us;
That iron chain, rent by our fathers of old,
Is not fit for their sons, though its links were of gold."

This was the last of Leander's poetical contributions to the *Centinel*. He was now approaching the time of his ordination as priest, and poetry was driven out of his mind by more important matters.

CHAPTER V.

1825–1827.

Ordination as Deacon—Letter from Father Hurley—Journey with Bishop Conwell—"The Cuckoo Sermon"—Answer to Nine Objections—Ordained Priest—At St. Augustine's Church—At Bedford—Called to Philadelphia—Troubles of St. Mary's Church.

MR. HUGHES was already in holy orders, having been made deacon in 1825. He had resolved to attach himself to the diocese of Philadelphia, then governed by the Right Rev. Henry Conwell; and it seems to have been arranged that when he left the seminary he should be placed for a time under the direction of the Rev. Michael Hurley, a distinguished Augustinian preacher, and rector of St. Augustine's Church in Philadelphia. Father Hurley conceived a strong liking for his destined assistant, and gave him many a useful hint for the direction of his studies. On a false rumor that Mr. Bruté had left Mount St. Mary's, and that the divinity school was to be broken up, he wrote to Mr. Hughes as follows, in November, 1825:

We are informed that Mr. Bruté has left Emmitsburg, and that, of course, the first blow has been struck.* Most sincerely and deeply do I regret it. . . . . This bold step will, I much fear, be injurious to you. By close and systematic application during the current collegiate year, and under such a man as the learned and pious Mr. B——, I had no doubt but that your proficiency in theol-

---

* The Archbishop of Baltimore several times proposed to close the theological classes at the Mountain, thinking it more expedient to have only one seminary in his diocese—that of St. Mary, Baltimore. The college authorities were strongly opposed to this measure, because, by depriving them of their tutors and prefects, they feared it would lead to the suppression of the whole establishment.

ogy at the expiration of it would justify your promotion to the priesthood. His removal must be a considerable drawback on your exertions, however great they may be. Although Mr. Dubois may undertake the deserted class, yet his avocations are so great and so various, that it is scarcely possible for him to find sufficient time or vigor to do it justice. What he can do I feel confident that he will, and that to the very last he will maintain his energy, his independence, and his cause. Under such circumstances, I need scarcely tell you that your own exertions must be redoubled and constant, yet so as not to injure your health. Should you at times find your nerves the least affected by the application of hours, immediately desist, betake yourself to the mountain air and exercise, and beware of enervating in any way that most delicate, and indeed the least understood of the human machine, and which, when once relaxed, it is almost impossible to brace up to its original tone. I am giving you the advice of experience, and wish you to profit by it. I am desirous, as I mentioned to you when here, that you should prepare at your leisure as many short discourses as you can, so that when you commence your mission you may be six or more months in advance of the *preaching* part of your duty. Do not make your sermons long—half an hour or thereabouts will be sufficient; you will then be able to deliver them with more energy and self-command, and to throw more soul into them, without which there is no true eloquence, and consequently little or no fruit from it. Make yourself *master* of the *End of Controversy* ; do that, and I shall be content. So far as regards scholastic divinity. With respect to moral divinity, I would have you to fix indelibly in your mind its great general principles and maxims, as it is by these that you will have to govern yourself in the great majority of cases, when you become a confessor and a guardian and director of souls. As to out-of-the-way, far-fetched cases of conscience, with which so many of our moral divines abound, I would have you pay no more attention than what may be necessary in the exercise of the class, as you would hereafter find them to be nearly useless. In a large portion of the cases to which I allude, there is more ingenuity discernible than knowledge of the world. Here again I write from experience, and therefore with confidence. My affectionate respects to Mr. Dubois. Smith desires to be remembered to you. Your friend,

M. Hurley.

While Mr. Hughes was deacon, he happened to be at Chambersburg one day with his parents, when Bishop Conwell arrived there on a visitation of his diocese. The venerable prelate, glad to be rid of a part of his task, commanded the young clergyman to preach. Though taken by surprise, Mr. Hughes acquitted himself well, and was invited to accompany the bishop on the rest of his journey. The compliment was not without its compensating penalties. The Pennsylvania roads were rough; there were neither railways nor coaches; and the bishop, the deacon, and the episcopal luggage were all carried on horseback. At Path Valley they were joined by Mr. Hughes's old acquaintance, Father Heyden, then pastor of Bedford. The bishop gave confirmation in the humble log church, and Mr. Hughes was once more requested to preach. Here was a dilemma. He had so far made little progress in following Father Hurley's advice, to "get six months in advance of the preaching part of his duty;" for one sermon was all he knew. He was not a man, however, to own himself at a loss, so he preached it again. At the next halt, he preached it for the third time; at Sinking Valley for the fourth; at Newry and Bedford for the fifth and sixth. And after he became priest and was called to Philadelphia, his first sermon in St. Joseph's church was the same he had preached all through the visitation. Dr. Conwell, who knew it at last almost as well as the preacher himself, used to call it "the cuckoo sermon."

During one of Mr. Hughes's Chambersburg visits a tract entitled "Protestantism and Popery," in which certain popular objections to the Catholic Church were set forth in the form of question and answer by a writer signing himself *Boston*, was handed to him with the suggestion that he should induce several of the students at the seminary to write a joint reply to it, each refuting a separate point. He did so; but on collecting the answers he found them so various in style and method that he threw them all aside, determined, as soon as he had leisure, to write the whole himself. It was not until 1827 that his reply was published, first in the (Charleston) *United States Catholic Miscellany*, and afterward in pamphlet form in Chambersburg and Philadelphia.*

On the feast of St. Theresa, October 15, 1826, he was ordained priest by Bishop Conwell in St. Joseph's church, Philadelphia. Two weeks afterward his preceptor, the Rev. Mr. Dubois, was consecrated Bishop of New York in the cathedral at Baltimore.

For a few weeks Father Hughes remained with Dr. Hurley at St. Augustine's, taking his share in the labors of the pulpit, schooling himself in the lessons of sin and sorrow and suffering which make up the daily task of the missionary priest, and learning those practical rules of clerical life which a seminary education cannot teach. To Mr. Dubois and Mr. Bruté he was indebted for the book knowledge necessary in his profession, and for precepts and examples of all the Christian virtues. From Dr. Hurley he learned how to make the best use in his daily duties of what he had accumulated at college; and he obtained such an insight into the troubled condition of the diocese, as would enable him to act prudently and justly in the future. Father Hurley used often to predict for him a glorious future. He saw in him a discretion beyond his years, an indomitable will, a courage that nothing could shake, and a zeal that never tired. Whatever he had once stored in his brain, he had a remarkable faculty of finding and using just when it was wanted. With a taste for controversy somewhat akin to the Irish love of a fight, with a natural aptitude for dialectics, and with studious habits, joined to this gift of making the most of all he knew, it is no wonder that he took his place from the first among the most promising young clergymen of the diocese. Very soon after his ordination he was sent by the bishop to Bed-

---

* *An Answer to Nine Objections made by an anonymous writer against the Catholic Religion. By a Clergyman of Chambersburg, Franklin County, Pennsylvania.* 57 pp. 12mo, 1827.

ford, to supply the place left vacant by the removal of Mr. Heyden to Philadelphia. The field of his mission was a rough mountainous region, peopled by the descendants of Lutheran, Calvinistic, and Wesleyan immigrants. He had to journey over a wide extent of country, to do battle with bitter prejudice, to suffer hardships of body and trials of the soul. His force of mind was equal to these tasks. The harder his work, the better he liked it. Shrinking from no fatigue, daring the attacks of his religious adversaries, never so happy as when he had a chance to fight for his faith, his fearless bearing gained him first respect and then friendship among a people never insensible to what they call pluck. Although he stayed only a few weeks in Bedford, he was there long enough to make a goodly number of converts, in whose welfare he retained a lively interest after he had been removed to more stirring scenes. He lived while here with the parents of Father Heyden, and laid the foundation of a lasting regard for the family. Two years afterward he wrote to Mr. Heyden, Sr.: "You will not be surprised at receiving a few lines from one who spent a brief but happy period of his life under your hospitable roof. The recollection of that short mission, when to me every thing was new, only fills me with regret that it terminated so soon, whilst at the same time it reminds me of the many obligations I owe to your kindness and that of your amiable family. My occupations here are too multiplied and incessant to leave time for writing often to my friends; but this is not a reason why I should forget them."

Early in January, 1827, Bishop Conwell, at Father Heyden's instigation, recalled him to Philadelphia. Before we study his career in that city, we must understand somewhat of the state of church affairs there; for though his name seldom occurs in the published history of the unfortunate disputes then rife between the bishop and some of his people and clergy, yet he had a most important agency in their final settlement; and there is no doubt, too, that they had their influence in shaping his policy when he himself was called upon to govern a diocese.

Philadelphia had been for several years distracted by ecclesiastical disorders, springing principally from the wretched trustee system, which placed the management of the churches in the hands of laymen. The trustees were chosen by the pew-holders, and it sometimes happened that, so far from possessing the requisite qualifications for their important trust, they were not even Catholics. Abuses of various sorts, and frequent conflicts with the bishop, were the natural result. After the death of Bishop Egan, in 1814, it was not found easy to induce any competent person to accept a mitre so thickly set with thorns. Three clergymen to whom it was offered refused it. At last, in 1820, the Very Rev. Henry Conwell, vicar-general of the diocese of Armagh, in Ireland, accepted the post, and was consecrated in London at the age of nearly seventy-three.*

On arriving at his see in the latter part of the same year, he found the cathedral church of St. Mary in charge of a young priest named Hogan, whose character was not above reproach. For reasons which were not made public, the bishop, on the 12th of December, forbade him the exercise of priestly functions within his diocese; and as Mr. Hogan, despite this prohibition, continued to officiate, he formally excommunicated him in May, 1821. Mr. Hogan, though a man of little education, was very popular with a part of the congregation, and they resolved that he should be pastor in spite of the bishop. By the charter of the church, the management of the property was vested in a board of trustees, consisting of the pastors, not exceeding three in number, and eight laymen, elected annually by the pew-holders. How the three pastors were to be chosen, the law did not say; the bishop claimed the right of appointment and removal, according to the usage and spirit of the Catholic Church, and

* *The Catholic Church in the United States.* By Henry De Courcy and John Gilmary Shea. Second edition, revised. New York, 1856.

the lay trustees as strenuously resolved to exercise it themselves. They accordingly installed Hogan as pastor, and took forcible possession of the church. The bishop, with the clergy of his household and a large part of the congregation, removed to St. Joseph's, a chapel of ease, about a stone's throw from the cathedral. Even after this exodus, however, Hogan and the trustees were not supported by a majority of the pew-holders of St. Mary's; so they built a number of new pews, and put into them one hundred and thirty voters of their own party, many of them professed enemies of the Catholic religion. The next election for trustees, in Easter week, 1822, was attended with horrible disorder and even bloodshed; the schismatics carried it by a small majority.* Efforts by Bishop England and others to bring about a reconciliation repeatedly failed, principally through the vacillation or insincerity of Hogan. He made promises, and immediately broke them; submitted to the bishop at night, and returned to the arms of the trustees in the morning. As a last method of securing peace, the bishop in 1821 determined to invite to Philadelphia the Rev. William Vincent Harold, an eloquent and popular preacher, who had formerly lived for several years in that city, but was now prior of the Dominican convent of Corpo Santo in Lisbon. He hoped that this priest would succeed in enticing the malcontents away from St. Mary's, and so leave Hogan pastor, if he pleased, of the church, but without a congregation. It was a sad mistake. The call was hardly given before the bishop learned that Mr. Harold had been one of the leaders in a vexatious opposition sustained by the trustees of St. Mary's against Bishop Egan. He revoked his invitation, but it was too late. Mr. Harold had already set sail for America, and in the month of December he arrived at Philadelphia.† His conduct at first was perfectly proper. He was appointed the

* *Works of the Right Rev. John England, First Bishop of Charleston.* 5 vols. 8vo. Baltimore, 1849.
† De Courcy and Shea, *The Catholic Church*, etc.

bishop's secretary, and took decided part against the schismatics, but his efforts to weaken them were utterly futile. The solemn condemnation of Hogan by the Holy See, in 1822, was unheeded. At last, about 1824, that unfortunate priest left the diocese of his own accord, turned Protestant, and took a wife. The books which he wrote against the Church after his apostasy did less mischief to religion than he had wrought by his disobedience and bad temper while he professed to be a zealous Catholic priest. Throughout his controversy with the bishop, he and his friends had been incessantly publishing violent pamphlets against Dr. Conwell, Dr. England, and the clergy of Philadelphia. Heartburnings, enmities, party spirit, scandals, separation of friends, not in St. Mary's parish alone, but all through the city, were but a few of the many evils which sprang from this schism, and lasted for years after the schism itself had been healed.*

To supply the place of Mr. Hogan, the trustees employed the Rev. Thaddeus O'Meally, of Limerick. Bishop Conwell offered terms of accommodation, but they were not accepted, and Mr. O'Meally set out for Rome to lay the complaints of the trustees before the Pope, and to petition for the bishop's removal. In Rome, however, he repented of his conduct and retired to a convent.

Worn out by these long conflicts, the bishop † at last yielded to injudicious advisers, and signed a treaty with the trustees, Oct. 9, 1826, by which a temporary peace was

* So intense was the feeling in Philadelphia about the St. Mary's affair, that little children copied the feuds of their parents, and school-boys divided themselves into hostile parties, one for the bishop, another for the trustees.

† Bishop Conwell was a good and amiable man, but unfit for his post. He understood little of the condition and wants of the American church. Though of a dignified and venerable aspect, he lacked all dignity of character. He was naturally a man of considerable ability; but age and trouble had weakened his mind until at times he seemed almost imbecile. It will readily be understood that such a bishop was of all men the least able to cure the inveterate disease which afflicted the church of Philadelphia.

secured at the sacrifice of certain fundamental principles of church government. The bishop was recognized as senior pastor, with the right of appointing the two assistants. Should the trustees object to either of the clergymen so appointed, they were to state their objections; and if the bishop persisted in his choice, he and two clergymen not connected with St. Mary's were to meet and consult with three of the trustees: a majority of votes in this committee was to decide the dispute; in case of a tie, the parties were to choose by lot another person who should give the casting vote. The salary of the bishop and pastors was left "to the liberality and discretion of the trustees." The bishop relinquished all claim for arrears of salary and emoluments; a general amnesty was to be published in the churches of the city; and all books, deeds, papers, and documents belonging to the corporation were to be delivered to the custody of the trustees. At the same time, the trustees protested, in writing, that they meant in no shape or form to relinquish what they considered "their *inherent* right of presentation," but that they entered into the above-mentioned agreement solely to restore peace and enable them more effectually to prosecute their claim to that right; they did not admit that the Bishop of Philadelphia in his own right was or could name himself a pastor of St. Mary's church; and finally they declared that they would "with all their energy prosecute their claim to the See of Rome to allow a bull or decree against any future bishop being appointed unless his appointment should have been made with the approbation and at the recommendation of the Catholic clergy of the diocese." *

Two days after the conclusion of this agreement, St. Mary's church, which had been for some time under an interdict, was formally reopened by the bishop, and Messrs. Harold and Heyden were appointed pastors. The liveliest dissatisfaction at the bishop's concessions was felt by the clergy in general, and a copy of the treaty was sent to Rome to be

* Bishop England's Works, vol. v.

submitted to the Pope. It was the conviction of those best
qualified to judge, that his Holiness would annul it. The
trustees made no effort to hide their triumph, and it needed
little foresight to perceive that the storm was ready to burst
forth again at any moment. Mr. Heyden begged leave to
return to his peaceful country parish, and proposed that Mr.
Hughes should be brought to Philadelphia in his place. The
bishop sent for Mr. Hughes, but would not dismiss Mr.
Heyden, preferring to retain him at St. Mary's, and employ
Mr. Hughes at St. Joseph's, which he had resolved to erect
into a separate parish. It was a trying situation for an inexperienced man, and it was one that of all others he would
have avoided had his own wishes been consulted. He was
ready enough to meet open enemies; but here he was obliged
to deal with foes who called themselves friends; to avoid
conflict; to be prudent and hold his tongue. It was a fortunate thing for him that at the beginning of his career he had
so many wise friends at hand to whom he could apply for
advice. Dr. Hurley and Mr. Heyden were always ready to
help and counsel him, and he often had recourse to good
Father Bruté, and to Mr. Egan, who had succeeded Bishop
Dubois as president of Mount St. Mary's. Mr. Egan writes
to him, Feb. 5, 1827: "It is but a few days ago that I
learned you had been recalled from Bedford and stationed
in that miserable city of Philadelphia. I was surprised to
hear it, and from my soul I pity you, for I have some idea
of Philadelphia. But as it is evidently the will of God that
called you, or rather which you obeyed, you have not so
much to fear as in a place of your own choice. You have a
vast field before you, in which you can exert your zeal and
labor for the glory of our common Beloved. I hope you
will pay particular attention to the children and the catechism, for I really believe that all the good to be done is by
that means. The rising generation have already witnessed
scandal enough to make them lose their faith; and were not
that even the case, ignorance would produce the same effect.

I feel deeply for the state of the Church in Philadelphia, and am convinced that it has need of zealous, disinterested, and holy priests to keep alive the spark of religion which still exists in the breasts of a few."

Mr. Hughes governed himself with a discretion far beyond his years. The indignation which he must have felt when at the outset of his sacerdotal life he saw contempt cast upon things that he had been taught to hold sacred, and his bishop terrified into unworthy concessions to usurping laymen, however it may have burned in his breast, found no public utterance from his lips. He would not make himself enemies and impair his powers of usefulness by taking part in disputes of which he could not influence the result. He would hold no conversation, except with his intimate friends, upon matters of church discipline, content to wait patiently for the decision of Rome upon the argeement with the trustees; and meanwhile to give up his whole soul to the discharge of his duties, to preaching, visiting the sick, and instructing children. He wrote his sermons with great care, and learned them by heart; and although he made his appearance in the pulpit at a time when Philadelphia had several eminent preachers, such as Dr. Hurley and Father Harold—although, too, he had as yet acquired but little of that graceful delivery and vigor of thought which gave such a charm to his later discourses, he made an impression on the public from the very first, and people began to forsake the other churches to go and hear him. Bishop Conwell was delighted with him. When he met any of the professors or students from Mount St. Mary's, he would accost them, in his rough way: "How are ye? How's Bruté? Ah, Hughes is the boy, isn't he? He takes all the wind out of our sails. We'll make him a bishop some day!" Dr. Conwell, with Mr. Hughes and two other priests, lived in the house attached to St. Joseph's, not having returned to St. Mary's when it was reopened. Mr. Hughes was only curate at this time. The senior priest, a good but rather dull man, took it into his head one day that the revenues of the church were not fairly divided; the three clergymen who composed the bishop's household drew, as necessity required, from a common purse, "whereby," said he, "the curates get as much as their elders." So the bishop and the three priests came together, and Father —— exposed his grievance, proposing that the bishop should allot to each a fixed salary. "To be sure I will," cried Dr. Conwell; "and I'll give Hughes twice as much as the rest of you. It's he that draws all the people. He's the only one of you that can preach decently." The question of fixed salaries was not mooted again, and matters remained on their old footing.

Trouble at St. Mary's soon broke out again. In the course of a few months, Dr. Conwell found it necessary to suspend Father Harold from the exercise of the ministry; but before taking this step, he desired, with his characteristic feebleness, to obtain from all the clergy in the city a written approval of it. Mr. Hughes refused to sign such a paper, though he fully believed the impending sentence to be a just one. He was the more unwilling to interfere in any way, because it had been proposed to make him pastor of St. Mary's in Father Harold's place. He wrote to Father Bruté and Mr. Egan for advice. "You know my full opinion," writes Mr. Bruté (March 22, 1827), "of the fatal articles of peace. It was evident that, sooner or later, evil would again come out of them. You tell me that the trustees are ready to see them mended. I would then entreat the bishop—humbly, but to the last most earnestly—to leave me in my situation until they are actually mended. You do good in your situation, and only good, by keeping, as I have no doubt you do, your blessed strict line of duty, free from interference with matters not belonging to it, avoiding curious or busy questions from persons out of your official call—so many people in large cities being continually planning and canvassing, without any vocation or grace for it, and too often without the pure intentions duly studied before God, which alone could bless such inquiries, complaints, or propositions. A zealous and diligent pastor in your vast cities has so much of real duty to perform, that he must easily find means to keep strictly to his only actual character, and leave Providence to dispose of everything else in a manner that subjects him not to undue responsibility. . . . My poor advice, you see, is to keep to your present situation as long as your bishop leaves you your powers in it." Mr. Egan wrote to the same effect: "Were I in your place, I would remain where I was doing good, and not meddle, either directly or indirectly, in the plans of either side. Were I sounded on the subject by the trustees, or any one else, I would refer them to the bishop. Were I pressed by the bishop, I would insist on a change in the articles of that strange concordat. . . . . When it comes to the last point, of command on the part of the bishop, your acceptance would then appear to be in the usual order of Providence. But I would protest against any claim of lay interference in my appointment; above all things, I would keep on the *best and most friendly terms* with Mr. Harold, and convince him that you never meddle nor intrigue in any way; nor would I accept, or declare my consent to accept, until he had actually been removed. As to the articles, if the bishop and trustees do not change them, I know from the highest authority that Rome will. There is a storm, I am afraid, gathering in the Vatican, which will burst on the good old bishop."

After some difficulty, Dr. Conwell prevailed upon Mr. Hughes to sign the document condemnatory of Dr. Harold, promising that it should not be made public. The next day, however, the contents of the paper and the names of the signers were known all over the city. It was said that Mr. Hughes and the other young priests had "conspired" against Harold, and the latter gentleman, having been formally suspended on the 3d of April, 1827, was urged by his friends to bring a suit for defamation of character. Bishop Conwell they called a dotard; Father Heyden had gone back to Bedford; of the other "conspirators" the most prominent was Mr. Hughes, and he accordingly was made defendant in the action. The cause was never brought to trial, for Mr. Harold soon saw the folly of his conduct and withdrew the suit. With all his faults—and they were chiefly the faults which spring from a hasty temper—Mr. Harold was a man of too much virtue to continue his ministrations in spite of the bishop's prohibition, and the trustees were reduced to the necessity of either closing the church or accepting any priest the bishop chose to send them. Accordingly, when Mr. Hughes, at the positive command of his ordinary, reluctantly accepted the pastorship upon Mr. Harold's removal, he encountered no decided opposition, though the trustees intimated that they did not recognize the validity of his appointment, and should pay no salary either to him or to his assistant, Mr. O'Reilly. He heard them quietly, and kept on, to use Mr. Bruté's words, in his "blessed strict line of duty, free from interference with matters not belonging to it, avoiding curious or busy questions from persons out of his official call." "I am perfectly sensible," writes Mr. Egan, "of the delicacy and unpleasant nature of your situation. I do not perceive how you could well have acted otherwise than you have done. I was much pleased to hear from Rev. Mr. Heyden that you made it a rule to decline any discussion or conversation with laymen on the subject of church differences. I think it a wise and prudent plan, though sometimes difficult to execute. You have entered upon the only method of doing good amongst the Catholics of that ill-fated city—the instruction of the children. The origin of so much scandal there and elsewhere can only be attributed to ignorance."

His wise and conciliatory course seems to have had a temporary effect upon the refractory trustees.

TO THE REV. THOMAS HEYDEN.

PHILADELPHIA, *May* 19, 1827.

REV. DEAR FRIEND :

I had much pleasure in reading your letter of the 14th. It was not the least source of my satisfaction to learn that all my Bedford friends, particularly your own family, were in good health. Give them the assurance of my fondest affections, and tell them that if it were *any use* to be sorry, I have much more reason to regret leaving them when I did than they could have for my departure. You need not expect so full a letter as you sent, because you were loaded when you arrived in Bedford, like a bee that sips the honey juice of every flower as it passes; whilst I am just where you left me. I am still *illic ubi sedimus et flevimus cum recordaremur Sion !*

Things are *in statu quo*. Rev. Mr. C—— has just returned from his northern tour, or, to use a less dignified phrase, from what Dr. Power calls "a peddling excursion." * Mr. H. has been to New York this week. Mr. Power is expected by the bishop to preach in St. Mary's next Sunday and the Sunday following. I have had a hundred messengers to ascertain whether I have heard from you; the days since you went and till you return have been often counted since your departure. The opposition is becoming extremely calm and gentle, and the fever of passion has in a great measure passed away. It seems their determination to demean themselves like good Catholics, until the "Court of Rome" puts all to rights, as the traitor hope has disappointed them in every other quarter. I have held forth this forenoon in St. Mary's, on the "pride and the abuse of human knowledge," and I assure you M. Carey's spectacles were not idle. He will, no doubt, think of his old adage, "Men of glass," etc. The church was full.

Give my best love to your sister, your mother, father, brother, Messrs. Harman, Brown, and above all, Mr. Osterlo; also Mrs. Brown, Mrs. Byrne, Miss Byrne, Miss Walter, Miss Reilly, and all Mr. Keefe's family. I remain Yours affectionately,

JOHN J. HUGHES.

---

* Mr. C—— was in the habit of publishing books and travelling about the country to sell them.

TO THE SAME.

Philadelphia, *July* 3, 1827.

Rev. Dear Friend :

When we parted, I understood something like a bargain between us to write to each other often during your stay in the country. I had the pleasure of receiving one letter from you since, and whether you received mine or not, I sent two. The weather is almost too hot to attempt writing in such an atmosphere as Philadelphia possesses; but still I will write, supposing you as anxious to hear from me as I and many others can be to hear from you.

Affairs have taken quite an unexpected turn latterly, or, to express it in Joe's phrase, we are all " in the catches." * The trustees had refused to have a meeting in consequence of Barry's affair. And as there was no one to be responsible for any remuneration to myself or Rev. Mr. O'Reilly, I gave the congregation my *ultimum valete* the Sunday before last.† This was a measure so prompt and unexpected, that it came like a shot upon them. I do not know what may be the ultimate result of it, but I do know that no one can blame me for doing it. The bishop gives them mass at 9 o'clock on Sundays; but I think the church will soon be shut. They had a meeting of the trustees yesterday; but the bishop, to avoid being present, or, as he expresses it, to avoid being insulted, just took a trip to Baltimore in the morning. As if they would never have an opportunity to insult him, provided he could contrive to escape this time! The trustees nearly all have passed over to the opposition, and it is not worth while looking after them. I am at St. Joseph's, as before my removal—as busy as a nailer every day.

Rev. Mr. H. is still passing the time in telling the people to be quiet. I recollect in Shakespeare that Iago cautions Othello against the very passion he wished to awaken—" beware of jealousy." Shakespeare knew mankind well.

We are all well. The inquiries about your return are endless. Give my best love to your family, and ask Miss Margaret "How does Mr. Heyden come on?" I wish I could spend six weeks of this month with you at the Springs. Oh, it's so warm here! How is

---

* Joe was a mulatto servant of Bishop Conwell's, who was subject to occasional fits of insanity; he used to call his attacks being " in the catches."

† June 23d.

Mr. Dopp, and Felix Cassidy, and all the other odd fishes on the rounds ! . . . . . I suppose you have a great many sermons written by this time ! Ah, Thomas ! I am afraid "you are playing your cards." I suppose Rev. Mr. Smyth is quite busy between Ebensburg and Huntingdon.

Give my best respects to all my good friends in Bedford, particularly Mr. and Mrs. Brown, Miss Juliana, Mr. Harman and family, Mr. O'Keefe, Miss Peggy, Miss Reilly, etc., etc.

Now, why do you not write ! If there is any thing which you would wish me to do, you know that nothing would give me greater pleasure than to know what it is. But really, I cannot account for your silence, otherwise than by supposing that you are coming soon, which could not be too soon if it were consistent with your own happiness. For my part, if I were to let care prey upon my mind as it might, I would be dead very shortly. But it is useless. These clouds will pass away in time.

I remain your affectionate brother in Christ,

JOHN HUGHES.

The voluntary retirement of Messrs. Hughes and O'Reilly was the hardest blow the trustees had yet received, for it left them masters of a church without a clergyman. The bishop determined to give them no one in Mr. Hughes's place, and, except for an early mass on Sunday mornings, the church was closed. A week or two after this event, the decision of the Holy See respecting the agreement of October, 1826, reached Philadelphia. It was conveyed in a letter from Cardinal Cappellari,* prefect of the Sacred Congregation of the Propaganda, to Bishop Conwell, and notified to him that an assembly of cardinals, held on the 30th of April, had condemned the articles of agreement as subversive of the episcopal power and ecclesiastical discipline, and that Pope Leo XII. had confirmed their decision. In obedience to a request in the same letter, Bishop Conwell made a verbal announcement of this decision in St. Mary's church on the Sunday after he received it, and also caused it to be published in

---

* Afterwards Pope, under the title of Gregory XVI. (1831-1846).

the papers. "Being bound in conscience," said he, in making the announcement, "to obey this decision, I do most willingly submit, and engage to act on that full canonical power, claimed and exercised universally by bishops of every nation in the world, as well as by my more immediate brethren, the bishops of the United States, whose favor and indulgence I crave on this occasion."

TO THE REV. MR. HEYDEN.

PHILADELPHIA, *July 22, 1827.*

REV. DEAR SIR:

I was not at home when your letter arrived, having gone to Washington, on a brief excursion to recruit my spirits and my health by breathing an atmosphere of piety and of peace. I suppose you have heard before this that the "articles have been condemned" by the highest tribunal in the Catholic Church—the Sacred Congregation and the Pope. Their condemnation was promulged yesterday in all the Catholic churches in this city—to the inexpressible joy of your humble servant. You see by this that the Court of Rome is determined that the bishop *shall be bishop*, in spite of him. It seems that Providence has directed your retirement and mine from St. Mary's church to take place in time. We should feel cheap enough at leaving it in consequence of the late document. It was anticipated that the opposition would triumph; and perhaps so they would, if the communication had not caught them attempting to smuggle their favorites into St. Mary's under the shelter of those very articles which they once condemned.

With respect to the suit, I cannot inform you *officially*, Mr. Randal having been abroad for some time, and not being expected until Saturday next. But the general impression is that you ought to be present, to avoid falling under "contempt of court," and many other phrases of terrific import in the hands of a lawyer.

With respect to the details which will be produced by this news from Rome, I cannot inform you any thing as yet, as we have not had time to see how the "cat will jump." Give my most affectionate regards to all.
Yours,
JOHN HUGHES.

Excuse brevity and haste.

Mr. Hughes writes as follows to Mr. Heyden in September:

Our affairs remain *in statu quo*. Rev. Mr. H. is apparently quiet, as well as his friends, except perhaps some occasional under-growlings. The tide begins to turn against them, and, having been too prodigal of their lungs at first, they will hardly have breath to stem it. As for our part, we are as busy and as happy as we can make ourselves. They call us boys now and then; but *time* will gradually wear away this objection. Besides, if it be age they want, the bishop is old enough for them!

The Holy See in the mean time had resolved to attempt a radical cure of the evils which had so long afflicted the church of Philadelphia. Accordingly in August the Cardinal Prefect of the Propaganda invited Bishop Conwell to come to Rome, and instructed him to surrender the administration of his diocese to Dr. Maréchal, Archbishop of Baltimore. As the best means of preserving peace during his absence, Dr. Conwell restored Mr. Harold, reappointed him pastor of St. Mary's, and associated with him another Dominican, the Rev. John Ryan, who was acceptable to the trustees. Many persons indulged the hope that the schism was now at an end; but Mr. Hughes never concealed his opinion that the fire was only smothered, not extinguished. Archbishop Maréchal was then dying: he refused to bear the additional burden that was laid upon him, and Dr. Conwell put off his departure until he should hear again from the Propaganda. The archbishop died January 28, 1828.

TO THE REV. MR. BRUTÉ.

PHILADELPHIA, *Jan.* 31, 1828.

REV. AND DEAR SIR:

With how much sorrow have I learned the news of the archbishop's death! It was expected, and yet when it is actually made known it strikes us as if we had not expected it. "Blessed are they who die in the Lord," and I trust in the mercies of God that this was his case; the length and the nature of his sickness were such as to leave him time to prepare, and convince him that the hour could not be far distant. I perceive by Rev. Mr. Whitfield's letter that he himself desired to be recommended to the prayers of the bishop and clergy of Philadelphia. In compliance with this request I shall have a solemn mass for the repose of his soul in St. Joseph's Church some day next week. In the selection of that day I shall have to consult the choir. I suppose the same will be in all the other churches.

. . . . .

It is probable you will receive this in Baltimore, and if so I hope you will write me by return of our good bishop. I wish you could come and spend a week in Philadelphia. It is not yet what I could wish it to be, but I believe at no time since the origin of these unhappy troubles would a visit give you so little pain as at present. There seems at present a subtraction of that fuel on which the flame of discord has fed so long. How soon it may receive a supply of material our gracious God, to whom the events of futurity as well as the past are equally known, can tell. As for St. Joseph's, it is so happily situated that it contains no bone of contention. St. Mary's is *apparently* in the same situation; but the parties, and the friends, and the enemies, and above all the approaching election, looked upon by these unhappy and mistaken Catholics with more intense feeling and interest than that for president—all these things give just cause of apprehension that disturbance will revive, at least once a year, until better notions of church government shall have been gradually introduced.

I send you a packet intrusted to me by Mr. Duponceau. He gave a little picture, on which I recognized your handwriting, to Miss Rodrigue, observing that you wished to "convert him;" to which she replied, that it is time he should be converted. He seems very partial to me, and in conversation with him some time ago religion was casually introduced; in which he began to tell me what objections he could make *if* he wished to play the philosopher; whilst I, thinking it a good opportunity, began to tell him what I should say in reply, *if* I had such a philosopher to deal with. The conversation ended by his inquiring what was the best treatise on the subject of Christ's divinity. I recommended Grotius *De Veritate Christianæ Religionis*. Perhaps the *Philadelphia Catechism* * would have been better.

* By Bishop Conwell.

Recommending myself and my ministry to your fervent prayers,
I remain Your brother in Christ,
JOHN HUGHES.

TO THE SAME.

PHILADELPHIA, *May* 2, 1828.

REV. DEAR FRIEND:

It is long since I had the pleasure of a letter from you, and yet I think you are still some in my debt. However, I cannot remind you of my claim without writing; and since I have found a half hour of leisure and a pen, I shall at the same time write something besides. As to our local affairs, of which you have heard little for some time past, they are still in an unsettled state; you know I mean the churches of St. Mary and the Holy Trinity. In the former the pastors are at issue with the trustees, and I fear where there is so much combustible matter already, some unlucky spark will catch and excite the flame anew. You must know that five of the lay members in the board will not recognize the bishop as pastor, and without him the other five cannot have any majority. The consequence is that each party, true to its colors, will not meet the other unless enticed by the prospect of some wily advantage by which to gain the upper hand. There is no treasurer; and as there is no likelihood of a board during the year, the strong ground of contention will shortly be as to who shall receive the pew rent. No one can receive it according to law except duly appointed by the board; and yet, according to the same law, the pew is forfeited which is found six months in arrears! Besides, who in this state of things will pay the clergy, the organist, the sexton, and others? These are the seeds of future strife, and I fear they will have a hotbed vegetation. The present clergy have got a slight advantage in the renting of 40 pews, which they rent to *their friends*, in order to have a better election next year; and by and by they will blame these same people for meddling in church matters! My own opinion on this measure is, that the clergy will excite opposition, injure their ministry, and in the end defeat their own purpose. The bishop has little to expect or fear from either side; each is ready to bow to or insult him, just as it suits the interest of the moment, and I may add, *sic fuit ab initio.* In Trinity they cry out for a German priest; "they *consented* to take Mr. Carroll merely to get rid of the French clergyman," etc., etc.

Fortunately, there is no great excitement abroad on these topics; but how long will it continue so ? What will become of the Church if laymen, sometimes as depraved as they are ignorant, have such virtual influence in her government ? What will become of the clergy, if they must descend from the dignity of their sacred character, and become parties and the tools of parties in the petty broils of contending rivals for the office of trustee ? And for what advantage ? Just to have the choosing of their masters. There is no remedy for all this until the time shall have come to aim the blow, not at the branches, but at the root of this abominable system of trusteeing churches. In St. Joseph's all is quiet; I received such encouragement that I was lately on the point of enlarging the church, which is much too small for the concourse of people that attend it. But I have declined for the present, for particular reasons.

With respect to myself, I am stationary, and the only chance I shall have is to take a furlough of about three weeks immediately after the consecration of the archbishop. I hope to spend some time with you at the Mountain, when we can talk *facie ad faciem.*

P. S.—On reading over this hasty letter, I find I have inserted more treasonable matter than I dare repeat in Philadelphia for the life of me ! To you, however, I need not say with what caution it is to be spoken of as coming from me. Here I keep myself as quiet as I can, but in writing to you I have given free expression to my thoughts, and *let myself out,* more perhaps than you yourself will approve of. J. H.

A few days after this was written, the expected answer was received from the Propaganda. Bishop Conwell was again summoned to Rome; the Rev. William Matthews of Washington was appointed administrator of the diocese; and at the same time Fathers Harold and Ryan, who had been guilty of various acts of insubordination, received from the Pope and Vicar-General of the Dominicans an order to repair to Cincinnati.

TO THE REV. MR. BRUTÉ.

PHILADELPHIA, Ascension day [*May* 14], 1828.

REV. DEAR FRIEND:

I received your kind letter yesterday, and am sorry that the duties of my situation will not permit me, as I had hoped when I wrote last, to be present at the consecration of the Archbishop.* You are probably acquainted already with what has taken place in regard to this diocese. Rev. Mr. Matthews has arrived this day with important despatches from the Holy See, by which the bishop is called to Rome, and the Rev Messrs. Harold and Ryan *ordered* to depart this place, and *recommended* to go to Ohio! Mr. Mathews is appointed to administer the affairs of the diocese, "*durante absentia episcopi*" or "*donec aliter constituatur*,"—with the title *Vicarius Generalis Apostolicus*. Almighty God alone knows what will be the consequence. The bishop means to imitate Fenelon; we know not whom the others will take for their model. I feel pity for each, and for Mr. Matthews I can feel more, if possible, than for either. I will offer no commentary. Perhaps we will be all in the grave before Divine Providence shall have manifested its mysterious designs by drawing great and lasting good from transient evil. The shepherds have been stricken because the flock was divided, whereas there ought to have been but one shepherd and one sheep-fold. They have all *preached* obedience to lawful authority, but now it is in their power to *preach effectually* by the practice of their own doctrine. I trust they will. I feel dejected. I was perhaps heretofore hasty and unmerciful in my judgments; but now, and since I heard this news, their faults seem to have escaped my memory, and I am almost tempted to ask (as if I had a right to do so), Why are they overtaken by this humiliation? I speak as if you saw my heart. Please write immediately on receipt of this. It always does me good to receive a letter from you, but particularly so when visited by dejection of mind, from which I believe few are at all times exempted. The *facts* I have communicated are not secret.

Your affectionate friend and brother in Christ,

JOHN HUGHES.

* Dr. James Whitfield was consecrated Archbishop of Baltimore May 25, 1828.

Bishop Conwell immediately set out for Rome, but Messrs. Harold and Ryan took the absurd resolution of applying to the United States Government for protection against the papal mandate. It does not appear how they expected the President to step between them and an authority which had no control except over their consciences, nor whether they believed that John Quincy Adams had power to absolve them from their vows of obedience. In the absence of Mr. Clay (then Secretary of State), President Adams, through a subordinate officer of the State department, instructed the American minister in Paris to communicate on the subject with the papal nuncio at that capital, and to request that his good offices might be employed to procure redress from the Holy See. The reply of the nuncio showed so clearly that the matter was one with which the civil power had nothing to do, that Mr. Clay informed the American minister that he "might consider his agency in the affair as satisfactorily closed." *

TO THE REV. MR. HEYDEN.

PHILADELPHIA, *Oct.* 21, 1828.

REV. DEAR SIR:

How comes it that you appear determined never to write to an old friend, if it were only to inquire about your old flock, or about some of your city friends, who are so numerous? But no; not a line, not a word, for more than one year! *Si inimicus hoc fecisset, sustinuissem utique.* But after all I do not blame you much. Engaged as you no doubt have been in the duties of your mission, and cherishing your happy peace, you have not desired to disturb it by even a correspondence with those who are engaged in the scene of trouble and of warfare. Another reason may have been a secret apprehension lest you should be called to serve another campaign. However, without *guessing* further at the motives of your silence, I will give you an idea of our present situation.

---

* Messrs. Harold and Ryan withdrew at once from St. Mary's, but not from Philadelphia. In 1829 they went to Ireland, where they mended their ways, and died universally respected.—*De Courcy and Shea.*

You are aware of what took place regarding the bishop and his reverend opponents. Since the bishop's departure those gentlemen have made formal application to the Executive of the general government for protection against the mandates of the Pope and of the "master of his palace" (the general of the Dominicans). They are "citizens," and as such they beg the President to interpose the shield of government between them and their spiritual superiors! Hogan *talked* about it, but they have *done* it. We have the copies of their letters and of the communication on the part of government to the minister at Paris. Both are anti-Catholic and diabolical. They are prostrated, and I apprehend the next communication from beyond the waters will be a thunderbolt. All the clergy are well. Mr. Hurley has been joined by one of his brethren, Rev. Mr. O'Donnell, and another is expected soon. Mr. Mayne is going to St. Augustine's in Florida. Mr. Keilly is pastor of St. Mary's *solus*, assisted *pro tem.* by Mr. Cooper; Mr. Carrol at Trinity, amidst many cries for a Dutch priest; Donaghoe and myself are still in St. Joseph's, although I have to hold forth occasionally to the Philistines over the way.

We have received letters from the bishop, dated Paris, Aug. 18; then setting out for Rome. He wrote in good spirits, *sicuti mos erat*. He may be back. Our Very Rev. Administrator is determined to keep a respectable distance from the diocese until he is made certain of his appointment.

Give my sincere respects to your father and mother, to Margaret and Nicholas. Remember me also to all friends in Bedford. And do write as soon as may be convenient to

Your affectionate friend and humble servant,

JOHN J. HUGHES.

P. S. "I tell you, Heyden, you are playing your cards." When have you heard from Uncle Jemmy?* Report says he had the yellow fever only five times since he went to New York.

Bishop Conwell passed eight or ten months in Rome. Cardinal Cappellari expressed a strong desire that he should not return to his diocese, at least until the angry feelings

---

* The Rev. James Smith, a good but very eccentric priest.

which had been rife there so long should have wholly passed away. The poor old bishop fancied that there was a purpose of detaining him by force, and he hurriedly left Rome for Paris, and thence after some time returned to America. His fears were groundless; no effort was made to stop him, but he never recovered his episcopal jurisdiction.*

* Bishop Conwell passed the rest of his life in retirement in Philadelphia. He died in 1842, aged ninety-four, blind and loaded with infirmities.—*De Courcy and Shea.*

CHAPTER VI.

1827-1829.

Intimate relations with Mr. Bruté—Reply to Dr. Bedell—Letters to Mr. Heyden—Establishment of a Tract Society—Andrew Dunn—Converts at St. Joseph's—Death of Mr. Lynch—Letter to Thomas Heyden, Sr.

DURING these stormy years Mr. Hughes had been gradually winning the affection of his own people, and the respect of many others to whom the very name of a Catholic priest would once have been abominable. His friends at Mount St. Mary's watched his career with affectionate delight. "My dear brother," writes Father Bruté, "God may bless such wise and prudent beginnings of your holy ministry amidst such difficult and perplexing circumstances as it had pleased him to try them by. May he bless such worthy sentiments as expressed in your letter. I would never have others. . . . 'A breviary, an altar, heavenly independence on earth.' I hope your dear Catholics, at least all that meant well, will by and by know how to find their best peace. . . . . We are much concerned to hear that M. Mayne is so ill: he has, I think, a good constitution, but you have all so much labor that you cannot stand it. Do, my dear M. Hughes, see prudently to it; for the word of St. Bernard is true, the greatest zeal without health does little, whilst keeping a sufficient care of it, much is done even by an inferior degree of zeal. . . . . Mde. Iturbide, with whom you travelled to Washington, arrived here to-day from Bedford. She brings her son here. She is with Rev.

M. Lopez, whom you have also known." In all his perplexities he had recourse to Mr. Bruté. He asks his opinion, now upon a point of theology, again upon some antiquarian subject; now he applies to him to find a passage in one of the Fathers; now consults him upon a question of philology, or asks from him a summary of the principles of canon law which bear upon the existing state of affairs in Philadelphia. Upon all points this extraordinary man was ready to satisfy him. Mr. Hughes at that time was a hard student. For works of a purely literary character he seemed to care little, but he gave every spare hour to such reading as he thought he could make the most effective use of in his ministry, and especially to books of controversy and doctrine. Now and then he wrote anonymously in various newspapers, always sending his pieces to Mr. Bruté after they were printed, and asking his opinion of them, which was given with freedom. In a controversy with Dr. Gregory T. Bedell, then rector of St. Andrew's Protestant Episcopal church in Philadelphia, his prudence seems to have got the better of his theology.

MR. BRUTÉ TO MR. HUGHES.

MOUNT ST. MARY'S, *Sept.* 18, 1827.

. . . . .

I thank you much for that "Friend of Truth and Justice." I would recommend to compress a little; what is too long, in gazettes, commands not so much attention from hasty readers.

I would object a little, not to the prudence of St. Paul, etc., etc., but the measure of humoring even such an old favorite of the public. Alas! his true friends would be those who, rather than flatter him, and so far encourage such a peace and serenity, might prevent the immense temptation such old men now feel to close their days in their settled indifference, and fully trust so much human praise and honor.

Oct. 8.

. . . . .

How glad I am for the excellent effect of the piece you wrote, and which has been so well received. It is a great encouragement, with the preceding ones, to cultivate properly that vein of good, and to remove occasionally as much as possible of the remaining prejudices.

Yet Mr. Bruté was too good a friend to flatter. In the same letter he warns his "beloved brother" against caring for the applause of men; and in another, recurring to the Bedell letter, he says:

You imparted to me so much like a brother, though you are really my better now, the use of the sequel to the controversy in which God gave to our friend the manifest advantage, that I feel again ready to make some observations simply meant to let you know my opinion. . . . I find not the reply to Bedell what I would like; . . . . my main objection is that you put on, may be, more of liberality about creeds than our own firm faith, as exclusive as truth, divine truth could be, would well consistently justify if a watchful adversary was calling us to account about framing our religious belief by authority, even an authority to which all should submit. I think that the very Catholic principle is too much at stake at the bottom of these ideas of liberality, bigotism, &c., not to require much caution in handling them. . . . . Probably after all the piece will have been acceptable to the Protestants at large, and more good than I expected done by the "Friend of Truth and Justice."

And as if he feared lest the excitement of controversy might lead his dear pupil to forget the more spritual occupations of the priesthood, he adds, on a little scrap of paper fastened to the back of the letter: "My dear brother and friend, I thus insist again on my main thought—my only thought almost as I grow old: make in all things *positive good, simple obscure duty*, your principal joy and crown." It was fortunate for Mr. Hughes—or was it not rather a special order of Providence in his favor?—that at a period when he was most exposed to be led astray by the blandishments of the world and the praise of men, a devout and loving friend was at hand who knew how to advise him well, and had no fear to offend by speaking plainly. "I assure you," says Mr. Bruté again, "that I more and more take my whole consolation in this world in adoring, blessing, and trusting all in all to our Lord; and so do you, much better than myself. . . . . How pleased, moved, and edified am I at your blessed St. Joseph's! *Gaudium et corona mea*, you may say; yet say it not (in any complacency, I mean); leave it to your good guardian angel, and of so many souls keep only their testimony ready."

Here is a letter in which Mr. Hughes announces the death of one of his fellow-laborers, an ex-Jesuit:

TO THE REV. MR. HEYDEN.

Ascension Thursday [May 23], 1827.

DEAR SIR:

I have very unexpected news to communicate. The Rev. Mr. Baxter died this morning at two o'clock. He had complained on Friday last of a sore throat, and, as usual with such persons, it terminated in an inflammation of the brain, and he is now a corpse, laid out before the altar in St. Joseph's. There was so little apprehension of his death on my mind that I did not think necessary to mention it in my letter of Sunday. He received the last sacraments on Tuesday, and it was fortunate, as his mind has been gone ever since. I have hardly any other news to communicate. We are all well, and if we have zeal, we have enough whereon to exercise it. Every additional day's experience shows us that unless we labor *for God*, we labor in vain. What does it now matter for him that he was persecuted or applauded, if he has merited the reception which the "good and faithful servant" shall receive from his Lord? The sufferings of this present time are not worthy to be compared to that eternal weight of glory that shall be revealed hereafter.

Give my warmest affection to your good parents, whose kindness to me I shall never forget. Remember me also to Margaret and Mr. Lyons, and all friends.

I remain your affectionate brother in Christ,

JOHN HUGHES.

The next letter refers to a college which Mr. Heyden attempted to found, and shows also the interest which Father

Hughes still felt in his first parishioners, especially those who were admitted into the church under his instructions:

TO THE REV. MR. HEYDEN.

PHILADELPHIA, *Sept. 24,* 1827.

REV. DEAR SIR:

I know not how to apologize to you for my apparent rudeness in not answering your kind letter sooner. But the fact is that I had not time. I received thirteen converts into the church yesterday, and their instruction, together with catechism for the approaching confirmation, sick, sermon, etc., etc., took up my time in such a manner that I had not a moment. But you know what Philadelphia is. How rejoiced I have been to hear of the purchase of the academy, and its appropriation to the cause of religion! I hope the forest shall smile under the cultivation of two such efficient laborers in the vineyard as you and Mr. Smith.

With respect to assistance, I know none who would suit you better than Mr. Varin, principally on account of his knowledge of German. He is, besides, an excellent Latin and French scholar. But if you want to rival St. Mary's, at Emmitsburg, I shall tell you how you can do it. I can inform you, from unquestionable, but as yet *secret* authority, that the C. Seminary in Washington, D. C., is about to be broken up. I can inform you further that the Rev. Mr. Keilly will very probably quit the Jesuits on account of it. I can inform you further that there is no diocese in the Union in which he would rather form a seminary than in Pennsylvania, though I am not certain that the location of yours would meet his views. The last thing I can inform you is, that his professors are ready to go with him wherever he may undertake such an institution. These are the materials with which you may build up a splendid and permanent edifice, if you can only work them in. Rev. Mr. Keilly is admirably calculated to superintend such an institution, as the experience of several years has proved in Washington. You would do well to write to him in a "general way," on the subject of your college, as if you knew nothing of what is going on in the society; and from his answer you can gather how his pulse beats, or, in the language of your old friend, you will "see how the cat jumps." . . . .

Rev. Mr. Hurley is well, and rejoices in the event which leaves it in your power to lay the foundation of a diocesan seminary. May Almighty God give his blessing to so laudable an undertaking!

Give my love to your good father and mother, to Margaret and Nicholas, and to little Bridget. Also, Mr. Keefe and family, Mr. Harman, Mrs. Byrne, Miss Ally, Miss Walters, Miss Reilly, etc., etc., and particularly to Mr. Osterlo. Do not forget my first penitent, Mrs. Chapman. I suppose Mr. and Mrs. Brown have started ere this. Please to let me know how my *converts* (as far as they were mine) come on. How does Miss W—— and Miss R—— do? And the man near Buckstown—I forget his name? Tell Margaret I impose on her (as a penance, if she pleases) to give me a detail of these matters, which are too minute for a person engaged in projects so grand as those which, I suppose, engage your thoughts at present. This, however, must not deprive me of the pleasure of receiving a letter from yourself as soon as leisure will permit. Write great things about your churches and colleges, etc., etc., and leave details for Margaret, who knows what I would like to learn. I hope she and you will do me that favor soon. In the mean time,

I remain your affectionate friend and brother in Christ,

JOHN HUGHES.

Mr. Hughes himself was engaged about this time in an undertaking from which he hoped for important results. This was the establishment of a tract society in Philadelphia, to be supported by voluntary contributions. The society was to publish in a cheap and attractive form short religious essays, chiefly of a controversial character, and sell them at cost price to such of the clergy as might feel disposed to distribute them gratis among the people. He commenced the enterprise by preparing an antidote to an English Protestant tale, which had lately been republished in Philadelphia, and very widely circulated. The scene of this story was laid in Ireland. Andrew Dunn, the hero, is a Catholic; but having presumed to question some of the doctrines of the Church, his priest horsewhips him. Still unconvinced, he procures a Bible, talks with a few godly persons, and ends by becoming a sound Protestant, and baffling the best theologians of the "Romish communion." Mr. Hughes resolved to take "*Andrew Dunn*" for the title of his story; and by an odd coincidence Mr. Bruté seems to have fallen upon the same idea. "I cannot but approve," writes Mr. Hughes to his old friend, "the skeleton of a new '*Andrew Dunn*' which you have framed; but I would recommend you not to occupy your time (otherwise so valuable) with it, until you have an opportunity of seeing whether that which I am preparing for the press will not answer the purpose of an antidote." *The Conversion and Edifying Death of Andrew Dunn* (12mo, Philadelphia, 1828), is the only attempt, I believe, at fictitious composition in prose which Mr. Hughes ever made. It is curious to contrast the style of this little book with that of the polemical writings which were so soon to give him a reputation. Looked upon simply as a story, it certainly is not well told. That facility which was afterward the most striking characteristic of his pen, had yet to be acquired by practice; but skill in argument and familiarity with the best weapons of controversy were his already. It will be worth our while to see a little of Andrew Dunn. In his early life, as told in the first chapter, there are one or two points which remind us of John Hughes's own boyhood:

Andrew Dunn was born of poor, but honest and industrious parents, by profession Protestants, and warmly attached to their persuasion. Anxious to instil the same principles into the tender mind of their son, they took him with them, as often as occasion offered, to hear sermons, both at Church and Meeting-Houses, and carefully taught him their Catechism.

Wishing also to give him a good stock of learning, they sent him to a day school, where he was instructed in reading, writing, and accounts. At the age of fifteen they took him away from school, and kept him at home, to assist them in their daily labors. His obedience to their orders, and his attention to their wants, made him extremely dear to them. Indeed, he was beloved by all that knew him; for he was naturally of a mild and amiable disposition.

He was also a very good liver; he had a great horror for cursing, swearing, drunkenness, and all such vices; and seemed indeed in earnest to save his soul, by loving and serving God in the best manner he could. He daily searched the Scriptures; he frequently attended sermons; and he always, with great docility, took for granted that every thing the Preacher told him was true. So exemplary was his conduct, that his neighbors looked upon him as a saint, and would often wish that they were like Andrew Dunn.

At the age of thirty, Andrew began to be troubled with very great *Doubts* about religion, which changed his former cheerfulness into dejection and melancholy. His friends having noticed this change, and occasionally observed him to be uncommonly serious, with his eyes often bathed in tears, at length made bold to ask the cause of his apparent trouble. "Oh! Andrew," said they, "excuse our boldness; do tell us the cause of those melancholy looks, and those floods of tears we so often witness. A life like yours, spent in the service of God, ought to be to you a source of joy, as being a *sure* token of joys that will never end. If the remembrance of your past sins causes your great grief, have confidence in the goodness of God, and in the merits of Jesus, who has bled and died for the expiation of your sins; remember that 'the blood of Jesus Christ cleanseth us from all sin.'"—1 John i. 7.

In answer to these questions, Andrew exposes at some length the doubts which perplex him. How do I know, he asks, that my interpretation of the Bible is the right one? What reason have I for being a Protestant, except that my father was one before me? Why is it that Protestants in their controversies with the Roman Catholics are so often guilty of misrepresentation, and so often beaten in argument? How can the Protestant Church be the Church of Christ, having made its first appearance fifteen hundred years after the time of Christ? And how can I say with truth, in the words of the Apostles' Creed which I am taught to repeat at morning prayer, "I believe in the Holy Catholic Church," knowing as I do that I am not a Catholic, but a Protestant?

He is advised to consult his minister; but from this

gentleman he gets little except an explanation of the origin of the term Protestant. A conversation with "John Smith, a neighbor of his, and a very good liver, but a Roman Catholic," leads to a happier result. John and Andrew discuss the chief doctrines of the Catholic faith; but before they begin, they kneel together, and Smith prays for heavenly direction: "O Lord, do thou who hast sent thine only Son Jesus to teach us the truths of eternity; who hast commanded us to believe those truths, under pain of eternal misery; who hast said, Mark xvi. 16,* 'he that believeth not shall be damned;' do thou in thy great mercy direct us to the true faith, and conduct us, we beseech thee, to that Church to which thou daily callest such as shall be saved." John Smith then proceeds to show the impossibility of taking the Bible alone as a rule of faith, and the necessity of pastors, duly commissioned to teach, and deriving their authority from Christ, through an unbroken succession of bishops reaching back to the Apostles. He shows that the Roman Catholic Church alone has such a succession of pastors, and that it alone has fulfilled the command of Christ, "Go and teach all nations." He enumerates the different countries that have received the faith from Roman missionaries, and speaks of the barrenness of Protestant attempts to convert the heathen. "Besides this," he adds, "the Catholic religion is the safest to die in."

Now it is a certain fact that thousands upon thousands of Protestants, on their death-beds, call for the assistance of Catholic Priests, and embrace the Catholic Faith; whilst it is equally certain that *no* Catholic, that is no person who had lived all his life-time a Catholic, was *ever known* to wish to die a Protestant; therefore, Andrew, I think this conclusion clear: the Catholic religion is the *safest and best.*

Again, whilst we see thousands of Protestants daily becoming

* The circumstance of Smith's quoting chapter and verse in his prayer is a curious instance of the polemical spirit cropping out where it is least expected.

Catholics, though, by doing so, they are exposed to the ridicule and persecutions of the ungodly; yet we seldom see or hear of any Catholic becoming Protestant, unless with a view to live a more unrestrained and licentious life. And so evidently is this the case that a Protestant Clergyman, *Dean Swift*, used to say whenever he heard of any Catholic becoming Protestant, "I wish, when the Pope weeds his garden, he would not throw his nettles over our wall." Of this class, it is true, there have been a few; but they have often met with the most awful judgments of heaven. Dr. Milner mentions the following, in his "End of Religious Controversy": Smyth was one of those wretched Priests who, wanting the grace necessary for living up to the strictness of their obligations, left the *Catholic Church* and became a *Protestant*. This unfortunate man *dropped down dead* in Canterbury Cathedral, about the year 1780. About the same time another unprincipled Priest of Staffordshire, of the name of Taylor, *met with the same fate* in stepping into a stage coach. Another still more unprincipled Priest, Dr. Geddes, with Lewis of Leominster, Holmes of Essex, and Rogers of Birmingham, *all met with sudden deaths*. James Quesnel and James Nolan also, having both been warned by their friends of the fate they might expect, but continued to waver about their duty, *both dropped down dead in the streets*, the former at Worcester, the latter in London. Awful and terrible judgments of God, Andrew, are these on the crime of Apostacy!

From this time Andrew Dunn's conversion is quick. He spends most of the night in prayer, and in the morning goes to the Catholic chapel, where he is struck by the devotion of the people, but horrified at the sight of a crucifix. "'Ah!' said he, 'this looks like *Image worship;* this cannot be right; when I once get out of this place, I will never more return.'" Smith, however, easily removes his doubts; talks with him about the sacraments of penance and the eucharist; and in the evening takes him to hear lectures upon the same subjects by a Catholic priest. So clear and powerful are this clergyman's arguments, that immediately after the lectures Andrew professes himself a Catholic. One chapter is devoted to an account of his preparation for the sacraments; one to his daily exercises of devotion; and another to his last sickness and death. In these three an opportunity is found to teach the practice of the principal Christian virtues; in the eight preceding chapters the author had developed the arguments in favor of some of the chief dogmas of the faith.

Such is "Andrew Dunn"—slight enough, compared with Mr. Hughes's other writings; but there are persons yet living who remember the effect produced by its appearance, especially among the poor people of the country districts, for whom it was principally written. The following letter from the author to his venerable friend at Mount St. Mary's gives his own views on the subject of this little tract:

TO THE REV. MR. BRUTÉ.

PHILADELPHIA, *March* 3, 1828.

REV. DEAR FRIEND:

It is a pleasure to have so direct an opportunity of sending you "*Andrew Dunn.*" I have just got a few from the printer. I have but a few minutes to spare, and time only to request you will read and let me know what you think of it. It will give me great pleasure if, as I hope, it will meet your approval. Please write to me as soon as you can after reading it, and if you like it you can have any reasonable quantity for your neighborhood at first cost; out of which number so many may be sold at $12\frac{1}{2}$ cents a piece as will bring back your money, and leave a quantity to give to the poor or Protestants gratis. I think the country is the place where such things will be most useful. If they should be the means of bringing only *one* soul to the knowledge of the truth of God, would it not be enough to authorize the attempt? I do not wish the thing to make any noise, because the Protestants will take the alarm; but managed properly it will leave in the hands of the clergy the means of diffusing the knowledge of religion in a way suited to the circumstances of the Catholics at large. These things, in addition to their pastoral exertions, may, with the blessing of God, be as the oil to supply from time to time the lamp of faith even among Catholics, and serve to ground them on the eternal rock of whose stability they have sometimes such faint conceptions.

The fund increases apace, and the great advantage is that the laity have no share in its management. It is one dollar, given once by those who wish the prosperity of the undertaking. I do not intend that it shall ever exceed $300. But I will write soon again and give you further particulars.

Wishing to be remembered to all the reverend gentlemen and friends, I remain   Yours in Christ,
JOHN HUGHES.

MR. BRUTÉ TO MR. HUGHES.

MOUNT ST. MARY'S, *March* 12, 1828.

MY DEAR BROTHER:

Like you extremely busy—excuse my short lines. I have not been able to read Dunn's happy conversion, but I rejoice for it, and request you to send me a number of copies to the charge of five dollars.   .   .   .   .   .

The success of *Andrew Dunn* was much greater than that of the project from which it sprang. It seems to have been the first fruit and the last of the association for the purpose of circulating cheap controversial tracts, from which so much was expected. Poor Father Bruté, with all his zealous interest in "Mr. Hughes's dear M. Dunn," as he used to call it, was not a little embarrassed by the five dollars' worth of copies he had ordered. More than two months afterward, at the end of a long letter about various matters, he wrote as follows:

"It seems as if I tried to avoid answering my old debt—that invoice of your tracts. Indeed, I ought to avoid it for shame! Your poor friend is at a loss what to say, except, with utmost simplicity, this: I have the disposition of no possible money, so that I first feel at a loss how to account myself; secondly, I am equally at a loss, from my corner of the second story, secluded with my old books, how to circulate the tracts. I have trusted them to MM. Egan and McGerry, and you may be sure of the $5 first. I took some, and paid M. Egan for them (say, 50 cents—all I then had of money; for it is a literal truth—only speak not of it—I have no more money from my dear friends than either Sourin, or Gartland, or any one—in fact, I want none); but when I heard the plan, I trusted that my gentlemen would support it, and so they surely will." Perhaps other clergymen in whom Mr. Hughes put his trust were as empty of pocket as Father Bruté; perhaps the Catholics of Philadelphia, to whom he looked for money to pay the necessary expenses, were not alive to the importance of his scheme. At all events, we hear no more of the project for disseminating religious knowledge by means of cheap and attractive pamphlets.

His sermons probably made more converts than his tract society. He speaks of one of his disciples in the following letter:

TO THE REV. MR. BRUTÉ.

PHILADELPHIA, *October* 21, 1828.

* * * * *

Miss M——, whose conversion to the Catholic Church I mentioned some time ago, made her first communion last Sunday two weeks, to the great edification of all who witnessed it. Her acknowledged talents, her family, her enlightened piety and prudent zeal are all calculated to produce a happy effect on all within the reach or influence of her example. It has excited a good deal of feeling among the Episcopal clergy, and the more so as she gave them repeated opportunities to prove the truth of the religion she abandoned, having had frequent interviews with Dr. Abercrombie and Bishop White for that purpose. She demanded *proof* when they thought to amuse her with *assertion*. She says that she did not permit them to explain the Catholic doctrine, but their own; and having hemmed [them] up by cutting short all subjects other than the proof of the Protestant religion, and of the Episcopal form rather than the Unitarian or Baptist, they were like dumb oracles—except that they said the priest must have given her lessons, and that she had lost her senses. In fact, I had told her to apply to them, lest it should [be said] that she had been led away without hearing the other side. She is of opinion that although they may be sincere, yet if they come to examine the question and compare notes they will be astonished to find, both clergy and laity, that there is no faith among them, or if there be, no one knows what it is. There are three or four others receiving from me private instructions, determined to say nothing about their intention to change until they shall have known enough of both religions to give unanswerable reasons for their conduct. Pray for them all.

In the next, he alludes to the death of the Rev. Mr. Lynch, one of his fellow-students at the Mountain:

TO THE REV. MR. BRUTÉ.

PHILADELPHIA, *Nov.* 18, 1828.

REV. DEAR FRIEND:

I received yours from Frederick this morning, and it has given me much pleasure, though I had been acquainted with the painful relation from other sources before. The occasion must have been solemn and melancholy. It has not, of course, made the same *vivid* impression on me as if I had witnessed it; and still the fact of our long acquaintance, and the circumstance of our having been anointed together, have filled my mind with reflections which it is unnecessary for me to mention. Even on that day Death had marked him. He obtained two years of respite, and it is a consolation to know that the indulgence was improved. I fear I shall not have so long a warning, and it is so difficult to be always prepared! especially when one lives in the world, and when even the exercise of the ministry is replete with danger and distraction of mind. Still it is in the world that the ministry must be exercised, and God knew our weakness before he intrusted us with it. He is, besides, our Father, and provided we go on quietly endeavoring to do his will, we may still hope in him with the confidence of children. For my own part, I am so incessantly occupied in the affairs of others that I am often discouraged at having so little time to attend to my own. The share of the ministry that devolves on me is more than I could well discharge. Besides the temporal affairs of the church, which are the business of every day, Rev. Mr. Matthews has put me in for the concerns of the house, marketing, servants, etc., etc.

MR. BRUTÉ TO MR. HUGHES.

SUNDAY, *Feb.* 1, 1829.

I am delighted to hear such good news of the returning piety of your vast Catholicity of Philadelphia. See in a short time what can be granted by God to the zeal even of a few priests as you are for that whole city!

The following, to the father of his friend Rev. Mr. Heyden, represents Mr. Hughes in a new character:

TO MR. THOMAS HEYDEN, SR., BEDFORD, PA.

PHILADELPHIA, *Feb.* 2, 1829.

I remember that some time during my preparation to come to Philadelphia, Mrs. Heyden observed, in the train of a conversation in which Nicholas and Margaret were successively the topic, that she wished I would look out for a good match for either or both. It arose from the scarcity of *respectable* Catholics in the range of their acquaintance at Bedford, and was made by Mrs. Heyden in a kind of half jesting way. Still I have thought of it from time to time; and at last I have found the very person who would suit Nicholas. She is the daughter of a merchant who has retired, perhaps as much as ten years, from business. She is accomplished in all the branches of female education. Having been deprived of her mother at an early age, the superintendence of the house devolved on her, and in this respect she acquits herself like a perfect matron. She has *prudence, education, respectability*, and religion in as great a degree as I have ever witnessed. In a word, she is worthy to be a member of your family, a sister and companion of Margaret; and when I say this, I don't know I could pay her a higher compliment. She has been a penitent of mine since I came to Philadelphia, and a monthly communicant since perhaps ten years—being now five and twenty. There are two or three things which it is impossible for me to say: 1st. With regard to her father's wealth, I only know that he lives in a private but superior style, and has, within three miles of the city, a small but beautiful country-seat, in which he spends a part of every summer. He has four children—two sons and two daughters. The sons have professions, and are pursuing them; one is a physician. The other daughter is still at school, being about fifteen. 2dly. I cannot say whether she would have him, although I do not know any reason to suppose the contrary, except the fear of making her father unhappy by leaving him; for this seems to occupy all her thoughts, the happiness of her father. 3dly. I know not whether Nicholas has not already made a choice. If not, let him come to Philadelphia to purchase *his spring goods;* and being a man of business, let him see and judge for himself. I promise to give him an introduction, to assist him in his selection, and if need be, to go his security to any amount!

If such a thing should take place, I have no fear of receiving your thanks, the thanks of the family, and of the congregation, when this lady's worth is known in Bedford as well as it is in Philadelphia.

Thus, dear sir, I have seriously discharged an obligation as far as in *me* lies, which I undertook perhaps as much in jest as in earnest. Please write me on the subject as early as you can. In the mean time give my love to Father Thomas, Nicholas, Mrs. Heyden, and Margaret. Tell her how much pleased I should be to receive a letter from her, since her brother will not write. Remember me also to all my old friends, and young ones too, and believe me,

Your affectionate friend and humble servant,

JOHN HUGHES.

P. S. Mr. Osterlo called on me. He said he had a letter from Mr. Heyden for me, but his trunk was stolen off the stage, and so I was robbed. J. H.

CHAPTER VII.

1829–1830.

St. John's Orphan Asylum.—Catholic Emancipation.—Controversy with Dr. Delancey.—Mr. Hughes recommended for Bishop.—Letters to his sister and Mr. Purcell.—Rev. F. P. Kenrick appointed Bishop of Philadelphia.—Miscellaneous Correspondence.—Letters to *The Protestant*.

In the year 1829 an incident which came under Mr. Hughes's notice in the course of his ministry among the poor, led to the establishment of St. John's Orphan Asylum. He gives the following account of its origin in a communication published in the Philadelphia *Catholic Herald*, in January, 1834:

It originated in the forlorn condition of one or two families of orphan children in the winter of 1829. Their parents, recently from Ireland, had died, leaving them helpless, without food, clothing, or a house to shelter them. There was no door of charity open for them, except the almshouse. St. Joseph's Orphan Asylum was already full. Their first friends, who had some knowledge of their situation, were themselves poor—some of them in families at service; still they raised a subscription among themselves to provide for the immediate wants of these helpless objects. But who was to take charge of them?

This was the difficulty which brought the case under the notice of the writer, who felt that there was benevolence as well as means enough abroad to keep them from going to the almshouse as their only escape from perishing. He accordingly engaged the ready co-operation of a few charitable persons in happier circumstances. A society was formed, composed chiefly of the poor, the subscription being only $1.50 a year. An application was made to the superior of the Sisters of Charity, and four sisters were deputed from the community to take charge of these children. There were already eight on the list, which soon after increased to sixteen. A house was then rented in Prune street at $400 per annum.

The zeal of a few benevolent ladies, whose charity on that as well as other occasions should never be forgotten, supplied the furniture and bedding which were immediately requisite. This was the commencement of what is now called "St. John's Orphan Asylum," and these were the circumstances which gave occasion to its existence.

What has been its history? It has since the period of its establishment afforded home, protection, food, clothing, and education to a number of destitute orphans varying from 20 to 28. It has besides this afforded the benefits of religious instruction and *gratuitous* education to more than 1,000 female children. The expenses of its support have been on an average about $1,600 per annum. This sum has been derived from the subscriptions of the original society (which, however, has been neglected in a great measure since the commencement of St. John's); from private donations; from the sale of fancy articles manufactured by the Sisters themselves; and from the proceeds of five charity sermons, ... together with one or two inconsiderable legacies of a hundred dollars each. The number of orphans at present is 28, and the number of children attending the school, 190; of whom 129 are gratuitous, and the others generally $2 each per quarter—which also goes to support the orphans.

From the outset a spirit of rivalry existed between this institution and St. Joseph's Orphan Asylum. Mr. Hughes tried all means to remove the hostile feeling, going so far even as to propose, in November, 1833, to place his asylum under the control of the managers of St. Joseph's, on the sole condition that the school for poor female children attached to it should be continued. The board would not accept the offer, unless it were made without any conditions whatever. In 1836, however, the three Catholic Orphan Asylums then existing in Philadelphia were reorganized; St. John's took all the boys, St. Joseph's all the girls, and St. Vincent's was abolished.

He writes thus to his college friend Mr. Purcell, who had become a professor at Mount St. Mary's:

TO THE REV. MR. PURCELL.

PHILADELPHIA, *April* 23, 1829.

REV. DEAR FRIEND:

I just begin to have a little leisure after the pleasing duties of Easter. They were very numerous. A remarkable accession of numbers has been observed at the holy table this year, not only in this church, but in all the others. There were, as near as I could estimate, between four and five hundred persons at communion in St. Joseph's on Sunday morning. Most of them had been preparing from the beginning of Lent, one evening in each week having been set apart for hearing confessions. Still, the proportion of those who approached, compared with those who should have approached, taking the whole city into count, is hardly one to fifteen ! . . .

We yesterday received a letter from our mutual dear friend Rev. Mr. Egan, concluded on the 27th of January. You no doubt received letters by the same arrival. His letter to us, having special reference to the ecclesiastical affairs of this place, was "confidential." He was well, and improved in his constitution. He mentions that he would leave Rome on this day, and sail 15th of June. God grant him a safe return.* You have seen, I suppose, that Bishop England is transferred to the diocese of Ossory, in Ireland. Poor Charleston!

I suppose that before this time the bill for the emancipation of the Catholics has passed into a law of the British Government, and certainly it is the commencement of a new era in the history of our hapless country. I hope too that, the penalties heretofore incurred by entering into the pale of our holy religion being now removed, the conversions from the ways of error will be numerous. Who would have thought, five years ago, that Peel, the Pharaoh of the

* Mr. Egan had gone to Europe for his health. He died on his way home, at Marseilles, May 29, 1829.

British Government, would have come out the advocate of Catholic rights, and put an end to their protracted bondage ? And now, who knows what happier changes in regard to religious belief will follow in the train of consequences ? It was stated yesterday in the papers (but it must be a hoax) that Dr. Doyle is to be made a cardinal.

* * * *

Give my love to Rev. Mr. Bruté, Mr. McGerry, and all my old companions, not forgetting Gegan. Hoping to hear from you shortly, I remain

Your affectionate friend and brother in Christ,

JOHN HUGHES.

The emancipation bill received the signature of George IV. on the 13th of April, 1829. We can imagine the delight with which Father Hughes heard the news. He writes respecting it as follows : " This was the result of O'Connell's inauguration of the doctrine of rights in the British empire; but it is only just to say that, notwithstanding his immense power in swaying the minds of his countrymen, the emancipation act itself could never have been carried through Parliament, against the prejudices of the British people, except by the influence of another Irishman—but at that period more English—named, by well-deserved title, Field Marshal the Duke of Wellington. Before this event took place, I had been already ten [twelve] years in the United States. I rejoiced with others over this event. In the city in which I then lived, Philadelphia, chimes of Protestant bells (if we can call them so) were ringing out notes of joy over the fact that England had at last surrounded with black lines, if it had not altogether obliterated, its unjust legislation toward the loyal Catholic subjects of the British empire." * On the 31st of May, a solemn thanksgiving service, in gratitude for the passing of this bill, was held in St. Augustine's church. The street, and the yards, windows, and doorsteps of the neighboring houses, were crowded with

---

* Unpublished letter to the editor of the Dublin *Freeman's Journal*, Dec. 11, 1861.

people who could not find standing room in the church. Mass was sung by Dr. Hurley, and Mr. Hughes preached a sermon from the text, "Lord, thou hast blessed thy land: thou hast turned away the captivity of Jacob. . . . Mercy and truth have met each other: justice and peace have kissed. Truth is sprung out of the earth: and justice hath looked down from heaven."—*Psalm* lxxxiv. The sermon was printed in pamphlet form, with a dedication to O'Connell. It was Father Hughes's first published discourse, and great was the excitement caused by its appearance in the little town of Chambersburg. One of his brothers writes to tell him how eager all the townspeople are to read it. "I was astonished," he says, "when Mr. C——, in company with his lady, stopped me in the street to shake hands with me, and proclaimed you to be an orator."

Catholic emancipation was made the subject of an article, on the 6th of June, in the *Church Register*, the organ in Philadelphia of the Protestant Episcopalians. "We shall be sorry for this measure," said the writer, "if the revival and dissemination of the trumperies and delusions of popery are to be the result of it." "The lion, who lies in his den, pining with famine, or wasted and weakened with disease, unable to raise his feeble limbs against even a helpless lamb, is still a lion, and with returning health and vigor will recover his wonted ferocity, and wait only for occasions to evince it." In the same paper was another article commenting upon the London *Catholic Miscellany's* report of the missions in Ohio. "If the funds by which such extensive and surprising results have been brought about," says the *Register*, "have been derived from the contributions of charitable persons in Europe—if such efforts are made by aliens to our country to establish in her western wilds a superstitious and corrupt church, shall Protestant Episcopalians be listless and indifferent to the urgent calls for their exertions and aid in imparting to those destitute regions the privileges and blessings of that church whose faith and worship and

ministry they regard as preëminently pure and scriptural?"
The *Register* was conducted by an association of clergymen,
each of whom in rotation directed it for a certain time. The
editorial chair, when these articles appeared, was occupied
by the Rev. W. H. Delancey, D.D. (late bishop of the Protestant Episcopal Church in western New York), and to him
Mr. Hughes accordingly addressed a note, announcing his
intention to review them, and to hold the editor personally
responsible for their language, unless he should designate
some other person as the writer. Mr. Delancey replied that
"the terms of the editorial association of which he was a
member did not permit him to disclose the authorship of any
particular articles in the *Register*," and that he should accordingly prepare himself to endure Mr. Hughes's meditated
assault "with as much composure as he could summon to
his aid." He seems to have had no fear of the young priest,
then just rising into notice, and as a writer utterly unknown
except to his immediate friends; but before the close of the
controversy he saw reason to respect his ability, if not to
agree with his conclusions. There was no Catholic periodical printed in Philadelphia, and Mr. Hughes accordingly
sent his letters, three or four in number, to the *United States
Gazette*, one of the leading daily papers of the city, then
edited by Mr. Joseph R. Chandler. Mr. Delancey replied
through the *Register*. The discussion lasted from the 14th
of July to the 22d of August, and seems to have attracted
a great deal of attention among Catholics. Its best result
probably was that it introduced Mr. Hughes to the arena of
theological conflict, and taught men to look to him as a
champion always ready to defend his religion. His previous
anonymous essays in the way of polemical writing were the
occasional occupations of a leisure hour. From this time he
may be said to have made it his business to fight for the
faith whenever it was attacked.

In October of this year he attended the first provincial
council of Baltimore, as an unofficial adviser, jointly with

Dr. Hurley, of Mr. Matthews, the administrator of the diocese of Philadelphia. Father Matthews was anxious to resign his burdensome office, and one of the duties of the council was to provide a successor for him. During their deliberations, Bishop Conwell arrived unexpectedly from Europe; and although he did not take a seat at the council, he was frequently in consultation with his episcopal brethren. While in Rome he had recommended Mr. Hughes to the Holy See as one of the fittest persons who could be chosen for the next bishop of Philadelphia; but the council preferred the Rev. Francis Patrick Kenrick, then president of a theological seminary at Bardstown, Kentucky, and accordingly advised his appointment as coadjutor to Bishop Conwell, with full powers of administration. Providence held Father Hughes in reserve for another work. We shall see, further on, how on two other occasions before his appointment to the see of New York, he was nominated for different bishoprics; how his consecration seemed certain; and how in one instance it was only defeated by an accident.

I am not sure that he knew of Bishop Conwell's recommendation. If he did, that knowledge was never allowed for a moment to interfere with the zealous prosecution of the labors of his ministry. His letters show how entirely schools, asylums, the instruction of converts, the visitation of the sick, the duties of the pulpit and the confessional, employed his thoughts. To Ellen Hughes, who had become a Sister of Charity under the name of Mary Angela, he wrote thus:

TO ELLEN HUGHES.

September 17, 1829.

MY DEAR SISTER:

I received your letter by Mr. Petray, and I cannot for shame allow him to return without writing to you. I had been seriously alarmed about your health in consequence of divers reports, but your letter removed my worst apprehensions. Mother's health has been worse than usual, but Margaret's last letter informs me of a considerable change for the better. I am generally well myself, thank God!—and it is well that I am so, for I am hurried every hour. Every thing goes on well here at present—persons joining the church from time to time, and others learning to *practise* its precepts.

I have been delighted with Bishop England, who is to start with Mr. Petray. . . . . I am always distressed, my dear sister, when I perceive in your letters expressions accusing me of neglect toward you. It is true, if you were to judge my affection for you by the *number* of my letters, you would have some reason for the suspicion; but I have explained it so often that, when you consider my situation and your own, you ought to make every allowance. I hope the time will come when I can write to you without any risk of neglecting more important duties; but at present, and indeed at all times since I came to Philadelphia, I am like a servant who has a thousand masters at once.

Give my love and respect to Fathers McElroy and Grace, to the Sisters, to the ladies and gentlemen of St. John's choir, etc., etc., and believe me

Your affectionate brother,

JNO. HUGHES.

TO THE SAME.

Nov. 11, 1829.

MY DEAREST SISTER:

I received your letter by Mr. O'Neill, but had not the pleasure to see the bearer. I have enjoyed good health generally since I wrote you last, and when I was in Baltimore I was strongly inclined to go to see you, and I believe I was prevented only by the fear of being tempted to go further, and so spend more time away than I could afford.

I received a few days ago a letter from Margaret. She is in good health and spirits. The family are well, except that mother, in addition to her other complaints, begins to be afflicted with rheumatism in her back. Cousin John Treaner sailed the other day for Ireland, after having *in vain tried* to recover a part of his brother's estate.

I hear great accounts of the success which attends all the undertakings of good Father McElroy in Frederick. Has the seminary commenced yet? How many pupils? and what prospects? Here every thing in the way of religion goes as well as might be expected, considering all things. There are still converts from the different denominations of Protestants; and if the Catholics themselves were what they should be, the number of converts would be astonishing. There is no place in the country where our holy religion would progress more than in Philadelphia, were it not for the obstacles that have been thrown in the way.

TO THE REV. MR. PURCELL.

PHILADELPHIA, *Dec.* 21, 1829.

REV. AND DEAR FRIEND:

I received your letter on my return from New York more than a week ago, and some apology is due for not answering, or at least acknowledging it sooner. I saw our poor friend* embark, and in a few hours the canvas of his ship seemed to mingle with the distant clouds. His departure, which excited a good deal of speculation here, has entailed upon you a responsibility which I trust you will have the fortitude, as I know you have the qualifications, to sustain. Your situation is one of great difficulty. Your institution has certainly taken the lead of every other Catholic establishment in the country; but recent circumstances are calculated to excite in its friends a degree of prospective solicitude. There is a spirit of unusual vigor—a species of revival—infused into the institutions at Baltimore and Georgetown, which, unless by wise management and renewed exertion, Emmitsburg is destined to feel. Of course there is patronage enough in the country for them all; but whether or not there will be a reaction in favor of those institutions at the expense of yours, will depend very much on the united zeal, prudence, and exertion of you and of your colleagues. I have had frequent opportunities to judge since I left there, and I do not know any thing so well calculated to make the institution flourish at home and popular abroad, as to make the boys happy, and the parents at ease, by frequent and judicious correspondence. In this, poor Mr. Egan was extremely felicitous, and Mr. McGerry extremely otherwise.

---

* Mr. McGerry, on whose departure for Europe Mr. Purcell became president of Mount St. Mary's.

You have been kind enough in your letter to say that you will receive with consideration any remarks I may deem proper in regard to the institution; and if a constant desire to see it prosperous could establish a right, I might say that I am entitled to the privilege. But after all, human exertion or human wisdom is in vain, unless that God support it who has rendered the administration of all your predecessors happy and successful. If there is any thing which I might suggest to you, it would be this: that being president *de nomine*, you would also be president *de facto;* for I am afraid lest your modesty or humility might induce you to be guided by the judgment of others, where *it will be necessary for you* to follow the sober dictate of your own. I think also that a regular and unbending course of discipline should be maintained among the professors as well as among the boys. I make this observation, because on my visit last year it appeared to me that things in that regard had very much retrograded from the time I was there. This I mentioned once to Mr. McGerry; and whether it was so or not, you must know. . . . . .

We remain in the usual way in this city of long-standing confusion. We are enjoying the quietude of suspense: how it will terminate, God alone can tell. At the little chapel of St. Joseph's there is peace and piety. They are generally poor, and Massillon says that the poor are the objects of God's predilection.

It would afford me great pleasure if you would correspond with me whenever you have time. Mr. Bruté, from whose letters I derived comfort and instruction, seems to have given me up. Give my love to him and all, and believe me

Your friend and servant,
JOHN HUGHES.

TO THE SAME.

PHILADELPHIA, *March* 24, 1830.

. . . . .

I received yesterday a letter from Rev. Mr. McGerry. He was in Paris when he wrote it, Jan. 23d, and was to start next day for Lyons; thence to Marseilles, and thence to Rome—by sea, I suppose, as far as Leghorn. He wrote in tolerably good spirits, and you see in every line what we have all felt, that distance only strengthens his attachment to his country. His passage was long and boisterous. He was astonished at the splendor and magnificence of the churches in Paris. I was amused with an observation of his on the "ornamental parts of those buildings," which he seems to have surveyed with the spectacles of political economy. He met with several Mountaineers in Paris—Bedford, C. Harper, and others.

I infer from your letter to Mrs. Arey that you have obtained a charter from the Legislature, the particulars of which I should be glad to have from yourself direct.

There is nothing new here at present. The poor bishop lives quietly, and writes to Rome by every packet. He received a letter the other day from Cardinal Cappellari, couched in terms of great kindness and charity, but without promise of reinstatement. The diocese is really in a deplorable plight. There has been no Jubilee yet—no word of it even now. No oils consecrated for us these two years—no one to attend to it except at the risk of being considered officious. It is said that "the bishops" recommended the appointment of a coadjutor, and whilst we pray that the appointment may be a judicious, we are bound also to pray that it may be a *speedy* one. Whatever I say on this subject I wish you to consider as confidential.

There is to be a splendid sale of foreign books at Freeman's Auction Room on or about the 10th of April. I will send you a catalogue the moment it is printed, and if you or Mr. Bruté see any works that you would like to have, you have only to command my services. Give my love to him, and ask him why he writes so often to Philadelphia, and so seldom to one who never reads his letters without delight and profit? I think he is in my debt, although I should declare myself a bankrupt at once if in our correspondence he were to act on the principle of a *quid pro quo*. Give my love to all, and my special congratulation to Rev. Mr. Stillinger, whose ordination I read in the *C. Press* the other day. Please to write soon and often to

Your affectionate friend and servant,
JOHN HUGHES.

REV. F. P. KENRICK TO MR. HUGHES.

BARDSTOWN, *April* 21, 1830.

REV. AND DEAR FRIEND:

Your favor of the 28th ult. was received above a week since, but I delayed a reply in the hope that each succeeding mail would bring me some Roman intelligence that would enable me to give you an explicit statement of my views. I had written to Cardinal Cappellari on a case of conscience; and as my letter was despatched from Baltimore before the close of the council, I anticipated ere this a reply. Your letter confirming the rumors and hints that had come from other quarters, my curiosity was awakened to ascertain what is to be my future destiny on this varied theatre of human action. If I know my own heart, I do not long for the honors of the mitre; and notwithstanding all your kind reasoning and the suggestions of some other kind friends, I cannot say that I am yet fully determined. It will be time enough to accept or decline when the offer is made, and it may be better for us all in the mean time to implore with earnestness that the divine will may be accomplished. I owe it, however, to you and to truth to state that you have overrated my qualifications for the high office, since, though anxious my self-love may be to realize them all, yet the vigor of health, whereof you speak, is certainly wanting. The labors of the Jubilee of 1826 gave my constitution a shock from which it has yet to recover. This consideration naturally damps whatever ambition for a mitre may lurk within my breast. If you would point out to me one, different from myself, and more likely to answer the desires of all, I would use every exertion to procure his promotion, and still remain in the loved obscurity of my retreat.

The difficulties of the situation rush upon my mind, though perhaps not so forcibly as they ought. I am aware, indeed, that there are materials for great good, and with a zealous and disinterested and united clergy I should think every thing possible. Your coöperation is pledged, and that of many others would, I trust, be given to any one whom the proper authority may appoint; but will all relish the nomination of an humble missionary that never labored in the diocese! This surely is almost too much to anticipate.

The essay on Prejudice I had already adjudged to your pen,

rather on account of its intrinsic merit than the initial letter which distinguished it, and which I knew to be arbitrary. *The Miscellany* has concurred with me in regarding it as a highly interesting piece. I hope your occupations will leave you leisure to pen occasionally some similar productions, calculated to smooth the ruffled surface of the prejudiced mind. Our religion will sweetly insinuate herself into the hearts of the sincere, if all her advocates adopt the same style.

Your labors for the education of youth are sources of consolation to us all who know what advantages are thence to accrue to religion. The enemies of our faith are no less sensible than we that their calumnies cannot long gain credence if the infant mind be preserved from the infection of the nursery-tales concerning Popery. What purity of morals will not crown the integrity of faith in many of those trained up to virtue by precept and example! Proceed then with the good work, but still contrive to devote an hour to the enlightening of the more mature, whom curiosity or a love of truth may lead to the perusal of the Catholic publications.

. . . . . .

The Rev. Mr. Kenrick's appointment was officially announced soon after this letter was written, and on the 19th of May he issued his first pastoral letter as bishop-elect of Arath *in partibus infidelium*, and coadjutor and administrator of the diocese of Philadelphia. He was consecrated at Bardstown by Bishop Flaget, June 6th, being then in his thirty-second year, or about six months younger than Mr. Hughes. He was a native of Dublin, and a graduate of the College of the Propaganda at Rome; and when only twenty-four years of age was recommended by his professors for the post of superior of the theological seminary which Bishop Flaget had just founded at Bardstown. He had held that position ever since his arrival in America in 1821, relieving the confinement of a studious life by occasional missionary tours in the half-settled regions of Kentucky. Once and again he had entered the field of religious controversy; but he shrank instinctively from the rough usage of newspaper polemics, and his reputation rests chiefly on works of a solid and scholarly character. He concealed a resolute will beneath a mild and timid exterior and a modesty of manner that was almost effeminate. The half-subdued schismatics of St. Mary's found in him a master; and Mr. Hughes hailed him, on his arrival, as a man after his own heart.*

TO THE REV. MR. PURCELL.

PHILADELPHIA, *June* 8, 1830.

REV. AND DEAR PURCELL:

The indulgence with which you have treated so worthless a correspondent as I have proved myself, has convinced me that friendship (yours at least) is like charity; it hopeth and believeth all things. I find with astonishment that already more than two months have fled since the reception of your kind letter of March 30th. It is unnecessary for me to trouble you again with apologies about want of time, but proceed immediately to what may be more interesting.

And first, the affectionate and friendly manner in which you speak of myself personally has awakened all the gratitude of my heart. It has also operated as an encouragement to struggle in the race of usefulness in which your *kindness* places me foremost. True, "we were fed with the same food, and refreshed at the same fountain;" but *mine* was the *hurried* repast. When I look back to the days we have seen together, to the time we first met, to all that has happened to ourselves and our friends since, I cannot but adore that amiable providence of our Blessed God which has stooped so low to lift us into so high a sphere of usefulness. Our lots have been differently cast. You, with your colleagues, called to form the officers who are to lead the armies of Jesus Christ; I, to train the simple soldier. Both honorable, both responsible. Yours the privilege of being always in the house of God; mine the more arduous

---

* After restoring order in Philadelphia and founding several valuable religious institutions, Bishop Kenrick was promoted in 1851 to the archbishopric of Baltimore. He died during the night of July 6th and 7th, 1863. He was a devout man, and the best scholar in the American hierarchy. His most important works were a course of Moral and Dogmatic Theology in Latin, and a revised translation of the Bible.

task to mingle among the ranks, and invade (at least enter) the camp of the enemy. We have both had good models as our respective predecessors; and both, perhaps, have witnessed the fragments of shipwreck, to remind us that there are rocks on the borders of our course. With regard to myself—in addition to higher motives, the advice and approbation of such friends as you and Rev. Mr. Bruté will support me powerfully. For in scenes so distracting, the high and original motive is not always present to the mind, or rather the mind is not always at home to cherish it; and poor human nature looks around for encouragement, more consoling, because more sensible. It was to Emmitsburg I naturally turned my eyes, and indeed for the last three years I would have looked elsewhere in vain. It required a protection from God himself to have preserved me, even so well as I have been preserved, for the last three years. And although I am not without my apprehensions as to the future good understanding of all parties, still I trust that in the zeal and learning and piety of Dr. Kenrick I shall have an arm to lean upon. If he will only allow himself not to be imposed upon by appearances, until he will have had time to lay the foundation of sound views from actual observation, I am satisfied that all will go well. If, on the contrary, he act hastily (I refer to St. Mary's, the only quarter from which he need fear trouble), I fear he will have occasion to repent it.

In the conclusion of your letter, you said you would write soon again; but my epistolary delinquency has no doubt hindered you from the fulfilment of your promise. I have much to say which I may not put to paper; but your vacation visit is so near.

I received a letter a few days ago from Mr. McGerry. It was written about the middle of March. He was well—overwhelmed with admiration of all he saw and all he need not attempt to describe. The last page of his letter is altogether about the Mountain. He "is not as yet settled any way, nor will he do any thing until he gets letters from America. He hopes he will be able to return with Bishop Dubois, or else——"

I was, of course, rejoiced at the facility with which your charter was obtained at Annapolis. I hope it will be an advantage. Please to congratulate Rev. Mr. Hitselberger for me on his promotion to the holy priesthood.

I had the charity sermon on Sunday, as mentioned in Mr. Bruté's letter. The morning was damp, and the salt and sugar people stayed at home. Still, we did pretty well. The collection was $330. Our school is doing well. We have above eighty day scholars.

I began this letter two days ago, and had to lay it aside no less than six times. Give my love to all. Hoping to hear from you soon, I remain, dear friend,

Your affectionate brother,

JOHN HUGHES.

TO SISTER ANGELA.

June 23, 1830.

MY DEAREST SISTER:

It is nearly a week since I received your last letter, which leaves me at least two in your debt. Finding it impossible to keep up every portion of my engagements, it happens so that my correspondence is not the most exact or faithful; and in this it happens also that my *friends* are the very persons who are most liable to be neglected. Because they *are my friends*, I calculate the more on their indulgence. This is the reason, if I have not written to you as often as we would both wish.

Our school comes on well; they count nearly 100 in regular attendance. The children that attend the school are all females, from the ages of 7 to 15 years. Many of them—say 50—pay, but all are obliged to be clean in their persons and decently dressed, so that the association of rich and poor children may have nothing in it to hurt the pride of either. We have 14 orphans, for some of whom we receive a partial compensation. Our house is very large and commodious, but you understand that on this very account it requires the more labor to keep it in order. We shall be obliged soon to ask two more Sisters. Hitherto we have prospered beyond our expectation; whether it will continue so, God only knows; for whilst our prospects are fair, we must not forget that every thing of this kind is popular at its commencement. We are adding about twenty feet to the other asylum, and this is the only enlargement of the building that is now to be expected from the wisdom of the managers. Sister Margaret, I believe, knows its present size. The new establishment is as large as five of it. It is also happily located in the centre of the churches, having St. Mary's but a few rods distant, and St. Joseph's and Trinity within a square and a half. Have you heard the extravagant representations that have been made and believed at St. Joseph's about the elegance of our furniture? Turkey carpets! gilt chairs! and all the rest mahogany and brass!—so that it would be impossible for the Sisters to keep their vow of poverty in so splendid a mansion! Have you heard all this? If you have, you have heard nothing but what some gossiping visitors told at St. Joseph's, and what the Sisters believed and *censured*, although it is false in the main. Sister Sophia has been very much annoyed by it. I must tell you, in a word, the Sisters had nothing to do with it. The people made presents, and I saw no reason to reject articles of furniture merely because they were not of white pine, nor carpets just because they were not made of rags. When Father Hickey comes, I am sure he will be much disappointed to find that we have none of the extravagant grandeur which they attribute to us.

. . . . .

We expect our new bishop every day. He is a most excellent man, and his appointment augurs great good to religion in this long ungoverned and almost ungovernable diocese.

. . . . .

My health is still good, but I am weak and debilitated. Give my respects to all friends in Frederick—Mrs. Low and family, Mr. Tormey, etc., etc.

Your affectionate brother,
JOHN HUGHES.

TO THE SAME.

Aug. 24, 1830.

MY DEAREST SISTER:

. . . . .

I intended to visit you this vacation, but my health was so far impaired by the hot weather and the double duties it brought, that I was obliged to go to the sea-shore. I have wonderfully recruited. I hope I shall visit you about the beginning of November. . . . Our school was reopened yesterday after a vacation of four weeks. There is little variety in our prospects since I wrote last, except that our numbers are on the increase, and we will have to get two more Sisters.

Give my love to sister Margaret, and tell her that I have delayed answering her esteemed letter by Mr. Armour, hoping to be able to give a better account about ———, for whom sister M. and Mr. McElroy are so solicitous. Poor ———! I have entreated her to come, appointed the day, extorted a promise; but all in vain. I have done every thing except going to the house for her; and even this I mean to try, although there are reasons why a clergyman in Philadelphia should make such visits, even for such motives, few and far between. I am afraid there is something in the way. I wish very much that the young ladies who become Catholics at ——— were converts more by *principle* and conviction, and less by *feeling* and the imitation of that example whose influence is irresistible. After my next essay I will write to sister Margaret upon it.

· · · · ·

About this time Mr. Hughes was led into a controversy of a rather unpleasant nature with a brother clergyman in New York; and although there is not much in the dispute itself which deserves recollection, the circumstances in which it originated call for a few lines of explanation. In November, 1829, a weekly paper was started in New York, under the title of *The Protestant*, and with the recommendation of a large number of ministers. Its avowed object was to attack the Catholic Church on every possible opportunity. It reproduced all the vulgar calumnies about priests and nuns, with so little regard for decency that other Protestant papers were compelled to denounce it. Perhaps as much for his own amusement as with an eye to any serious results, Mr. Hughes resolved to test the credulity or good faith of *The Protestant* by sending it some preposterous communications, as if from one of its own creed. Over the signature of "Cranmer," he accordingly wrote from time to time the most "alarming reports of the progress of Catholicity" in Pennsylvania, exaggerated statistics, and ludicrously false accounts of Catholic ceremonies and institutions, interspersed with appropriate reflections. In one letter he told how the "four mass-houses" in Philadelphia, being each filled three times on the Sabbath, were made to accommodate twelve congregations; while for those who could not attend in the morning there was an extra "mass in the afternoon." In another he gave an account of an imaginary nunnery in Cambria county, Pennsylvania, and described a Jesuit academy at Pittsburg which never existed. The experiment succeeded. *The Protestant* took all he gave, and asked for more. "Mark," said Mr. Hughes, "how he bespatters me with his dirty eulogy":

> Our Philadelphia friend communicates his melancholy intelligence in a very Evangelical spirit of sensibility and fervor. We trust Cranmer will remember that his letters are sermons of momentous importance, and they are now read with intense and increasing interest by a rapidly augmenting host of Protestants of a like spirit. The oftener we decorate our columns with such pathetic appeals and heart-stirring facts, the more encouragement we shall feel to blow the trumpet in Zion, and sound the alarm in the Holy Mountain. We hope our correspondent will supply us with a plenty of Gospel ammunition, and it shall be discharged so as to produce the desired effect.—*The Protestant, March* 13, 1830.
>
> We have received a number of inquiries for our friend Cranmer, and in reply we are highly gratified to exhibit this genuine Protestant of the city of Penn *in propria persona.—June* 12, 1830.

A correspondent in Philadelphia writes: "I sincerely hope 'Cranmer' will give us another of his intelligent surveys of our city and its environs;" and another exclaims: "Oh, that we had such an observer in Baltimore!" After the deception had been carried on for four months, Mr. Hughes threw off the mask, and over the signature of "A Catholic" printed in the New York *Truth Teller*, in July, 1830, a letter "To the 'Ministers of the Gospel' who have recommended *The Protestant* to the patronage of a Christian public." First animadverting severely upon the character of the paper, he then continued:

> I must now inform you that the writer of this is the author of

those letters in *The Protestant* signed "Cranmer," which have attracted so much notice and elicited so much praise. I must be candid, gentlemen, and tell you, like two or three other Catholics of that city who have been writing for that paper under different signatures, I have woven in as many lies as possible. And it is remarkable that the greater the slander the greater was the eulogium bestowed on me by the editor, and the better Protestant he said I was! . . . He saw in my anonymous communications a number of falsehoods, which I rendered obvious and palpable *on purpose;* but they were against the Catholics, and he immediately pronounced me a "genuine Protestant;" and your recommendations entitle him to belief. In this, gentlemen, you pay a dear-bought compliment to your religion.

But perhaps you ask how my conscience would allow me to gratify, even in jest, the editor's craving for slanderous matter wherewith to season his weekly dish. The fact is, I had a scruple at first; and at last I was obliged to quit, lest the hungry expectants should commit gluttony. I imagined myself into the belief that I was writing romance, like Dr. Ely in his "Dreams" and "Visits of Mercy," Carter in Letters from Europe, or Brother Christmas in his account of the Montreal controversy. I thought, too, I was justified by the example of the missionaries writing to their societies from all parts of the world when their money is run out; and the more so as I did not write for filthy lucre. I knew that you, gentlemen, and the editor alone, would be responsible for any falsehood you might think proper to publish. I was satisfied that no enlightened man would believe a line published in *The Protestant*, except he knew from other sources that it was true; and that no modest woman who had read it once by accident would ever read it again by design. I wanted to ascertain whether or not *conscience* had any thing to do with the columns of *The Protestant*. I found it had not: I found that from the moment I spoke against Catholics, and adopted the signature of the coward, cruel, but hypocritical "Cranmer," I might write any thing, however false (nay, the falser the better), and it was published under the sanction of your names. In a word, I could not find a line deep enough to fathom the editorial depravity of *The Protestant*. It is time now, by putting him and you, gentlemen, and a few of the falsehoods you have mutually adopted, in juxtaposition, to see how you stand.

He then placed in parallel columns extracts from "Cranmer's" letters, the comments of *The Protestant* on them, and the recommendations of a few of the clerical patrons of that paper. *The Protestant* affected to believe this communication a forgery by a Catholic priest in New York. Mr. Hughes thereupon, in another letter to *The Truth Teller*, July 15th, offered a wager of five hundred dollars that there were "in the city of Philadelphia alone not fewer than four Catholics who had been in the habit of communicating all manner of suitable trash for its columns." His triumph was complete; but he felt little satisfaction in it. He was afterward sorry for the whole affair; and many Catholics did not hesitate to express their disapproval of the trick. Among others, the Rev. Thomas C. Levins of New York attacked him through *The Truth Teller*, over the signature of "Fergus McAlpin," and the result was an angry personal controversy which lasted more than a year. Mr. Levins was a man whose bad temper often carried him to great lengths; and Mr. Hughes, when his feelings were deeply engaged in a dispute, was apt to give a bitterness to his pen which was really foreign to his heart. At least one of his communications was so severe that the editor would not print it.

TO THE REV. MR. PURCELL.

PHILADELPHIA, *Sept. 27, 1830.*

. . . . .

I regret, my dear friend, that circumstances have compelled me, in the case of "McAlpin," to depart from my own resolution and your excellent advice. If you remember, there was a long quotation imbedded in the midst of his tirade, as an extract from my letters to *The Protestant*. I never wrote any such passage. And not wishing to take any notice of him at all, I requested Denman to disclaim the extract on my authority. He did not, and I was obliged to do it myself, as you saw by the *T. Teller* of Sept. 11. On the Saturday following, 18th, McAlpin again asserts the falsehood that I am the author. I conceived there was no alternative, and accordingly I sent a communication which should have been in last Saturday, and which is as powerful against McAlpin as my pen could render it. Experience has proved to *my* satisfaction that the dread of scandal, which usually restrains good men from defending themselves, is in its operation a kind of encouragement to that aggressive spirit which triumphs by its recklessness. If the birch had been applied to McAlpin's back ten years ago, it would not be necessary for me, as it now is, to apply it. I have certainly been severe, and however the present affair may terminate, still I am confident that McAlpin will take care how he meddles with what does not immediately concern him hereafter. In doing so, I was consoled for the personal consequences by the belief that it would save, or rather prevent, evil effects to religion in other cases, as the gentleman had his pens already whetted to attack Dr. England.

.   .   .   .   .

Adieu.
JOHN HUGHES.

CHAPTER VIII.

1830–1832.

Journey with Bishop Kenrick—More trouble at St. Mary's—Foundation of St. John's church—Death of Mr. Hughes's mother—Letters to Ellen Hughes and Mr. Purcell—Article on the will of Stephen Girard—Dedication of the new church and removal from St. Joseph's—Mr. Hughes at the synod—Fourth of July celebration at St. John's—Letters to Ellen Hughes.

VERY soon after taking possession of his see, Bishop Kenrick began a visitation of the diocese. At Chambersburg, about the end of September, he fell sick. Mr. Hughes was sent for, and on the Sunday after his arrival preached from the text, "Thou shalt love the Lord thy God with thy whole heart." His father, still a hale old man, and his mother, now sinking fast to her grave, were among his auditors. He remained with the bishop until his recovery, and then accompanied him on the rest of his tour; visiting Bedford, where he preached again, and enjoyed for a few hours the society of his friends the Heydens; thence proceeding to Pittsburg and Blairsville;* and sharing for a brief time at Loretto the hospitality of the venerable missionary, Prince Gallitzin, the apostle of the Alleghanies.† The

---

* He used to tell, with keen enjoyment, how, after a sermon at Blairsville, in which he was conscious of having done his best, one of the most intelligent of his hearers grasped his hand and exclaimed, "Your Reverence has preached a *rouser!*"

† Demetrius Augustine Gallitzin was the offspring of a princely Russian family, and was born at the Hague, where his father was ambassador, in 1770. At the age of twenty-two he set out for a tour in America; but soon after landing in this country, he resolved to embrace the ecclesiastical state, and entered

roads and conveniences for travelling in the interior of Pennsylvania were not much better at this time than when Mr. Hughes went about preaching with Dr. Conwell. In journeying from Loretto to Newry, Bishop Kenrick managed to obtain a seat in some public conveyance; Mr. Hughes and Father Heyden were left to follow him with the baggage in an open wagon. Night overtook them long before they reached their destination. A few miles distant from Newry they examined their baggage to see if all was safe. Behold, the mitre and crosier were missing; they had fallen out of the wagon. "We must turn back," said Father Hughes. But to this Father Heyden and the driver objected. The road was dangerous; the night was very dark; and it would be impossible to find the lost articles. Father Hughes cut short the discussion by seizing the reins and turning the horses himself. The mitre and crosier were picked up before they had gone far. A believer in omens might have thought this little incident prophetic; for while Father Hughes, who insisted upon searching for the mitre, was destined to wear one himself, Father Heyden, who wanted to go on without it, twice afterward refused a bishopric when one was offered him.

We find him, after this trip, laboring with increased diligence in the various duties of his profession. He acted as secretary to the bishop, and assumed the troublesome office of agent in Philadelphia for Mount St. Mary's college—

St. Mary's Seminary at Baltimore. He was the second priest ordained in the United States, having received orders from Bishop Carroll in 1795. After a few years' labor as a missionary, he founded a Catholic settlement which he called Loretto, on a high bleak part of the Alleghanies, in Cambria county, Pennsylvania. He bought an immense tract of land, and divided it into farms which he gave away, or sold at very low prices, to poor emigrants. This charitable undertaking cost him no less than one hundred and fifty thousand dollars; but the colony prospered, and at the death of its founder in 1840 it numbered six thousand souls. Prince Gallitzin was simple and austere in his manners. He dressed in homespun, lived in a humble log-cabin, and concealed his noble origin under the assumed name of Father Smith.

executing various little commissions, and sometimes receiving or paying money on account of the institution, or serving as the medium of communication between the president of the college and the parents of the pupils. He delivered a series of lectures on the evidences of the Christian religion, to which great numbers of the most intelligent people of the city, Protestants as well as Catholics, came to listen. He still found time to continue his studies, and once in a while to exercise his pen. A friend of his having prepared for the press a new translation of Bossuet's *Exposition of the Doctrine of the Catholic Church in Matters of Controversy*, he wrote for it a short preface, in which he spoke of the usefulness of controversial works, and briefly related the history of Bossuet's little treatise.*

TO THE REV. MR. PURCELL.

PHILADELPHIA, *Jan.* 12, 1831.
REV. AND DEAR FRIEND:

I just stop in the midst of writing a sermon for next Sunday, to satisfy the inquiries in your letter, and if it be considered an atonement for past neglect, to answer *promptly for once* the communication of a *friend* I must confess that I have treated the letters of those who do not come within the meaning of that endearing term with much more attention than I have treated yours; for, next to the members of my own family, you have been most neglected.

. . . .

I will discharge with pleasure the commission to the "O's," and even appoint an agent, if I can get one to accept the office. *The Catholic*, however, falls under the general rule of having many critics. The articles, it seems to me, do not recommend themselves by being "original." They are heavy. The grand secret in this age is to get, not matter, but *readers*.

The affairs of Europe are indeed important, and whilst those

---

* This book was published at Chambersburg, with *The Life of John Mary Decalogne, Student in the University of Paris. Translated from the French.* 12mo, 1831.

who are better acquainted with them are led to contemplate the darker aspect, my mind generally turns to the possible good which Almighty God knows how to draw out of the worst of them.

Mr. Bruté *used* to write me, but whether he thinks me now unworthy of his correspondence, or, what is more probable, is better employed, I have not received a line from him since my return from the country. My last to him was one of apology and asking pardon (in the which you were included). Can it be that he never received it?

You will be surprised and afflicted to learn that the trustees of St. Mary's have again become refractory. Dr. Kenrick signified to them, the other day, his intention to take charge of the congregation, as its chief pastor. They kicked immediately. He made a statement of their proceedings in the pulpit last Sunday, which filled them with exasperation, and the people with disgust for *their* proceedings. In their anger they summoned a general meeting of the pew-holders for this evening at 7 o'clock—of the result of which I will inform you before I close this letter. They revive the old question about the choice of pastors. Dr. Kenrick is universally and deservedly popular in the city and throughout the diocese. Yesterday, and these very men seemed ready to bear him on their shoulders!! To-morrow I hope they will be under his feet. Poor M—— has the misfortune to be one of them. Be kind to John, and write to his father and mother even more frequently and more feelingly than ever. His good, good mother—she called on me the other day, and cried bitterly about her son, and all things.

. . . . .

As to Bishop England, I am sorry that he is made the butt of so many attacks. Walsh was more than usually severe. I told him he would have to recant; that B. E. never supported the political doctrine ascribed to him, etc., etc. He told me that Mr. Poinsett had written to him on other occasions that the bishop, in all his ministerial peregrinations, was in the habit of introducing politics; and therefore he had no doubt but the statement in this instance was correct. "At all events," said he, "I intend to give Dr. Beecher a lashing in a few days, for his enmity toward the Catholics, and (after censuring Bishop England) it will not be considered as emanating from religious feeling"!!!

The rest of this will be little enough to give you an account of the meeting.

(THURSDAY MORNING.) *Gloria in excelsis Deo, et in terra pax hominibus!* The neck of the bad principle was *broken* last night. Dr. Kenrick attended the meeting himself. His presence (in his cassock, and his cross displayed on his breast) disconcerted them. He then proved, to the satisfaction of the meeting, that the trustees were misrepresenting. He made them eat their own words. He told them they must not dare to control him in the exercise of his episcopal authority. He said he was their pastor and their bishop; that St. Mary's *was* and *should be* the cathedral of the diocese; and *he* was supported, and the *trustees* were put down by their own meeting—and I may say their own party! The hope of the other page is realized. They are under his feet. Last night he whipped them with fair arguments, until they were fairly beaten; and when they gave up, and declared the withdrawal of their opposition, and when their friends were about to fall on them, he interposed, and set them on their legs again. He said he wished no other trustees, so long as these gentlemen would confine themselves within their proper limits, and not presume to meddle, directly or indirectly, with his authority. There was finally a kind of shaking hands between the vanquished and the victor—with what sincerity on their part, time only will tell. At all events, it is the first time within ten years that an attempt has been made to pluck up the *root* of the schism—and I assure you Dr. Kenrick did it with a giant's hand.

Give my love to all. Pray for us, and write soon again to
    Your affectionate friend and brother,
                      JOHN HUGHES.

The trustees, however, soon rebelled again; and as they persisted in interfering in the appointment of pastors, Dr. Kenrick felt himself obliged, in April, to order "the cessation from all sacred functions in the church and cemeteries of St. Mary's." This brought the trustees to terms. "On the 21st of May," says the bishop, "we received a communication dated the 18th, and signed by five of the lay trustees, wherein they disclaimed all right to interfere in the spiritual concerns of this church, and distinctly stated that they considered the right of interfering in the appointing, rejecting, or removing of pastors, as being included in these spiritual concerns. They added, however, that they reserved to themselves the right of regulating the salaries of the pastors, and even of withholding them, should the power of appointment be (contrary to their expectations) not exercised in accordance with the declarations of the prelates in the Baltimore council, 'so as to meet not only the wants, but the wishes, of the people, so far as the conscientious convictions of the prelate, and the just desires and expectations of meritorious clergymen, will permit.' . . . . Although a portion of said communication appears to us highly objectionable, and calculated to afford matter for future dissension, yet as it contains an explicit disclaimer of all right of interference in pastoral appointments or removals, we are unwilling to withhold any longer from you the consolation of worshipping in the church which you have so long frequented."

TO THE REV. MR. PURCELL.

May 24, 1831.

. . . . .

Dr. Kenrick is confined to his bed by fever since Sunday morning. It is somewhat abated to-day under Dr. Jackson's treatment. It seems to be a remnant of the Chambersburg attack, which has been lurking in his system and survived the winter. I trust it will pass off in a few days. St. Mary's has no doubt had its share in the cause; as I perceive by close observation that his mind is of too sensitive a character for such shocks, although I have no doubt but he will pass triumphant through the ordeal. The trustees have made concessions entirely consistent with the discipline of the Church. They have in a written document disclaimed formally all right of interference "in the appointment, rejection, or removal of pastors in St. Mary's, or in any other spiritual concern." This, however, is accompanied with a kind of intimation that dominion over the purse and the right of grading salaries belong to them. In fact, the course that was pursued was well calculated to weaken them. They were left to *themselves*, and they could not stand it. Every thing tending to excite the passions was kept back from the question. The bishop called a meeting; but in consequence of his sickness it has not yet been held. In it I hope every thing will be settled.

Poor Mr. C—— is gone! He died this morning at 8 o'clock. His condition for the last two months has been a succession of recovery and relapse. I visited him in the early stage of his illness, and he told me that "he could not go the whole length of the Catholic religion." Mr. Bedell had been with him that morning, and I found him too far gone to bear my exhortation. I left him, despairing of his conversion *at that time*, and could only pray that God would restore him, so I might have an opportunity; but others must have prayed, for he was restored several times. But he always avoided that topic. He had received the Protestant communion, and seemed to have made up his mind. On Sunday he was up and about. Yesterday I was engaged to preach at Mr. Kelly's church, eight miles out of town; but just as I was waiting for the gig, a messenger came to let me know that Mr. C—— was worse and wanted to see me. Supposing it was something about the new church, of which he was to be organist, I sent word that I would go immediately on my return from the country. The boy came back, and I went. The moment I entered the room he told the attendants to retire, and seized my hand. "Oh! Mr. Hughes, how I have been hoping to see you! My mind has been so tossed about, and I want a place to rest my foot!" He was very low. I proposed to him a brief profession of the Catholic faith, which he pronounced with fervor—as also contrition for his sins. He then made a general confession of his sins, with great compunction and distinctness of recollection, and I had the consolation of giving him absolution. I asked him if he would not desire to receive the body of our Saviour? "Oh, you know, Mr. Hughes, I am not worthy!" He was much exhausted, and after exciting him to composure and confidence, I promised to call in the evening; which I did, but had no opportunity of seeing him. This morning as I approached, the arrangement of the shutters informed me that the soul of this second Cornelius had departed. It will be a consolation for Sister A—— to know that she can say, "Lord, have mercy on it!"

I shall have business to your neighborhood in the course of the ensuing month, and if I can I shall attend your exhibition. Let me know on what day it will take place.

    I remain affectionately your brother in Christ,
                 JOHN HUGHES.

 The final overthrow of the trustee system in Philadelphia was due in no small measure, as I have already intimated, to Mr. Hughes himself. He put an end to the long warfare, not by openly taking part in it, but by building a new church, without lay corporators, and drawing to it nearly all the best people of the city. St. Mary's was reduced to an humble and obscure condition, and at one time was on the point of losing its cathedral privileges. The quarrelsome trustees, unable any longer to excite party spirit, ceased to interfere with the spiritual concerns of the congregation, and at last there was peace. The new church, which was to be a means of effecting so much, was begun in the spring of 1831. In the early part of the preceding winter, Mr. Hughes, who for some time past had felt the necessity of a new edifice for the accommodation of the rapidly increasing congregation that crowded the little church of St. Joseph, obtained the bishop's authority to undertake the work. As soon as he found a piece of ground that seemed suitable, he announced his plan from the pulpit of St. Joseph's, and urged all his parishioners to give according to their means. On Monday he waited at home to receive subscriptions; but he waited in vain. On Tuesday he was likewise disappointed; he began to feel discouraged. On Wednesday a servant woman called upon him. "This is the first day, Father," said she, "since you spoke to us on Sunday, that I have been able to come out. I have brought my contribution for the new church." The sum was three shillings.

 "I took the money," said he, "ran to my bedroom, and throwing myself upon my knees, thanked God that the work was done. From that moment I never had a doubt of the success of my enterprise."

Money after this came in rapidly. Meetings of the Catholics of the city were held at St. Joseph's from time to time to further the undertaking, and committees were appointed to solicit subscriptions. A benevolent person having given Father Hughes $5,000 to be applied to any religious or charitable purpose he thought proper, he devoted it to the new church. Above all, Mr. M. A. Frenaye, a French West Indian, who had accumulated a competence by trade in this country, gave his whole fortune to aid the good work. He became a very dear friend of Mr. Hughes, and after the new church was built he lived with him as long as Mr. H. remained in Philadelphia.

TO THE REV. MR. PURCELL.

Feb. 14, 1831.

. . . . .

I hope Almighty God will put it into the heart of Bishop Dubois to place the money which he will have collected in Europe in your institution, as a perpetual fund, and let the interest educate with you candidates for his diocese, instead of attempting, *at his age*, the establishment of a seminary. By expressing a wish that I should visit you, you seem to be unacquainted with my having undertaken to build a church in the western part of the city. I had dallied a long time on the brink, weighing the consequences, but I have finally made the plunge. I have engaged a lot in 13th, between Chestnut and Market. It is 97 feet front on 13th, by 150 deep; but has the advantage of three fronts—affording a site for the Sisters with their orphans and day school for female children. I have a prospect also of having, connected with the church, a Catholic school for boys, which is very much wanted. The ground will cost about $13,000! When you have read thus far, you will see how improbable is my visit to the dear Mountain. The church is to be under the invocation of St. John the Evangelist, the documents authorizing its erection having been given by the bishop on the festival of that saint.

. . . . . .

The corner-stone was laid by Bishop Kenrick in May.

In those days of plain architecture and cheap churches, the plan seemed of almost unparalleled grandeur, and the expense something prodigious. Catholics then in Philadelphia were neither numerous nor rich, and it required all the energy of Mr. Hughes, and, I may add, all the generosity of Mr. Frenaye, to prevent the work from being stopped for want of funds.

It was at this time that Mr. Hughes gave up the practice of writing his sermons and committing them to memory. He had no leisure for such laborious preparation; and besides, he used to say that he found he made his sermons *too sharp* when he wrote them. He always had a great many Protestants to listen to him; and now that he was building a costly church, for which he hoped to make all his hearers subscribe something, he found it necessary to give over hard knocks and adopt a policy of conciliation. He could do this much better when he spoke without preparation. He changed his method of preaching by degrees, beginning by interweaving unpremeditated passages with his written discourses, and coming gradually to abandon altogether the habit of writing even notes of his sermons. His first attempts at extempore speaking were not happy. The oral discussion with Dr. Breckinridge was what first placed him wholly at his ease in the pulpit.

TO THE REV. MR. PURCELL.

June 8, 1831.

· · · · ·

The report which is prevalent here, and which seems to have reached you, respecting Dr. P——'s being a Catholic, is one of the strangest, and to me the most unaccountable. Poor man! His mind is in perpetual torture on the subject of religion, but no man can tell where his difficulties commence. He came to St. Joseph's one Sunday afternoon in the winter, and it was such a miracle to see him in church, that possibly it gave rise to the report. He has since been reading Milner's *End of Controversy* and Fletcher's *Compara-*

tive View; and on one or two occasions when our doctrines were assailed, he brandished in their defence the arms of which these works put him in possession.

I will accept with gratitude the literary honors * which you are pleased to offer me in the name of the faculty. I would not add any thing to your stock of knowledge by telling you that they are unmerited. I hope to be present at your exhibition, as I shall set out from here on Monday, 20th, and be with you Thursday evening—having to call by the way at Chambersburg.

TO THE SAME.

[*September*, 1831.]

It would have been difficult for you to have paid me a greater compliment than by inquiring after the new church. It will certainly produce some of the effects at which you hinted. It will shame the Quaker meeting; make all the bishops of all the churches jealous; cause those who give nothing toward its erection to "murmur" at its costliness, and those who did contribute to be proud of their own doing. Whilst it will make the Protestant wish it were his, it will expose the godly Presbyterian to the danger of squinting in his effort to look the other way as he passes. The roof is raised, and we shall have service in it about Christmas. As a religious edifice, it will be the pride of the city. There are crowds who go to see it every day, and the leading Protestants and infidels proclaim it the only building in the place that is entitled to be called a *church*, "inasmuch as its appearance indicates its use, and there is no danger of mistaking it for a work-shop."

TO SISTER ANGELA (ELLEN HUGHES).

CHAMBERSBURG, *Sept.* 30, 1831.

MY DEAREST SISTER:

The Rev. Father McElroy has no doubt prepared your mind for the melancholy intelligence which I have now to communicate. God has dealt kindly with us; and whilst he has taken from us a most kind and tender parent, he has accompanied the affliction with

---

* The degree of Master of Arts.

so many consoling circumstances, that it is difficult to say whether we have not greater cause for joy than for sorrow. Our dear mother departed about two o'clock this morning. It is about a week since she was taken with a fever, accompanied with a pain in the head and back. On Sunday evening Margaret, who despaired of her recovery from the commencement, wrote to me, and I started by the 12 o'clock steamboat on Wednesday, about an hour after I received the letter. I arrived in Baltimore at 2, and took my passage in the Chambersburg stage, where I arrived about 7 o'clock. I hurried home without daring to ask any questions, and found them all around her bed weeping, for she was dying. The coldness of death was in her hands and on her cheek when I kissed it; and yet she knew me, and spoke to me with perfect recollection. I knelt down immediately and read the prayers for the departing, in which she joined with earnestness and emotion. I do not believe that she was deprived for an instant of her recollection and consciousness from that time until the last throb of her breast gave notice that the scene was changed. She ceased not until the last to move in prayer to her God those lips which were already cold in death. Oh, may my last end be like to hers! and for you, dear sister, I desire nothing more. She has bequeathed to us an obligation which you will consider sacred. It was during her sickness that she told Margaret the message to be sent to you and me, as her last request, "that we would never cease to pray for her."

She is gone, my dear sister, and whilst we pray for her soul, we must prepare to follow her. I would be glad to go and see you on this sorrowful occasion, that we might mingle together tears of pious and filial affection; but my duties forbid. I must hasten back and devote myself to the labors of my ministry. *We* "must not be sorrowful as those who have no hope."

The rest are well;—much weighed down with grief, as you may suppose; but that will wear away. Margaret has done her duty. All desire to be remembered to you. The burial will take place to-morrow at 2 o'clock. The mother of Rev. Mr. McCosker was buried some ten days ago; and old Mrs. Mahony, Mrs. Jeffries's mother, has died this morning. Give my love and respects to Mr. McElroy and the Sisters, and write as soon as you can to

Your ever affectionate brother,

JOHN HUGHES.

TO THE REV. T. J. DONAGHOE.

CHAMBERSBURG, *Oct.* 1, 1831.

REV. AND DEAR FRIEND :

You have already anticipated the subject and the contents of this letter. My beloved mother departed on Thursday night, and was buried this afternoon. Almighty God has been good to her and us in the circumstances of sickness and death. She had every consolation that the divine institutions of our holy religion can impart to a mind of the strongest faith and a heart of the most ardent devotion. She had the almost constant attendance of a good and kind physician, and Margaret was her nurse. The affection and devotedness of such a child toward such a parent would of itself have plucked many thorns from the pillow of sickness and of death.

These were *her* consolations; and *ours* were to mark how steadily she kept her eye on the star of her hope, which seemed to brighten on her mind in proportion as all other objects became more dim and shadowy. Thrice she endeavored to make the sign of redemption whilst I was reading the departing prayers; and her lips continued to move in supplication to her God long after the coldness of death had chilled them forever. She seemed to possess her recollection and consciousness until the last moment. There was no convulsion—no apparent agony; but the gradual and progressive ebbing of life until it passed almost imperceptibly into the eternal ocean.

She had told them, from the commencement of her sickness, that she would not recover; and yet she was unwilling that I should be sent for, "*lest it would interfere with the discharge of my duty.*" She is gone to rest.

The church is to be consecrated in Gettysburg to-morrow, and I intend to say mass early in order to attend; but I must return and spend a few days with my afflicted father. He bears it with wonderful fortitude considering his age, being now seventy years. She was in her sixty-fourth. I will be in Philadelphia toward the latter end of the week; in the mean time you will discharge as much of my duties as you can, and believe me ever

Your affectionate friend and brother in Christ,

JOHN HUGHES.

P. S. It is hardly necessary for me to request that you will give my love to the Rev. Mr. Hurley and the rest of the clergy. They will all, I am sure, offer up the holy sacrifice for the repose of my mother's soul. Give my love also to all those dear friends who may inquire for me and would share in any grief of mine—the Sisters in particular. J. H.

TO SISTER ANGELA.

Dec. 15, 1831.

With regard to our beloved father, nothing has been done but with his consent and approbation. Brother Patrick and his wife will move to the house, and father will have the two rooms upstairs fitted up and made comfortable for himself alone. Patrick cannot move till spring. In the mean time, they have a person to cook and keep house. His health and spirits were good, and this arrangement is the one of his *choice*.

The new church will be finished I hope by Easter. It bids fair to be the handsomest in the United States. In point of grandeur it is not of course to be compared with the cathedral of Baltimore, but as far as *beauty* is concerned it will exceed it. I have a place designed in the plan for the Sisters and orphans exclusively. And if you should ever be sent on the Philadelphia mission, you will find your seat prepared. . . . Our institution is flourishing, but I suppose Father Hickey gave you a general account of all the foreign establishments.

The project of suppressing the theological department at Mount St. Mary's was revived this year, and called forth the following letter:

TO THE REV. MR. PURCELL.

PHILADELPHIA, *Feb.* 21, 1832.

REV. DEAR SIR:

As Mr. White is to return this way shortly for Emmitsburg, I must not allow him to pass without writing to you. The effects of the intended suppression of your establishment—for it will be tantamount to a suppression—have been to my mind a subject of much speculation and regret. Have you cast in your mind what you shall do? How will you dispose of *yourself?* What will be done with your ecclesiastics, especially those who do not belong to Baltimore! Is the institution which it took so much pains and labor to raise, and which was becoming the hope of the American Church, to be smitten by the hand that should protect it, and prostrated in a day? Or does God mean to display another instance of the folly and short-sightedness of human wisdom, by bringing something better from its ruins?

If the mind of your archbishop and his determination in your regard be like the laws of the Medes and Persians, then I tell you what—have the back door open, and back out; not forgetting, as you cross the Maryland and Pennsylvania line, to shake off the dust of your feet. Neither do I want you to come alone; but bring all the zeal, disinterestedness, and talent of your establishment, and have the glory of instituting the diocesan seminary of Philadelphia. There is adjoining the new church a building which will suit admirably, both as to location and internal arrangements. You may either rent or purchase it. I will have means provided, without your being obliged to furnish them in advance. After enjoying this building and its advantages for a few years, you will be able to dispose of it at considerable profit, and to remove, if you wish it, to some favorable place in the neighborhood of the city, with the advantages of an established school and reputation.

The project may perhaps startle you by its novelty, but it is altogether practicable. Let me know your ideas in reference to the subject generally, and then I shall have more to say. In the mean time circumstances compel me to think of what concerns myself more immediately. The new church will be opened for divine service on Passion Sunday (and, by the way, try to be here), and I find that, for a time at least, I shall have to discharge the duties of the pastorship *solus*. At first it was understood, in my mind at least, that my present colleague would accompany me; but Dr. Kenrick has determined otherwise. . . . The consequence is, that I shall be left alone to bear a burthen which will be too heavy for one—but which I would rather sink under than divide with any —— of an associate. Now if the ruling powers will have it so that you cannot be better employed after the 25th Sept. 1832, what would you think of coming to join me? Or if you would not, whom would you recommend that could? A man of sound but not enthusiastic piety; mild in his temper; honest, open, and sincere in his disposition. As to his learning, I should not think it an objection if he resembled Sir Roger de Coverley's chaplain in some respects,* provided always nevertheless that he is capable of writing and pronouncing well his sermon, and does not—as the New England critic on pulpit-oratory has it—think himself privileged to "talk nonsense in the name of the Lord." Now, if you know any such person, won't you let me know it? for I have reason to believe that Bishop Kenrick would put no obstacle in the way of my desire in this matter.

We are all well; Bishop K. not yet returned from Harrisburg. The new church is verging toward its *complete* finish in the interior. I received a letter to-day from *our* representative in Congress, which says that the committee will report favorably on the duties of the articles imported—about 350 dollars. The Hoganites are quiet, and well they may [be]. The Haroldites are mad to think that such a church could be built not only without their aid, but in spite of their opposition—and so costly too!!! They had anticipated a triumph in seeing the work stop short—and they have been disappointed. Poor people! They mistook factious attachment to a man for fidelity to their religion, and the curse of their error is upon them. They are, however, but two or three; but the havoc which their language and example have made, especially in their own families, is frightful.

I remain, very sincerely, your brother in Christ,

JOHN HUGHES.

The Philadelphia press just at this time teemed with articles on the will of Stephen Girard, who died December 26, 1831, bequeathing two millions of dollars, a plot of ground, and the residue of certain portions of his estate out

* Sir Roger "asked me how I liked the good man whom I have just now mentioned? and without staying for my answer told me that he was afraid of being insulted with Latin and Greek at his own table; for which reason, he desired a particular friend of his at the university to find him out a clergyman rather of plain sense than much learning, of a good aspect, a clear voice, a sociable temper, and, if possible, a man that understood a little of backgammon. 'My friend,' says Sir Roger, 'found me out this gentleman, who, besides the endowments required of him, is, they tell me, a good scholar, though he does not show it.'"—*Spectator, No.* 106.

of which legacies were to be paid, for the foundation and endowment of a college for orphans, into which no ecclesiastic, minister, or missionary, of any denomination, was to be admitted even as a visitor. Mr. Hughes published in the *United States Gazette*, February 25, 1832, a letter signed "Fenelon," in answer to a correspondent of the *Pennsylvania Whig*, who had charged the clergy in general with "assailing Mr. Girard's memory with the tongue of slander and the shafts of ridicule." After analyzing his adversary's statements, he attacked the will on its merits with great sharpness.* He anticipated a reply from the correspondent of the *Whig*, and began to prepare himself for a long controversy; but his expectations were not fulfilled.

TO THE REV. MR. BRUTÉ.

PHILADELPHIA, *Feb.* 21, 1832.

REV. DEAR FRIEND:

It is unnecessary for me to inform you that for some time past I have been a faithless correspondent. To you also, who know my situation and engagements, I trust it is equally unnecessary to offer any apology.

Our city authorities are utterly at a loss for an *answer* to the opposite questions that are put about the *infidel fund* bequeathed by Girard. They seem to think that silence is their safest course, touching a will the difficulties of whose execution will devolve on their successors. I doubt very much the expediency of attacking the will openly, or entering into any public discussion of the merits of its provisions. Reason and religion, though unconquerable in

---

* The following extracts will give an idea of the spirit of this letter:

"It may be said in answer to all this, that Mr. Girard had a right to attach whatever conditions he thought proper. True, he might have required as a condition that each boy on entering must submit to have a piece of his ear cut off; and even then, two millions would secure him an apotheosis with such writers as 'Sparta.'"—"The next is a sneering paragraph at the ordination of ministers. The writer says, 'We never read that the Apostles were ordained by a convocation of learned prelates.' . . . . He might as well have sneered at the relation between parents and children, by telling us, with an air of great complacency at the discovery, that he never read of Adam's ancestors."

themselves, will yet stand but a poor chance before an *interested* tribunal of this semi-infidel community, when opposed to an argument of from two to five millions of dollars. Bishop White entered elaborately on the question whether the *acceptance* of this enormous bequest could be reconciled with the belief of Christianity or the principles of the constitution. I do not believe he made a single convert. Even Mr. Walsh, who never loses an opportunity of throwing incense at the "venerable"—even Mr. Walsh opposed his views. Being enabled myself to judge of the general feeling of the people, and of the effect which any public discussion of the question would have, I have deemed it expedient to abstain; unless, as in the article which I send you, it can be done in the shape of self-defence and under the plea of repelling aggression. My object in this article is to excite the attention of the clergy. The extent of abuse to which the exaction of money for fanatical purposes has been carried by these *parsons* has prepared the way for a powerful reaction, of which religion itself will be the victim, and to which the spirit of Girard's will is destined, perhaps, to give the first decided impulse. If the clergy can be roused to a settled purpose of opposition, it will be impossible, as the advocates of the will themselves acknowledge, to carry its provisions into effect. For my own part, although I regret that he has excluded religion, still I should have been sorry if he had left a prey to the voracious mongrels of heresy who, under the plea of propagating religion, are absolutely attempting to devour every thing. It was not, however, the abuses which are carried on under pretext of religion that Girard wished to exclude, but, as I have it from his niece (by a species of confidence), his intention was to originate means for the gradual extinction of Christianity in this country, and to strip man of every attribute except such as become a mere operative and productive animal. It is probable that my adversary will provoke a discussion of the general question, and that is what I desire. Be pleased to furnish me with your ideas, *and arguments to support them,* for the fact is that my engagements are too numerous and imperative to allow me leisure sufficient for reflection on this or almost any other subject that requires study.

The new church progresses rapidly, and will be opened on Passion Sunday. Mr. Powers is to preach the opening sermon. I would have asked Bishop Kenrick; but the fact is that he does not seem to understand what *suits* such an occasion. He, however, expressed his entire approbation, which I was careful to obtain before I invited Mr. Power. Could you not be here on that day? It would add to the solemnity of the occasion, and be a subject of joy to all your friends, who are all that know or ever heard of you. Every thing is provided for the new church, down to the cruets and towels for the altar—except a small crucifix, the figure of which should be about 15 to 19 inches, to suit the place it has to stand. Have you, or could you procure for me, this essential article? I have sent to Bishop Dubois for it, and he sent me one in bronze, but it is too small. Joseph Bonaparte has made us a present of a "Flagellation of Christ" by Hannibal Carracci, which I am told by judges would fetch 1,000 guineas in London. An Italian, a Roman artist, is decorating our sanctuary for the purpose of showing advantageously the power of his pencil, without any expense to us. A French sculptor also has made a model of an angel, from which we have taken six castings, to stand in so many arches of the ceiling which have been left for them in the architecture. Clouds rising from the caps of six columns are the pedestals. The effect will be fine. In a word, God seems to have brought forth facilities for the perfect accomplishment of the work, which even the most sanguine could scarcely have anticipated. Every thing is quiet. The Sisters all well—their school overflowing with poor female children, mostly Catholics. Yours sincerely in Christ,

JOHN HUGHES.

REV. MR. BRUTÉ TO MR. HUGHES.

MOUNT ST. MARY'S, *March* 12, 1832.

I was wishing every day to answer your kind and interesting letter by Mr. White. The excellent piece on Girard's will came to my hands a few days after, and it seemed to me well calculated indeed to fulfil the object that you had in writing it.

. . . . . .

I have heard from all quarters of the great success that God grants to your noble undertaking. The details you give me are of the most pleasing nature. The invitation you add for the day of the consecration I acknowledge with all my heart; but be sure that my good obscure corner here is my true place, and a couple of miles of radius, reaching just to St. Joseph's, the true space of my usefulness; for the rest, *nesciri et pro nihilo reputari.*

Father Hughes preached his farewell sermon at St. Joseph's on Sunday, April 1, 1832. He was much affected in bidding adieu to the little congregation among whom he had always found peace and happiness, and they on their part gave audible expression to their sorrow. The new church was dedicated on the following Sunday by Bishops Conwell and Kenrick Father Hughes had founded golden expectations upon the dedication sermon by the eloquent Dr. Power of New York. He knew that many Protestants, including several clergymen, would be present at his invitation, and he proposed to take up a collection at the close of the ceremony toward paying some of the most pressing debts upon the church. To his consternation, Dr. Power chose for his subject "the four marks of the true Church," and preached a bitter polemical discourse. At the end of the service, Father Hughes shook him heartily by the hand, and exclaimed, "My dear sir, you have ruined me!" The sermon caused some irritation and provoked controversy; but its effect was not so bad after all: the collection amounted to eight hundred and fifty dollars. Still there was matter enough for anxiety in the pecuniary affairs of St. John's. The cost of the ground and building was about seventy-three thousand dollars, and long after Father Hughes had become Bishop of New York it was struggling under a load of debt which threatened to crush it. To a gentleman who had some control over the pecuniary affairs of the church, he wrote thus in 1840, at a time when its finances were in an especially embarrassed condition: "What a triumph your exhibition must furnish to the advocates of trusteeism—to those who from the beginning were hostile to the undertaking, in every degree of hostility, from open opposition down to polite indifference! To what idle purpose did I toil in the broiling sun to collect money for it! You tried it *one* day, and it was enough. But I had it for months and months." Father Hughes had little business talent. He could frame a comprehensive plan of money operations, but be needed the help of others to put it in execution. He could think out a great system of collection and disbursement; but for the details of finance he had no head. The affairs of St. John's were therefore a heavy burden for him to bear, and the wonder is that he bore it so bravely and so well. There were no lay trustees, and the deeds were in the pastor's own name.

When the diocesan synod of Philadelphia assembled in May, 1832, he was appointed *promotor*, that is, an officer whose duty it is to bring before the council the questions which require deliberation. He preached at the opening of the synod on the constitution of the church and the order of church government. With his old friend Father Hurley and the Rev. Nicholas O'Donnell, he was appointed to deliberate respecting the establishment of a diocesan seminary. He spoke with great earnestness of the need for such an institution, but the most that could be accomplished at that time was the opening of a theological class at the bishop's own house. At the close of the synod he was chosen to make a complimentary address to Dr. Kenrick in the name of his brother clergymen.

TO THE REV. MR. BRUTÉ.

PHILADELPHIA, *Saturday morning, July* 28, 1832.

REV. DEAR BROTHER:

I prefer to write in a hurry and briefly rather than prolong your anxiety, if any thing I have to say can remove or diminish it. With regard to the fourth of July, when I was waited on for the church, I gave no answer until I had laid the request before the bishop as it was made to me. He saw no impropriety in granting it, as the object was not political, but purely *patriotic*, and as the association is composed of the most respectable young gentlemen of the city. The selection of St. John's was intended as a compliment to the Catholics and to the church. I took no pleasure in granting it; but when the request was made, I believed that, with the restrictions I put, the grant would be less injurious than the refusal.

I am not aware that the use of a church has ever been refused or solicited either in Baltimore or Boston. And as far as I have an opportunity of judging, the increase of Catholics by conversion from sects is greater here than in either of those cities. It happens, curiously enough, that I have had more converts since the day in question than I had for a year previous. Within two weeks there have been ten who applied to me for instruction to be admitted into the C. Church—all respectable, one an extensive merchant. It is the same with the bishop. This circumstance, however, would not prove any thing, as it must be the work of God.

The platform was in the middle aisle in front of the altar, made by resting boards on the pews of either side. The prayer at the commencement was a prayer written for the occasion by myself. The first part acknowledging our sins and unworthiness, and imploring the mercies of our offended God. The second part was a petition for humility, and against national pride and arrogance; and the conclusion invoked the protection of Almighty God for the country. The prayer at the close of the celebration was that of Archbishop Carroll, read from the prayer-book. The oration was an apology for, or rather a panegyric of revolutions. It was foolish, and pronounced so by nearly all that heard it. But it was in *its spirit* such an one as might have been expected, and in this country could do no harm. It was severe on the old governments of France and of England, and equally so upon the spirit of sectarianism in this country, containing an attempt to vindicate the revolutionary spirit from the charge of irreligion. On the whole, there was as much good order and respect to the place as could have been expected. But I do not mean that it shall ever be repeated where I am. Nor would I have granted it at this time (because I look upon such occasions just as you do), did I not fear that the refusal would have added to the bitterness of feeling produced by the very harsh texture of an injudicious sermon some months before.

I enclose you a copy of my regulations for the church and congregation. With regard to the confessions, my fixing particular hours was intended to inform the people when they could calculate *with certainty* on finding me in the confessional. You seem to have understood it as exclusive, and that I would never be there except at those particular hours. This is not the case; I am there, I might say, every morning, and at all times when I am wanted. Parties of pleasure are not frequented by me, and except one I am sure I visit less than any clergyman in this city. Everybody acquainted with my situation knows I have no time, and I am as well pleased it should be so, for in fact I have no inclination. I am just called to visit a sick man in the Penitentiary, and must conclude by requesting your prayers for

Your affectionate brother in Christ,
JOHN HUGHES.

TO SISTER ANGELA.

Sept. 1832.

MY DEAR SISTER:

Margaret has left me room, but it was not in her power to procure me what is equally necessary to write much—time. I am really ashamed to put forward always the same excuse, but really it is the true one. I am obliged to attend a congregation in the country tomorrow, and I write this while my penitents are in the church, believing me at tea. St. John's is flourishing, and acknowledged to be the handsomest and best attended church in Philadelphia. I trust that about the middle of November I shall have all the finishing improvements of church, school, and dwelling completed. Until then, I need not expect any respite. Give my love and respects to all, and believe me, just as if I wrote *twice a week*,

Your affectionate brother,
JOHN HUGHES.

TO THE SAME.

Nov. 28, 1832.

All our Sisters are well. In St. John's Asylum, which they here call by my name, there are 25 orphans destitute, and 25 more for whom some small compensation is received, making a family of 50,—besides the Sisters who have charge of them,—and a day school of 150 children. In Mr. Donaghoe's, where Sister Ann is, there are 300 children at day school, and no orphans. In St. Joseph's, the old establishment, there are some 43 orphans, but no day school. In the almshouse there are eight Sisters, whose services in reëstablishment of order have been duly acknowledged by the Board of Managers.

St. John's church goes on prosperously, but its affairs leave the pastor little time at his own disposal. This will be the case for many years, perhaps after I am dead; for it is so much in debt, as you may suppose, that no small revenue is necessary to pay interest and meet expenses. Now, over and above the duty of preaching in a spiritual view, it will be necessary for the pastor of this church to preach well—or to work miracles. I must depend on the former—and in order to accomplish it, study is absolutely necessary; so that what between study for my sermons and the external duties of the mission I shall not have a moment for myself. Perhaps, on the whole, this is an advantage, as well as the under-snarling of certain little curs for whom I have been either too prosperous or too independent. Their attacks will operate as a counterpoise to that flattery which on my account you dreaded so much. In both I perceive the goodness and mercy of God, who would thus remove from me all temptations to pride and idleness. Either of these is bad enough, but both together would destroy an angel.

Let me hear from you soon again, and pray for

Your affectionate brother,

JOHN HUGHES.

Whatever may have been his temptations to pride, there was little danger of his being spoiled by idleness. He was now about engaging in a public controversy which must have taxed his powers of application to the utmost.

CHAPTER IX.

1832-1835.

First Controversy with Breckinridge—Establishment of *The Catholic Herald*—Review of Bishop Onderdonk on the Rule of Faith—Father Hughes's position in Philadelphia—Nominated Bishop of Cincinnati—Letters to Sister Angela, Mr. Bruté, and Bishop Purcell—Letters to Rev. Henry M. Mason on Infallibility.

THE Reverend John Breckinridge, with whom Father Hughes was about to measure swords, was a Presbyterian clergyman of high standing, and well versed in theological disputes. He was born at Cabell's Dale, Kentucky, July 4, 1797; his age was consequently only ten days less than that of his opponent. He had been tutor at Princeton College, chaplain to Congress, editor of a religious paper at Lexington, Kentucky, pastor of churches in Lexington and Baltimore, and at the time of the discussion with which we now have to do, was secretary and general agent of the Board of Education of the Presbyterian Church. So far as natural talent for discussion and fondness for polemical theology went, the two disputants were well matched. Mr. Breckinridge had been the longer in the ministry by four or five years, and had the advantage of the more thorough education. In 1831, while he was pastor of a church in Baltimore, a lady of his congregation handed him a review by an anonymous hand of a well-known anti-Catholic tale called "*Father Clement*," and begged him to answer it. "I chose to reply in writing," said he, "and at the close called for a written rejoinder to a number of objections stated in the reply; and insisted on one from a *responsible* author, stating my readiness, at the same time, in view of these 'objections,' to meet such a person on the whole field of controversy between Roman Catholics and Protestants." The anonymous reviewer was ascertained to be a Catholic layman, "and did not appear to me," says Mr. Breckinridge, "an *accredited* defender of his principles, though in all likelihood as wise as his teachers. . . . There are priests and bishops. . . . We are willing to meet any of them on the broad field of this important and vital discussion." In the autumn of 1832 he published the letter from which the above words are taken in *The Christian Advocate*—"impelled to it," as he said to Mr. Hughes, "in part by the frequent and sometimes insolent attacks that were made upon the Protestant churches,* and in part by the very unwarrantable course pursued at the consecration of the house of worship in which you officiate." † A copy of *The Christian Advocate* containing Mr. Breckinridge's letter was brought to Father Hughes by Mr. L——, one of his congregation. "My Presbyterian friends exult over this," said Mr. L——, "and ask me, 'Why, if these things are untrue, does not your great Mr. Hughes reply to them?' I have pledged myself that you would reply."

"I fear you have gone too far," was the answer, "in committing me; but since you rely upon me, I will not fail you."

To combat the desultory charges contained in the *Advocate* he soon found would be a waste of time. "There are

---

* Special allusion was here made to a letter from Mr. Hughes, signed J. H., and published in *The United States Gazette*, Sept. 7, 1832. It was addressed to the Rev. Ezra Stiles Ely, D D., editor of *The Philadelphian*, and referred to the conduct of the Catholic as contrasted with the Protestant clergy during the prevalence of cholera.

† So far from proving the "ruin" of Father Hughes, Dr. Powers's dedication sermon was therefore one of the remote causes of his reputation and skill as a controversialist, and perhaps of his ultimate elevation to the episcopacy.

first principles at the bottom of every subject," wrote he to Mr. Breckinridge, "the application of which never fails to throw light on questions in detail springing out of such subjects. I saw in your letter that you had entirely overlooked those first principles of Christianity by the application of which truth may be distinguished from error. I saw our doctrines incorrectly stated, arraigned, tried, and triumphantly condemned; but then you were conducting these proceedings in the absence of every tribunal except that of your own opinion and the opinion of those who might happen to agree with you." He proposed to begin by discussing the "rule of faith." The conditions of the controversy were settled partly in personal interviews between the two antagonists and their respective friends, and partly by a preliminary correspondence protracted through three months. Mr. Hughes first proposed that they should "write and publish alternately in the same paper, never allowing any communication to exceed two columns." Mr. Breckinridge preferred an oral debate, but was willing that the discussion should be carried on through *The Presbyterian*, a weekly paper published in Philadelphia. The preliminaries were finally arranged as they are given in the following letter:

TO THE REV. MR. BRUTÉ.

Dec. 14, 1832.

REV. DEAR SIR:

When I shall have made you acquainted with the position in which I find myself, you will not be surprised that I should turn my eyes to you for help and counsel.

At a future time you will be made acquainted with the occasion of a regular controversy in which I am about to engage, and the preliminaries of which have been amicably arranged with my antagonist, a Mr. Breckinridge, a Presbyterian clergyman of considerable reputation and standing among them. The time fixed for opening the controversy is the first week of January; and as I look to you for much powerful ammunition, I must make you acquainted with the written conditions of the warfare. They are to stand as a constant heading to the discussion, and are certainly as favorable as I could have expected. They are as follows:

"The undersigned, agreeing to enter on an amicable discussion of the great points of religious controversy between Protestants and Roman Catholics, do hereby bind themselves to the observance of the following rules:

"1. The parties shall write and publish alternately in the weekly religious paper called *The Presbyterian*, and a Roman Catholic paper to be furnished by the first of January; it being understood that the communications shall be published after the following plan: one party opening the first week, the other party replying the next week, and every piece to be republished in the immediately succeeding number of the Roman Catholic paper. The communications not to exceed four columns of *The Presbyterian*, nor to continue beyond six months without consent of parties.

"2. The parties agree that there is an infallible rule of faith established by Christ to guide us in matters of religion, for the purpose of determining disputes in the Church of Christ.

"3. They moreover agree that after giving their views of the rule of faith, they shall proceed to discuss the question, 'Is the Protestant religion the religion of Christ?'

"4. The parties agree respectively to adhere strictly to the subject under discussion for the time being, and to admit no second question until the first shall have been exhausted. Each party shall be the judge when he is done with a subject, and shall be at liberty to occupy his time with a second subject when he is done with the first; leaving to the other party the liberty of continuing to review the abandoned topic as long as he shall choose; subject, however, to be answered if he introduce new matter.

"5. Mr. Hughes to open the discussion, and Mr. Breckinridge to follow according to the dictates of his own judgment.

"(Signed)   JOHN BRECKINRIDGE,
                                             JOHN HUGHES.

"*Dec.* 14, 1832."

You perceive that he admits the necessity and existence of an infallible rule of faith for the settlement of disputes in the Church. The question then with which I shall have to commence is—"What is that infallible rule?" The next question is that stated in the conditions. Thus, Rev. dear Sir, you see the parts of the adversary's fortress that are to be attacked, and please to give me all the aid in your power. Please also to show this to the Rev. Mr. Purcell, with my love and respects, requesting him also to think of my situation. But above all, I entreat you both to pray to Almighty God that this affair may turn out to the advantage of souls and the promotion of his glory. It is near 10 o'clock, and the person hurries me; so I must conclude in haste.

    Yours sincerely and affectionately in Christ,

                                          JOHN HUGHES.

The situation of Mr. Hughes seemed far from enviable. Bishop Kenrick, Mr. Bruté, in fact nearly all his clerical friends, strongly disapproved of what he had done. The laborious duties of a parish priest were enough to occupy his time, without the superadded task of a long and exhaustive public discussion; but when we reflect that there was no Catholic paper printed in Philadelphia at that time, and that before he could begin his controversy he had to found a journal in which it might be published, his energy and courage seem truly wonderful. A few of his personal friends having supplied the necessary funds, he established *The Catholic Herald* in January, 1833, and for a few weeks acted as editor. At the end of that time he carried what money remained to the bishop, and washed his hands of all further responsibility for the paper, though he continued to write for it frequently. His first letter on the Rule of Faith was dated January 21, 1833. It was a vigorous and well-planned attack upon the Protestant principle of private interpretation of the Bible. In a postscript he says, alluding to the preliminary correspondence: "You take great pains to show in all your letters how much you have to do, and how much leisure, 'sanctuary quietude,' remains on my hands, intimating thereby the advantages which my situation gives me over you in the conducting of this controversy. Be assured, Reverend Sir, that if I thought the public could be interested in the detail of my avocations, I also could make out a tolerable list of duties; enough, perhaps, to turn the scales of comparison. But to make your mind easy on the subject of your official occupations, I beg to state that I am prepared, if God gives me health, to sustain the Catholic argument against any or all the clergymen of the Synod or General Assembly, provided he or they write with your signature and adhere to the rules." The introductory discussion on the Rule of Faith was not finished until the end of June, and only one month of the time to which the debate was originally limited remained for the consideration of the second question, "Is the Protestant religion the religion of Christ?" By mutual consent, however, the time was extended to the first of October. Mr. Bruté, though he did not approve of the discussion, was liberal with his assistance. By every mail he furnished Mr. Hughes with notes, suggestions, references, quotations, outlines of argument, all jotted down in his rapid style, and needing, we can hardly doubt, some ingenuity to understand them.

TO THE REV. MR. PURCELL.

PHILADELPHIA, *Feb.* 14, 1833.

REV. DEAR SIR:

You know too well the value of apologies about long silence, great occupations, etc., to expect that I should begin this by invoking them. I have just finished a letter of 13 pages foolscap to Mr. Breckinridge, which I think (authors, you know, are never vain) will shiver his Rule of Faith. The Protestants here are excessively anxious to see the questions fairly tried. There are no less than three publishers making arrangements to publish the controversy in monthly numbers. Pray for the success of the cause of God.

I enclose ten dollars at the request of Mrs. ——, which I understand is intended for the travelling expenses of her son, who is to come home at the close of his present six months. This is almost the last act of her life in widowhood, as she was married on last

Sunday evening to a Catholic widower, of Trinity church, whose name I do not now recollect.

I am afraid my excellent friend Mr. Bruté thinks unfavorably of me for not acknowledging the receipt of his letters. Here again I might excuse myself by referring to my want of time; but besides, although his letters abound with good materials for argument, and great erudition, still there was such a tone of apprehension pervading them, that they began to produce doubt of propriety and general discouragement in my mind. Situated as I was, retreat was impossible, except in obedience to superior command. I myself, considering the prospective arrangements I had made as to rules, order of subjects, etc., never felt a scruple or doubt as to either the utility or issue of the controversy. The opportunity of placing my letters under the eyes of certainly not fewer than 30,000 Protestant readers, is too precious to be allowed to escape unimproved. I do not pretend to say that it will make many converts; but the perusal of them now may be the destruction of prejudice in some minds; and the first seed, reflection, and still more *afflictions* of the heart, may ripen into actual conversions when I and my letters shall have been forgotten. Pray for me, and write soon.

There is a kind of demi-official impression among us here that the mitre of Cincinnati is waiting for a head from the Mountain. What think you? Yours sincerely in Christ,

JOHN HUGHES.

TO THE REV. MR. BRUTÉ.

March 8, 1833.

REV. DEAR FRIEND:

Your very welcome letter has relieved my mind from the apprehension that my apparent neglect of your former letters had determined you not to write to me any more. I have now to thank you for the excellent hints and information which they contained; but I was really embarrassed by the doubts of utility which they expressed in reference to the controversy in which I was *bound* to engage. The very first thing I did was to advise the bishop of the whole affair, when he was still at Pittsburg; and on his arrival it was my first care to tell him that I would extricate myself from all the pledges, in case he did not approve of my proceeding. But I knew that the calumnies of B.'s first letter, and the call addressed to "Priests and Bishops" to deny or answer, would have scandalized the weak Catholics, many of whom have been tottering under the *shock* of all that has taken place in this city. The Protestants were pushing that document into their very eyes, and saying, "If it is not true, why don't some of your ministers answer or deny it?" But how could I have exposed its author by any other course than that which I have adopted? As you probably have not seen this letter, I will send it to you. And you can render me a great service by *verifying* the references—which will be *falsifying* them. This I have done myself in two or three instances. But having the original works, if you would be good enough to copy the passages to which he has made reference, in order that I may give a whole letter to show his *dishonesty*, and point out the character of the weapons by which *truth* has been assailed and Protestantism defended ever since the Reformation, the effect on the public mind will be astounding. But then to make it successful it must be done triumphantly. The controversy has excited all attention here. It is published *entire* in four religious papers, and partially in seven or eight. It is published in pamphlet form in four different offices—one stereotype. The Episcopalians are trembling lest they should be brought in, and their periodicals are crowded since it began with *accidental* essays on the possibility of "Protestant certainty." Poor old Bishop White has convened his clergy, and enjoined them, with all the little authority he has, to keep quiet and take no part in it. In the mean time they are *circulating in the form of a tract* the catechism of Bishop Bowen—refuted by Bishop England. The refutation is indeed as prolix as it is powerful.

You will have seen, ere this reaches you, my third letter to B. I was obliged to defend the Catholic principle which he had assailed, but I shall return to my former ground. The Protestants generally are dissatisfied with his answer. They pronounce him unfair and *flinching*.

I have but little time to write. My love and respects to all. Please investigate the references.

Yours sincerely in Christ,
John Hughes.

MR. BRUTÉ TO BISHOP KENRICK.

PALM SUNDAY [*March* 31], 1833.

Oh! may God bless M. Hughes to the end, and any fear about what has now to go on to the results, hidden in God's, whose thoughts are not our thoughts, be spared. God may bring much good as easily as prevent scandal; let us but pray and do for the best.

TO THE REV. MR. BRUTÉ.

PHILADELPHIA, *Holy Thursday* [*April* 5], 1833.

REV. DEAR FRIEND:

I have received your favor by Mr. Gillespie, and seize a leisure moment to thank you for the pains and interest you have taken. You will have perceived by the last *Herald* that I have used your notes in the faith of their *infallibility;* and yet, if I were questioned as to my authority, I should be at a loss to name the *book* that furnishes it. I suppose that a reference to the "*Tractatus Speciales de Controversiis Fidei*" of the two Bishops Wallemburgs would do; but I have not the work, and I do not believe it is in the city.

You see also that I have *intimated a review or rather exposure* of my adversary's authorities and references before the close of the controversy. For this I must depend on you and Bishop Kenrick. I have not the books; and if I had, not being *familiar* with them, I should not find time to investigate. I wish you would *review* from the commencement every reference, and *refute*, either by a brief quotation from the passage referred to, or by a clear explanation of its meaning in the *context*. Of all things, be *clear;* for neither myself nor the readers to whom it is to be submitted possess *your* intellectual discipline and habits of familiarity with books—and for our sakes make every thing *lucid*, even to excess.

There are some encouraging circumstances connected with this controversy. There are no less than three converts under instruction in this church now, in consequence, *as they say*, of its perusal—one a Baptist, one an Episcopalian, and one a *Duncanite* Presbyterian, who was moved to pity the Catholic Church by the language in which her minister warned the "flock" not to venture inside of St. John's, nor listen to the sophistical lectures. The famous Parson McCalla has paid me two or three visits, without disclosing any other intention than a professed desire to know the *real* doctrine of the Church, and the books from which he might learn it. I have no anticipations in reference to him; but God may improve his heart and head, which have been those of a fanatic, to a better knowledge of the truth.

Love and remembrance to all. Yours sincerely in Christ,

JOHN HUGHES.

In September Mr. Breckinridge informed his antagonist that "his duty imperatively called him to leave the city and travel at large through the country for several months." He renewed his proposal of an oral debate, to be held after his return. Mr. Hughes would not consent to this. "If your business carry you abroad," said he, "you are free to discontinue when you please, and to resume when you find it convenient to do so. But you must not deprive me of my right to return the arrow which you shoot—in retreating. When you return you may resume the contest, and I shall be prepared to receive you." The thirty-fifth and last letter of the controversy was accordingly written by Mr. Hughes October 3d. The Rev. William L. McCalla, a Presbyterian divine, answered it in his own name, but Mr. Hughes did not feel called upon to notice his communication. Angry traces of the long discussion may be found in the *Presbyterian* and *Catholic Herald* for some months after this; but it was not formally renewed, although both parties professed a readiness to go on with it. Like almost all other controversies, it abounded in personalities and recriminations, for his share in which Mr. Hughes afterwards expressed his regret. He published the letters on both sides in a single volume without comment.*

---

* *Controversy between Rev. Messrs. Hughes and Breckinridge on the subject*, "*Is the Protestant Religion the Religion of Christ?*" Phila., 472 pp. 8vo, 1833.

Several side issues sprang out of this famous discussion. For instance, there was the question, debated during a month or more, whether Bishop Kenrick did or did not caution the faithful against reading it. The bishop's dislike of the proceedings was well known to Protestants as well as Catholics; but he explicitly denied having given such a warning either in public or in private. At the opening of the Convention of the Protestant Episcopal Church of Pennsylvania in May, 1833, the Right Rev. Henry U. Onderdonk, assistant bishop of the diocese, delivered a charge to the clergy on the Rule of Faith, in the hope, as he said, "that his remarks might not be without their value when the claims of the Church of Rome were brought into notice." Mr. Hughes reviewed it in a little pamphlet,* and in his preface spoke thus of the discussion with Breckinridge:

It is not for me to say one word in the way of opinion as to the manner in which my opponent has sustained the Protestant Rule of Faith, or acquitted himself in the arguments and authorities adduced to disprove the Catholic principle of religious guidance. He seems to be highly satisfied with himself.

But for some months back there has been a considerable undertone of dissatisfaction among the better informed Protestants generally, not excepting Presbyterians themselves. They had never suspected the strength of the Catholic position on the Rule of Faith, nor the weakness of their own. And in this mood of feeling, they ascribed the sufferings of the cause to the incompetence of the advocate. Even some of the Protestant clergy did not hesitate to say that Mr. Breckinridge was not "the man" that should have been selected; that he had no business to engage in such a discussion without being authorized by those whom he undertook to represent, and in utter contempt of the poet's admonition:

> Sumite materiam vestris, qui scribitis, æquam
> Viribus; et versate diu quid ferre recusent,
> Quid valeant humeri.

---

* *A Review of the Charge delivered May 22d, 1833, by the Right Rev. Bishop Onderdonk, on the Rule of Faith.* By the Rev. John Hughes. Phila., 19 pp. 8vo, 1833.

It is not for me to say whether it was these considerations that moved Bishop Onderdonk to take up the Rule of Faith, and make it the subject of his "charge" to the assembled convention of the Protestant Episcopal Church of Pennsylvania. The public attention was called to it in various newspapers, and not only the charge, but also the *subject* of it, contrary to custom, was announced as something important and interesting "at *this* time."

The Church Register took up Bishop Onderdonk's defence, and was answered by Mr. Hughes in one of his letters to Breckinridge.

It would not be easy to overrate the reputation which Father Hughes acquired by his triumphant vindication of the Catholic faith. Vilification of Catholics was just then in fashion all over the United States. The religious newspapers of all denominations teemed with polemics to an extent which nowadays would not be tolerated. In Pennsylvania the Catholic Church had so far found no defender able to grapple with her adversaries and fight them in a fair field. When Mr. Hughes stood forth, the faithful soon felt that a strong arm was striking blows for them, and thenceforth they looked to him whenever they were attacked. Besides courage and skill, there were other qualifications which made him a valuable champion. He was held in higher reputation among Protestants than almost any other priest in that city had been for many years. He had often taken part in theological fights; but it was to defend his own creed, seldom to attack others. "I have had intercourse," he said, "with society of all denominations; I have preached nearly every Sunday, oftentimes on controversy, when hundreds of Protestants were present; and I venture to assert that I have not done one action or used one expression, in the pulpit or out of it, to warrant the charge of malignity. I have wounded no man's feelings; I have ridiculed no man's religion; I have injured no man's character. . . . I am proud to believe, and have reason to believe, that, though a Catholic and a priest, I stand as high in public, even Protestant, estimation as Mr. Breckinridge himself." Even before his controversy with Breckinridge, he had come to be regarded as the representative man of his religion in Pennsylvania. He left upon all who came in contact with him an impression of his ability, which previous to that discussion was not justified by any of his public acts. He was a good preacher, but so far not a great one, and his published writings were of a slight and ephemeral character. What Dr. Johnson said of Burke, that "no one could meet him by accident under a shed to avoid a shower without being convinced that he was an extraordinary man," might have been said with nearly equal truth of Father Hughes.

While the controversy was going on, his name was under consideration at Rome in connection with the vacant bishopric of Cincinnati. Of the candidates suggested to the Holy See by the American prelates, there were two whose claims seemed equally balanced—Mr. Hughes and Mr. Purcell. Bishop England, who was then in Rome, had been requested by his episcopal brethren to hasten the appointment as much as possible. He had frequent interviews upon the subject with the Cardinal Prefect of the Propaganda, and urged the importance of making a choice without any unnecessary loss of time. One day the cardinal said to him: "There are two candidates, bishop, between whom the Sacred Congregation are utterly at a loss how to decide; these are the Rev. John Hughes and the Rev. John B. Purcell. If you can mention any particular, no matter how trifling, in which one seems to you better qualified than the other, I think a decision may be reached at once."

The bishop hesitated; for he was really perplexed. At last he answered:

"There is one point, your Eminence, which may deserve to be considered. Mr. Hughes is emphatically a self-made man, and perhaps he would be on that account more acceptable to the people of a Western diocese than Mr. Purcell."

"Ah!" said the cardinal, "I think that will do."

The next day he met Bishop England again, and exclaimed, with an air of satisfaction:

"Well, bishop! the question is settled. As soon as I told the cardinals what you said about *Mr. Purcell's* being a self-made man, they agreed upon him unanimously, and the nomination will be at once presented to his Holiness for approval."

"I was about to explain the mistake," said Bishop England to the clergyman from whom I have this anecdote, "but I reflected that it was no doubt the work of the Spirit of God, and was silent." The cardinal never knew of his blunder. Mr. Purcell was consecrated in October, 1833, and he and Mr. Hughes were both present at the second provincial council of Baltimore which met in the latter part of that month. Mr. Hughes attended in the capacity of theologian to Bishop Kenrick. The council recommended to the Holy See the erection of the diocese of Vincennes, to embrace the whole State of Indiana and the eastern part of Illinois, and Father Bruté was mentioned as the fittest person to be the new bishop.

TO SISTER ANGELA.

Jan. 20, 1834.

We hear about once a month from Chambersburg. Father's health continues good. He has built a small house on his place out of town, and lives, or at least spends most of his time there.

We were all delighted with your excellent Bishop Rosati, and edified at the account which he gave of the state of religion and piety in the West. Write me a letter about your new establishment, and every thing concerning yourself. Pray for me, and cherish carefully, my dear sister, the grace of your vocation. The time is short; and if we meet not in this world, let us endeavor to meet in a better. God bless you. Your affectionate brother,

JOHN.

TO BISHOP PURCELL.

April 16, 1834.

RIGHT REV. AND DEAR BISHOP:

I am afraid that my neglect of your kind letter, received several months ago, has injured me in your estimation. I often thought of it with remorse; but although my contrition was sincere, yet my resolutions of amendment were not prompt. In fact, dear friend, I never felt that I had time, *just then*, to write; and so days and weeks and months have passed away. On the eve of my departure for the council, I had agreed to take the "Gothic mansion" for the orphans, and the pressure of that engagement has kept me down ever since, until I find, as is the case at present, that the first crisis is over. Five Catholic gentlemen, at my request, gave their notes, each for one thousand dollars, to meet the payment which was to be made in hand. The fair, of which you have seen, no doubt, the result in the *C. Herald*, has relieved me of that burthen. But to get up the fair, with the discordant materials which the combination of female effort on so large a scale is sure to develop, and to carry it through in the teeth of sectarian opposition, such as I had to contend with, required all my attention and perseverance. Fortunately, every thing has gone off in the very happiest manner. The Protestants deserted their own fairs, and flocked to us in crowds; and ours was the scene of wealth, fashion, pride, and aristocracy, as well as of humble piety and devotion to Catholic charity. The net proceeds were about $4,500, amidst what are called bad times, and certainly very unpropitious weather.

We have yet $4,000 to pay in a few months, for which I had calculated on the legacy of Major Dugan. I am sorry to learn by report that there are lawsuits, which may prevent the settlement of the estate for some time. But I should hope that in our need the executors would advance the legacy for the orphans, and the more so as the board will be ready to grant a bond of indemnity in case it is required. . . . . .

For myself, I am well, but not strong. I have now, for the first time since my ordination, a *prospect* of comparative leisure, which I intend to employ, not in building churches, but in repairing the interior edifice. Please to remember in your prayers

Your affectionate friend and servant,

JOHN HUGHES.

He accompanied Bishop Kenrick on another episcopal visitation in April and May of this year, in the course of which he preached on the occasion of the dedication of St. Paul's church, Pittsburg, on the 4th of May.

TO BISHOP PURCELL.

PITTSBURG, *May* 8, 1834.

RIGHT REV. AND DEAR FRIEND :

How much I regret that, being so near, you did not make it convenient to join us on the occasion of dedicating St. Paul's; and that, although you remain two weeks in Somerset, it will not be in my power to visit you! Pressing affairs call me back to Philadelphia; and as for Bishop Kenrick, he had made his appointments for the next three or four Sundays in different parts of the diocese.

St. Paul's excels every thing, as a Catholic Church, that I have seen—not excepting even St. John's. The occasion passed off with great satisfaction to the bishop, the pastor, and congregation, and indeed the citizens generally, if I except the implacable Presbyterians. There was solemn high mass by Rev. Messrs. O'Reilly, Stillinger, and Masculet, with good music in the choir. The sermon was by your humble servant, and I believe gave no offence, which is about as much as I can say in its favor. But altogether, it is highly consoling to reflect that Catholicity has been able to raise such a temple in such a place, and in so short a time from its first appearance; for it is said that fourteen years ago there were not above one hundred and fifty Catholics in this city.

. . . . .

TO THE REV. MR. BRUTE.

June 10, 1834.

. . . .

With regard to any thing's being done for the education of clergymen, I despair of it until the bishops and colleges, or college, shall understand each other and themselves better. It is a subject on which there is too great a variety of opinion, and on which each superior looks only to the boundaries of his own jurisdiction.

This state of ecclesiastical education seemed to be the choice of both bishops and priests at the late council; and although it may do during the continuance of remittances from Europe (which should be sent; it strikes me, for the support of missionaries in the East), it will not do without some such support. I maintain that there are resources enough in the country for the education of priests and the establishment of a college, or colleges. But if nothing is done by the bishops, those resources cannot be reached. For instance, the bishop's domestic seminary here—I am sure that not one out of five of the Catholics in the city are aware of its existence. Yet the bishop would desire that the clergy and people should support it. But no plan proposed—no system organized—no prospects held forth—nothing to direct, nothing to encourage. And in reference to the general subject of clerical education at the council, it was identically the same.

How, then, with all my solicitude, I might add apprehension, for your house, to which I am bound by so many ties of attachment—how can I do any thing? I do not, indeed, believe that in the present distress any thing could be done, no matter how great might be the effort, and I am really at a loss to see how poor Bishop Kenrick expects to succeed with his establishment.

But the indifference or supposed hostility which is felt in Baltimore for the Mountain has weakened the confidence of all at a distance. And it will be difficult to find inducement for the people to espouse warmly a cause which is conceived to be neglected, if not thwarted, by those who should most delight in its prosperity. I make these remarks only to yourself, and I should not like them to go further. But if nothing is done by the people, I have no hesitation in saying it is because the superiors choose to have it so.

. . . . .

MR. BRUTÉ TO MR. HUGHES.

No DATE [1834].

. . . . .

I think much of your letter on the seminaries. Think well on it; digest some plan; let not the first council pass without realizing more for it. This is the *all in all.* Else *in vanum laboraverunt;* harvest on all sides, and no laborers, or too few, and imperfectly prepared.

. . . . . .

Adieu, à Dieu—God alone! all in all, God and our eternity! God and our sacred altar! *altaria Domini virtutum!*

S. Bruté.

Very soon after this letter was written came the official intelligence of Mr. Bruté's appointment to the see of Vincennes.

TO BISHOP BRUTÉ.

PHILADELPHIA, *Aug.* 14, 1834.

Right Rev. dear Sir:

I have been unusually engaged since I received the news of your elevation to the episcopacy. My congratulations are on this account *later*, but not less sincere. The place which you have hitherto occupied seemed to me so important for the Church, that I confess it is with regret I see it vacant. But when I think of the ways by which Almighty God accomplishes his designs, especially in reference to the Church, I can have no doubt but it will be found according to his will.

I have been attending a poor man who was to be executed tomorrow, but is now reprieved until 7th of next November.

My friend Doctor H—— will pay you a visit about the time this reaches you; and I can have no doubt you will pay him that attention which his merit demands; and to which a *request of mine* would be entitled. He is all Catholic but the profession, and some "*doctor-prejudices*" on the H. Eucharist. He is particularly desirous to make your acquaintance, and I am sure you will be pleased with him.

I shall soon write you a long letter; the duties of the day must be my excuse for making this short communication, which has for object mainly to advise you of my friend's visit, and to secure your particular attention to him.

Yours humbly in Christ,
John Hughes.

His anonymous contributions to the *Catholic Herald* were still frequent; but most of them were on subjects of temporary interest. Controversy was the staple of the

Herald, as it was indeed of all the other religious papers of that day, and there were few discussions of religious topics upon which he had not something to say. He resumed the question of the Rule of Faith in a series of ten letters to the Rev. Henry M. Mason of the Protestant Episcopal Church, whose published sermon on that subject had lately caused no little excitement and displeasure among the members of his own sect by its strong high-church tendency.*

---

* *The City of God. A Sermon preached by Appointment in Trinity Church, Newark, before an Annual Convention of the Church in the Diocese of New Jersey, on Wednesday, May 18, 1834.* By Henry M. Mason, Rector of St. John's Church, Salem.

CHAPTER X.

1835.

Oral Discussion with Breckinridge—Death of Mr. Mayne—Proposal to publish a Catholic Annual—Affairs of St. John's—Contemplated visit to Mexico.

It may seem strange that, after the unpleasant circumstances which attended the controversy described in the last chapter, Mr. Hughes should consent to engage in another with the same person. He was not so keenly alive to applause as to be influenced by ambition to win fresh laurels. The bishop and other respectable ecclesiastics who had discountenanced his former contest were none the more ready by reason of its fortunate result to approve of a new one. The valuable assistance which he had derived from Father Bruté of Mount St. Mary's he could not hope to obtain again from Bishop Bruté of Vincennes. Moreover, though in private he spoke of Mr. Breckinridge as an honorable and a high-minded man, personal questions had arisen between that gentleman and himself which rendered a renewal of their dispute particularly distasteful to Mr. Hughes. But in fact he was in a manner forced into an oral discussion with his former adversary—into doing what for three years he had steadily refused to do, "because," as he said, "I dislike personal contention with any one, and most of all with him, for reasons which I have not concealed." The origin of the second discussion was in this wise: A society of young men in Philadelphia, called the Union Literary and Debating Institute, and composed of Catholics and Protestants of various denominations, had chosen Mr. Hughes an honorary member, and invited him to attend their meetings. In January, 1835, they adopted for debate the question, "Is the Roman Catholic Religion, in any or all its Principles or Doctrines, inimical to Civil or Religious Liberty?" "Having attended on the occasion," says Mr. Hughes, "I took the liberty to suggest, in the most respectful manner, the inexpediency of treating such a question in such a place. Prejudice and popular calumnies might make many members eloquent in attacking; whilst incompetency to detect sophistry, and want of specific information on that subject, might render others unequal to the task of defending. The consequence would be so far injurious to the Catholic body in their civil and religious rights. I did not imagine, nor do I now believe, that the members of this society could be induced to be employed *knowingly* as the tools in the hands of a combination of bigotry and malice,* whose centre is New York, and whose contemplated circumference is the boundary of the land. . . . We find, by a coincidence too striking to be natural, that the same question which was selected for debate in this society was at the same time undergoing discussion in New York, Ohio, Kentucky, and the Eastern States." Mr. Hughes was invited to deliver an address at the next meeting, January 22d, on the principles involved in the discussion, and the distinction between the doctrines of the Catholic religion and the sayings or doings of its nominal members; but when he appeared on the appointed evening, he found the Rev. Mr. McCalla there to meet him, and the society pledged to the resolution that he should not lecture before them, though he might, if he chose, debate. The whole matter had been arranged between Mr. McCalla and Mr. Breckinridge with a view of dragging Mr. Hughes into a public discussion. The night before the meeting Mr. Breckinridge wrote the following note from New York, which Mr. Hughes called "the most unwarrantable letter he ever received in his life":

* The "Protestant Association."

MR. BRECKINRIDGE TO MR. HUGHES.

NEW YORK, *Jan* 21, 1835.

SIR :

I have just been informed that you are expected to address a society to-morrow evening on a question of which the following is the substance, viz. : " Whether the Roman Catholic Religion is favorable to Civil and Religious Liberty ?"

I write a few lines in order to say that I will meet you, on the evening of the 29th instant, before the same society, Providence permitting, on that question;—or if that be not *agreeable* to you, in any other place where this vital question may be fully discussed before our fellow-citizens.

As I shall not be present, I request that you will yourself make the necessary suggestions to the society to-morrow evening, and give me as early a reply as convenient. I can conceive of only one reason for your refusing, and I hope time has overcome that.

I remain your obedient servant,

JOHN BRECKINRIDGE.

Mr. Hughes took no notice of this communication, but he resolved to overcome his repugnance to meeting Mr. McCalla at all events ; "because," said he, "I knew that if I did not, the trump of triumphant falsehood would proclaim my defeat, and ascribe it to a wrong motive. In fact, as it was, the veracious *Presbyterian*, and another paper published in New York, called *The Protestant Vindicator*, proclaimed that I was pulverized, annihilated, and that after having been reduced to nothing I fled." The debate on the 22d was confined to a discussion of certain conditions, such as the affixing of definitions to the terms "doctrines," "civil liberty," and "religious liberty," without which Mr. Hughes was unwilling to proceed. On the 29th Mr. Breckinridge was present, with Dr. Brownlee and other clergymen. At their request the conditions proposed by Mr. Hughes were accepted, and a committee was sent to inform him of that fact. A few moments afterward he entered the room. The debate was opened by a young gentleman, a member of the society; others followed briefly, and the rest of the evening was occupied in a courteous discussion between Mr. Breckinridge and Mr. Hughes. The two antagonists afterward had a private interview, in which they agreed upon the rules of the debate. The question, "Is the Roman Catholic Religion, in any or in all its Principles or Doctrines, opposed to Civil or Religious Liberty?" was to be discussed before the Institute for any number of evenings not exceeding six; the question, "Is the Presbyterian Religion, in any or in all its Principles or Doctrines, opposed to Civil or Religious Liberty?" was then to be discussed for an equal number of evenings. No person except Messrs. Hughes and Breckinridge was to take part in the dispute. Each party was to have the privilege of inviting one hundred hearers. A short-hand writer was to be employed by the Institute to take an impartial report of the proceedings.

Under these rules the debate was opened by Mr. Breckinridge, and six nights were given to each of the questions. The courtesy which marked the preliminary proceedings was forgotten. Mr. Breckinridge's first speech was in the highest degree offensive; and Mr. Hughes, despairing of a calm, gentlemanlike, and candid examination of the questions at issue, was soon fain to defend himself with his adversary's own weapons. Here is a choice extract from Breckinridge's second speech

> Allow me, thus early in the debate, to say that nothing but the love of liberty as an American and of truth as a Protestant Christian, could induce me to subject my feelings to the coarse and ill-bred impertinence of a priesthood whose temper and treatment toward other men alternate between servility to their spiritual sovereigns and oppression of their unhappy subjects. I can and will bear, for the sake of the great cause, whatever may be made necessary—though, thank God, I am not forced to do it either as a minion of the Pope, or the subject of an arrogant and vulgar *Jesuitism.*

And Mr. Hughes replies to him thus:

Do you not, sir, pity the gentleman! The Chesterfield of the Presbyterian church—the *magister elegantiarum*—to be exposed to the retorts of a Catholic priest!

After calling his adversary a *blackguard*, coarse, vulgar, and impertinent, Mr. Breckinridge uses the following mild language:

It ill becomes me to retort Mr. H.'s vulgar and unchristian assaults; for the Sacred Scriptures forbid us to "render railing for railing." The low abuse and indecent personalities of the *gentleman*, if I can consent to call him so any longer, reflect most unhappily on his spirit and his origin, and confirm, what I have long known, that he is really ignorant of what gentlemen owe to each other and to themselves.

I consider this a sufficient answer (and more than he deserves) to all his scurrility. Poor St. John's! It was set up for the fashionable and the refined world, who wished to go to heaven without the trouble of being holy; and the priest at the altar was supposed by some to have sprung from a band-box. As for breeding, they would have found a real gentleman in the Rev. Charles Constantine Pise. As it is (if any of that people venture on the *mala prohibita* of a controversy with heretics, or if, like the devouter Papists, they read Mr. Hughes's argument alone), I am sure they will find in his last speech that his breeding is skin-deep, and it is only want of resolution that keeps him from the frequent and free use of the ecclesiastical shillalagh.

And Mr. Hughes replies:

There are some men in whom VULGARITY and PRIDE are inseparably blended—alternately betraying each other. . . . Lest the gentleman should mistake my motive for abstaining, I wish him to know that as to FAMILY, ORIGIN, GOOD-BREEDING, EDUCATION, PRIVATE HISTORY, PUBLIC CHARACTER, I have no reason to shrink from a comparison with HIM, the said Rev. John Breckinridge.

Even these extracts do not give an adequate idea of the strong language used on both sides; for when the speeches were prepared for the press they were, by mutual consent, considerably modified. Mr. Breckinridge's arguments were of a piece with his personal remarks. Roaming over the whole field of disagreement between Protestants and Catholics, he brought forward all the common vulgarities about Popish immorality; all the scandalous lies about priests, and convents, and Jesuits; bugbear stories about the Inquisition and Papal conspiracies; any absurd falsehood which he thought would disconcert his adversary, or provoke a laugh from his audience. And both these effects he did sometimes produce. Very few intelligent people attended the debates; but the room was crowded with the lower classes, who could not appreciate a good argument, but caught eagerly at a bouncing slander. Some one afterwards asked Mr. Hughes how he felt in speaking before such an audience. "Felt!" exclaimed he; "I would rather have taken a good flogging than have discussed divine truth before those people."

There was another point in which Mr. Breckinridge had greatly the advantage of his opponent: Mr. Hughes had too logical a mind to be a good debater on such a rostrum. He would dissect his adversary's arguments, and after exposing their fallacy would be content to leave them;* as if he forgot that his object should be not so much to convince Mr. Breckinridge as to influence his hearers. So, when the Presbyterian divine repeated arguments which had already been demolished, or travelled out of the record, or brought up silly and trivial questions, Mr. Hughes often disdained to

* Mr. Hughes's excessive confidence in the effect of sound logic was strikingly exemplified in a circumstance which happened while he was pastor of St. John's. A Sister of Charity having punished a troublesome child in the free school attached to the church, the child's mother brought an action for assault and battery. Mr. Hughes employed counsel to defend the suit, and attended the trial. When the testimony was all in, the Sister's vindication appeared so complete, that he insisted upon letting the case go to the jury without argument. His counsel, who knew the ways of the multitude better, remonstrated, but yielded to Mr. Hughes's advice. The consequence was a verdict for the plaintiff with six cents damages. Judge Bouvier, who presided in the court, severely rebuked the jury, and offered the defendant a new trial.

answer him; and the uneducated multitude misinterpreted his silence, supposing him overpowered when he was only indignant. Mr. Hughes fought for victory, Mr Breckinridge for effect; and each got, at least to a certain degree, what he wanted. Mr. Hughes unquestionably vanquished his opponent in sound reasoning, and Mr. Breckinridge not unfrequently produced a more vivid impression on the multitude.

When the stenographer's report was examined, it proved incomplete and incorrect. Of the first three nights there was no report whatever. It was agreed, after some dispute, that instead of amending the report, each speaker should write out his own speeches for publication, and submit them to his adversary. Each was allowed full liberty to amplify and even to introduce new topics. Under this arrangement the speeches grew to such a length, that when the work was one-third finished the amount of matter reduced to writing already exceeded the amount originally spoken. The society became impatient at the delay, and alarmed at the prospective cost of printing. They begged the Reverend gentlemen to condense and to hurry. Mr. Hughes proposed to stop short, and publish only what was then ready—that is, the substance of twenty-four speeches, twelve on each branch of the question. This course was finally adopted. The manuscript was sold by the Institute to Messrs. Carey, Lea & Blanchard, and the volume appeared in 1836, under the title, "*A Discussion of the Question, Is the Roman Catholic Religion, in any or in all its Principles or Doctrines, inimical to Civil or Religious Liberty? and of the Question, Is the Presbyterian Religion*, etc. By the Reverend John Hughes of the Roman Catholic Church, and the Reverend John Breckinridge of the Presbyterian Church." (Philadelphia, 8vo, pp. 546.) The Catholic members of the debating club presented to Father Hughes a richly bound copy of the book, and a piece of plate. In his letter acknowledging the compliment, he says:

The people require only correct information, and, so far as I was able, I deemed it a public duty to impart that information on the exciting question of civil and religious liberty. I believe that good has resulted from the effort, and as a proof I might mention the fact that the book which has grown out of the discussion finds no patronage among the anti-Catholic crusaders who provoked its publication. It contains both sides of the question of civil and religious liberty—their doctrines and our doctrines—their history and our history; and if they are sincere in their pretended zeal for the enlightenment of the public mind, let them aid to circulate the work among their adherents. Their refusal to do so shows that they feel their position, and are afraid of the light.

He was not a man to bear long the sore feelings which this discussion engendered. The book after a time passed into the hands of a Catholic publisher, and it is characteristic of Mr. Hughes that when he heard, after Mr. Breckinridge's death, that a new edition of it was to be put to press, he expressed his regret; "because," said he, "I should be glad to soften the asperity of my language, but I cannot in justice do it, since Mr. Breckinridge is no longer living to do the same."

For assistance during this discussion Father Hughes had frequent recourse to a learned Jesuit, the Rev. Mr. Kenney, who happened to be at the time in Philadelphia. Bishop Kenrick was no better pleased with this controversy than with the previous one. He tried to stop it by every honorable means in his power short of absolute prohibition, and it is a significant fact that the *Catholic Herald* carefully abstained from alluding to it during its progress.

Father Hughes visited a great deal in Protestant society at this period of his life. He was welcomed in the best circles; and he had a peculiar faculty of adapting himself to his company which made him, wherever he went, a most delightful companion. Whether in mixed assemblies, or in the society of scholars, artists, literary men, or politicians, he always seemed at home. After the Breckinridge discussion he was elected a member of the Wistar Club in Philadelphia, an association of gentlemen who met for social purposes at one another's houses—an exclusive and rather aristocratic club, to which only persons of consideration were admitted. Father Hughes had not enjoyed opportunities for thorough scholarship; but he had the knack of bringing forth his stores of information so aptly that they seemed much greater than they were. He knew how to illustrate almost every subject with an anecdote, or a few scraps of knowledge, always introduced just at the right moment and in the most effective manner. He talked well, but he was careful to take less than his share of the discourse. He delighted rather in dropping a word here and there, to start or turn the flow of conversation, than in taking a very conspicuous part in it himself. It was his pleasure to draw out others, to sound their depth, and to find out their character. Sometimes he took a sly gratification in setting two of the guests by the ears, and watching their skill in controversy. His manners were courtly, pleasing, and remarkably easy. He frequently dined out; but he had no taste whatever for the pleasures of the table. He could sing a good song, and did not think it beneath his dignity now and then to entertain chosen circles of friends in that way.

At the same time he was a model of a conscientious, hard-working priest. He was indefatigable in visiting the poor and sick, hearing confessions, and instructing children and converts. He was not a student; but he read a great deal, and he had a wonderful memory. During the Breckinridge discussion he had begun to collect a theological library. He added to it from time to time, as he had occasion, in the course of his public disputes, to make use of books; and before he died his collection—though incomplete in all branches—was large and valuable. He was, of course, well grounded in the common principles of theology; for the rest, he laid in his stock of dogmatic and polemical lore only as he had immediate use for it. But then he never forgot what he had once learned.

The literary project mentioned in the latter part of the following letter was not carried out. Mr. Mayne, whose death is here mentioned, was one of his most intimate college friends:

TO BISHOP PURCELL.

PHILADELPHIA, *Feb.* 6, 1835.

RIGHT REV. DEAR SIR:

I received with delight the excellent little letter which you put in the hands of Mr. Repplier, dated January 23. It was written with one of your old Mountain pens, and in the style that recalls the memory of olden time. Poor Mr. Mayne! The very last letter he ever wrote, I suppose, was to me, dated October 27, in which were mingled the sentiment and drollery of the happiest days at the Mountain. Among the dreams of futurity that then amused us, there was one which seemed more fixed than any other—it was a voyage to Europe, in which we were to visit Ireland *first*, and next Strabane, where he was born. Early in autumn I wrote to him, telling him that an individual who intended to leave me a legacy of $3,000, and who is very old, was willing to give me the money now, for the purpose of making the contemplated tour; but that I could not get any one to take my place in St. John's. I did not reflect that the allusion to it was calculated to depress him. In his reply he says: "Would to God that the mind, body, and other circumstances of poor Mayne allowed *visions of old* should be realized, *by you* at least!" And then he adds, in that humor which spoke in his eye, as well as by his words: "Is that $3,000 body any relation of mine? I like the idea of receiving the legacy in 'anticipation.'" He too is gone!—making the fallen of the ranks of those days as numerous as the survivors, with the certain prospect of soon bringing the majority over to the side of the grave.

But I did not intend getting among the tombstones, neither have I read Hervey's *Meditations* since I left the Mountain; still the ray of friendly recollection which came to me from the West connected itself, somehow, in my mind, with that which has been so recently and prematurely extinguished in the South. I am sure he is not forgotten by you at the holy altar. . . . . .

With regard to the two papers you mention, it so happens that I do not see either of them. So far as the defence of religion is concerned, I believe them to have done vast injury; and moreover, although it does not make the crime of the incendiaries less, I am sincerely of opinion that the application of the torch might be traced to the wild harangues of Doctor O'Flaherty and the fierce language of *The Jesuit*, as well as its inexpedient title—not as the cause of the outrage, but as the occasion of the cause.

I am sorry that G—— should play the F—— of the West, in *any respect*. But the Church is very strong, and those who run against it will break their heads and fall. If Mr. Jeanjean believed his assertion, he should have put on his mitre, taken up the staff of the Lord, and whacked the criminals of the sanctuary, instead of running about, nobody knows where or why. Let him take that.

. . . . . .

Our asylum prospers. We have forty orphans and about one hundred day scholars, who are taught, among other things, to make the sign of the cross and to say their beads. This is a great deal. We have paid, since the beginning of last April, about $12,000 on the place—viz.: fair, $4,200 clear; one legacy, $3,000; another, $4,600. The mortgage interest on the balance is more than paid for by the rent of two small stores on the premises. Still there is little excuse for withholding the legacy of Major Dugan, as we offered an indemnity bond to secure the executor; he did not even deign to notice the proposal, nor to reply to it.

. . . . . .

By-the-by, I have a notion on which I wish to consult you and [Mr. H.]. If about half-a-dozen of old Mountaineers would set to, and write each a good religious or pious story, we might bring out a very pretty and useful Catholic Annual for next year. What do you think of it? We have prose and poetry writers enough. I have thought seriously of it. Will Mr. H. be a contributor for one good article—and I know he will not send any other than good! Will friend Collins send us the productions of his pious muse? I am willing to play editor, and write an article myself. Would bishops condescend to aid? I could calculate on the Messrs. McCaffrey, Sourin, Mr. Pise (have you seen *Letters to Ada?*); and your Rev. successor Mr. Butler should sketch the engravings, by way of reparation for the abuse of his pencil in painting lyres and long ears in the days of Mount Rascal. Mac had a hand in that too. I mean to write them on the subject.

I had the pleasure of seeing your brother a few days ago. He is well, and looks well—but a hot politician.

Have you taken the trouble to read the letters "to Rev. Mr. Mason"? What do you think of them? I think of adding about six more, and then publishing them together, as a tract, on the infallibility of the Church. As for Smith,* Breckinridge, *et id genus omne*, I mean to have nothing to do with them, personally or by name, any more. I am told they are despised among their own, except in the newspapers for effect; and many Protestants flatter me by saying they are not worthy of my notice. I am disposed to try and think so too. By the way, I wrote a little biographical sketch of Smith some time ago, in *The New York Diary*,† signed B. I think you would do well to put it in *The Telegraph*, that the Catholics at least should know who and what he is.

. . . . .

The debt on St. John's church was now becoming a source of great perplexity. "Statements from the pulpit and in print, appeals, meetings to which every pew-holder was invited in general and in particular, were tried," but still very little money was obtained. "I found," said Mr. Hughes, "that further application would be exposing myself uselessly to the uncharitable remarks to which such topics generally give rise in such circumstances, and determined with myself to seek abroad for the means necessary to accomplish the object in view, which is to put the church and ground out of the power of creditors, and if possible to finish the building." He resolved to go to Mexico, and for six months prepared himself by studying Spanish, which he learned to speak fluently. When all his preparations were made, he gave notice to his congregation one Sunday that he was about going, and expected to be absent five or six

---

* Samuel B. Smith, a fallen priest who had recently apostatized.
† September 13, 1834.

months. At the close of his remarks, his colleague, Mr. Gartland,* rose, on the impulse of the moment, and made an urgent appeal to the congregation to exert themselves, and not to allow their pastor to undertake such a long and, as it was thought, dangerous journey. His words produced an effect. The pew-holders devised means of paying the most troublesome debts, and the Mexican expedition was given up.

* Afterwards Bishop of Savannah.

CHAPTER XI.

1835–1838.

Project for translating Bishop Kenrick to Pittsburg—Mr. Hughes nominated his successor in Philadelphia—Correspondence with Bishops Kenrick, England, and Purcell—Death of Mr. Hughes's father—Letter on the use of the Bible as a school-book—Mr. Hughes appointed coadjutor to the Bishop of New York—Letter from Bishop Dubois—Letter to Bishop Purcell—Letter from Bishop England—Consecration.

THE great progress which the American Catholic Church had made during the few preceding years called for the creation of new bishops. Dr. Dubois, burdened with age and infirmities, and harassed by serious troubles, required the aid of a coadjutor, and Bishop Kenrick desired a division of his diocese, and the erection of a new see at Pittsburg. Mr. Hughes was proposed for each of the bishoprics which would have to be erected under these arrangements. It was well known that Dr. Kenrick was anxious to leave Philadelphia, and Bishop Dubois pressed him to accept the coadjutorship of New York; but he preferred going to Pittsburg. The next choice of the venerable bishop of New York was the Jesuit Father Mulledy; and the third was his old pupil Father Hughes. Bishop Kenrick had written to Rome in the latter part of 1835, stating his wishes with regard to his own diocese, and recommending Father Hughes for either Philadelphia or Pittsburg, as might seem more expedient to the Holy See. His request was granted, and the Sacred Congregation, in January, 1836, actually made out the appointment of Father Hughes as coadjutor to the bishop of Philadelphia (Dr. Conwell), and the transfer of Dr. Kenrick to Pittsburg. But when the matter was laid before the Pope, he decided, in consequence, as it would seem, of certain canonical objections suggested by Bishop England, to defer the division of the diocese until after the meeting of the next council of Baltimore.

The news of the appointment, but not the news of the subsequent postponement, soon got abroad, and was copied from a Paris paper into the Philadelphia journals. But in the mean time trouble had arisen between Dr. Kenrick and Bishop Conwell (whose mind was somewhat affected by old age); people began to accuse Dr. Kenrick of a cowardly abandonment of his post, and he wrote accordingly to Rome in July to request that, if no final action had been taken on his previous application, the whole matter might be left to the decision of the approaching council. This would relieve him of the imputation of cowardice; but it placed him in a very delicate position with respect to Mr. Hughes. The fact that he had withdrawn his recommendation was not long a secret; and as the reasons for his doing so were not generally known, it was rumored that there was some unkind feeling between Father Hughes and the bishop.

Mr. Hughes addressed Dr. Kenrick in a very frank and good-tempered letter of remonstrance, not because he had withdrawn his recommendation, but because he had allowed the person most deeply interested in it to learn of his action for the first time through the public prints. "You could not suppose," he says, "that it would have pained me, since you remember that last spring I wished you to write such a letter in my name and at my request." . . . . "I had studied the inside as well as the outside of a mitre, and I regarded him who is obliged to wear it as entitled to pity, not envy. I had, if not humility, at least sense enough to be satisfied that the man who is qualified and willing to be a bishop in the United States, deserves a recompense which he may not expect from this ungrateful world." He ends by repeated assurances of his regard and respect:

It is my simple and sincere desire to be united with you as before, so that no charity may be broken, and that the example of union among the clergy, at least so far as I am concerned, may counteract any tendency to disunion among the people. The man who is your enemy cannot and shall not be my friend. I shall be happy to pay you my respects when we are at leisure, when we may talk more freely on the subject; after which I shall strive to forget it.

Your humbled, but yet sincere and attached friend and servant in Christ,

JOHN HUGHES.

BISHOP KENRICK TO MR. HUGHES.

PHILADELPHIA, *Jan.* 19, 1837.

REV. AND DEAR SIR:

The simple statement of facts will be the best means of removing the impressions which have been made on your mind. The pressing solicitation of Bishop Dubois to accept the office of his coadjutor, and his expressed determination to urge the matter with the Holy See, led me, on the 27th of February, to address the Cardinal Prefect, and state my reasons for objecting to that situation; but I did not in the least degree retract my proposal, though I consented to postpone the measures till the next council, should the Holy See think fit, that both dioceses might be provided for. I had not previously written a word, except to urge the measures, and subsequently I have not communicated with the Cardinal Prefect, until the 15th November, when I simply signified that the resolution of the Holy Father, to postpone it until the council, had been made known to me, and that I continued of the same mind as to the expediency of erecting the new see. Neither letter contained a word unfavorable to you, unless in reference to a concomitant proposal of Bishop Dubois in your regard, I stated that I feared the influential clergy of New York would see with pain a clergyman placed over them who they might not conceive had an equal title to that mitre as themselves. In July I found . . . . that a coloring had been given to my application at Rome, as if I was abandoning my post in despair, when on the 23d of that month I addressed Dr. Cullen to correct this latter impression, and authorized him, in case no final action had taken place, to leave the whole matter until the council. In this letter, which was the only one which could have been deemed calculated to suspend the proceedings, I did not say any thing that could derogate from the high commendations I had given you, nor did I ground the suspension on any change of opinion in your regard. . . . . This letter was written long after the news of your appointment had reached us through the *Ami de la Religion*, and contained an express assent to any arrangement that had been previously made by the Holy See. Neither it, nor even the letter of the 27th February, could have influenced the determination of the Holy Father, which was taken in spring, I suppose before the February letter reached the Holy See. I communicated with no other person save with Father Dubuisson, who having informed me by his letter of the 1st January that your appointment would take place in the next assembly of the cardinals, I authorized him in a letter of the 27th February to signify my unconditional assent to the measure. My letter to Bishop England was written on the 16th August, and contained nothing disrespectful to you, or signifying any revocation of the measures.

From this simple *exposé* you may see that either Bishop England or your informant has mistaken my assent to a suspension, which originated in the proposal of Bishop Dubois, for a revocation. The proposal of the good bishop of New York is still urged by the archbishop, to whom I have stated my strong objections to that post, but have declared my willingness to go wherever my colleagues might choose—even to New York. The Propaganda has written to him lately, with a view to know how Philadelphia and Pittsburg should be provided for, in case of my translation. Thus the matter rests, and I have in a recent letter urged you to be placed first on the list for Pittsburg, in case you should not be selected for Philadelphia. Bishop England is proposed by me for New York or Philadelphia, in order to leave Dr. Clancy at ease at Charleston.

Yours affectionately in Christ,
FRANCIS PATRICK KENRICK,
Bp. Arath and Coadj. Phil.

BISHOP ENGLAND TO MR. HUGHES.

CHARLESTON, *Jan.* 24, 1837.

REV. AND DEAR SIR:

I shall give you as much as I know of the history of the affair to which you allude.

I received a letter from Dr. Kenrick, more than a year ago, stating that he had written to Rome requesting a division of the diocese of Philadelphia, the erection of a see at Pittsburg, and also that he had sent forward names therein specified for the purpose of enabling the Holy See to select one for the additional see, old or new as it should deem proper after considering wishes of his own therein expressed. Your name was very honorably placed on this list. I sent no answer to Dr. K., but I wrote to Rome, stating that I supposed from the recommendation of Dr. K. the division must be useful, if not necessary. I gave my opinion of the names, but I urged some canonical and other difficulties which appeared to me to exist respecting an immediate division, and recommended a delay until after the meeting of our provincial council, at which I supposed every difficulty could be removed. I have since learned that the Congregation of the Propaganda acceded fully to Dr. K.'s request in all its parts; but upon their determination being reported to his Holiness for his approval and the order for execution, he concurred in the view that I had given, and desired its further consideration to be laid aside until after the celebration of the council. Things were in this state when I arrived in the city of Rome on the 1st of last September. I left on October 11, and I said not a word upon the subject; but previous to my leaving that city I got a letter from Dr. K., stating among other things that he saw reason to change his intentions and to withdraw the application for dividing the diocese. I never learned, nor do I suspect, what these reasons were. And I have suffered so much from intermeddling in other people's affairs, that I had no desire to learn what they were.

As to your name, I am under the impression that it was treated in Rome with the same kindness that it was in the document which emanated from Philadelphia, and that up to the period of my leaving Rome it was held in favor and respect. Nor have I any reason to think otherwise since, or to believe that it has been since then treated in any other way. This communication I leave you at liberty to use as you please.

I am so pressed for time that I must abruptly conclude by assuring you of the esteem and regard of

Yours most sincerely,
✠ JOHN,
Bishop of Charleston.

TO BISHOP PURCELL.

January 2, 1837.

RIGHT REV. AND DEAR FRIEND:

Although I have not had the pleasure of a direct correspondence with you for some time, I still see or hear enough of you to know that you are better engaged in the high and holy duties of the state to which God has called you. The season brings back the memory of all friends, and hurried as you may be, I will engage your attention for a moment. I will write you a letter whilst old Time is here at my elbow, cutting another notch in his infallible calendar. But what shall I say first? Why, first, may you be happy, now and forever. May Divine Providence fell down all the big trees of opposition to your ministry, and give you the strength of a giant to pluck up the underwood by the root; and when you shall have made the number of heretics as few as the Catholics were when you took up the crosier, then may you exchange the insignia of contest for the tokens of triumph, and the mitre for the crown of glorious recompense.

Is it a very delightful thing to be a bishop? Are there not difficulties that touch the quick, and make it painful to be invested with authority which it is obligatory to exercise? The contingency in which I was led to believe during a part of last year, had the effect to make me examine more closely the lights and shadows of episcopal honor; and if the result has been a settled disposition to prefer an humbler state, I fear that cowardice has more to do with the preference than humility. Happily, however, as I anticipated in my last to you, at a time when all were credulous but myself, I am not likely to be put to the test. The division of the diocese is adjourned, and in fact I do not see any real necessity for it. Every thing goes on very well; and as to the remoteness of episcopal authority from the western section, it could be remedied by the appointment of a V. G. in Pittsburg. Bishop Kenrick is deservedly loved and respected in every part of the diocese, and the whole case comes under the sage maxim, "Let well enough alone." The unpleasantness of his situation in St. Mary's as a cathedral would have been a reason; but even that has passed away, and the apprehension of being stripped of an honor of which they had rendered themselves so supremely unworthy, has wrought a most salutary change for the better.

From some notices I have seen, it appears that you are likely to be involved in a controversy with Mr. Campbell. I have no apprehension as to the result; but from my own experience I sympathize with you in the trials to which your feelings will be exposed by the grossness to which the desperation of defeat will drive these men. Let them triumph over you, and they will be polite as possible; but show their ignorance and expose their reasoning, they will become vipers. That you will do both, I have not the least doubt; and it is precisely on this account that your personal feelings will be exposed. Will you not have the kindness to cause some of the young men to forward me from time to time an account of the progress of the controversy? It would gratify me very much; but if it should be inconvenient, do not think of it.

. . . . . .

We have turned our asylum into an establishment for male orphans exclusively, having transferred the girls to St. Joseph's. Our present number is 36; but our markets are so high that it requires a great deal to support them. I have not heard any thing of Major Dugan's legacy or the lawsuits since your last letter, which has been a great many months. How is our good friend Bishop Bruté coming on? The care of all the churches (that are to be) has banished his old friends from his recollection. I used to receive an occasional letter from him, which was always an occasion of delight as well as of edification; but latterly he has forgotten me. I see, however, that he does not forget the Pope of Boston—Channing. It does me good to read his pieces in the *Telegraph*.

The waters of religious strife here have not been agitated since the discussion. I do not mean to say that the discussion has produced this effect; there are other causes. The division in the Presbyterian ranks seems to engage the attention and engross all the malice of both parties, for the purposes of mutual crimination and hostility. Breckinridge is at Princeton, in the keeping of his father-in-law Miller. Both are rubbing their hands over the desolations of Zion; the latter because the honors and emoluments of his chair will be in danger if, in the final issue, he should not be found with the majority; and the former because in the beginning of our controversy I told him it *must* come to this with the Presbyterians—for the which he has repeatedly called me a "croaking prophet," and begged his brethren in synods and assemblies to heal their differences, lest they should confirm my ill-omened prediction.

Among ourselves there is nothing new. The bishop purchased a Presbyterian church some time ago, but he has not yet obtained possession of it, owing to the opposition made by some of the members. The clergy are all well—all busy. There have been few converts within the past year, yet the Catholic religion is manifestly gaining on the enlightened mind of the community. It is very generally acknowledged by the better educated sort among Protestants to be as rational and as consistent with piety as any other. The storms of abuse which it had to encounter have purified the waters of opinion which they agitated, and the succeeding calm has occasioned the sediment to settle quietly at the bottom. If I may judge from the papers, it does not appear that the fanatical excitement has yet subsided in your western country.

. . . . .

TO SISTER ANGELA.

BALTIMORE, *April* 19, 1887.

MY DEAR SISTER :

As we have both been taught that we must look to another world for all that is perfect and unchanging, I write in the confidence that *you* will not give way to immoderate grief, on the news that God has called his servant from the scene of labor to the place of rest—the laborer from the field of toil to the harvest of repose and recompense.

Our good father has been called away from a world for which he cared little, to that better world for which he lived. His age might have prepared us for this, but his excellent health had inspired us with a kind of security that the evening of his life would not have been closed so abruptly. Still, all was serene and calm and tranquil, as became the sunset of such a life as his had been. He had, on the Tuesday after Easter, arranged all his affairs, so that nothing further might distract him from the thought of his God and his soul—as if he had a presentiment of what was about to take place. The Wednesday week following he was taken with a bilious pleurisy, and the Monday after slept with his God. You know he had always been attentive to his religious duties, but for the last years he was almost every Sunday at communion. He was resigned to the divine will, and enjoyed the use of all his mental faculties to the last moment. As you will be anxious to see the details, I enclose you a letter from Michael, who was sick at the same time. The memory of his virtues, dear sister, is to us a treasure of consolation. Margaret bears it with that fortitude which you might expect from her good sense and piety. Michael, too, does well, as you will perceive by his letter. I am here attending the council, and shall go to Chambersburg before my return. From there I will write you a longer letter.

I have been unwell ever since I came, but am now much better. In consequence of my indisposition, I have engaged Bishop England to preach the consecration sermon of Mr. McElroy's new church, which he had invited me some months ago to do, but which I am now glad to escape; as the doctor says I require rest of mind and body, as he considers my little attack nothing more than a cold aggravated by anxiety and fatigue.

I know, my dear sister, that you will be afflicted by the news which it is my melancholy duty to communicate; but let your grief expend itself in the fervency of your prayers for the repose of the souls of our dear, dear departed parents. Let your tears fall at the foot of the cross. You have learnt to regard the things of life and of death, of eternity and of time, as they are.

I am interrupted, and must conclude.

Your affectionate brother,

JOHN HUGHES.

TO THE REV. THOMAS HEYDEN, ST. PAUL'S, PITTSBURG.

FEAST OF CORPUS CHRISTI [*May* 25], 1837.

REV. DEAR FRIEND:

Many thanks to you for your kind and consoling letter of sympathy with me on the death of my father, whose respect and fondness toward you were greater than I could well describe. You were his "man of God;" and as such, in the pulpit or out of it, it seemed he never could say enough in your praise. No doubt the kindness with which you used to listen to his plans and enter into his feelings had its effect in securing his admiration, which, like all he did and said, was cordial and sincere. I trust he is enjoying, or soon to enjoy, the reward of a virtuous and, I may say, religious life. His daily communion was with God, and it was on this account that solitude was so dear to him. Recollecting how much you were instrumental in preparing him for the unforeseen change which has taken place, I am sure that you will sometimes make a memento of him at the holy altar.

But what a world this is! Poor Mr. Hurley, but yesterday in the enjoyment of perfect health, and to-day consigned to the sepulchre! A few weeks more, and he will be scarcely spoken of, except as the nature of the conversation may make it necessary to mention his name. You must have been very much shocked, and Mr. Whelan still more so, to hear of his death without having your mind prepared by any knowledge of his sickness. Under all the circumstances, however, his friends have great reason to be thankful; for, although the time was short, he was early made sensible of his danger and the more than probable issue of his disease, and he prepared for it with much devotion—his mind and faculties generally continuing sound till the last.

. . . . .

But I have one thing to communicate which, if you have not heard it, will edify and entertain you not a little. It is that your predecessor, the late little bishop * of St. Paul's, has been caught by a vocation in Philadelphia, and is consequently saved the trouble of journeying to Rome in quest of one. St. Augustine is likely to

---

* "The little bishop" was a college sobriquet of the Rev. Mr. O'Reilly, which clung to him for years.

triumph over St. Ignatius in the acquisition of a subject, who, after all, will be a credit to either. In plain language, Mr. O'Reilly is about to enter on duty in St. Augustine's church, toward supplying the vacancy created by the death of its late pastor. We are, of course, all delighted, and the bishop in particular, at having this queer, good little man among us, and securing the services of an efficient and zealous laborer in a portion of the vineyard in which they are wanted much more than in Rome.

Please remember me to Mrs. and Mr. Fetterman, and believe me
Ever your sincere friend and brother in Christ,
JOHN HUGHES.

TO BISHOP PURCELL.

June 27, 1837.

DEAR BISHOP:

I should like exceedingly to comply with your kind invitation to visit Cincinnati, and then with mutual explanations give you my full opinion of the whole matter in which you are so much interested. Any thing I should write would be founded on abstraction; whereas to give a sound and practical opinion, it should rest on the basis of actual circumstances such as surround the question. Hence, unless you wish it particularly, I should rather decline, on the ground that I am not conversant with the matter. The principle on which schools are constituted; the powers of the college of teachers; the tendency of the public mind on the subject of sects; the character of the element which in any collision or struggle for ascendency must predominate; the use or abuse which might be made for special purposes of privileges guaranteed or concessions made for a general end;—these are all matters of which I am not able to form any judgment; and I think, ignorant of these, my opinion would be given in the dark. One of the things which struck me most in the council was the diversity of opinion of the different speakers on certain points of discipline. This I could trace to nothing else but the difference of the circumstances in connection with which each speaker gave his opinion. Things were decided by each, just as it appeared they would be applicable, or otherwise, in *his* congregation; forgetting that the point was to affect the Catholics of the whole province, and that these consist of every variety of minds and habits, from the artificial life of our fashionables in the great cities, down to the primitive manners of the good but simple people of the country, in times and places at which Mr. Badin, *e. g.*, could lecture them on the stool of repentance before the whole assembly of the faithful.

This will suggest to you the principle of my diffidence in giving an opinion on the subject of putting the Bible, as a school-book, under the auspices and with the sanction of the Western College of Teachers. If you allow me, however, to state a few of the conclusions to which I have come without giving any reasons for them, I shall proceed to state them.

1. The *Punica fides* that characterized the enemies of Rome in former times, belongs eminently to the Protestants. Their enmity to Rome is their great overruling passion, which they are willing to gratify in every degree, and by every means. With this conviction on my mind, you will not be surprised that I have no confidence in their religious friendship; that I dread their favors.

2. In religious coalition they have *nothing to lose*, whatever may be the effect of the experiment. Their creeds, so called, are so ambiguously defined that the addition or subtraction of half-a-dozen dogmas cannot destroy their identity—except, perhaps, one of the tenets adopted should be atheism!

3. They know that we have a creed which cannot exist but *in its integrity*.

4. We cannot, therefore, meet them on equal grounds. If then, in addition to this, we consider their bad faith, their little to lose, their purpose to withdraw all they can from our faith, their numbers, their means; it becomes to my mind evident that even *a good thing*, which *might* be perverted, should be dispensed with, rather than encounter the risk.

5. There are certain outworks in the discipline of the Church, which are conservative of her integrity and safety. These keep her enemies not only from entering her gates, but also from approaching too near her walls *outside*. One of these is, to prevent the uneducated, the children, and the faithful at large from receiving any of the things of religion through any other channel except the Church herself exclusively. Hence the bishops in Ireland never pronounced a wiser decision than when they refused to allow their people to re-

ceive the *Catholic Scriptures, with Catholic notes, explanations, and approvals,* from one of those rascally societies that hit on this last expedient to obtain access to the Catholic people.

6. In these coalitions there is no advantage. If we join them for instance in education, they will not expurge their abominable books. And if they should yield to correct some things, they will retain others. What has been excluded will be more than compensated by the *implied* sanction of what will be retained.

Finally, with regard to the Bible as a school-book, I think the selection one of the worst possible. The style is not good. The subjects treated of are sometimes such as, if they were found in any other book, would be considered as immoral and injurious to the minds of youth. The sacredness of the book renders it unfit for the levities and sometimes profaneness of schools. Its meaning too, far above the scholar and the teacher—the version also—every thing makes it in my opinion objectionable as a common school-book.

Write me again; and if seriously you think my going to Cincinnati would increase the chances of getting our legacy, just say so. I shall then feel justified in going; but as it is, we are contented to be represented by you, and to share your lot. All well. Respects to your brother and Mr. Collins. I am delighted to hear that Edward is studying for the Church. I don't know what you will make out of this contemptible little sheet.

Ever yours,

JOHN HUGHES.

(Can you make it out?)

P. S. I have submitted your letter on Major Dugan's case to our Board, and they have authorized me to go and see about it. Let me know at what time between this and the 15th of August it would be most advisable for me to be in your city. Please not to mention my going, as I wish to be quiet—and write by return of post.

J. H.

The council met at Baltimore on the 16th of April, 1837, and determined for the present to leave the diocese of Philadelphia intact. For coadjutor to Bishop Dubois they nominated Mr. Hughes and two other priests, leaving the Holy See to choose between the three. It was not until November

3d that Mr. Hughes received formal notice that the choice had fallen upon him. Before the announcement had been officially made, Bishop Kenrick wrote as follows to Bishop Dubois:

BISHOP KENRICK TO BISHOP DUBOIS.

PHILADELPHIA, *Oct.* 4, 1837.

. . . .

Your prospects of a coadjutor are, I believe, certain, though I have reason deeply to regret your choice. The loss of Rev. J. H. is likely to make the church which he erected bankrupt. Nearly forty thousand dollars debt are upon it. In any other circumstances than those in which I was placed, I should have opposed the measure; but as Providence requires the sacrifice, I rejoice that you are to have his efficient aid for the administration of your vast diocese. I trust that his useful ministry will be now succeeded by a more extensively useful and long coadjutorship.

Your devoted brother in Christ,

✠ FRANCIS PATRICK KENRICK, *Bishop, etc.*

Mr. Hughes himself was the first to make known his appointment to his old friend and master. In the good bishop's reply, we see the piety of the humble Christian who felt no pain at the elevation to an equality and close association with himself of his former protégé and pupil; but we see, I think, at the same time, something of the spirit of the "little Bonaparte":

BISHOP DUBOIS TO MR. HUGHES.

NEW YORK, *Nov.* 6, 1837.

MY DEAR FRIEND:

Your favor of the 31st ultimo, which is the only information (official) I received of your nomination by the Holy See to the coadjutorship of New York, afforded me much consolation, in the hope that you will find in it, as I do, an expression of the divine will. One part of your letter only created in me a painful sensation: I allude to the apprehension of a contingent disunion which might take place between the bishop and his coadjutor. You surely could not suppose a moment that I would encroach upon the rights and privileges attached to that sacred office, and I have too great an opinion of your merit and affection for me to suppose that you would encroach upon mine. As a counsel, I shall the more readily yield to your wishes, as our resolutions will pave the way to the course which you will have to pursue hereafter; but when conscience or experience would demand a dissent of opinion on any subject, this dissent of opinion could not produce a division of hearts or arrest our proceedings. That scandals should have arisen between Bishop Conwell and his coadjutor, who is ex-officio sole administrator of the diocese, is no wonder, with a man of the bishop's disposition; but I am neither reduced to the nullity of Bishop Conwell—a circumstance rather painful to human pride—nor would I be disposed to struggle for the mastery if I had been placed in his situation; I would have considered this nullity as a warning from the divine goodness that henceforth all my time must be exclusively devoted to my preparation for death; but as it is, you may be sure that I will always be happy to act in concert with you.

Whilst you are in Baltimore and have an opportunity to extract from the canonical books the rights and privileges attached to the coadjutorship, you will oblige me to take a copy of the same, and you may be assured that I am more disposed to extend than to restrain them.

. . . . .

May Almighty God guide you, for his greater honor and glory; and be assured that, as I already proved to you, you have a sincere and devoted friend in

Your humble servant,

✠ JOHN,

Bishop of New York.

TO BISHOP PURCELL.

PHILADELPHIA, *Nov.* 28, 1837.

RIGHT REV. AND DEAR FRIEND:

You, at least, could not have been among the surprised at the return of appointments from the Holy See, which were the result of in part your own recommendation. The consequence has been, as regards myself, to deprive St. John's of its pastor, and me, I have much reason to dread, of the peace and happiness which I have hitherto enjoyed in my comparatively humble and obscure situation. They have persuaded me that it is the manifestation of the Divine Will, and that the graces which God has designed for me are attached to that situation, and I would do wrong if I expected them in one of my own choosing. I have yielded accordingly; but God knows with what sorrow and affliction of heart. Time and absence from this place may change or at least otherwise occupy my feelings. But there is grief enough around me to make a coward of a sterner heart than mine.

I fear that the guilt of all my former sins toward my friends in the West has been much aggravated by my seeming forgetfulness of them, and constructive ingratitude for their many marks of kindness and hospitality during my visit. When I returned, news from Rome was stated to be on the very eve of arrival; and waiting for it day by day, I allowed weeks, and then months, to my shame I confess it, to pass away without writing. And then, when it did arrive, it brought with it such a crowd of perplexities, that it seemed to me no one had a right to expect letters from one in my situation. But now that, through many an inward struggle, I have arrived at a conclusion, and have determined, for the future as well as the present, in every emergency to "look aloft," I shall begin, not only to pay my creditors, but also—if that be any thing—to acknowledge their patience in waiting so long.

Would it be possible for you, my dear friend, to assist at my consecration? I dare not ask it, attended as it would be with so much fatigue and inconvenience; but if you could, I need not tell you how much it would console and how much it would oblige me. It will take place in New York, on the feast of Epiphany. Bishop Kenrick has promised to assist, and Bishop Fenwick, I trust, will not refuse. May I *hope* that you too will assist—to recall old associations, and give the right hand of episcopal fellowship in the name of the West? Would that I might!

I have endeavored to fill the measure of your wishes in relation to the amiable convert whom you did me the pleasure to introduce. But I regret that her stay is so short; and owing to a mistake of her residence, I spent two days of the first week looking for her in a part of the city different from that in which she resided. She returns, or at least sets out to return, to-morrow; pleased with the *eastern*, but more so, I perceive, with the *western* Philadelphia.

Bishop Kenrick is to reside at St. John's, and make it the cathedral. After all, this consoles me: first, because I love the church, and hold it worthy of honor; and secondly, because in giving it up, I strike from the limbs of another the fetters which are henceforth to bind my own in the degrading bondage of *trusteeism*.

Has Mr. Heyden accepted? He has at least resigned his charge in Pittsburg, and Rev. Peter R. Kenrick is about to enter on the discharge of its duties. The Rev. Dr. Barron, brother of the M. P. for Waterford, with a neat little income of £500 sterling annually, is now at the head of the seminary. He is a worthy, amiable, learned, and pious man.

And now, after this *mélange*, what shall I say of my friends in the West?—among whom the worthy Mr. Considine stands at the head of the list. I send him his sermon. But please, dear bishop, to remember me to all—your Rev. brother, Rev. Mr. Collins, Sister Seraphina and her associates, Mr. Rogers and family, Doctor Bonner, and all friends whose names I forget, but whose kindness I have not forgotten.

There are a few things I would wish to say to you if I could have the pleasure of doing so *viva voce*. They relate to matters and things here in general, and form a host of little annoyances that might have been spared—painful as they have been—but of which it will not do to unburthen the heart on paper. My health is good; and whilst I have been solicitous for yours, on account of your many duties and much susceptibility, it makes me glad to hear our friend of Vincennes, for whom I felt really alarmed, is recovering. I must write to him and others soon. In the mean time I am, as ever,

Your sincere and affectionate brother,

JOHN HUGHES.

P. S. Now that I *have* written, I perceive and confess that I might have done so long since, were it not for that thief of fame as well as time, procrastination.

Bishop England writes to Mr. Hughes on the 21st of December: "I was not surprised by your appointment, though *I* had no share in it. I was the only bishop who declined signing the document." He believed that the Very Rev. Dr. Power, of New York, who had some years before been temporary administrator of the diocese, was entitled to the appointment, and he wrote to that effect to the Holy See—giving Mr. Hughes a copy of his letter. He adds:

> I was fully aware, from my knowledge of the partiality of his Holiness to you, that whenever your name was presented to him the appointment would be made. . . . . I did wish to see you placed in the episcopal body, and perhaps to the general attaining of that object I have done some little. . . . . I acknowledge that your task is by no means light; but I feel convinced that you are more likely to perform it usefully and creditably than any other that I know.

On Sunday the 26th of November the bishop elect announced to his congregation that he had accepted the appointment, and would soon leave them. The scene in the church when he delivered his farewell sermon is said to have been extremely affecting. The 7th of January, 1838, was the day fixed for his consecration, and on the second day of the new year he removed to New York, and took possession of the apartments provided for him in the episcopal residence in Mulberry street opposite the cathedral. It was characteristic of him that he refused invitations from many distinguished persons, in order to pass his last evening in Philadelphia at the house of an humble friend whose acquaintance he had made when he was a day-laborer in the village of Emmitsburg.

TO MR. M. A. FRENAYE, PHILADELPHIA.

NEW YORK, *Jan.* 3, 1838.

MY DEAR FRENAYE:

I arrived safe at half-past one yesterday. My cold and hoarseness had increased somewhat, but I feel better to-day.

I should not have left yesterday morning without asking pardon of you all for my many imperfections and for any pain I may have given you; but my feelings would have overpowered my utterance.

I find them badly off for *copes*, even for the occasion of next Sunday. There are two copes in the cathedral; the other churches have none. Mention this to Bishop Kenrick. You will have to bring on my gold vestments and cope, as there are none here suitable for me to use in my consecration. If you can, also bring another cope (white). I fear the hurry may expose them to be injured in packing, but they are indispensable. Bring my best alb also; and bring the episcopal chapel,* it may be wanted for me on the occasion; and as it is easily packed, I should like you to *loan* it, at least for this time. We shall understand each other on the subject when you come on. Any other thing you or Mr. Gartland can think of, you will do well to bring. Do not forget the *loaves* and *barrels*.

Remember me cordially to Miss Miller, Mary Ann, the other Mary, and little Billy; also my second mother Mrs. McMahon, and all friends. Let them all pray for me next Sunday.

Ever sincerely and affectionately yours in Christ,
JOHN HUGHES.

The consecration was performed in the cathedral of St. Patrick in Mott street, by Bishop Dubois, assisted by Bishop Kenrick and Bishop Fenwick of Boston, and the sermon was preached by the distinguished Jesuit Father Mulledy, sometime president of Georgetown college. So great was the crowd of people who came to witness the ceremony, that the windows of the church were thrown open, and platforms were built in the grave-yard in every position from which a glimpse of the sanctuary could be had. The new prelate received the title of Bishop of Basileopolis † *in partibus infidelium*, and coadjutor to the bishop of New York. People did not fail to remark the dignity and self-possession with which he performed his part in the solemn ceremony, and the firm, distinct utterance with which he pronounced the

---

* A *chapelle* is a case containing all the vestments and sacred vessels necessary for the celebration of mass.

† Basileopolis was an ancient see in Cappadocia, the first bishop of which was consecrated by St. John Chrysostom. Bishop Hughes, I believe, was the seventh.

words prescribed for him in the ritual. "I remember," says Archbishop McCloskey, "how all eyes were fixed, how all eyes were strained to get a glimpse of their newly consecrated bishop; and as they saw that dignified and manly countenance, as they beheld those features beaming with the light of intellect, bearing already upon them the impress of that force of character which peculiarly marked him throughout his life, that firmness of resolution, that unalterable and unbending will, and yet blending at the same time that great benignity and suavity of expression—when they marked the quiet composure and self-possession of every look and every gesture of his whole gait and demeanor—all hearts were drawn and warmed toward him. Every pulse within that vast assembly, both of clergy and of laity, was quickened with a higher sense of courage and of hope. Every breast was filled with joy, and, as it were, with a new and younger might." *

* Funeral Discourse, 1864.

CHAPTER XII.

1838–1839.

Condition of the Diocese—Health of Bishop Dubois—Foundation of a seminary at Lafargeville—Trouble with the trustees of the Cathedral—Their final overthrow—Bishop Hughes appointed administrator—Foundation of St. John's college.

THE diocese over which he became the ruler, practically, from this hour, embraced the whole State of New York and a large portion of New Jersey. It comprised a Catholic population of nearly two hundred thousand, scattered over an area of fifty-five thousand square miles. There were only forty priests, and but little more than half that number of churches.* Of these, eight churches and some fourteen or fifteen clergymen were on New York island. The Sisters of Charity had a few schools in New York and Albany, and orphan asylums in New York, Albany, Brooklyn, and Utica. Except these, there was no religious institution of either charity or education in the whole diocese. Bishop Dubois had founded at Nyack, on the Hudson river, in 1833, a college on the plan of Mount St. Mary's; but it did not prosper, and when it was destroyed by fire, before it was quite finished, he confessed himself on the whole rather glad to be rid of it. The trustee system was in full force in all the New York churches, and bore the same bitter fruit which we have seen it bearing in Philadelphia. The churches were overwhelmed with debt, and several of them were on the verge of bankruptcy.

* In the same territory there are now (1865) five bishoprics.

Bishop Dubois had for some time past been too feeble to bear the heavy load of trouble and anxiety which such a condition of things entailed upon him. About a fortnight after his coadjutor's arrival he suffered a stroke of paralysis. He partially recovered; but other attacks followed, and he never after took a very active part in the affairs of the diocese.

TO MR. FRENAYE.

NEW YORK, *Feb.*, 1838.

MY DEAR FRIEND:

I wrote the day after the bishop's second attack, but owing to some disappointments the letter remained here till the last of the week. Bishop Dubois does not recover so fast this time as after the first. His appetite is not so good, and his spirits have sunk. He insists on seeing every one that comes to inquire for him, and the consequence is that toward the evening of every day he is extremely feeble, both in mind and body. There have been physicians attending him, but they do and direct nothing. His complete restoration they do not look for. But no apprehension is felt for immediate consequences of a different kind, although we are warned to be prepared for them at any moment.

The church of St. Peter's has been this day consecrated. It is a splendid edifice, somewhat spoiled in the details. Grand ceremonies, grand music—as the custom is here—and a fine sermon, all contributed to make the occasion impressive. We have nothing new.

. . . . . .

Ever yours affectionately in Christ,

✠ JOHN HUGHES,
Bp. Belps. and Coadjr. N. Y.

TO THE SAME.

NEW YORK, *March* 18, 1838.

. . . . . .

Bishop Dubois has said mass three times since his return; but his right side is manifestly affected, and his mind continues relaxed. He is better, on the whole; but his progress is not very encouraging.

Love and kind remembrance to all friends. I shall like New York in proportion as I forget Philadelphia; and to this latter the Philadelphians seem disposed to allow every chance.

Ever yours,

✠ JOHN,
Bp. Bslps. and Coadjr. N. Y.

TO THE SAME.

March 22, 1838.

. . . . .

I perceive that you entirely misunderstand the "last part of my letter." It never came into my mind to think about my popularity. I simply complained of their not writing, and that by their silence they afforded me *every encouragement to forget them.*

I was at Nyack yesterday to witness the ruins of the splendid folly, of which I had no conception before. The whole effect upon my mind has been a conversion to the opinion of Bishop Dubois, that the burning of it was providential. Some good stone and lumber may be yet saved, and used elsewhere.

Mr. Rodrigue will soon come on, and by him I expect the books.

Ever your sincere friend in Christ,

✠ JOHN,
Bp. Bslps. and Coadjr. N. Y.

The first few months after his consecration he seems to have spent chiefly in visiting the churches in and about New York, making himself familiar with the wants and condition of the diocese, and studying the character of his clergy. He preached in many places, delighting everybody by his eloquence in the pulpit, and his agreeable manners in society. What was better, he showed no disposition after his elevation to lay aside the laborious habits of his previous life. He continued to hear confessions regularly, and perform all the other duties of the missionary priest. It was the custom in Bishop Dubois' house for all his domestic clergy to unite with him in saying their daily office together, after the fashion of religious communities. Bishop Hughes joined in this exercise with the rest.

"The whole clergy and people," he writes to Cardinal Fransoni, prefect of the Propaganda, "appear, so far as I can judge, to receive my appointment with great satisfaction. The bishop himself seems every day better and better pleased. Notwithstanding his advanced age and feeble health, he retains his episcopal rights rather too rigidly and cautiously; but he has left to me, from the first, the administration of the temporal concerns, to which I assiduously devote myself. The trustees of the cathedral are now building a decent and convenient episcopal residence."* Occasionally he visited Philadelphia to preach a charity sermon, his old flock receiving him, as might be supposed, with a warm welcome.

The subject that of all others he had nearest at heart was education. Soon after the destruction of the college at Nyack, Bishop Dubois attempted the establishment of a new one in Brooklyn. A quantity of stone was removed to the spot from the ruined edifice on the Hudson, but the project was abandoned on account of some difficulty about the title to the land. In the mean time Dr. Hughes had set about founding a theological seminary at Lafargeville, Jefferson county, in the extreme north-western part of the State of New York, near the Thousand Isles in the St. Lawrence river. Bishop Dubois, from his happy experience at Emmitsburg, was in favor of placing seminaries as far as possible from the excitements and temptations of large cities; and certainly Lafargeville was remote enough, being three hundred miles from New York, and well removed from all great lines of communication. The project met with Bishop Dubois' approval, and an estate was consequently purchased by his coadjutor in his name.

* This was the same house still occupied by the rector and other clergymen of the cathedral. It had been the episcopal residence for some time before Bishop Hughes came to New York; the "building" of which he speaks was an enlargement of it.

TO MR. FRENAYE.

May 3, 1838.

My dear Friend:

It is some time since I had a letter from you, although still in your debt myself, as I believe I have not written since I received your last. I have been absent at Lafargeville, where I was induced to accept a tempting offer of a tempting place, viz., a plantation, highly improved, of 460 acres excellent limestone land, with buildings in quality superior, and in extent not much inferior, to Mount St. Mary's at Emmitsburg. The buildings were put up in 1834 and 1835, and cost 30,000 dollars. The land itself would sell for 35 to 40 dollars an acre; and the whole has been purchased for 20,000 dollars, to be paid at intervals in ten years. The college was enough at one time, but it would have been a pity to miss the offer, especially as it will be of great advantage as a house of retreat for the clergy and a place of ecclesiastical education for poor boys, as provisions are so cheap that the expense of one here would support three there. The board and tuition will be only 112 dollars per annum, for those who can pay; and, if possible, none but Catholic boys will be received. Rev. Mr. Guth, whose mission is in the neighborhood, will take charge of the premises for the present, but it will not be organized entirely for some time. I intend to send —— there, if he should wish, and there be no obstacle to his one day becoming a priest. The farm and farmhouse, with barns, etc., are rented, except forty acres, the most improved, which is attached to the mansion. This was built and arranged by Mr. Lafarge for his own residence; but he is grown so rich that he wishes to come to the city, and gives it so low in the hope that his improvements may be preserved and perfected in this way, instead of being called "Lafarge's folly" if he disposed of them in the land-market. He is a Catholic in name; but his wife is remarkably pious, and at her instance he made a present of the furniture and appurtenances, except a few costly articles which we do not require. If it should not answer the use I intend, I shall dispose of it to some religious community of men, like that in Missouri. . . . . . .

You will all be sorry to hear that Bishop Dubois had another slight attack to-day, from which, however, he is now partially relieved. But his restoration from the former attacks was not complete, and his entire recovery is, I think, more than doubtful.

I intended to pay you a short visit about this time on business, but I shall have to postpone it two or three weeks longer. I cannot be absent on Sunday however, as the only efficient clergyman at the cathedral is at present in poor health.

Love and respects to all. What is Mr. Heyden about? Where is he, and what does he intend to do with himself?

Ever your sincere friend and servant in Christ,

✠ JOHN HUGHES,
Bp. Bslps. and Coadjr. N. Y.

The abandonment of the Brooklyn plan led to some change in the Lafargeville establishment, and it was determined to make it a college for secular education as well as a theological school. It was opened, under the name of "St. Vincent of Paul's Seminary," September 20, 1838, by the Rev. Messrs. Guth, Moran, and Haes, and three tutors. "With the assistance of my two excellent colleagues," writes Mr. Guth on the 25th, "I have launched your small vessel with a most limited number of passengers—six young men and two boys. We hope to pick up some more travellers, or else we could not go far. . . . . Mr. Moran will tell you our rules and regulations; they are those of Mount St. Mary's Seminary." A few "more travellers" were picked up, but very few. A short trial was enough to prove that whatever advantages Lafargeville might possess as a site for a theological seminary, it was too remote for a house of general education. "Yesterday," writes Mr. Guth in September, 1839, "we commenced our classes again with a handful of children. Is it not a pity that for so few you should have such a burden, and we so much labor and classes? We might be compared to a big stage-coach drawn by four horses, and no passengers."

But before we come to the bishop's next attempt to establish a college, we must devote a few pages to a matter which brought into notice the sterner side of his character, and demonstrated in a remarkable manner his fitness for the station to which he had been chosen.

A long-standing dispute between Bishop Dubois and the trustees of the cathedral had reached the point of open warfare. One of the clergymen attached to that church (the same Mr. Levins whose attack upon Mr. Hughes over the signature of Fergus McAlpin was noticed in a previous chapter) had been suspended by the bishop for insubordination;* but he was a favorite with the trustees, and they resolved to recognize no other as their pastor. They made him rector of the parochial school, voted him a salary, refused to pay the priest who was appointed pastor in his stead, and threatened to cut off the bishop's own salary unless he yielded to their demands. They authorized the suspended priest to forcibly expel from the Sunday school a teacher whom the bishop had sent there, and to employ the assistance of a constable in removing from the school-rooms " any persons who might, either on Sundays or week-days, conduct themselves in a manner that should be deemed objectionable by him." The civil law, it is true, gave them authority to do all this. "But it gives them the same right," said Bishop Hughes, "to send a constable into the sanctuary and remove the priest from the altar." He appealed from the trustees to the congregation. "Is it your intention," he asked, "that such power be exercised by your trustees? If so, then it is almost time for the ministers of God to forsake your temple, and erect an altar to their God around which religion shall be free, the Council of Trent fully recognized, and the laws of the Church applied to the government and regulation of the Church." Bishop Dubois was too old and too feeble to carry on the contest, but he rightly judged that his coadjutor had all the courage and firmness which the occasion demanded, and he committed the whole matter to him. Bishop

---

* Mr. Levins was a hot-tempered but virtuous man. He was subsequently restored to the ministry by Bishop Hughes.

Hughes felt that the battle must be a decisive one. It was not an affair of the appointment of school-teachers or the payment of salaries; it was practically the question whether the Church should be governed by the bishop or the legislature. If the charter of incorporation could give laymen the right of interference when the bishop deemed it necessary to inflict canonical censures upon one of his clergy; if it entitled them to appoint catechists and expel from the premises anybody who did not please them; why might it not go further, and commit to the trustees the entire management of the spiritual concerns of the congregation? If they might demand the services of a suspended priest, why not of an excommunicated priest? of a Methodist minister? a Jew? a pagan? an atheist? The trustees, in fine, were acting on the Protestant principle, which puts all church matters into the hands of the people; they may call whom they please to preach to them, and if they do not like him, may send him away and call another. The Catholic principle supposes that pastors are sent by God to teach and govern their flocks. We have seen how clearly Mr. Hughes perceived the radical evils of the trustee system at the time of the troubles in St. Mary's, Philadelphia, and how he wrote to Mr. Bruté in 1828: "There is no remedy for all this until the time shall have come to aim the blow, not at the branches, but at the root of this abominable system of trusteeing churches." He believed that the time was come now. The great mistake of the bishop of Philadelphia was, that by attempting to secure the election of trustees who would carry out his wishes, he tacitly admitted the propriety of lay interference in spiritual concerns. Bishop Hughes determined to put matters at once upon their proper footing—neither to submit, nor to compromise, nor to threaten any thing that he could not execute.

On the 10th of February, 1839, a constable was employed to eject the bishop's catechist from the cathedral Sunday school. The next Sunday Bishop Hughes spoke of the occurrence from the pulpit in such a tone as to invite an apology from the trustees and smooth the way for a reconciliation. No apology, however, was made. On Sunday the 24th he read to the congregation a Pastoral Address written by himself, but signed by Bishop Dubois. It called upon them to disavow the course of their representatives, and threatened with ecclesiastical penalties those who persisted in their insubordinate conduct. It told them in effect that the bishop ought to be and would be master. The law gave them control over the church edifice and the revenues; but it gave them none over the clergy or the sacraments. They might do what they pleased with the building; but unless they acted in perfect conformity with the canons and spirit of the Catholic Church, the priests should all be withdrawn and the cathedral laid under an interdict. The charity of pious Catholics would keep the bishops and clergy from want until they could establish themselves elsewhere. The pew-holders were invited to meet Bishop Hughes in the school-room the same afternoon.

At the appointed hour, from five to seven hundred persons assembled. After the meeting had been called to order by a member of the congregation, Bishop Hughes came forward. "The object of this meeting," said he, "may be comprised in the simple question, whether it is your will that, in any clash or collision between the doctrines, discipline, and ecclesiastical authority of your religion, and your civil powers as a corporate body, the freedom and integrity of the former shall succumb and be sacrificed to the latter?" He then went on to show that it was the duty of every good Catholic to vindicate the freedom of religion in all its relations with the outward world. The power which the trustees enjoyed was given to them by the civil law, not that they might interfere with the discipline and spiritual authority of the Church, but that they might transact its temporal affairs in a legal and convenient manner. Hence, when the trustees expelled the Sunday-school teacher appointed by the bishop, they did what they had indeed a technical right to do; but they acted against the spirit of the civil law, besides violating their religious duty, invading the rights of the clergy, and damaging the spiritual interests of the congregation. Speaking of the danger to be apprehended from encroachments upon religion in the name or by the authority of the civil power, he took occasion to contrast the state church of England, "a gilded slave, chained to the crown," with the persecuted religion of "poor Ireland, who upheld the freedom of her faith at the sacrifice of all that men hold dear beside." It was a happy allusion; he well knew the character of his listeners; and when he pictured the Irish Catholics in the time of the penal laws "assembling in the solitude of the mountain or the dampness of the secret cave around their priest, for whose head the laws offered the same premium as for that of a wolf," he seemed to move the very depth of feeling in every breast. The whole assembly was his; he could do what he liked with it. The people had been well disposed toward him from the first; but with the skill of a consummate orator he had brought them to a state of such perfect sympathy with him, that they seemed to think only his thoughts, and look at every thing with his eyes. When he next proposed a preamble and resolutions, they were adopted by acclamation, without one dissenting voice. The most material part of them was this: "Resolved, that we know no difference between the authority of the Holy Church and that authority with which she has invested the bishops, for carrying on her mission and for our spiritual good; and that we hold it as unworthy of our profession as Roman Catholics to oppose ourselves or to suffer any one in our name to oppose any let, obstacle, or hindrance—no matter how legal such act may be—which would hinder or prevent our bishop from the full, free, and entire exercise of the rights, powers, and duties which God has appointed as inherent in his office, and the Church has authorized him to preserve, exercise, and fulfil." The trustees were requested to enter the preamble and resolutions on the records of the cathedral, and to accept them as a fundamental rule of action for themselves and their successors. Any member of the board who might feel unwilling to do this was invited to resign.

Some of the members did resign—though not until after a faint resistance; others came over to the bishop's side; and the regular election which soon followed placed in office a board which was not disposed to make trouble. The cathedral has always continued under the temporal management of trustees; but Bishop Hughes had killed the spirit of rebellion among them forever. Now and then he experienced similar but less serious difficulties in other parishes: he had generally but to say a few words to the congregations, in his determined way, and at once there would be a great calm.*

TO MR. FRENAYE.

March 20, 1839.

DEAR SIR:

We have brought the trustees so low that they are not able to give a decent kick! The congregation have unanimously requested me to deliver a course of six lectures in the church, on the evils and dangers to religion of that system, and I have consented. I shall publish them, and if it were not out of fashion now, I would dedicate them to yourself; for I am sure that no one will rejoice more over the death and grave of their power. The poor old bishop is revenged for their treatment of him. He can hardly believe it. And the best of it is, there is no controversy, no party, no one to say one word in their favor loud enough to be heard.

But what is this that I hear? that you are going to give away the rich, beautiful, and valuable chandeliers, *a part of the church*, for the introduction of GAS!!! You will ruin it, and be sorry for it when it will be too late. Leave gas to the theatres, fancy-stores, and toy-shops, but do not desecrate the church with the association

---

* Some years afterward, his secretary thus recorded an incident of the kind in another city: "The archbishop went to —— to give the trustees of St. ——'s a blowing up. The only way will be to blow them out of the church entirely.— N. B. He turned them out."

which it will present to the eye. If not for my sake, I would beg for God's sake that you will not do this. If you have taken any steps, try to retrace them as quietly as you can. The people will pay any expense you have been at; but if not, I will give 100 dollars myself toward it. But do not give away the chandeliers at any rate. They are perpetual ornaments; belong to the plan of the church, and are worth, even as brass, 1700 dollars. And why will you banish them to give place to a feature of the museum or theatre? Do not, I entreat you.

Your sincere and attached friend in Christ,

✠ JOHN HUGHES,
Bp. Belps. and Coadjr. N. Y.

TO THE SAME.

April 22, 1839.

* * * * *

The trustees and all are quiet. The three new ones *and the congregation* will take care of all. The others would resign if they were not ashamed. But they will make no opposition. They know there is no confidence in them. One, ——, has resigned. They must be reformed in their principles through the whole diocese; and I do not think it will be at all difficult. My second lecture on the subject [was given] yesterday; but I am cramped, not wishing to give offence on so delicate a subject.

Yours sincerely in Christ,

✠ JOHN HUGHES, *Bp., etc.*

In getting together materials and searching out references for these lectures, he had some help from Bishop Bruté. The good old prelate was then very near heaven; but weak and sick as he was, he drew up for his dear pupil a catalogue of all the principal schisms and disorders which had arisen from the trustee system in this country, and sent it to him with a number of pamphlets and a characteristic letter, dated "Vincennes, 28th March, the very 'Holy Thursday,' the day of all apostleship, priesthood, and Christian blessing for all Christians." "Full of joy," he says, "as I read your letter of the 20th, and that triumph of true, divine principles over those of the Gates of Hell. . . . . A review of cases or of general principles is more easy than the truly delicate task now before you. . . . . Treat it with piety and charity, with a view to instruct, not to humble, to rail. . . . . . Let it be evident that the whole purpose is of a superior order, settling here the Church on its proper ground, and securing Catholics in the enjoyment of their religion against designing or misguided men. So will you succeed."

He writes again, April 19th, only a few weeks before his death, to congratulate Bishop Hughes on the success of the lectures, and the excellent effect of the pastoral letter of their "common father and friend" Bishop Dubois:

I finish reading your first page delighted—God's own spirit and promises to his Church—all the true mixture of firmness, prompt action, and charity—given to you from above. But you are too kind to remember me, and grant me such an excellent letter—second and third page my increasing consolation. What you say of Bishop Dubois affected me to tears. . . . . I love and respect him, and you now so faithful to him and to your God, with increased affection.

What was the remark about Bishop Dubois at which Dr. Bruté was so much moved, I have no means of knowing; but it is not difficult to conjecture. Repeated paralytic strokes had produced their natural effect upon the venerable prelate's mind: he was no longer the clear-headed, far-seeing, energetic man that he had been. He became ready to trust and quick to be deceived; his confidence was continually abused; and the mournful conviction forced itself upon the minds of those about him, that the interests of the Church required his retirement.

Bishop Hughes wrote to the cardinal prefect of the Propaganda, describing the evils which resulted from Dr. Dubois' state of health:

He is now better, now worse. His faculties both of mind and of body are impaired: his memory especially fails him. . . . . Devoted to him with my whole heart, as he is to me, I have made no attempt to interfere in the government of the diocese, except in the way of advice and persuasion, which are of little avail, because he is very set in his purposes. . . . . . I write of these things, most eminent and reverend father, not that any authority for governing the diocese may be taken away from him, or conferred upon me; but in order that you may be informed of the state and circumstances of ecclesiastical affairs. On the contrary, I should be deeply grieved if any thing should be done or ordered by the Holy See to diminish his authority or dignity. I know that it is my part to assist the venerable Bishop of New York, "so far as he himself wishes," and I know not whether I ought to have said what I have. If I have done wrong, I beg your Eminence to hold me excused.

In August, 1839, Archbishop Eccleston arrived in New York, with instructions from the Holy See to take the administration of the diocese out of the hands of Dr. Dubois, and confide it to Dr. Hughes. It was a terrible blow to the good old Bishop of New York. When the news was first communicated to him, his imperious spirit rebelled at what seemed an undeserved humiliation. "What wrong have I done?" he cried. "They cannot take away my authority unless I am guilty of crime! I will never give it up, never!" There fortunately happened to be another bishop in New York just then, who had been one of Dr. Dubois' favorite pupils. The old man loved him with all his heart, and used to speak of him as his dear son. Bishop —— threw himself on his knees before Dr. Dubois. He reminded him of his age and infirmity. He pointed out how the diocese was suffering for the want of a young, energetic, fearless governor, who could exercise a personal supervision over even its remotest parts. He begged him to submit promptly and patiently to the will of the Sovereign Pontiff. His words were not in vain. The momentary outbreak of human nature was repressed by the influence of divine grace, and

Bishop Dubois yielded up his authority with the most exemplary meekness. To use his own words, "he obeyed the bit, but not till he had covered it with foam." From this time, though he officiated occasionally, he took no further part in the government of the Church. There is, to my mind, something inexpressibly touching in the last scene of this venerable life—consecrated through so many years of hardship and trouble to the service of God's Church, and finding its reward not in the applause or gratitude of man, not even in the approval of the Holy See, but in the record of a good conscience and the smile of Heaven. He who had done so much for the education of the priesthood, who might almost be called the father of the American clergy, saw his bishopric taken from him by one whom he had received twenty years before as a poor Irish lad. He bowed to the stroke; but in his infirm state of mind he could not conquer a natural repugnance toward "Mr. Hughes," as he persisted in calling him. They lived in the same house; but they met no oftener than was necessary. We have seen what Bishop Dubois wrote concerning Dr. Conwell, little thinking that his own case would be the same as that of the Bishop of Philadelphia. "I am neither reduced to the nullity of Bishop Conwell—a circumstance rather painful to human pride—nor would I be disposed to struggle for the mastery if I had been placed in his situation: I would have considered this nullity as a warning from the divine goodness that henceforth all my time must be exclusively devoted to my preparation for death." So he passed the rest of his life in pious exercises. "He appears reconciled and cheerful," writes Bishop Hughes; "of course I leave nothing undone to make him so." *

When his appointment as administrator arrived from Rome, Bishop Hughes was visiting the northern and western

---

* Bishop Dubois was taken suddenly ill on the 15th of December, 1842, and died on the 20th. From the time of this last attack until the moment of his death, says his panegyrist Mr. Quarter, he never ceased to pray.

portions of the diocese. In Onondaga county he found a little colony, composed entirely of converts from Protestantism, of which he wrote an interesting account, the next year, to the central committee of the Society for the Propagation of the Faith, at Paris:

The congregation consists of eighteen souls already received into the Church, and two who, as catechumens, are preparing for baptism. Nearly all are members or immediate relatives of the principal family; and when the first conversion took place, the nearest priest was at a distance of sixty miles. Even at present they have no priest nearer than eighteen miles. The head of this family is a farmer of large wealth and property; a man of good education and strong understanding, who has been a representative of the county in the legislature. From himself and his excellent lady I had the account of their conversion, which I shall give as nearly as possible in their own words. But *written* words can convey no idea of the expression of spiritual joy and peace of soul which beamed on their countenances whilst they related it.

He then proceeds with the story of Colonel D——'s conversion, through the instrumentality of a pedler, who spent a night at his house in 1836, and of the subsequent conversion of a number of his relatives and neighbors. The bishop then continues:

At Christmas Colonel D—— and his wife took their private carriage, and in the coldest weather, and over roads that were almost impassable, travelled to Utica, where the nearest priest was stationed, in order to be at mass on Christmas morning, and to receive their new birth in the waters of baptism on the nativity of our Redeemer. They also engaged the clergyman to visit them for the purpose of baptizing the others, who desired it with equal ardor. The sister and brother-in-law of Mrs. D——, their two daughters and son, and others of their neighbors followed the example, and embraced the faith, until at the period of my visit in July last they were in all sixteen who had abjured Protestantism and been received into the communion of the Church.

They have now a church and priest within eighteen miles, where they attend mass on Sundays, whenever it is possible. But, besides this, Colonel D—— has fitted up a private chapel in his house, separated from the parlor by folding doors, and the priest visits them to say mass and administer the sacraments occasionally on a week day. There they have their altar, adorned and decorated in the richest manner that the resources of the country would allow. Silver candlesticks, a very neat ivory crucifix, white fine linen, and beautiful fresh flowers at the foot of a small picture of the Blessed Virgin, constituted its decorations when I had the pleasure of paying this excellent family a short visit last summer. Evening and morning the family, and on Sundays and festivals, when they cannot go to mass, the whole little flock assemble before this altar, and unite in the prayers and devotions of our holy religion; but when the priest comes, their joy is complete. Colonel D—— throws his rooms open, and invites all his Protestant neighbors to attend. "And," said he, "in spite of their prejudices, they are forced to acknowledge themselves struck with a feeling of awe, in witnessing even the *outward ceremonial of the holy sacrifice*, and the profound attention of those who assist at and believe in it."

I had but a few hours to spend with them, the journey going and returning on the same day having been thirty-six miles. I hardly spoke; I listened in silence, and with secret emotion, wishing my own heart to share in all the *feelings* of faith and joy which I saw abounding in theirs. I was reminded of the first Christians; they appeared and spoke as persons who, by a special grace of God, had been put unexpectedly in possession of the heavenly treasure, and who were still in the freshness of their joy and gratitude.*

From these peaceful and edifying scenes he hurried back to New York to take up the additional responsibilities thrust upon him by the Holy See, and throw himself more energetically than ever into that warfare which was henceforth to be the occupation of his life. There was no longer a Mentor to whom he could turn in time of perplexity. The saintly Bishop Bruté slept in the Lord on the 26th of June this year; and our young prelate, in his trying situation,

* "Annals of the Propagation of the Faith," 1840.

could not look abroad for advice or help. We shall see that his own strength and judgment were sufficient.

The first thing that engaged his attention was the establishment of a new college. A suitable place was found at Fordham, in Westchester county, about ten miles from New York. Rose Hill, as the estate was called, was a beautiful spot, in every way well adapted to the bishop's purpose. The buildings consisted of an unfinished stone house, on the summit of a gentle eminence, and an old wooden farm-house which had been in its day rather a fashionable mansion. A beautiful lawn, some fifteen or twenty acres in extent, occupied the slope in front of these buildings, and along the edge of it was a fringe of magnificent elm trees, the seeds of which—so the proprietors of the place were fond of telling—had been brought in old times from Holyrood palace. Behind the stone dwelling lay a large and productive farm, and back of that a beautiful wood, through which ran the river Bronx. Rose Hill, besides, was not without its historical associations. It was within a stone's throw of Fordham Heights, celebrated in revolutionary history as the position occupied by General Washington during the movements which preceded the battle of White Plains in October, 1776; and a mound of earth covering the remains of a number of soldiers was a conspicuous object on the north side of the lawn, seeming to indicate that a skirmish had taken place on or near the estate. While the American Congress was in session in New York, just after the peace of 1783, Rose Hill was the residence of the celebrated Lady Mary Watts, the daughter of Lord Stirling; and the old farm-house must have witnessed in those days many a brilliant scence of gayety and fashion.

The purchase was soon made. Bishop Dubois was not in a fit state to take any part in the negotiations; but it was one of the effects of his mental weakness that he was tenacious of his dignity, and extremely sensitive to any thing like a slight. A clergyman to whom he was particularly attached undertook the delicate task of informing him of the intended purchase by his coadjutor. "You see, bishop," said he, "it was better that he should appear in the matter than you; he has just come here, and is not known yet." "Ah!" replied the good old man, "but they soon will know him."*

The cost of Rose Hill was about $30,000; to fit the buildings for the reception of students would cost, it was supposed, $10,000 more. To meet these demands the bishop had, of course, not a penny; but he concluded the bargain, and immediately opened subscriptions throughout the diocese. A large part of the money was obtained in this way by voluntary subscription; a considerable sum was collected in Europe; and the rest was finally raised by loans in small amounts, for which interest was paid at the rate of five per cent.

TO MR. FRENAYE.

Sept. 19, 1839.

DEAR FRIEND:

I know not what you will have thought of my long silence. But I have been so much engaged that scarce a moment remained. You can easily imagine this from the events that have occurred within the last few weeks.

The college and seminary go on prosperously. Of the 40,000 dollars which *must* be raised before we begin, about 15,000 are already subscribed. When it exceeds 20,000 I shall go to Europe, to engage professors, etc., probably about 16th next month. . . .

About the charity sermon, I shall not be able this year. Get some other; Dr. Moriarty will do well, as I understand he is famous for such occasions. Make any arrangement you please with Mr. Cummiskey.† The sum you mentioned in your last will do well enough. But whatever you do, I will ratify.

Why can't you come and pay us a visit? I am happy to hear

---

* Bp. Bayley, "Discourse on the Life and Character of the Most Rev. Archbishop Hughes."

† This refers to an offer for the sale of the copyright of the Hughes and Breckinridge Discussion.

that Bishop Kenrick is so much recovered from his indisposition. Give my respects to him, to Mr. Gartland, Mr. Sourin, Mrs. McMahon, and the Sisters of the asylum; and believe me

Very sincerely your friend and servant in Christ,

✠ JOHN HUGHES,
Bp. Belpls., etc.

On the 14th of October he published a pastoral letter, in which he strongly commended the new institution to the liberality of his people, and at the same time announced that Bishop Dubois had resigned the administration of the diocese, in consequence of his great age and feeble health. "Having passed through more than half a century of apostolical labor and boundless as well as untiring zeal, he was entitled, at the age of seventy-six years, and it was natural for him to seek the privilege of repose, by leaving to younger energies to take up the burden which he had so long and so zealously sustained."

CHAPTER XIII.

1839-1840.

Voyage to Europe—Letter from Rome—Letter to the Leopoldine Society—Interview with O'Connell—Letters from Dublin.

BISHOP HUGHES sailed from New York for Havre, in the packet ship Louis Philippe, on the 16th of October, 1839. The object of his visit to Europe was to obtain assistance in men and money for his diocese.

From a letter of sixteen closely written pages to his sister Mrs. Rodrigue, I select the following passages:

TO MRS. RODRIGUE.

ON BOARD LOUIS PHILIPPE, *Nov.* 6, 1839.

MY DEAR SISTER:

I shall not finish this letter until after we reach Havre, which we hope to do by next Sunday. But this is no reason why I should defer till then to write you all that I have thought worth preserving of my notes and observations of the voyage, especially as I have leisure now, which may not be at command after our arrival. . . . . You recollect we did not sail on the appointed day; we had to remain at anchor from the 16th to the 20th off Staten Island, owing to light or adverse winds. A stout breeze from the north on Sunday morning enabled us to go to sea.

Our passengers are as civil and polite, and withal as good-for-nothing a set, as you need desire to travel with. . . . Although all seated at a convenient distance for purposes of conversation at table, I never remarked any thing like a general topic introduced or sustained. Once, indeed, there was a discussion which, from the earnestness of the speakers, seemed to engage the attention and interest of the listeners also. It was on the comparative merits and character of oysters at New York and at Havre.

On the 31st I was gratified with a spectacle which I had often desired to witness—the condition of the sea during a tempest.

After a breeze from the north and north-west of about sixty hours' continuance, the wind died away about 4 o'clock the afternoon previous. The calm continued until about 9 o'clock in the evening, as if the winds had ceased to blow, excepting a few puffs that were floating about, bewildered and not knowing what to do with themselves. In the interval, the mercury in the barometer had fallen at an extraordinary rate, and the captain predicted that we were likely to encounter "a gale" from the south-east. I did not hear the remark at the time, or I should not probably have gone to bed. The gale came on, however, at about 11 o'clock—not violent at first, but increasing every moment. I slept soundly, as usual, until half-past five in the morning, although I had a confused and dreamy recollection of a good deal of rolling and thumping through the night, occasioned by the unsteady course of the ship and the dashing of the waves.

On the deck most of the passengers had by this time congregated. I found them clinging to whatever they could hold on by, around the doors of the hurricane house, and looking on in silence and consternation. "Ha, ha!" I said to myself, "this is what I have been wanting; but *c'est un peu trop*." It was still quite dark. Four of the principal sails were already in ribbons. The winds were howling through the cordage—the rain dashing along furiously and in torrents; whilst the noise and whirl-gusts of spray reminded one of the scene behind the great cataract of Niagara. In the midst of all this were the captain with his speaking-trumpet, the officers and sailors screaming out to each other in efforts to be heard, and, incredible as it may seem, and should be, swelling the gale with their oaths and curses; all this taken together, in the darkness or rather twilight of the hour, and the fury of the hurricane, combined as much of the *terribly* sublime as I ever wish to witness concentrated in one scene.

This was but the commencement of the gale, which, however, had taken us by surprise, and borrowed additional terrors from the darkness and suddenness with which it came upon us. It lasted for 24 hours, so that through the whole of that day I had an opportunity of enjoying at leisure a scene which (apart from the danger) would be at any time worth a voyage across the Atlantic.

The hurricane did not acquire its full force until about 9 o'clock. By that time there was no more work to be done. The vessel "lay-to," as they term it, and those who had charge of her stood by, only to see and meet whatever disaster might occur. It was now breakfast time; but cooking had been out of the question, and appetite was nearly so. My own was excellent, especially for the small allowance of a fast-day. By this time the sea had put on its hurricane-billows; and not to lose the opportunity, after having fortified myself with appropriate clothing, I took my position on a part of the quarter-deck from which I could survey the whole scene around the ship undisturbed, and with entire safety to myself so long as her strong work should hold together. I had often seen and admired paintings of a storm at sea, and my recollections of them enabled me to compare them with the original by which I was now surrounded. Those paintings in general are true, so far as they go. But after all, how feeble is the representation, and how destitute of those accompaniments which art cannot supply! In the painting you have, it is true, the ship and the sea agitated by the storm; but *motion*, the very life and spirit of the subject, is lost in the imitation—it is arrested, and the whole becomes stationary as the canvas itself. Imagination, indeed, comes to the painter's aid, in this perhaps more than any other subject of the merely physical order. But not for the eye alone has the sea-storm the many parts by whose wild harmony it becomes at once beautiful, terrible, and sublime. For even could the pencil be successful in repesenting it so far as the eye is concerned, there would still be wanting the rushing of the tempest, the groaning of the spars and masts, the quick, shrill whistling of the cordage and rigging, and more than all, the ponderous dashing of the uplifted deop.

The weather was thick and hazy, more especially along the surface of the sea. It was impossible to see more than three-quarters of a mile in any direction. But within this contracted horizon you saw the mountain waves rising suddenly out of the darkness on one side, and rushing and tumbling across the valleys that remained from the passage of their predecessors, until like them they rolled away into the darkness on the other. These waves were not either numerous or rapid in their course. But their massiveness and elevation were such as, it seems, a tempest alone has power to produce. It must have been the refraction of light falling on their sides that gave to these waves, especially near their summit, the most beautiful, clear, green color—as if they were composed of irregular and disturbed heaps of molten and transparent emerald—crowned with a toppling of white foam, which, as the wave approached, would spill itself over on the side nearest you, and come tumbling down with the dash of a cataract. Not less magnificent than the waves themselves were the valleys of different and varying dimensions that remained between them. Their waters had lost for a moment the onward motion of the billows, but they were far from being at rest. Under their scarf of foam they preserved the same green color of the mighty insurgents that had passed over them. But the symptoms of violence which they presented to the eye, boiling up and wheeling about rapidly in currents and eddies, with the surface glowing and hissing as if it had come in contact with red-hot iron—all showed that even these low places were not unvisited by the storm, but that its angry spirit had descended into their depths, ready to heave them up into all the rushing violence of the general commotion.

. . . . .

It was impossible not to be impressed with a deep feeling of awe at the universal majesty of that God who has created and preserves all this wondrous combination of the elements. The Scriptures speak of Him in the midst of thunder and lightning, as riding in the whirlwind and walking on the great deep; and at such a moment how could I forget *His* presence who alone unbinds or restrains the fury of winds and waves at His pleasure! Here they were raging with indescribable fierceness; and yet man, of such limited strength as to his physical structure, was now in the act of triumphing over their fierceness. By using his reason, that feeble ray of the Divine Intelligence which has been imparted to him, he builds his house on the foundation of the waters, and the tempest cannot overturn it.

TO MR. FRENAYE.

HAVRE, *Nov.* 16, 1839.

MY DEAR FRIEND:

I have just time to write a line before the sailing of the packet of this date. We sailed on the 20th Oct., and arrived only yesterday. The Iowa entered the basin with the same tide; and as the steamboat came to take the passengers of both ships, the first persons I saw were those whom you mentioned from Philadelphia. They appeared desolate enough. I was not in the least sick, although the weather was very stormy, and we had a magnificent gale of twenty-four hours, which was worth the whole voyage.

Mr. Starrs will forward you a package for my sister, which you will be kind enough to send by some opportunity. Instruct her also how to direct her letters. I am much pleased with what I have seen of France. I lodge with the curé of Notre Dame, and am to officiate to-morrow. You shall hear from me in Paris; but do not wait to write. Give my respects to everybody at St. John's, the asylum, etc. Ever yours in Christ,

✠ J. HUGHES, *Bp., etc.*

He spent some time in Paris, and was presented by General Cass to King Louis Philippe and the royal family at a private audience. Toward the beginning of the year 1840 he went to Rome. "The Holy Father," he wrote to the Very Rev. Mr. Power, "made me valuable presents. Nothing could exceed the kindness of all to whom I had occasion to present myself. The Pope inquired most particularly and affectionately for Bishop Dubois, and charged me to present the respects of his Holiness to the bishop." He had several audiences of the Sovereign Pontiff, to whom he exposed freely the wants of his diocese. The Pope gave him a handsome golden chalice, and a valuable collection of some four hundred engravings, from paintings in the Vatican. He writes as follows to the Rev. Felix Varela of New York:

Rome is the only city in which I spent any considerable time, or which I felt regret at leaving. I had not much business to transact there, but even the little which I had proceeded so slowly as to furnish me with no unwelcome plea for protracting my departure. And when the hour came at length that I must pass its gates, I felt that a hard destiny which obliged me to turn my back upon all that it contains, and my face toward a world that (for the moment) seemed cold and cheerless.

The associations which are awakened within its walls are a perpetual feast of sentiment. Such a collection of all that great men have bequeathed to the world of genius, arts, and sciences, mingling and combining with the brighter and better legacies of confessors, saints, martyrs, apostles, makes Rome what no other city is, or ever can be—a city of the soul. Even in its outward relation to the senses, it is like a mighty harmonicon of all music, giving forth its sweet sounds from the dawn of the morning till the close of the day, and sinking into silence only when the light ceases to play upon it, and it is overspread with the darkness of night. There is but one Rome in this world. Other cities are beautiful, if you please, but to me insipid if compared with Rome.

I have not taken much pains to observe of this or any other city things appertaining to the material order, which have been described by so many travellers. But what has delighted me more was to behold on every side, and in every country, the young spirit of Catholic fervor which is penetrating the masses of society. In France and Italy the piety of the people—not all—but of millions and millions struggling by zeal, by deep devotion, by prayer and charity, to sanctify themselves and make others sharers in the blessings of religion. In Germany the quickening spirit is abroad; and in spite of the persecutions of Protestant and the indifference of Catholic governments, the return to the faith of many converts, and to more ardent piety among the people, are the consoling evidence of its power. The same may be said of England and Scotland, where religion is making almost miraculous progress.

He spent nearly three months in Rome, and then made a rapid tour through northern Italy. In April he was at Vienna, soliciting pecuniary aid from the Leopoldine Society.

This association was organized in 1829 for the special purpose of promoting the activity of Catholic missions in America, "and to keep in lasting remembrance her deceased majesty Leopoldina, empress of Brazil, born archduchess of Austria." It somewhat resembles, in its object and mode of operation, the Society for the Propagation of the Faith. Its funds are derived from small weekly contributions of its subscribers, and in the distribution of alms special favor is shown to those portions of America in which the greatest number of German immigrants have settled. Bishop Hughes was received by the society with great favor, and obtained a liberal donation in aid of his college and seminary. In a letter to the society, he gave a sketch of the history and wants of his diocese, from which I add a few extracts:

There are many privations, especially of a moral character, incident to the life of the poor emigrant in America, even when he is conscious of improving his temporal comforts. The wealth, the manners, sometimes the language, and generally the more elevated condition in society of the people by whom he is surrounded, remind him constantly that he is not in the land of his fathers nor among the companions of his youth. It is only when he has the consolations of his religion within his reach that he feels comparatively happy in his new position. If on the Sunday he can be present at the holy sacrifice of Mass, if he can only see the minister of his religion at the altar and hear the word of God in the language to which his ear was accustomed from childhood, he forgets that he is among strangers and in a strange country. He can approach the sacraments; he can have his children baptized by a minister of his own creed; he can indulge the hope that, under the guidance of their pastor, they will not forsake that creed when they grow up; and when sickness overtakes him, and death gives warning of its approach, he can call the same minister to his bedside, and receive at his hands the sanctifying unction and the bread of life.

Hence in the diocese of New York the cry for priests comes to the bishop's ears from almost every quarter; often, alas! when he has no priest to send. And as the people judge that one of the greatest inducements for a priest to come among them is the existence of a suitable place for the celebration of the divine worship, their first effort in every new settlement is to erect a church, now larger, now smaller, according to their means and numbers. They do not reflect that to provide the minister of the sanctuary is often much more difficult than to erect the temple. These remarks explain to us the reason why the Catholics of this diocese have built so many churches in so short a time, notwithstanding their poverty.

. . . . .

The zeal of the Catholic emigrants springs, as has been already remarked, from their ardent desire to have a priest; and the consequence, which is foreseen and unavoidable in their circumstances, is that the churches generally are *in debt*. The people contribute liberally according to their means, but it must be remembered that they are only poor emigrants, just commencing in a new country, and struggling to supply the first great want of their condition, viz., the want of religion. They are able to contribute just enough to make the ground and church, when finished, *good security* for the borrowed money necessary to complete it. If they can accomplish this, they expect to have a clergyman among them. This is the great point. Then the congregation will flourish by his zeal. Others will join them. They will be enabled to pay the interest of their debt from year to year; and after a time, when their numbers will have increased and their industry will have enlarged their private means, they will be enabled to pay the principal also. This is their reasoning; and this is an outline of the history of almost every church in the diocese. For instance, nine additional churches have been built in the city and suburbs of New York within the last fifteen years. But the debt on these churches united exceeds half a million of florins!! and the interest on this debt amounts annually to thirty thousand florins! The other churches of the diocese, with few exceptions, are more or less in the same situation. Still, *time* will enable the Catholics to overcome all these difficulties, for their means will be enlarged and their expenditures diminished. But it is manifest that so long as this state of things continues, the onward progress of religion, so far as it depends on *their* means, is necessarily retarded. If they could appropriate to the building of churches or other necessary institutions what they are obliged to pay for those already erected, the case would be very different. But unhappily, what should belong to the *present* and the *future* is already mortgaged to the *past*.

* * * * *

Neither is this all. There should be one church at least, and one pastor, for every two thousand souls. And the moment this is admitted, it follows that fifty more churches and fifty more priests would be requisite to supply the spiritual wants now existing! How are these wants to be supplied? The providence of God indeed has many resources, and we must trust in him. But in this state of spiritual destitution, think of the souls who must find themselves deprived of the blessings of religion. Think of the children of the poor Catholics who, in their exposed state, must fall a prey to the false zeal of wealthy Protestants; of those who, brought up in remote parts of the country, without the care and instruction of the Catholic pastor, without the habits of their religion, will be ignorant of the truth or indifferent about it; and who, in becoming heads of families, will entail upon their offspring the same spiritual misfortunes. How can a bishop be without deep [concern], charged with a diocese in which such consequences threaten his people on every side?

The least reflection will convince you that the progress of religion in the diocese of New York is left far behind the progress of the Catholic population, and that the number of the Catholics, in their present situation, is precisely the evidence of their need. If they were fewer, their spiritual wants could be more easily supplied. And if there is any thing calculated to excite the charity and zeal of pious Christians in Europe, it should be that in this diocese there are so many of their brethren as "sheep without a shepherd,"—the bishop not having means to educate or send out missionaries to take charge of them. It would have been perhaps an advantage if they had not increased so fast. But what is to become of them, if so great a disproportion between the number of priests and the amount of population is to continue? It is easy to foresee that ignorance of religion, especially among the rising generation, indifferentism, apostasy from the faith, irreligion, and immorality will prey upon that surplus portion of the Catholic people for whose spiritual wants the bishop is unable to provide.

There is as yet no house of religious education in the whole diocese; and the consequence is that the youth of wealthier families are exposed to lose their faith by being educated in dangerous intercourse with Protestantism. There is no theological seminary for the training up of the future priests under the bishop's inspection; and hence he has hitherto been obliged by the wants of the people to accept such clergymen from other countries and other states as offered themselves. They are happily good and generally zealous missionaries; but is it not a painful and dangerous necessity which obliges him to send laborers into the vineyard of the Lord *without knowing them?* It is clear, therefore, that until houses of religious education and a theological seminary are established, religion in the diocese of New York is deprived of the very *sources*, the *life-spring*, on which its real progress and prosperity must, under God, depend.

He was treated with great distinction at Vienna, and presented to most of the notable persons of that capital. He made the acquaintance of Monsignore Bedini, who afterward visited the United States as papal nuncio. He saw his gallant countryman Marshal Nugent, the first officer of the Austrian army. "What endeared him to me still more than his being an Irishman," said the bishop, "was that in his speech he did not, like some, try to get rid of the brogue as quickly as he could." Among other distinguished men, he was introduced to Metternich, and in the course of a conversation asked him what he thought of the progress of Catholicism in America? "The Catholics and the Protestants in your country," replied the prince, "are like the iron pot and the earthen pot floating down the stream together: when they clash, the earthen pot must be broken."

From Vienna he went to Munich. In May he was once more in Paris, where he engaged a community of the Ladies of the Sacred Heart to found a school in New York. On the 20th he left Paris for London. In the latter city he obtained an introduction to Daniel O'Connell, whom he admired with an ardor almost amounting to enthusiasm. From the following account of the interview it will be seen that the bishop's sentiments on the slavery question had undergone some change since Leander wrote verses for the Gettysburg *Centinel:*

I was introduced with a determination to have a struggle with him on a certain question—that was on the asperity, I thought, with which he spoke of certain social institutions in this country, and I told him, after the ordinary introduction :

"You are not surprised, Mr. O'Connell, that while you have many friends in America, you have some who are much displeased with certain of your public remarks."

And he asked, "Which?"

"Well," I replied, "they think you are too severe upon an institution for which the present generation, or the present government of America, is by no means responsible—I mean slavery."

He paused, and said: "It would be strange, indeed, if I should not be the friend of the slave throughout the world—I, who was born a slave myself."

He silenced me, although he did not convince me.

I afterward heard him in the House of Commons, and there he was, the great, grave senator. You would suppose he had been brought up from childhood an Englishman, he was so calm and unimpassioned. But he was listened to with profound respect. I heard him again at one of those "monster meetings," as they were called, at Donnybrook. He had been preceded by several able and clever orators; for Ireland, and especially the city of Dublin, is seldom deficient in able orators. When he spoke, it was like casting oil upon the troubled waters. Those who had preceded him had aroused and awakened the passions of that crowd of not less than two hundred thousand people. But when he spoke he stilled their stormy passions, and allowed them all to go home in good humor.

At another time I had the honor of being invited to dine at his table. Nothing extraordinary occurred until after the dessert, when a little group of his grandchildren—I suppose—were permitted to enter. They closed around him just as some of his political satellites, but with the innocence of childhood. He had a hand for each; one clinging to his shoulder, another climbing upon his knee. And he had an epithet of tenderness, varied from one to the other, which surprised me more than any eloquence I ever heard. In the language of the continent of Europe, there are diminutive epithets of tenderness, but I never dreamed that they belonged to the English language, until I heard them from the lips of O'Connell.

I met him again on another occasion, in London, at a large dinner party, where there were a number of members of Parliament, and distinguished members of the Catholic nobility. He was near the lady who presided. Toward the end of the entertainment, a very warm discussion sprung up at the opposite extreme of the table, on a question with which they all at first seemed to be perfectly familiar, but in reference to which, the more they discussed it, the more they seemed to become involved in cloud and fog. The dispute had reference to a character in one of Mr. Cooper's novels ("The Pioneer"), named Leatherstocking, and the specific part which the novelist had made him play in the work just alluded to; and when they were fairly "at their wits' end" (O'Connell in the mean time conversing with the lady of the house), a reference was, by common consent, made to him. After hearing both sides, he commenced to stake out the whole subject. He began with the beginning, traced the characters, distinguished one from the other time and place, till at last they all wondered; and one said, "How is it, Mr. O'Connell, that you, who have to govern Ireland, and who have to meet the Tories in Parliament, and do this, and do that—how is it that you are so perfect in a matter of this kind?" He said—and I mention it for the benefit, perhaps, of some young person who may be engaged now or hereafter in the same career—he said, "It is probably owing to this, that the habit of my life has been to arrange all matter of knowledge according to chronology; that is, to see the order of time in which the events took place. As a lawyer, during the period when I have devoted seventeen hours daily to my profession, I always began by studying the chronology of the case—what thing took place first—what the next—until at last it has become such a practice with me, that although I just glanced over that novel of Mr. Cooper's, it has fixed itself upon my mind as if it were a law case."

Of his first interview with O'Connell the bishop has recorded another incident, as follows:

A few minutes after I sat down, and whilst the conversation was on mere commonplace topics, a silence ensued on his part, sufficiently long to make me think that I ought to retire. I observed his eyes swimming in tears. This astonished me still more, and I was about to withdraw, when he addressed me, as nearly as I can remember, in the following words—but in a voice which, though almost stifled with grief, yet sounded as the softest and tenderest that ever struck upon my ears: "Dr. Hughes, I have been forty years a public man—I have been engaged in political strife with men of every party and of every creed—I am, by all odds, the best abused man in the world; but through all this time neither Tories, nor Whigs, nor even Orangemen themselves, ever made an attack on the mother of my children. She was mild and gentle; she was meek and charitable. She was loved and respected by friend and foe. My bitterest enemies would have spared me, if they could not reach me without hurting the lamb that slept in my bosom. The only attack that ever was made on Mrs. O'Connell, came from your side of the water and from your city, in a paper called ——. Some mistaken friend, I suppose, thought to do me a service by sending me the paper. It reached me just after Mrs. O'Connell's death. Of course, the poisoned arrow missed the gentle heart for which it was intended, but it reached and rested in mine."

He heard O'Connell speak at the annual meeting of the Catholic Institute of Great Britain, held at Freemasons' Hall, London, in May of this year; and at the close of the exercises, he himself made an address in which he briefly sketched the history of the American Church. Next he went to Ireland, whence he wrote the following letters to friends at home:

TO MR. FRENAYE.

DUBLIN, *June* 1, 1840.

MY DEAR FRENAYE:

Yours of Feb. 6 was the only letter I received at Paris on my return, and I need not tell you how welcome it was. I found other letters waiting for me here, which have given me an idea of the progress and condition of affairs in America, and especially in New York. They have advanced but little since I left; but on the whole, matters seem to have gone on smoothly enough. The good Bishop Dubois is still able, or at least willing to officiate, and it is quite a satisfaction to me to see that he does so. I regret extremely the remarks of the *Miscellany* in his regard—so perfectly gratuitous and unnecessary.*

As I have several letters to write by the Great Western, I shall not enter into any details of my journey. I have had every success that I could have anticipated; some anxiety of mind; much fatigue of body; and now and then little fits of spleen that *you* were not with me, as you should have been. Then we might have gone to the Holy Land, and been back by this time. One of the things that puzzled me most was the ordering of my meals whenever *items* were to be specified; and many a time I suffered on the continent in consequence of my unconquerable ignorance of living as my constitution would require. This brought on dyspepsia, and with it depression of spirits, and then I was right down angry with you. But do not suppose me so selfish as to regret your not being with me entirely on my own account. How often have I thought of you when present at scenes and in circumstances which you would have enjoyed so much! I could not describe to you the pleasure and satisfaction which I have experienced on those occasions; and they would have been heightened had you only been with me to share in the feelings which they inspired.

I left Rome on the 10th of March. . . . I will give you an idea of my route since I left it: Florence, Lucca, Pisa, Leghorn, Bologna, Modena, Ferrara, Venice, Trieste, Vienna, Presburg in Hungary, Munich, Stuttgard, Strasburg, and on so to Paris. I left Paris on the 20th of May, and in 36 hours was in London, where I remained a week. It is a mighty big city of gloom and gorgeousness. Its proper emblem would be one of those gigantic cart-horses that are seen in its streets. I visited the tunnel—a great *under*-taking—and St. Paul's, which, after you have seen St. Peter's, is only fit to be blown up with gunpowder.

* "We are now aware that the jurisdiction of the see of New York is in Bishop Hughes, and not in Bishop Dubois, who has the title with the honors due to that station, whose duties his age and infirmities have prevented him from discharging. We have learned this for the first time from France. Bishop Conwell of Philadelphia and Bishop Dubois of New York are then precisely in the same position."—*U. S. Cath. Miscellany,* April 25, 1840.

Twenty-four hours more brought me to the capital of poor old Ireland! Alas for the people of this country! the stripes of their martyrdom are everywhere visible. They have been crushed by an apostate nation, which prospers withal. But God is just and merciful. He has said, "The world shall rejoice, and you shall be sorrowful, but your sorrow shall be turned into joy." Blessed words! which are found within the heart of this people, as a compensation of all that has been taken from them.

I shall sail for New York in the British Queen on the first of July. Give my kindest love and remembrance to all my Philadelphia friends. I made as long a list as I could think of [of] their names, and obtained the special blessing of the Holy Father for them all. Particular remembrance to the Sisters and Mr. McMahon. Say to Dr. Nancrede, with my best respects, that I saw his father last Tuesday week. He was slightly indisposed with a sore foot, but otherwise cheerful and kind as usual.

I know it will be a satisfaction to you as it is to me to think that I shall be home so soon after the receipt of this. It might however possibly happen that I cannot get off by the first of July.

Yours in Christ,

✠ J. HUGHES.

TO THE VERY REV. FELIX VARELA.

DUBLIN, *June* 1, 1840.

VERY REV. AND DEAR SIR:

Many thanks for the constancy of your kindness in furnishing me with copies of *The Catholic Register* at so many points of my wandering in Europe. To appreciate the value of this attention, one must be, or imagine himself, in my situation, absent from the scene which claims the solicitude of his mind and the affections of his heart. His eye may be delighted with what he sees—his ear charmed with what he hears—but his memory and inward feelings are perpetually reverting to other sights, and sounds, and objects, to him more dear and interesting. Now, of all these a newspaper is a kind of daguerreotype impression; and nothing can be more pleasant than to be met or pursued by such missives in distant countries.

Among the items of intelligence thus acquired, the first that would naturally attract my attention is the progress of the college and seminary undertaking. I perceive that but little has been done since I left. This does not discourage me, because I think it is owing to causes different from any want of zeal on the part of the Catholics of the city and diocese. The only effect it will have will be to delay the commencing; for as we have to begin only *once*, we must wait till we can begin well—and this cannot be before we shall have the buildings and ground paid for. When that shall be accomplished, the men necessary to carry them on with abundant blessings to religion will not be wanting. I have been as successful in the object of my visit to Europe as I could have anticipated. The rest must be with ourselves.

Since I left you I have not ceased to labor for the object which is so important for the interest of religion in New York, and which is so near to my heart. I have been absent longer than I intended, but not longer than has been essential for the purpose of my journey.   .   .   .   .

I am in the capital of poor old Ireland, and they tell me wonderful things of the moral revolution which has taken place on the subject of temperance.

It is remarkable that this nation, which has been thought the most in need of this reformation, has embraced it with a unanimity and cordiality resembling that with which they received the Christian faith. Already, I am told, the number is one million and a half of those who, lest they should violate the divine command prohibiting *excess*, have embraced the counsel to abstain altogether. Another astonishing fact has been mentioned to me by high authority, viz., that the Scotch, who are considered a sober people, have been, in times past, in the habit of consuming, man for man, nearly double the quantity of spirituous liquors that was consumed by the Irish! This has been established repeatedly by parliamentary documents and evidence. At all events, as we said the other day at the meeting of the Catholic Institute, Ireland has now a proud distinction before her, if, "after having triumphed, by her patient fidelity, over the persecution of the British empire for 300 years; after having proved herself the most *faithful* nation on the earth; she should now prove that her people are also the most *moral* people."

Alas for this nation! it is well for them that the Master to whose doctrines they have been faithful, has left on record the blessed words: "The world shall rejoice, and you shall be sorrowful, but your sorrow shall be turned into joy." The persecution has now ceased, but on every side you see the unhealed wounds and stripes of their martyrdom. Formerly, when the confessors of Christ were permitted to return from their exile, or the mines in which persecution had buried them alive, having lost, some their ears, others their nose, others again having their tongues cut out; these deformities, so far from drawing upon them the contempt of mankind, were rather titles to respect and veneration. They were hailed as true and valiant soldiers of Christ, covered with "honorable scars."

How easy it is to trace kindred moral results among the Irish people, proceeding from the same cause. If they had been as faithless and false as their gloomy and gorgeous oppressor, they might have been as prosperous in this world as he is. They were faithful and true; but the degenerate world does not understand the worth of constancy founded on such unprofitable principles, and therefore their virtue is without honor in the estimation of the world.

This you will find a curious epistle; but my pen has run on, and it is not worth while to correct or alter. I shall sail in the British Queen on the 1st of July, so that I hope I shall soon after your receipt of this have the pleasure of seeing you all.

In the mean time, believe me most sincerely your friend and servant in Christ,

✠ JOHN HUGHES,
Bp. of Basileopolis and Coadjutor and Administrator of New York.

CHAPTER XIV.

1840–1842.

The School question—Injudicious efforts of the Catholics to obtain a portion of the school fund—The Bishop enters the lists—Petition to the Board of Aldermen—Debate before the Common Council—Memorial to the Legislature—The Secretary of State proposes a plan of school reform—The Bishop supports it—The question postponed—Candidates for the Legislature pledged to oppose any change—The Bishop advises the Catholics to nominate an independent ticket—Mr. Maclay's school-bill passed—The Bishop's house attacked by a mob—Establishment of Catholic schools—St. John's College opened.

THE bishop arrived in New York on the 18th of July, and found that his flock had laid out a plenty of work for him during his absence. The Catholics of the city were trying, with more zeal than judgment, to obtain a modification of the common-school system.

The common schools of the State of New York were supported partly by taxation, partly by the revenue of a fund created by act of the Legislature in 1805, and afterward several times increased. The schools were managed and the expenditures regulated by commissioners, inspectors, and trustees, elected in each county, township, and school-district, over whom the secretary of state, as superintendent of public schools, exercised a general supervision. Such at least was the system throughout the country districts; but in the city of New York it was somewhat different. The Legislature seems to have acted on the belief that the public welfare was more nearly concerned in the education of the poor of a large city than in the establishment of free schools in the country; for while at the beginning they left it optional with all the rest of the State to conform to the school system or not, they enforced its adoption in the city. The taxes, moreover, for school purposes were much higher in the city than in other parts of the State. The money, however, was appropriated not to the establishment of new schools, but to the support of those already existing. The right of designating the institutions so favored was retained by the Legislature, and in 1813 the trustees of the following schools and societies were named as entitled to a share of the revenue, viz.: the Free School Society, the Orphan Asylum, the Economical School, the African Free School, and such incorporated religious societies as then supported or might thereafter establish charity schools. Under this arrangement various churches obtained a portion of the school money for some nine or ten years, when gross abuses, frauds, and misapplications of the money, especially in the case of the Bethel Baptist church, were brought to light, and led to a change in the system. The mayor and Common Council prayed the Legislature to take away from religious societies all control over the free education of the poor. "If religious societies," said they, "are to be the only participators of the portion of the school fund for the city of New York, a spirit of rivalry will, it is thought, be excited between different sects, which will go to disturb the harmony of society, and which will early infuse strong prejudices in the minds of children taught in the different schools. Moreover, your memorialists would suggest to your honorable body whether the school fund of the State is not purely of a civil character, designed for a civil purpose; and whether, therefore, the intrusting of it to religious or ecclesiastical bodies is not a violation of an elementary principle in the politics of the State and country." The committee of the Assembly to whom the matter was referred concurred in this view, and an act was accordingly passed in November, 1824, empowering the Common Council of New York to designate from time to time, at least once in three years, the "institutions or schools which should be entitled to receive the school moneys." The intention of the Legislature in this enactment undoubtedly was to guard against a repetition of such frauds as those just alluded to, by taking away from the churches all control over the school money, and giving it to corporations which were directly responsible to the State. Whether they intended also to withhold henceforth the public money from all schools that were not purely secular in their character, became a point of dispute between the Catholics and the Public School Society; but if such was their intention, the Common Council did not respect it; for at the time of which I am now writing, the Catholic Orphan Asylum, the Catholic Benevolent Society, and one or two other religious institutions, received money from the school fund. The disbursement of the greater part of this money, however, was intrusted to the Public School Society. This association was originally incorporated in 1805 under the name of "The Society for Establishing a Free School in the City of New York, for the Education of such Poor Children as do not belong to or are not provided for by any Religious Society." In 1808 its power was extended to all children who were proper objects of gratuitous education, and its name changed to "The Free School Society of New York." In 1826 it adopted the designation of "The Public School Society of New York," and its trustees were authorized to provide for the education of all children in New York not otherwise provided for, "whether such children were or were not the proper subjects of gratuitous education." Any person could become a member by contributing toward the funds of the Society, and the sum of ten dollars was sufficient for the purchase of a life-membership. The members chose fifty trustees, who were authorized to add to their own number fifty more. The Common Council were members *ex officiis*. This corporation was empowered by its charter to hold property to the value of $10,000 per annum; and its annual expenditure, from its own and the public fund together, was about $130,000. Up to the year 1840 it had established nearly one hundred schools, professing to impart a purely secular education, or at least to teach no more than those general principles of religion and morality which all Christian denominations hold in common. The members of the Society were of various religious denominations, and two or three of them were Catholics.

It might seem, at first view, that under such a system the free schools would commend themselves to all religious bodies alike. The Catholics, however, objected to them on two grounds. In the first place, they believed that, as there is no true morality which is not founded on religion, the very basis of a Christian education ought to be a knowledge of positive religious truth. So a teacher who leaves out of view this great essential, or dilutes his doses of theology so as to make them taste good to everybody, starts wrong, and will never do his work well. The Public School Society professed, indeed, to teach religion without sectarianism. "But," said the bishop, "if you exclude all sects, you exclude Christianity. Take away the distinctive dogmas of the Catholics, the Baptists, the Methodists, the Presbyterians, and so on, and you have nothing left but deism."

Bad as this profession was, the practice of the Society was still worse. Instead of teaching religion without sectarianism, they may almost be said to have taught sectarianism without religion; for in spite of their professions, the books used in the public schools abounded in false and contemptuous passages respecting the Catholic Church. The testimony of the clergy was unanimous that the influence of the public schools was highly unfavorable to the faith of the Catholic pupils. Even suppose that they heard nothing directly against the Church; they yet insensibly imbibed an uncatholic spirit in many ways. They listened every morning to the reading of the Bible in a translation which the Church condemned. In some cases the teachers were in the habit of commenting upon and explaining the chapters as they were read. The very phraseology used in speaking of religious matters was different from that to which Catholics are accustomed. And when they heard religion (such as it was) taught without reference, except now and then by way of reproach, to any ecclesiastical system, they naturally came to suppose that religion and the Church had no necessary connection with each other, and that it made little difference to what creed they belonged.

So in every parish where a little money could be scraped together, a Catholic free school was opened, either in the church basement, or in some other poor and inconvenient place. But the churches had great ado to provide for the expenses of the altar and the interest on their debts. They were utterly unable to provide fit school-rooms, nor in many cases could they afford to pay for competent teachers. The Sisters of Charity superintended, as far as they could, the education of the girls; but there was no religious community, as there is now, to look after the boys. The number of Catholic children in New York city, of "school age," was, according to the bishop's estimate, from nine to twelve thousand. The church-schools, crowded to their utmost capacity, provided for four or five thousand; a very few—perhaps two or three hundred—attended the public schools; the rest —that is, about half—received no education whatever.

While the bishop was in Europe, a priest of Albany, in conversation with members of the Legislature, became impressed with the conviction that the Catholics could easily obtain a portion of the school fund if they applied for it. He wrote to that effect to the Very Rev. Dr. Power, vicar-general, and, in the absence of Dr. Hughes, administrator of the diocese. Dr. Power called a meeting of the trustees of all the city churches, and laid the matter before them. By their advice he went to Albany, and satisfied himself that there was a disposition on the part of the Legislature to give the Catholics their rights. The governor of the State, Mr. Seward, alluded to the subject in his annual message, and seemed disposed to favor the Catholic claims. It was judged necessary, however, to bring the matter before the Common Council rather than the Legislature. A Catholic Association was formed in the city for the purpose of securing concert of action, and presenting their claims with all possible force; weekly meetings were held for several months; and finally, a formal petition for a share of the school money was laid before the Board of Assistant Aldermen. Immediately other religious denominations presented similar petitions, and, as might have been expected, all were denied. The matter, however, was not suffered to rest here. The association continued its meetings, and if all the Catholics of New York could have been brought to act with unanimity, their imposing numbers (they were about one-fifth of the whole population) would, it is very probable, have secured them a favorable hearing. But this was not to be. It was charged in *The Truth Teller* (Catholic) that the leaders in the movement were acting with political designs. Whether the accusation had any foundation or not, matters little now; but it was a brand of discord thrown into the assembly, and an excellent weapon of attack for the opposite party. And this was not all. The meetings were characterized by intemperate language, and disorder almost amounting to violence. The people most interested in the movement—that is, the poorer class of Catholics—were fast becoming the dupes, to use the bishop's expression, of those " political underlings who had been accustomed to traffic in their simplicity." The respectable priests who, from motives of pure charity and patriotism, had inaugurated the movement, were being shoved aside by ambitious and unprincipled partisans. Not only the success of their effort to obtain justice, but the good name of the Catholic body, was imperilled by these noisy assemblies.

Thus, when the bishop returned from Europe, he had several motives for throwing himself into the agitation of the school question. In the first place, he was profoundly sensible of the importance of the issue; in the second, he was conscious that the Church was in danger of becoming embroiled in political squabbles from which he must at all events preserve her; and finally, it was not in his character to let his people go out to fight, in any good cause, without their bishop at their head.

A meeting had been summoned for the 20th of July, the second day after his return. He resolved to lose no time in putting things on a right footing. He attended the meeting; "and the first thing I did," said he, "was to take measures that all politics should be excluded." First, he requested the chairman, Dr. Power, to explain the origin of the movement, as I have told it; then, amid tumultuous applause, he rose to address the meeting. No one can read the long speech which he then delivered, imperfectly as it was reported, without being struck by the adroitness with which he quickly assumed the entire direction of affairs. He began by expressing his gratification at finding reason to believe that a higher and holier feeling than mere politics was the soul of this agitation; he dreaded political feelings as most destructive of internal peace, and of that calmness of mind which disposes a man either for just judgment or the discharge of his religious obligations; he came to the meeting because he believed that the question which brought the Catholics together was infinitely above any thing that could be found in politics. And so he went on, assuming that the meeting was all that he wished it to be, and the people applauded every thing he said. So far as the populace and the clergy were concerned, he had no ill-will nor opposition to fear; but we can imagine that there were others who listened to him with less satisfaction.

He observed that had not the matter of the public schools been taken up during his absence, he should himself have called attention to it before he had been at home three weeks; he had already given thought to the question; he had examined some of the school-books; he had consulted the clergy as to the influence of the schools upon the faith of Catholic pupils. He then discussed the whole question of the Catholic claims; and when he sat down, it was plain enough to everybody that he had taken the matter into his own hands, and meant to keep it in them. Once after this (and I believe only once) the discussion assumed for a moment a political character. The bishop immediately arose. "Politics," said he, "must not be introduced: first, for the perhaps insignificant reason that if they be introduced I disappear from amongst you; and secondly, for the very important one that your prospects would thereby be defeated. . . . If you have any regard, then, for my feelings or your own interests, do not introduce politics. We do not meet for political purposes. I defy our enemies or our friends to show that one word of politics was ever tolerated in our meetings. . . . I trust, therefore, that it will be after I have received notice to retire that politics will be introduced."

The agitation was kept up by meetings every fortnight in the basement of St. James's church. The bishop always spoke, and generally at great length. The Catholics were delighted with their leader. The assemblies were crowded and enthusiastic. On the 10th of August an "Address of the Roman Catholics to their Fellow-Citizens of the City and State of New York," written by the bishop, was read, and adopted by acclamation. It contained the following statement of the reasons of their opposition to the public schools:

Besides the introduction of the Holy Scriptures without note or comment, with the prevailing theory that from these even children are to get their notions of religion, contrary to our principles, there were in the class-books of those schools false (as we believe) historical statements respecting the men and things of past times, calculated to fill the minds of our children with errors of fact, and at the same time to excite in them prejudice against the religion of their parents and guardians. These passages were not considered as sectarian, inasmuch as they had been selected as mere reading lessons, and were not in *favor* of any particular sect, but merely *against* the Catholics. We feel it is unjust that such passages should be taught at all in schools, to the support of which we are contributors as well as others. But that such books should be put into the hands of *our own* children, and that in part at our own expense, was in our opinion unjust, unnatural, and at all events to us intolerable. Accordingly, through very great additional sacrifices, we have been obliged to provide schools, under our churches and elsewhere, in which to educate our children as our conscientious duty required. This we have done to the number of some thousands for several years past, during all of which time we have been obliged to pay taxes; and we feel it unjust and oppressive that while we educate our children, as well we contend as they would be at the public schools, we are denied our portion of the school fund, simply because we at the same time endeavor to train them up in principles of virtue and religion. This we feel to be unjust and unequal. For we pay taxes in proportion to our numbers, as other citizens. We are supposed to be from one hundred and fifty to two hundred thousand in the State. And although most of us are poor, still the poorest man among us is obliged to pay taxes, from the sweat of his brow, in the rent of his room or little tenement. Is it not, then, hard and unjust that such a man cannot have the benefit of education for his child without sacrificing the rights of his religion and conscience? He sends his child to a school under the protection of his Church, in which these rights will be secure. But he has to support this school also. In Ireland he was compelled to support a church hostile to his religion, and here he is compelled to support schools in which his religion fares but little better, and to support his own school besides.

Is this state of things, fellow-citizens, and especially Americans, is this state of things worthy of *you*, worthy of our country, worthy of our just and glorious constitution? Put yourself in the poor man's place, and say whether you would not despise him if he did not labor by every lawful means to emancipate himself from this bondage. He has to pay double taxation for the education of his child, one to the misinterpreted law of the land, and another to his conscience. He sees his child going to school with perhaps only the fragment of a worn-out book, thinly clad, and its bare feet on the frozen pavement; whereas, if he had his rights he could improve the clothing, he could get better books, and have his child better taught than it is possible in actual circumstances.

Nothing can be more false than some statements of our motives which have been put forth against us.

It has been asserted that we seek our share of the school funds for the support and advance of our religion.

We beg to assure you with respect, that we would scorn to support or advance our religion at any other than our own expense. But we are unwilling to pay taxes for the purpose of destroying our religion in the minds of our children. This points out the sole difference between what we seek and what some narrow-minded or misinformed journals have accused us of seeking.

If the public schools could have been constituted on a principle which would have secured a perfect NEUTRALITY of influence on the subject of religion, then we should have no reason to complain. But this has not been done, and we respectfully submit that it is impossible. The cold indifference with which it is required that all religion shall be treated in those schools—the Scriptures without note or comment—the selection of passages, as reading lessons, from Protestants and prejudiced authors, on points in which our creed is supposed to be involved—the comments of the teacher, of which the commissioners cannot be cognizant—the school libraries, stuffed with sectarian works against us—form against our religion a combination of influences prejudicial to our religion, and to whose action it would be criminal in us to expose our children at such an age.

This was followed, a few weeks later, by a petition to the Board of Aldermen, also written by the bishop, and adopted at a meeting on the 21st of September. After rehearsing the objections of the Catholics to the public schools, it thus went on :

Your petitioners will now invite the attention of your honorable body to the objections and misrepresentations that have been urged by the Public School Society to granting the claim of your petitioners. It is urged by them that it would be appropriating money raised by general taxation to the support of the Catholic religion. Your petitioners join issue with them, and declare unhesitatingly, that if this objection can be established the claim shall be forthwith abandoned. It is objected that though we are taxed as citizens, we apply for the benefits of education as "Catholics." Your petitioners, to remove this difficulty, beg to be considered in their application in the identical capacity in which they are taxed—viz.: as citizens of the commonwealth. It has been contended by the Public School Society, that the law disqualifies schools which admit any profession of religion from receiving any encouragements from the school fund. Your petitioners have two solutions for this pretended difficulty. 1. Your petitioners are unable to discover any such disqualification in the law, which merely delegates to your honorable body the authority and discretion of determining what schools or societies shall be entitled to its bounty. 2. Your petitioners are willing to fulfil the conditions of the law so far as religious teaching is proscribed during school hours. In fine, your petitioners, to remove all objections, are willing that the material organization of their schools, and the disbursements of the funds allowed for them, shall be conducted, and made, by persons unconnected with the religion of your petitioners, even the Public School Society, if it should please your honorable body to appoint them for that purpose. The public may then be assured that the money will not be applied to the support of the Catholic religion.

It is deemed necessary by your petitioners, to save the Public School Society the necessity of future misconception, thus to state the things which are *not* petitioned for. The members of that Society, who have shown themselves so impressed with the importance of conveying *their* notions of "early religious instruction" to the "susceptible minds" of Catholic children, can have no objection that the parents of the children, and teachers in whom the parents have confidence, should do the same, provided no law is violated thereby, and no disposition evinced to bring the children of other denominations within its influence.

Your petitioners, therefore, pray that your honorable body will be pleased to designate, as among the schools entitled to participate in the common-school fund, upon complying with the requirements of the law, and the ordinances of the corporation of the city— or for such other relief as to your honorable body shall seem meet— St. Patrick's School, St. Peter's School, St. Mary's School, St. Joseph's School, St. James's School, St. Nicholas's School, Transfiguration Church School, and St. John's School.

And your petitioners further request, in the event of your honorable body's determining to hear your petitioners on the subject of their petition, that such time may be appointed as may be most agreeable to your honorable body, and that a full session of your honorable Board be convened for that purpose.

This petition was presented to the Board of Aldermen the same evening. The Public School Society replied by a "Remonstrance," and a committee of pastors of the Methodist Episcopal churches in New York city did the same. Bishop Hughes resolved to speak in support of the petition. "It has been suggested to me," he said, in one of his speeches at St. James's "by a gentleman very deeply interested in the success of this question, that it might not be expedient for me to appear in such a place on such an occasion, for it was possible that some language might be used toward me which, though I might bear it with patience, might be painful to others. I replied that I was willing to give up my own opinion, but at the same time I stated that I had no apprehensions on the subject, either on questions of propriety or any other. I have, however, considered whether I should not there be out of place, and whether even in meetings like the present I am not; but so vital and important do I consider the question, that I conceive I cannot be anywhere more in keeping with my character as a bishop than when I stand before you pleading the cause of the poor and the oppressed. And so near is the question to my heart, that I can bear insult from morning till night. For such a question I may venture to the furthest limits to which propriety will allow a bishop to go."

It had been arranged that in the discussion of the legal points of the question, the bishop should have the assistance of a lawyer; but the gentleman to whom the cause was intrusted was prevented by the bursting of a blood-vessel from attending the debate; so Bishop Hughes had to fight the battle alone. The Public School Society was represented by counsel, namely, Theodore Sedgwick and Hiram

Ketchum; the Methodists by the Rev. Drs. Bond, Bangs, and Reese; the Presbyterians by the Rev. Dr. Spring; and the Reformed Dutch Church by the Rev. Dr. Knox. The public had become greatly excited over the question at issue. On the afternoon appointed for the debate, the City Hall presented a scene to be long remembered. A vast crowd filled and surrounded the council chamber and blocked up the passages, and the speakers had great ado to force their way to the room. The bishop was attended by several priests and prominent Catholic laymen. The assistant aldermen were present by invitation of the upper Board. Proceedings were opened by the reading, first of the petition of the Catholics, and then of the remonstrances of the Public School Society and the Methodists. The Public School Society did little more than reply briefly to the principal points mentioned in the petition; the remonstrance of the Methodists was expressed with a great deal of temper, and bristled with sharp epithets. The bishop then rose, and spoke for three hours. He began by dissecting the two remonstrances. He went through them, sentence by sentence. He proved that all their arguments were either founded on false premises or directed against a false issue. He showed that the fundamental error of the remonstrances was the supposition that the Catholics wanted the public money for the support of their religion—or, as their opponents were fond of saying, for "sectarian purposes." This was an error which had already been anticipated and answered in the petition of the Catholics. "It is objected," said the bishop in that paper, "that though we are taxed as citizens, we apply for the benefits of education as 'Catholics.' Your petitioners, to remove this difficulty, beg to be considered in their application in the identical capacity in which they are taxed, viz.: as citizens of the commonwealth. It has been contended by the Public School Society, that the law disqualifies schools which admit any profession of religion from receiving any encouragements from the school fund. Your petitioners have two solutions for this pretended difficulty. First: Your petitioners are unable to discover any such disqualification in the law, which merely delegates to your honorable body the authority and discretion of determining what schools or societies shall be entitled to its bounty. Secondly: Your petitioners are willing to fulfil the conditions of the law so far as religious teaching is proscribed during school hours. In fine, your petitioners, to remove all objections, are willing that the material organization of their schools, and the disbursements of the funds allowed for them, shall be conducted and made by persons unconnected with the religion of your petitioners, even the Public School Society, if it should please your honorable body to appoint them for that purpose. The public may then be assured that the money will not be applied to the support of the Catholic religion."

The legal part of the question—that is to say, whether the Common Council had or had not the power to grant the petition of the Catholics—he touched very slightly. His whole speech, in fact, was rather a refutation than an argument. He felt that the work before him was simply to overcome the prejudices of his listeners and to answer the misrepresentations of his adversaries. He had only to explain the true meaning of what he asked: the right to grant it seemed to him too clear for dispute. And besides, I think there was another reason why he gave so many words to the intrinsic equity of the Catholic claim, and so few to the constitutional lawfulness of granting it. He had no expectation of succeeding with the Board of Aldermen; right or wrong, he felt certain that they would decide against him—for this reason perhaps, among others, that they were *ex officiis* members of that very Public School Society against which he was fighting. He went before them only as a preliminary step to going before the Legislature. He was more anxious therefore to disabuse the public mind of false impressions respecting the purpose of this Catholic movement, than to defeat the ministers and lawyers who had come here to meet him.

Mr. Sedgwick, who followed Bishop Hughes, spoke chiefly to the question of the law. He traced briefly the history of the common-school system of the State and city of New York; alluded to the Bethel church affair, which led the Common Council to petition the Legislature for a change in the school law, so as to deprive religious societies of the control of any portion of the public money; and argued that the act of 1824, which was passed in consequence of this petition, and which empowered the corporation to designate from time to time "the institutions or schools which should be entitled to receive the school moneys," was expressly intended to remove from the corporation "the right or authority to apportion the fund among religious societies." He attempted, moreover, to show that the objections of the Catholics to the public schools were not well taken, and that the system of purely secular education which the School Society professed to impart was a sound one. His speech—if correctly reported—was in the main temperate and dignified. I cannot give the same praise to the argument of his colleague Mr. Ketchum, who spoke of the bishop as "the mitred gentleman," and rebuked him for "descending into the arena" (as he called it), and "appealing to the popular prejudice or passion to influence the judgment of the board." His whole speech was devoted to the defence of the Public School Society. The bishop replied very briefly, and the board then adjourned to the next afternoon.

On Friday, the 30th, the debate was resumed. The public excitement was greater than it had been the day before. Many prominent clergymen, Catholic and Protestant, were present as spectators. The first speaker was Dr. Bond, of the Methodist Episcopal Church. He was followed by David Reese, M. D., a preacher of the same denomination; Dr. Knox, of the Reformed Dutch Church; Dr. Bangs, Methodist; and Dr. Spring, Presbyterian. The privilege of closing the debate was granted to Bishop Hughes, with the understanding that he should restrict himself to answering the arguments of those that had gone before him: if he introduced any new matter, the remonstrants were to be allowed to reply. The discussion took a still wider range than on the previous day. However anxious the bishop may have been to keep close to the point, he could not do so, for his opponents dragged him over nearly the whole field of Catholic and Protestant controversy. He spoke for three hours and a half. Mr. Ketchum claimed the privilege of answering certain points of his speech, but he was soon called to order by the chairman, and the debate was declared closed. The Catholic petition was referred to a committee of aldermen, in whose custody it slumbered for ten weeks. During this interval the Public School Society were not idle. They first proposed terms of accommodation, offering to submit their school-books to the bishop, and allow him to expurgate them. But the bishop doubted their good faith. "As if," said he, "we have nothing to do but to mark out a passage, and it will disappear! Are we to take the odium of erasing passages which you hold to be true? And have you any right to make such an offer? If we spend the necessary time in reviewing the books to discover offensive passages, you give us no pledge that you will even then remove the objectionable matter. After all our trouble, you may remove it or not as you see fit. And even if you should remove it, another board of officers may succeed you to-morrow and restore every thing that you have marked out." The Society next offered to buy from the Catholics the only school-house which their humble means had permitted them to build; but this proposition of course was not entertained.

On the other hand, the Catholics promised, if they were allowed a share of the school money, to appoint no teachers except such as, after examination by a committee of the Public School Society, should be pronounced fully qualified; to give any authorized agent or officer of the State or city government all facilities for inspecting their schools, teachers, books, and system of education at all times; to conform rigidly to the requirements of any and every law of the State, or ordinance of the Common Council, designed to correct or prevent abuses in the matter of common-school education; to organize and conduct their schools after the same plan as that pursued by the Public School Society; to teach no dogma during school hours; and finally, to teach nothing against the creed of any other denomination. It soon became evident, however, that no compromise or agreement was possible.

On the 12th of January, 1841, the committee reported adversely to the prayer of the petitioners, and their report was adopted by the Board with only one dissenting voice.

The bishop afterward acknowledged very frankly the personal courtesy with which he was generally treated during this affair; but he spoke bitterly of the character of the discussion. "Was there a single inquiry," said he, "respecting the truth of our alleged grievances, or any attempt to redress them? No; but the Rev. Dr. Spring, and the Rev. Dr. Bond, and the Rev. Dr. Bangs and company, came with an old volume of antiquated theology, and exclaimed, 'What monstrous people these papists are!' The Common Council heard them; and instead of examining the facts in which the rights of their constituents are involved, entered on the consideration of abstract theological reasoning. Eight or nine hours were wasted in the discussion of a theological tenet, but not one half hour was given to the only questions which the Common Council should have permitted to come before them—namely: Are the rights of this portion of the citizens violated or not? If so, is there in our hands the means to apply a remedy?"

The Catholics now looked to the bishop for the signal for further action; and when he summoned them to assemble at Washington Hall on the 11th of February, the largest meeting came together that had ever yet been convened on the subject of the school question. His appearance on the platform was greeted with tumultuous cheering. "My friends," said he, "take care of your cheering, for if the advocate of the School Society be passing by, he will say this is a meeting of whigs and democrats. You know he is not obliged to reason like ordinary men!" He gave a humorous review of the course of the controversy up to that time, and besprinkled his speech with many sprightly illustrations and an Irish anecdote. "And now," he continued, "what remains for us to do? We must not fold our arms and rest. We must take measures. I trust that no such defeat as we have experienced—the defeat of justice by authority—will make you give up your principles. Spread it abroad that you ask no favor, no preëminence, no boon, from their honors of the Common Council; but that you have rights, and these rights you claim. Let them reserve their favors for those who want them." He entered into some details respecting their future course of action, and recommended the appointment of a committee to present a memorial to the Legislature. In the mean time, he resolved to continue the public meetings.

The memorial was duly presented, and was referred by the Senate to the Hon. John C. Spencer, secretary of state, and ex-officio superintendent of public schools, who made a report on the 26th of April, recommending a complete change in the school system of New York city. The plan which he suggested comprehended the election of a commissioner of public schools in each ward of the city; the extension to the city of the general school laws of the State; and the transfer to the commissioners of the powers then exercised by the Public School Society. The public money was to be paid directly to the commissioners, and applied by them to the support of the schools under their jurisdiction. This was an improvement upon the system actually in vogue. Education would no longer be under the management of a close corporation; and Catholics might hope, by their vote at the polls, to keep sectarianism out of the school-rooms, if to do nothing more. The bishop accordingly supported the measure; although, as we shall see hereafter, he considered the whole system of "Godless education" radically unsound. Circumstances, in fact, had placed him in the curious position of an advocate of a class of schools which he could not approve, and which he some years afterward denounced. But Mr. Spencer's plan might answer until the Catholics were rich enough to have schools of their own. At any rate, it was useless to expect any thing better at that time.

It was during the agitation of the school question that the bishop formed an intimacy with Governor Seward which lasted for life. He had been introduced to the governor on a railway train, during one of his episcopal visitations in the western part of the State. Mr. Seward, by his position on the school question, was brought into frequent communication with Dr. Hughes, and throughout the discussion the bishop and the governor were in friendly correspondence with each other. Mr. Thurlow Weed was another distinguished politician with whom this school controversy brought Bishop Hughes into lasting relations of familiarity. It was from this time also, notwithstanding the straightforward, determined, and honorable course which we have seen that he adopted on his first appearance at the meetings of the Catholic Association, that the attempt was made to fasten upon him the character of a political intriguer. It was of all characters the very furthest from the truth, yet with a certain class of people he never lost it. He tells an amusing incident showing how persistently and absurdly his actions were misinterpreted. "It was my duty," he says, "on the day succeeding the debate before the Common Council, to proceed to Albany, for the purpose of giving confirmation. I went—preached three times next day, Sunday. On Monday, a very stormy day, I drove to Troy, for the purpose of visiting the churches there; and on Tuesday I returned to New York. Well, what was the story? Why, it was said that I having taken tea with the aldermen, a bargain was struck between us, and I was to go to Albany to get the Catholics to vote against the governor, and then all would be right!"

The Public School Society followed the Catholics to Albany, and the Senate appointed a committee to hear the arguments of both parties on the 8th of May. The petitioners were represented by James W. McKeon and Wright Hawkes; the remonstrants by Hiram Ketchum. About a month afterward a full report of Mr. Ketchum's argument was published in a New York paper. As the Catholics had not taken the precaution to have the speeches of the advocates on their side preserved, the bishop gave notice that he would undertake, at Carroll Hall, an oral "review and refutation" of the remonstrance of the Society and the argument of Mr. Ketchum. He devoted to this task the evenings of the 16th, 17th, and 21st of June, speaking before a large assemblage of people, among whom were Lieutenant-Governor Luther Bradish and a number of the state senators. His speeches were printed in *The Freeman's Journal*, and afterward published in a pamphlet. Mr. Ketchum replied through the columns of a city newspaper, and the bishop wrote for *The Freeman's Journal* a "review" of his opponent's "rejoinder."

Within the purlieus of the Senate chamber the school question was agitated with much animosity. The adversaries of Mr. Spencer's project had no scruple in appealing to the religious prejudices of the Protestant public, although that project had placed the school question in a position where it would seem that religious considerations could have nothing to do with it. The question had been made the special order for a certain day in May. On the previous day the New York *Journal of Commerce* published an article full of threadbare calumnies against the Catholic faith, and containing, among other choice morsels, the famous mock "bull of excommunication" from "Tristram Shandy." The agent of the Public School Society in Albany, just before the debate was expected to open, placed on the desk of each senator a copy of this paper, with the article I have referred to marked.

The Senate seems to have been unwilling to take the responsibility of deciding a question upon which feeling ran so high, for in the course of that month (May) they voted to postpone it to January, 1842, before which time there would be a new election for members of the Legislature, and so the determination of the dispute might be referred directly to the people.

The short interval of rest which followed this postponement was employed by the bishop in a visitation of his diocese. He started in the early part of August, and spent seven weeks in traversing the northern and western portions of the State, preaching every day when he was not actually travelling, and sometimes three times a day, organizing new congregations, and administering confirmation in ten or twelve parishes. He returned to New York about the end of September, ready to carry on the school-battle with more determination than ever. His opponents had made every preparation for an active campaign. The election was to take place at the beginning of November. A paper was established in the interest of the Public School Society, calling upon Protestant voters to be careful, even in their primary meetings, to nominate none but those pledged to oppose the Catholic claims. The religious newspapers were filled with political homilies to the same effect; and even some of the Protestant pulpits rang with denunciations of the bishop and defence of the public schools. If, therefore, the Catholics of New York, for the first and only time, seemed to mingle their religion with their politics, they were compelled to do so by their adversaries. "My position in this matter," said the bishop, "is a peculiar one. I stand alone and isolated in a degree; obliged, as it were, to step partially aside from the direct line of my sacred calling, and appear before my people on this subject. I have found myself imperatively called upon to take the position which I have assumed for the protection of the religious rights of those intrusted to my charge." A meeting of the Church Debt Association was to be held at

Carroll Hall about a week before the election. He took that opportunity to warn the Catholics that there was danger their cause might be lost unless they disregarded all party ties and gave their votes to the friends of the new school system, and to them only. "I have pleaded the cause of the destitute and oppressed children before the aldermen of this city," said he; "I have supported it in another form before the senators of the State; I have now to plead for it before the Catholics themselves. For the time has now come when it is necessary to learn their sentiments, and to know whether they are willing to vote for or against it. The question to be decided is not the strength of party or the emolument and patronage of office, but a question between the helpless and ill-used children and the Public School Society. . . . . An issue is made up between you and a large portion of the community on the one side, and that monopoly which instils the dangerous principles to which I have before alluded on the other. The question lies between the two parties, and you are the judges; if you desert the cause, what can you expect from strangers? . . . . . I have been given to understand that three out of four of the candidates presented to your suffrages are pledged to oppose your claims. They may perhaps triumph; but all I ask is, that they shall not triumph by the sinful aid of any individual who cherishes a feeling in common with those children. I wish you, therefore, to look well to your candidates; and if they are disposed to make infidels or Protestants of your children, let them receive no vote of yours."

In fact, it was ascertained that with two or three exceptions all the candidates then in the field, of whichever party, had pledged themselves to vote against any change in the school system. The bishop was urged by some of his people to recommend the formation of an independent ticket upon which the Catholics might throw away their vote, since Whigs and Locofocos were equally hostile to them. He consented; and on the 29th of October, four days before the election, a general meeting of Catholics was summoned at Carroll Hall. An independent ticket for senators and assemblymen, including the names of the few candidates already before the public who were understood to have refused to sign the pledge required by the School Society, and others taken from among the Catholics themselves, was then proposed, and received with a tumult of acclamations. "I am not acquainted," said the bishop, in his address in support of the nominations, "with any of these individuals; but they have been selected by gentlemen as much interested in this question as I am; and now if you are unanimously determined to convince this community that you are in earnest—that you sincerely feel that there is a *bonâ fide* grievance of which you complain, you will support the candidates thus offered for your choice; because if you do not, you have no alternative left but that of voting for the declared enemies of your rights. . . . . You have often voted for others and they did not vote for you, but now you are determined to uphold with your own votes your own rights. Will you then stand by the rights of your offspring, who have so long suffered under the operation of this injurious system?"

He was answered by loud cheering. "Will you adhere to the nomination made?"

"We will! we will!"

"Will you be united?"

At this the whole assembly rose to their feet, waving their hats, cheering, shouting, and testifying their satisfaction with every possible emphasis.

"Will you let all men see that you are worthy sons of the nation to which you belong?"

"Never fear—we will!" "We will till death!"

"Will you prove yourselves worthy of friends?"

Loud cheers.

"*Will none of you flinch?*"

The excitement which followed this last question is said to have been indescribable. The cheers and shouts, the stamping of feet, the waving of hats and handkerchiefs, were such as even an Irish assemblage in its most enthusiastic moments seldom gives way to. It was some time before the speaker could go on.

"I care not for party men. Bring them to the test, and you find great promises, lean performances. It is time that you should convince them—perhaps for the first time—that you are not the pliant body they mistake you to be. You will have nothing to do with the men who go to the Senate and Assembly pledged to act against you?"

"No, no, no! That we won't!"

"They may find votes enough to send them——"

"No, they sha'n't!"

"Let them go. But they will, in that case, be obliged to confess that they were sent by your enemies. I ask then, once for all—and with the answer let the meeting close—will this meeting pledge its honor, as the representative of that oppressed portion of our community for whom I have so often pleaded, here as well as elsewhere—will it pledge its honor that it will stand by these candidates whose names have been read, and that no man composing this vast audience will ever vote for any one pledged to oppose our just claims and incontrovertible rights?"

There was no possibility of mistaking the answer to this question. The applause was long and furious. Silence was at last restored; the nominations were ratified by acclamation; and the meeting then dispersed without the slightest disorder.

Naturally enough, the bishop's conduct horrified both the friends of the School Society and the old-fashioned sticklers for "propriety," who seemed to think that an ecclesiastic had no business anywhere outside of the sanctuary. A few Catholics even blamed him; but to the bulk of his people his conduct had forever endeared him. At this time he probably had more influence over the Irish population of New York than any man, in the Church or out of it, had ever possessed before, or has ever held since. The people felt that he was one with them—not only their bishop, but their friend; that his sacred office had not raised him above an affectionate interest in their general welfare, or rendered him either unable or unwilling to meet their worldly as well as their spiritual adversaries. They learned to look up to him for direction not only in affairs of the soul, but in those dubious questions which belong half to this world and half to the next. He did not always answer them. He was always cautious of intermeddling with matters that did not belong properly to his ecclesiastical office; but when he did speak, he spoke to some purpose. He was obeyed, when another bishop would not have been heard. And three years afterward, during the Native American excitement, the influence which he had acquired by means of the school controversy saved New York from a bloody riot.

Among the newspapers which attacked the bishop most violently for his Carroll Hall speech was *The New York Herald*, in which appeared on the 30th of October a garbled report of the address, together with editorial comments. These are not worth reproducing, nor would the matter be worth mentioning except for the sharp controversy between the bishop and Mr. James Gordon Bennett, which afterward grew out of it.* Bishop Hughes was sensitive to newspaper criticism, and he looked upon the *Herald* of this date as "the fountain of all the vituperation, calumny, and slander" which were poured out upon him for many years. Certainly, from 1840 to 1844, he was one of the best abused men in the country.

The election took place the first week in November. The bishop's manœuvre was perfectly successful. The independent candidates polled 2,200 votes; not enough, of course, to secure their election—they did not expect to do that—but enough to show that the Catholics were resolved to withhold

---

* See the bishop's letters to Mayor Harper and Col. Stone during the Native American excitement in 1844.

their assistance from every party which denied them justice Although small in comparison with the number of Catholic voters, the vote was a large one if we consider that it was cast only *pro formâ*, and that the ticket had been only four days before the public.

Governor Seward, who had been abused almost as much as the bishop for his views on the school question, and had narrowly escaped a defeat in the election for governor the preceding year in consequence of his support of the Catholic claims, wrote to Bishop Hughes a few days after the events just mentioned:

I thank you very sincerely for your kind letter of the 8th, and am exceedingly gratified in learning that you bear with true philosophy the buffetings of the short-sighted leaders of faction. I have no concern for your ultimate vindication. It is your fortune as well as mine that philanthropic conceptions for the improvement of society come in conflict with existing interests founded in existing prejudices. . . . . I have noticed several very gratifying indications of a determination among your people to vindicate and sustain you. If this should be the case, you will see henceforth a rapid transition among the people at large. The session of the Legislature approaches. I will say to you with all freedom, that I propose to reassert my opinions and principles with firmness, and to submit the subject of the educational system to the direct action of the Legislature. May I not hope that your concern on that great subject will induce you to accede to my wishes by making me a brief visit before the close of navigation ! Do not say nay.

It was partly on account of the dissatisfaction expressed by a few Catholics with the bishop's conduct, that a meeting was held at Washington Hall on the 16th of November, and an address was prepared and signed by the most prominent Catholic laymen of New York, conveying " a direct and earnest expression of their unwavering confidence in his zeal, judgment, and acknowledged ability," and testifying " to the respect which his fearless, independent, and judicious course in relation to the subject of education had excited in their minds." When this meeting was held the bishop was in Philadelphia, where he delivered a lecture on "The Life and Times of Pius VII.," before the Mercantile Library Association, on the 12th, and assisted Bishop Kenrick in the consecration of the Right Rev. Paul Lefevre as Bishop of Zeela, and administrator of the diocese of Detroit, on the 21st. As soon as he returned to New York he prepared a "Reply" to the address, briefly defending and explaining his conduct.

Governor Seward did not forget his promise of urging the school question upon the notice of the new Legislature in January, 1842. "The most gratifying indications," he wrote to the bishop, soon after the opening of the session, "present themselves on every side." Politicians began to be alarmed. The Locofoco party, which had so long counted with confidence upon the Irish vote, awoke to the wholesome conviction that the Catholics would not support them unless they deserved support. Many people no doubt believed in the fiction circulated by the *Herald*, that Bishop Hughes was attempting "to organize the Irish Catholics of New York as a distinct party that could be given to the Whigs or Locofocos at the wave of his crosier."

A bill embracing the principal features of Mr. Spencer's plan was introduced into the Assembly early in the year by the Hon. Mr. Maclay, a member from New York city. It was drawn up after frequent conferences with the bishop and the governor, and also with Mr. Thurlow Weed and Mr. Horace Greeley. The bishop, as I have already said, was far from believing that any form of common-school education from which positive religious teaching was excluded could be a good one; but almost any change from the system of the Public School Society would be for the better. He accordingly assented to Mr. Maclay's "Bill to extend to the city and county of New York the provisions of the general act in relation to Common Schools." It provided for the election annually of two commissioners, two inspectors, and five trustees of the common schools in each ward of the city, who should enjoy the same powers and have the same duties as similar officers in other parts of the State, and should constitute a Board of Education for the city of New York. No school which should teach any religious sectarian doctrine was to receive any money from the common school fund. There was not much difficulty in carrying this bill through the Assembly, which it passed in March by the decisive vote of sixty-five to sixteen. In the Senate it encountered more opposition. Fortunately, an election for mayor and other municipal officers was about to take place in New York. Parties were very nearly balanced, and the Catholics determined to resort to the same tactics which they had practised so successfully in the previous November. They again nominated an independent ticket, proposing for mayor Mr. Thomas O'Connor, a Catholic gentleman who had acted as chairman at nearly all the meetings on the school question in St. James's church, Carroll Hall, and elsewhere. The bill accordingly passed the Senate on the 9th of April, three days before the election; and on the 11th the Catholic candidates withdrew from the contest.

During the election a riot occurred at the polls in the Sixth ward, and in the midst of the disturbance a voice called out to the mob to pay a visit to "the political bishop." A party of the rioters accordingly proceeded to the bishop's house in Mulberry street, about eight o'clock in the evening, threw brick-bats and paving stones at the doors and windows, broke a few panes of glass, and then fled. The bishop was not at home at the time. "I am glad to hear," writes Governor Seward, "that you excuse the outbreak of passion which occurred at the close of the election, and I regret that your generosity on that subject cannot yet be appreciated. I agree with you in regarding the passage of Mr. Maclay's bill as fortunate; since, notwithstanding the ill grace with which that measure was adopted, and the offensive and grudging spirit which marks it, the proceeding is an acknowledgment of the vices of the old system, and its unequal operation. It is, perhaps, not unfortunate that the bill has, quite unnecessarily, been rendered so obnoxious that the public attention will still be directed to the subject. Every stage in the history of this strange controversy increases the strength of those who demand reform, and the weakness of those who cling to error, lest the good connected with it may be lost."

The ward schools established under the provisions of the new act took the place of those formerly controlled by the Public School Society; and the Society itself, a few years afterward, having made over its effects to the city authorities, quietly went out of existence.

So ended Bishop Hughes's famous contest with the Public School Society. It had lasted two years. Though it was by no means his most signal service to the Church, it was what chiefly made his reputation. It was only partially a victory. It utterly overthrew the rich and powerful Public School Society, but it left the Catholic schools as poor as they were before; it left untouched the fundamental vice of the system of State instruction—education without religion; and if it was the means of driving sectarianism out of the common schools for a time, it secured no guarantee that sectarianism should be kept out of them—and in point of fact it was soon introduced again. The bishop himself was conscious that he had not succeeded. Ceasing from further opposition, because he saw that it would be useless, he exerted himself to establish a system of Catholic education in the diocese, hoping that his people would soon be able to withdraw their children entirely from the public schools. He exhorted his priests to spare no labor in founding parish schools, and in 1853 he called a meeting of all the clergy of New York and Brooklyn in the sacristy of the cathedral, in which he read an address, urging them to increased zeal in " diffusing true education among the children of the flock " over which they were placed as pastors.

During his visit to Ireland in 1840 he had seen some of the schools conducted by the "Christian Brothers," and had been very much pleased with them. He determined, if possible, to bring a community of the brethren to New York; and in May, 1841, while he was in the midst of his contest before the Legislature, he sent the Rev. Andrew Byrne (afterward Bishop of Little Rock) to Europe to make the necessary arrangements. The brethren, however, were few; their services were much valued in Ireland; and the negotiations were not successful.

The seminary was removed from Lafargeville to Fordham in the autumn of 1840, and the college was opened in June, 1841.* The former institution was placed under the patronage of St. Joseph, the latter under that of St. John the Baptist. The seminarians occupied at first a small stone dwelling-house west of the college. The large building afterward used for a seminary, and the church adjoining it, were begun in 1845. The bishop not only labored and begged indefatigably to raise money for the foundation and support of St. Joseph's, but also devoted to that institution a considerable part of his own salary.

In the spring of 1841 a little community of Ladies of the Sacred Heart, whom he had engaged during his late visit to France, arrived in New York and founded their school for girls, which has since become so celebrated. They were under the direction of Madame Elizabeth Galitzin—a Russian princess, and cousin of the Prince Demetrius Augustine Galitzin, who was so long a missionary in the Alleghany moun-

---

* The first officers of the college were: President, and Professor of Rhetoric and Belles Lettres, Rev. John McCloskey (now Archbishop of New York); Vice-President, and Professor of Greek and Mathematics, Rev. Ambrose Manahan, D. D.; Professor of Moral Philosophy and Hebrew, Rev. Felix Vilanis, D. D.; Treasurer, and Professor of Natural Philosophy and Chemistry, Rev. Edward O'Neill; Professor of Spanish, Rev. Bernard A. Llaneza; Professor of Latin, Mr. John J. Conroy (now Bishop elect of Albany); Prefect of Discipline and Professor of Bookkeeping, Mr. John Harley; Professor of German, Mr. Oertel; Professor of French, Mr. McDonald; beside six tutors.

tains. Madame Galitzin was born at St. Petersburg in 1795, became a convert to the Roman Catholic Church at the age of twenty, and was received into the community of the Sacred Heart at Metz in 1826. She was for several years "visitor" of the houses of the Sacred Heart in America, founded a number of schools and a mission among the Potawatamie Indians, and died in the odor of sanctity at St. Michael, La., December 8th, 1843.

CHAPTER XV.

1841-1844.

The Church Debt Association—First diocesan synod—Controversy with David Hale—Difficulty with the trustees of St. Louis' church, Buffalo—Rules for the administration of churches without trustees—Visitation of the diocese—Visit to Europe for the purpose of raising money—Odd mistake of an English officer—Incident at Liverpool—The *Emprunt Catholique de New York*—Lectures in New York—Bishop McCloskey appointed coadjutor.

NEXT to the subject of education, the pecuniary affairs of the city churches seem to have caused the bishop the greatest anxiety. I have already said that the diocese was overloaded with debt. The Catholic population had increased with extraordinary rapidity, but the increase had been chiefly by the arrival of poor immigrants, who added very little to the revenue. For these poor people new churches had to be built on credit. It was all the congregations could do to pay the interest on their debt, and the more numerous the Catholics became, the poorer they found themselves. In 1841 there were ten churches in New York city, the aggregate debt on which was about $300,000. The annual interest on the debt was $20,000, or almost enough to build a new church every year. At that time $20,000 was a heavy sum for the Catholics to pay.

The burden, however, was by no means equally divided. One or two congregations were in comparatively prosperous case; others, like that of St. Peter's, were on the verge of ruin; the heaviest load of course rested upon the weakest shoulders. Now it occurred to the bishop that if he could bring the 60,000 or 80,000 Catholics of New York city to regard themselves as one great congregation having an equal interest in all the ten churches, they might with a little systematic effort pay off the whole debt in a very few years. He spoke of the matter at some of the meetings in Carroll Hall on the subject of the common schools in March and April, 1841, and his views were favorably received. He assembled his clergy, and obtained from them a written pledge to support his plan. On the 3d of May, 1841, he called a general meeting of Catholics at Carroll Hall for the purpose of explaining his project, and organizing a "Church Debt Association." He proposed that the pastor of every congregation which chose to take part in the work should appoint collectors to visit if possible every Catholic in the parish once a month, and receive subscriptions. All the money collected should be paid over by the pastor to the bishop; and once in three months the whole amount received during the previous quarter should be divided equally among the churches which had contributed; it being understood that this money was to be applied for the purpose of diminishing the principal of their debt, and for no other purpose whatever. It might be objected that it would be unwise or unfair to give an equal share to each church, whatever the amount of its debt; but, said the bishop, "suppose that there are ten churches to derive benefit from the fund; then the first division of money may pay the debt of one, and accordingly on the next periodical division of the funds the share of that one will be distributed over the others. The people of the church thus freed from debt do not cease to contribute to the funds of the association. Their honor is pledged that they will continue to contribute until all the debts of all the churches are paid."

The rules which the bishop proposed for the government of this association provided for public meetings at short intervals for the examination of accounts, so that the smallest misappropriation of money by any of the officers, from himself as president down to the collectors, might be readily detected. No objection was made to any part of his plan. The people entered into it with great zeal, and about $2,500 was collected before the meeting broke up.

TO MR. FRENAYE.

May 17, 1841.

. . . . .

I think you are mistaken about the plan. The churches that are built are in fact to pay their own debts; but this would prevent the people from contributing if those debts were left out. I do not by any means assume the debt of $300,000. It remains as before. But this means will stimulate the people, pew-holders and all, to labor for its extinction. Even to reduce it until it shall leave the churches out of danger, and thus take away a pretext for not giving to other things, will be a great deal. Besides, this *unites* them all. And it will be by its organization a valuable means for other purposes: the scaffolding is almost as important as the edifice. There is no danger of their zeal abating from this cause, for the supply of the wants of the people will always furnish enough for its exercise. The regulation in St. Peter's is poor enough; but the fact is that whilst there is space, and even empty pews, in the galleries, there are many who would prefer crowding the aisles of the church. Why should this be, after all!

The thing is exceedingly popular. Not a murmur. It will do something.

Yours as ever in Christ,

✠ JOHN HUGHES, *Bishop, etc.*

Seven out of the ten churches joined the association— the three which held aloof being the German churches of St. Nicholas and St. John the Baptist, and the new church of St. John the Evangelist, which was not quite finished when the society was organized. In the course of a year the sum of $17,000 was collected, and the expenses during the same period were but little over $300. If the work could have been carried on with the same energy with which it was begun, the debt might easily have been paid in nine or ten years, and Bishop Hughes would perhaps have left a reputation which he was far from deserving—that of a great financier. But the zeal of the people soon grew cold; the churches which stood most in need of assistance were the most negligent; and the others were not disposed to help those who would not help themselves. At the end of the year the association was accordingly abandoned.

The bishop's next efforts at reform were more successful. They were bent toward matters more or less closely connected with church discipline; and whereas we have seen him thus far looking to the people for support, we now find him, almost for the first time, asking the coöperation and moral assistance of his clergy. On the 29th of August he convoked the first synod ever held in the diocese. The clergy met at the cathedral, after having spent the previous week in spiritual exercises at St. John's college. The synod lasted three days, and enacted several important regulations proposed by the bishop, with a view of assimilating the discipline and customs of the diocese as far as possible to the decrees of the Council of Trent. He frankly told his brethren of the clergy that "these statutes were such as it was competent for the bishop to enact by his own sacred office, from which, in fact, their force was exclusively derived;" but he felt bound "to avail himself of their experience and knowledge of the circumstances of the different congregations over which they were placed, before he should enact any disciplinary statutes that might be in violent conflict with those circumstances, or might be premature and too difficult to be executed." It does not appear that objection was made to any measure which he suggested.

The first enactments related to the administration of the sacraments, and especially of matrimony. In order both to guard against bigamy, and to give the parties ample time to prepare themselves for the holy state of wedlock, the clergy were forbidden under severe penalties to perform any marriage of which notice should not have been given at least four days previous,* and were moreover required to exact proof that the candidates were not impeded by previous ties from entering into the married state.

"Secret societies" were severely denounced, and priests were forbidden to admit members of them to any of the sacraments, or to officiate at their funerals. It was generally supposed by Protestants that the bishop aimed this regulation at the Freemasons, Odd Fellows, and kindred associations. He afterward explained that these had not been in his mind at the time; he referred chiefly to the famous Irish societies of "Corkonians" and "Connaught men," or "Far-ups" and "Far-downs," whose factional riots and disturbances were then more widely celebrated than they are now. "Three or four years ago, and since," he said, "I had occasion to believe that many poor Catholics, especially when assembled in large bodies on public works, are perverted and marshalled into combinations, bound together by the solemnity of oaths administered to them by some of their more depraved or more designing countrymen. . . . . Both of these societies had most benevolent purposes and beautiful features displayed in the programme of their constitution." The circumstance to which he here alludes as having first called his attention to these associations, was probably a letter from Bishop Bruté, written at Chicago in August, 1838, and giving an account of some horrible disorders among the laborers on the Illinois canal. Bishop Bruté told him how the rival factions shielded their members by perjury from the punishment of their crimes; how with pistol and dagger they compelled the newly arrived emigrants to join their societies and swear fidelity to them; how difficult he found it to persuade these poor men that an oath taken unlawfully or unwillingly was not binding; how the "Corks" and "Fardonians" (as he called them) hated each other so fiercely,

---

* It is no very uncommon thing for a man and woman of the lower class to be married after a single day's acquaintance.

that they would not hear mass under the same roof; and how the Rev. Mr. Shaw, an American priest, who had exerted himself successfully to obtain a reprieve for two Corkonians condemned to be hanged for the murder of a Connaught-man, narrowly escaped being mobbed by the enraged and disappointed "Far-downs." He begged Bishop Hughes to devise some means of deterring the emigrants when they first landed in New York from enrolling themselves in these associations; and also to discover the leaders, who were said to be in New York, and "to find his way to their conscience." This, after some trouble, he seems to have done. "More than a year ago," he says, in 1842, "certain prominent officers of both promised me to abolish every kind of oath or solemn appeal to God, as the tie of membership binding their respective fraternities together. This, I have reason to think, they have observed since then most religiously. But I had occasion to discover further, that in many remote parts of the diocese and country, others who had been initiated previously into the societies still retained their oath, and deluded the unwary into joining those societies by asserting that they had my approbation. Now, this was true so far as the benevolent object of the society was concerned, but utterly false so far as those objects were to be secured by an appeal or an adjuration to the living God. Under these circumstances it became necessary for me . . . . to undeceive them, and to caution others upon this subject."

Finally the synod took into consideration the trustee system, and enacted that thenceforward no body of lay trustees should appoint, retain, or dismiss any person connected with the church—such as sexton, organist, singers, teachers, &c.—against the will of the pastor; that the moneys necessary for the maintenance of the pastors and the support of religion should in no case be withheld if the congregations were able to afford them; that no board of trustees or other lay persons should use the church, chapel, basement, or other portion of grounds or edifices consecrated to religion, for any meeting having a secular or even an ecclesiastical object, without the approval of the pastor; that no board of trustees should vote, expend, or appropriate for contracts any portion of the property they were appointed to administer (except the ordinary current expenses), without the approval of the pastor, nor, in case the sums to be thus expended should exceed $100 in any one year, without the approval of the bishop also. The clergy were required to keep an inventory of church property, and to exhibit annually to the bishop a synopsis of the financial condition of the Church. For this purpose they were to have access whenever necessary to the books of the treasurer and the minutes of all official proceedings of the board of trustees. Should any board of trustees refuse to comply with these statutes, the bishop declared that he "should adopt such measures as the circumstances of each case might require;" but in no event should he "tolerate the presence of a clergyman in any church or congregation in which such refusal should be persevered in."

These statutes were published in a Pastoral Letter, dated September 8th, in which the bishop reviewed the evils of the trustee system at some length. The Catholics themselves hailed the appearance of this document with almost unanimous approbation. The trustees of several churches offered to surrender their trust into his hands, if he wished them to do so—a proposition which he declined; but the secular press assailed the bishop very severely, and waxed warm with indignation at what they deemed his violation of the rights of the Catholic laity, who were on their part quite unconscious of their injuries, and not at all grateful to their self-chosen champions. The bishop published an "Apology" for his pastoral letter, in the form of a letter to "David Hale, Esq., who is a Congregationalist in religion; W. L. Stone, Esq., who is some kind of a Presbyterian; M. M. Noah, Esq., who is a Jew; and the editor (whose name I do not know) of a little paper called *The Aurora*." This led to a controversy with Mr. Hale, the editor of the New York

Journal of Commerce, which extended to three letters on each side. It was characterized, on the bishop's part, by his usual caustic tone.

I have said that the Catholics generally were well pleased with the pastoral letter. All the boards of trustees in the diocese acquiesced, except that of St. Louis' church, Buffalo. When the pastoral letter was published in this church, a meeting of the congregation was held and a committee appointed to draft resolutions, and communicate the sense of the meeting to the bishop. After stating their grounds of objection to the rules for the government of the temporal affairs of the church, they "respectfully declined" to submit to the proposed change, and "most sincerely regretted not to be able to comply with the bishop's *request*." The bishop's reply did not leave them long under the delusion that he had made any *request*. "I read your letter," he says, "with surprise. My pastoral letter was an intimation of an ecclesiastical law which is to be general throughout this diocese. It is not yet in force; but when it will be, I trust it will be of the greatest advantage to the peace of our congregations. . . . . Should it prove otherwise, however, in your judgment, you will have it in your power to resist its execution; and when you do, it will be time enough for me to ascertain what shall be my duty in the case. Should you determine that your church shall not be governed by the general law of the diocese, then we shall claim the privilege of retiring from its walls in peace, and leave you also in peace to govern it as you will. Indeed, we must keep our peace at all events, and charity also."

Having given the trustees a reasonable time for reflection, Bishop Hughes addressed a letter to the pastor of the church on the 28th of January, 1843, enjoining upon him to put in force the obnoxious regulations. "This you will please to do so long as the congregation, or the persons who act as its trustees or managers, shall permit you. But if they shall attempt to put such obstacles as will deprive you of the power of complying with the statutes, then I enjoin upon you to withdraw from St. Louis' church, bringing the sacred vessels and other things which are yours, and leaving that edifice entirely to the people who shall have rebelled against the regulations already referred to. Let there be no disputes or controversy about it. . . . . I shall appoint you to another congregration more deserving of your ministry, and no priest shall have authority to officiate in the Church of St. Louis until the congregation shall have decided whether they are Catholics or not." The pastor was also instructed to read the bishop's letter from the pulpit, without comment, on three successive Sundays.

The trustees persevered in their opposition, and moreover treated their clergyman—a respectable German priest named Pax—so ill, that he begged to be removed without further delay. The bishop wrote to him as follows:

NEW YORK, *Feb.* 23, 1843.

REV. DEAR SIR:

I received your letter of the 13th instant, together with the account of the meeting held by the disturbers of your congregation. Their resolutions are all stuff and nonsense, not worthy to be noticed, and to which I shall make no reply. I shall not, however, oblige you any more, under pain of obedience, to remain among such worthless people. But I leave it with yourself to remain or leave, whenever you think proper—observing, however, that it is probable I shall pay a short visit to France and Belgium in the course of the summer, and that I should be much pleased if you could find it convenient to be my travelling companion. I am not quite positive yet that I shall go, but I think it probable. In the mean time, should you think it adviseable to remain where you are, I would have you take no kind of notice of those proceedings, or the persons connected with them, but to follow on, in the quiet discharge of your duties, as if there were no such persons in the congregation.

I remain, with sincere regard,

Your father in Christ,

✠ JOHN, *Bp. N. Y.*

Mr. Pax immediately resigned and went home to Germany. The church remained without a clergyman. After a short time the trustees requested the bishop to send them one or two priests. "You have destroyed the peace and respectability of your congregation," he replied; "you have annoyed your pastor until he felt himself obliged to leave you; you have attempted to injure the character of your bishop by authorizing the circulation of falsehoods and calumnies against him in the newspapers; and in the midst of all this you ask me for a priest! You shall not govern your bishop, but your bishop shall govern you in all ecclesiastical matters. When you are willing to walk in the way of your holy faith, as your forefathers did, and be numbered among the Catholic flock of the diocese, precisely as all other trustees and congregations are, then I shall send you a priest, if I should have one." A few months afterward the bishop sent two priests to Buffalo with instructions to undertake the building of a new church. They succeeded without much difficulty. The trustees sent one of their number to Europe to complain to the pope, but he went no further than Paris, where Cardinal Fornari, the papal nuncio, persuaded him to return and attempt a reconciliation with the bishop. Bishop Hughes, of course, would accept nothing short of absolute submission. The Buffalo rebels then drew up a statement of grievances to be forwarded to His Holiness. But in the mean time the trustees, either repenting of their fault, or alarmed at the consequences to their treasury of a prolonged suspension of divine service in the church, called upon the bishop during his visitation of the diocese in the summer of 1844, promised obedience for the future, professed sorrow for the past, and begged him to open the church on the following day. He did so, having first required them to make a public acknowledgment of their errors, by a card in the newspapers. The bishop wrote this card himself.

Thus peace was restored in St. Louis' church, and it was not again broken so long as Buffalo remained under Bishop

Hughes's jurisdiction. But several years afterward, when the diocese had been divided and Buffalo erected into a separate see, trouble occurred there again, and out of it came the church property bill, which passed the New York legislature in 1855.

This unhappy Buffalo business afforded matter for a great deal of comment in the public journals, and the bishop was persistently held up to odium for his attempt, as many called it, to wrest from the trustees the title to their property. Of course he never attempted any thing of the kind. As we have seen, he refused to accept transfers from them when they were offered. He was too keenly sensible of the evils which seemed to spring naturally from lay-management of the Church's temporalities not to wish to limit the powers of trustees as much as he could, and to have control of all ecclesiastical property himself whenever he could have it prudently and justly. But he never sought to abolish the trustee system in any church in which it had once been established. The only instances in which the titles to church property ever passed from lay incorporators to him, were in the cases of four of the city churches which became bankrupt, were sold by the sheriff, and were bought by the bishop. He made it a practice, however, henceforth, and it became finally his invariable rule, to require that the title of every new church should be vested in him. In 1845 he published "Rules for the administration of churches without trustees," which, with some modifications, have ever since been in force. He required the pastor to keep an account of all receipts, and to appoint two members of the congregation to assist him in managing the temporal concerns—the one to act as treasurer, the other as secretary. Neither of these officers should expend any money without the pastor's written order. The salaries of organist, singers, sexton, and other persons employed about the church, as well as the other expenses necessary for the support of public worship, were to be determined by the pastor. The pastor's own salary was fixed at $600 throughout the diocese, and that of the assistant priest, if there should be one, at $400. The assistant was to bear one-half the expenses of housekeeping, and to receive one-half the perquisites (that is, fees for marriages, funerals, and baptisms), which were not to be included in the salary before mentioned; or he might pay a weekly sum for board, and receive one-third of the perquisites. Congregations were urged to prepare a suitable dwelling for the pastor and his assistants, and were expected to provide for it a decent supply of furniture, which should ever afterward be kept up as church-property at the expense of the pastor for the time being. If there should be no dwelling-house belonging to the church, the pastor was to receive $100 a year for house rent. Every six months a detailed report of the condition, income, and expenditure of the church was to be printed and distributed among the congregation, and a copy of it furnished to the bishop.

These rules proved very beneficial. A stop was put to careless expenditures; the plan of raising money by deposits, which had been followed in some congregations, was discouraged; divine service was conducted with more solemnity and decorum than ever before; and in the course of a very few years the churches began to free themselves from the load of debt under which they had groaned so long.

During the three or four years which passed in the discussion and settlement of these questions of trusteeism and debt, Bishop Hughes had been busy at many other matters. He had delivered several lectures for the benefit of charitable or literary institutions in New York, Baltimore, and Philadelphia—including one on "The Influence of Christianity on Social Servitude," in which it is curious to note that he made no allusion to negro slavery; and he had published a little essay on the Oxford movement, in the form of an introduction to Mr. Vanbrugh Livingston's "Inquiry into the Merits of the Reformed Doctrine of 'Imputation'" (New York, 1843). In the autumn of 1842 he visited the northern and western parts of the State. A picture of his life for two or three days, on this trip, gives us an idea of his wonderful activity, and of the strength of constitution which enabled him to bear almost incredible fatigues. He reached Binghamton, for example, late one Saturday night, and the next day administered confirmation, dedicated a church, and preached four times. On Monday he was unwell, but for all that preached twice and consecrated a grave-yard. On Tuesday he rode thirty miles in an open wagon to Oxford, where he preached again; and the same evening he set out for Utica.

TO MR. FRENAYE.

Ogdensburg, *Oct.* 12, 1842.

Dear Sir:

Your letter of the 16th ultimo reached me in my travels, and this is the first day of rest I have had since it came to hand. This is the first time I visited this northern section of the diocese, and I am quite surprised at the number of the Catholics which it contains, and the progress which has been made in forming congregations, building churches, etc. There are eight churches and congregations, attended only by two priests! And in one of these churches the number for confirmation was three hundred and sixty-two—in another three hundred and fifteen. I have just returned from Montreal, where I was received with the utmost kindness and hospitality. Having returned thus far, on my way westward, I have to stop a day for the boat. . . . . Amidst staging and boating, bad roads and good joltings, my health, thank God, is still good.

My respects to all friends at Philadelphia, especially good Mrs. McMahon, from whom I have not heard—I know not how long.

Yours in Christ,

✠ John Hughes, *Bp.*, *etc.*

His health finally gave way under all this hard work, and he was obliged to acknowledge that he needed not only rest and relaxation, but some permanent relief from the augmenting cares of his station. He took part in the deliberations of the fifth council of Baltimore, which met in May, 1843, and he asked in that assembly that a coadjutor bishop might be appointed to assist him.* The Rev. John McCloskey, then pastor of St. Joseph's church, New York, was accordingly recommended to the Holy See for the proposed office.

Immediately after the close of the council the bishop made preparations for the visit to Europe of which he had spoken in his letter to Mr. Pax, quoted a few pages back. Of his purposes in making the voyage he wrote thus to Father De Smet:

> The principal motive of my journey to Europe at this time, besides some relaxation from duties that were beginning to affect my health, and the hope of obtaining some good missionary priests, was to obtain a loan, if possible, at a cheaper rate of interest than we are now obliged to pay. I persuaded myself that there would be, in the old countries of faith, Catholics possessed of capital, who, if they be satisfied that their interest should be paid punctually, and that their capital should be safe, would be happy to employ it for the glory of God, in aiding those who are laboring to plant the Church in our great and rising country. The belief is becoming general on both sides of the Atlantic, that the Catholic religion is destined to become, if not the dominant faith, at least the most influential, in the United States. And whilst it is the duty of those who are charged with the government of the Church in that country to preserve what belongs to the present time, they must also look forward, to lay the foundations, to plant the first seeds of religion in that fertile soil, from which, with the blessing of God, the future will reap a mighty harvest. If we had as much money and as many priests as could be employed advantageously for the glory of God in the United States, I have no doubt but in less than half a century the majority of its inhabitants would be Catholics. The Almighty is pleased to deny us these temporal means for promoting the Church, to teach us, no doubt, that her triumph is his work, and not ours.

His plan was to consolidate the debts of the New York

---

* On the death of Bishop Dubois in December, 1842, Bishop Hughes had of course succeeded to the full title of Bishop of New York.

churches, negotiating a loan in Belgium at three or four per cent. interest, and with the money paying off the old mortgages. New mortgages would then be given to the European creditors. With a part of the sum saved annually in interest by this arrangement, he calculated that he could support his theological seminary; with the rest he proposed to create a sinking fund, to which would also be devoted the proceeds of an annual collection throughout the diocese. In about seven years he thought the whole debt might be paid off.

TO MR. FRENAYE.

SUNDAY, *June* 4, 1843.

MY DEAR FRENAYE:

I sail in the George Washington from this port on Wednesday next, at noon. Why are you not ready to come along? At all events, for the sake of old times, you and Father Gartland might come and see a body off.

The weather has been exceedingly unpleasant during the visit of Messeigneurs the bishops, which I regretted very much; but I think it will be better this week.

You will not forget to pray for me while I am gone—neither will the Sisters and orphans forget me. I am, as you may suppose, in much hurry of preparation.

Yours faithfully in Christ,

✠ JOHN, *Bp. N. Y.*

The bishop had for company in this trip his old friend Bishop Purcell, Father De Smet, the celebrated Indian missionary, and Mr. Thurlow Weed, the well-known New York politician. These four were much together on the voyage; and when their ship was becalmed in Courtmacsberry Bay, on the coast of the county Cork, they determined to go ashore there together, and travel overland to Dublin. It so happened that just before their arrival a rumor had gone about that French officers proposed coming over to Ireland in the disguise of priests, in order to stir up and organize the disaffected peasantry. The authorities of the little fishing village of Courtmacsherry made slight doubt that these were the foreign emissaries, and they had hardly set foot on shore when an English officer waited upon them to ascertain their character. They seem to have had no trouble in convincing him that they were harmless travellers, but when they reached England they found that the circumstances of their landing had been reported there with various embellishments, and the London newspapers had unhesitatingly written down the two bishops, at least, as apostles of the repeal movement.

They arrived in Dublin a day or two before a great repeal meeting at Donnybrook, which Bishop Hughes and Father De Smet attended in company with O'Connell. From Ireland they crossed over to Liverpool, and there an incident occurred, which I cannot relate better than in the words of Mr. Weed:

"We had some amusement, but not much difficulty, at the custom-house, where those of us who landed in Ireland found our trunks, &c. The officers were very courteous to me, and though I had a package of sealed letters that ought to have gone into the mail, and a few contraband periodicals, they allowed them to pass. Father De Smet, who has a trunk full of Indian wardrobes, war implements, medicine bags, &c., was let through for a trifle, but Bishop Hughes, for whom a friend had put up two small bottles of snuff (about a pound), had to pay a duty of eighteen shillings, or four dollars.

"'You must do this, sir,' said the officer, 'in honor of the queen.'

"'For which I should like to give her majesty a *pinch*,' replied the bishop."

The following letter was written by the bishop to a friend in America:

LONDON, *July*, 1843.

REV. AND DEAR SIR:

Constantly on the go since I landed in Europe, I have put off from day to day writing to you. Thrown by accident into the stir ring scenes of a most interesting and eventful period of English, and more especially Irish history, I have been almost bewildered at what is passing around me; one day amidst the thousands at Donnybrook, listening to the eloquent and patriotic liberator of Ireland, and the next in the House of Commons, listening to the masters of the world, I might almost call them, attempting to cope with and defeat one man. They have enough to do, I assure you. Never was a cabinet more perplexed than is that of Sir Robert Peel. But, though O'Connell has the right, alas! they have the power, and God grant that the crisis may not end in adding another blood-stained chapter to the history of Ireland's misfortunes!

Repeal, the government will not grant until the last extremity; and nothing short of Repeal will be of much use to Ireland, or will satisfy the Irish people. But there is one melancholy consolation, that, until it be granted, Ireland will continue in the eyes of all nations England's weakness and shame. The Parliament and the leading journals speak of nothing else, and yet the question seems to make but little impression on this iron-hearted people. But the truth is, that the Irish must depend on themselves. If they follow the advice of their great leader—keep peaceful—and carry on the great fight for national independence, not with their hands, but with their heads, their hearts, their abiding and indomitable *will*, they must be ultimately successful.

We landed on the coast of the county Cork on the 28th ult. It had been my plan to visit Ireland after I should have transacted my business on the Continent. This I may still do, but my feelings got so much excited by the poverty and oppression, the patriotism, the indifference, and the perfidy which I witness in that lovely land, that it is a relief to escape from the spectacle.

I shall visit France, Belgium, and perhaps Holland, and hope to set out for my diocese in the steamer of the 1st of October. Rev. Mr. Curran will, of course, have told you of all that could interest you among ourselves in America.

Before the close of the month the bishop was at Antwerp, making strenuous efforts, with Father De Smet's assistance, to induce Belgian capitalists to subscribe to his loan. He proposed that it should be known as the *Emprunt Catholique de New York*, and taken in shares of, say, one thousand francs each. He drew up an elaborate explanation of the scheme, in the form of a letter to Father De Smet, which he caused to be translated into French, but his project met with little or no encouragement. He succeeded, however, in persuading several missionaries to come over to New York, and in the latter part of September he set sail for America.

In December of this year he lectured in New York for the benefit of the Irish Emigrant Society, before an audience of thirty-five hundred people. His subject was, "The Mixture of Civil and Ecclesiastical Power in the Middle Ages." He treated it with even more than his usual ability, but it would appear from the following letter that his lecture did not escape criticism from some of the Catholic clergy:

TO REV. J. O'CALLAGHAN.

[NO DATE, *Dec.* 1848.]

REV. DEAR SIR:

I write not to enter on a discussion of your letter in reference to my lecture, but to acknowledge the receipt of it, and to make a few remarks which my station authorizes and which your letter invites. I am not displeased at your candor, though I cannot agree in your conclusions.

1. My lecture was on the "mixture" of two distinct "powers" in government, and not on what you call mere temporal affairs. 2. The Gallicanism of which you speak was altogether different from any idea which your letter gives of it. It was not a separation of Church and State, but supposing their union, it was a weakening of the *ecclesiastical element*, and transferring its strength to the *civil element*. It was keeping the union, but depressing the pope in order to exalt the king. This was its object and essence. The degrading union still continued, giving at one time a cardinal-bishop for secretary of state, and at another an infidel layman for a *ministre du culte*. Hence you or I must read history again before we can agree on this point of Gallicanism.

The people regarded the civil authority of the popes as a protection from the oppressions of their rulers; but you or I shall have to study logic again before I can admit that whoever declares this indubitable fact "therefore" holds that "the populace are the inventors or leaders in morality."

Neither can any one who has a notion of what I conceive to be sound logic, infer from my lecture that "the clergy have no divine right to interfere in temporal matters." In one sense, every act of their ministry is an interference in temporal matters. But it is not by the medium of *civil power* they do so. This distinction is obvious.

The encyclical letter of his present holiness had reference to the Carbonari and revolutionists of the Continent, and also to the wild schemes of De Lamennais, whose principles tended to revolution. All this does not show an approval of the union as it is.

In February, 1844, he began a series of Thursday evening lectures at the cathedral on doctrinal subjects. They were continued during three months, and were resumed the following winter. I believe that none of them was ever published, although they had an extraordinary popularity.

On the 10th of March the Rev. John McCloskey was consecrated coadjutor to Bishop Hughes, under the title of Bishop of Axiern *in partibus infidelium*, and at the same time the Reverends Andrew Byrne and William Quarter were elevated to the episcopate, the former as Bishop of Little Rock, the latter as Bishop of Chicago. The ceremony was performed in the cathedral of New York by Bishop Hughes, assisted by Bishops Whelan of Richmond and Fenwick of Boston.

CHAPTER XVI.

1844–1846.

The Native American movement—Riots in Philadelphia—Excitement in New York—The Bishop ready to fight for his churches—Letters to Mayor Harper and Colonel Stone—Third voyage to Europe—Reflections on the state of society abroad—Visit to his birthplace—Sisters of Mercy and Jesuits brought to New York—The diocese divided—The Bishop refuses a diplomatic mission to Mexico—Intimacy with statesmen.

THE formation and growth of the Native American party about this time called for the exercise of all the bishop's foresight and prudence—the more so as many of the leaders, in their harangues against the Catholics, showed a disposition to make capital out of the bishop's controversy on the school question, and out of a similar discussion on a much smaller scale which had recently taken place in Philadelphia. They pretended, among other things, that the Catholics sought to exclude the Bible from the common schools—though for this charge there was not the slightest foundation. They repeated the accusation of *The New York Herald*, that Bishop Hughes was attempting to organize the Catholics as a political body, to be given to this party or to that, according to his own good pleasure. They pointed to his efforts to break up the trustee system as evidence of an avarice of power which must make him, with his great influence and unquestionable ability, a most dangerous enemy to the community. He seems to have understood that while the masses of the people were so much excited as they now were, and their leaders so eager to twist his most harmless actions into confirmation of the slanders by which they had aroused the excitement, his best policy was to keep as quiet as he honorably might. "From a very early period, I prevented the only papers which affect to represent Catholic interests from opposing either the principles or the progress of the new party. .... I even caused certain articles to be published which should fall under the eyes of a large portion of my own flock, and which might caution them against the temptation of retaliating insult, in arraying themselves in opposition to the principles of this new party. I caused them thus to be reminded that, if those principles were wrong, time and the good sense of the community would be the best remedy; whilst Catholics, and, above all, the Irish Catholics, were entirely unfitted to apply a corrective."* So too, he adds, "When the private interest or enterprise of individuals urged them to establish newspapers intended expressly to oppose the progress of Native Americanism and to uphold the constitutional rights of foreigners of all religions, I peremptorily refused to give either patronage or approbation; foreseeing, as I imagined, to what point such antagonism must lead."

At the time of the city election in April, 1844, he had the satisfaction of witnessing the good effects of his advice, and the extent of his influence over his flock. On the night of the election a body of some twelve hundred Native Americans, yelling, groaning, and hooting, bearing illuminated banners inscribed with the words "No Popery," and armed with canes and bludgeons, traversed the streets of the Sixth and Fourteenth wards—streets occupied almost wholly by Irish Catholics. Their wish evidently was to provoke a riot; but the Irish, not often backward to accept an invitation to fight, and never more bellicose than when their religion is insulted, remembered the bishop's injunctions, and looked on in silence. "I am grateful to Almighty God," said the

* Letter to Mayor Harper.

bishop, "that, notwithstanding these injudicious exhibitions, no accident or disturbance occurred. .... Yet, notwithstanding all my solicitude and efforts, so feverish and morbid, so bewildered and diseased had the public mind become in certain quarters on the subject of 'popery,' that a lie of not more than five lines, circulated through any of our papers which might desire to create riots, would have been sufficient to produce the most fearful results." He was willing to practise patience and conciliation almost to the last extremity; but he was prepared to show a bold front, too, whenever he thought it expedient to do so. There were threats of burning some of the Catholic churches: this he resolved at all hazards should never be done; and so, as it was rumored that the men who paraded on election night proposed to attack the cathedral, some three or four thousand Catholics—among whom were the most prominent lay gentlemen of that denomination in the city—assembled in the churchyard, armed to the teeth. The Native Americans did not make an attack—"for a reason they had," said *The Freeman's Journal.*

Far different was the course of affairs in Philadelphia. There several disturbances, more or less serious, had occurred at open-air meetings of the Native American party, which, as if for the express purpose of provoking bloodshed, were held in the midst of the Irish quarters. At a meeting in the Kensington district, on the 6th of May, firearms were used, and a young American named George Shiffler was shot through the heart. This proved the signal for a horrible riot, which raged during three days. Many persons were killed on each side, and the house of the Sisters of Charity of the Blessed Virgin, St. Michael's church, and St. Augustine's church and rectory, with the valuable library of the Augustinians, besides a number of houses occupied by Irish families, were destroyed. Public worship was suspended in all the Catholic churches, and priests were forced to conceal themselves, or fled the city in disguise. At last the tardy arrival of a body of militia put a stop to the outrages.

A good priest who had escaped from Philadelphia advised Bishop Hughes to publish an address urging the Catholics to keep the peace. But the bishop thought the time for meekness and inaction had passed. He declared that "if a single Catholic church were burned in New York, the city would become a second Moscow." Some of the public authorities begged him to restrain the Irish. "I have not the power," said he; "you must take care that they are not provoked." He openly blamed the Catholics of Philadelphia. "They should have defended their churches, since the authorities could not or would not do it for them. We might forbear from harming the intruder into *our house* until the last, but his *first* violence to our church should be promptly and decisively repelled." He was ready for a desperate struggle if the mob forced one upon him. He caused each church in the city to be occupied by an armed force of one or two thousand men, "resolved, after taking as many lives as they could in defence of their property, to give up, if necessary, their own lives for the same cause." Yet he was careful all this time to warn his people against striking the first blow, or doing the least unlawful act to provoke a riot. It is a remarkable proof of the influence he had acquired over them, that in the midst of so much excitement his warnings were strictly obeyed. There were even some Catholics who had made preparation, in case of the occurrence of outrages such as those in Philadelphia, to fire their own houses for the sake of destroying those of their "no-popery" neighbors. *The Freeman's Journal* at this time was under the immediate control of the bishop, and he often wrote for it.[*] It was the medium through which principally he threatened

[*] It had been for some time supported at his expense, when in June, 1846, it became his property. For the next two years it was conducted by persons directly responsible to him, most of the time by his secretary. He sold it in 1848, and it has ever since then been managed by its present editor, Mr. James A. McMaster.

the Native Americans, and instructed the Catholics how to act. "We knew," he wrote in this paper, "the nature of a mob, especially a mob of church-burners, convent-sackers, and grave-robbers; that with it a firm front is the best peace-maker, and that to let it know that, be the authorities as supine as they pleased, the scenes of Philadelphia could not be renewed with impunity in New York, would do more for order than all the twaddle that could be poured out by all the papers in the country. . . . . We have not found any cause to doubt the sound wisdom of our course. Even had we wavered, we should have been fully assured by the hearty approbation bestowed upon it, not only by our readers, but by many candid and influential gentlemen of Protestant denominations. . . . . It is true that even in our own body a few were found to d-o-u-b-t, but these were generally good, cautious souls, who believe in stealing through the world more submissively than suits a freeman. Those, on the other hand, who most warmly approved, were precisely those whose opinions we are wont to receive with most deference, including among them, as we happen to know, all the most trusted and distinguished of our native-born Catholics—men who feel no consciousness of inferiority to any portion of their fellow-citizens, but who are, in every sense of the word, thoroughly American."

A delegation of Native Americans was expected to arrive in New York from Philadelphia, bringing with them a national flag, which, as they alleged, had been trampled upon by the "savage foreigners" during the riot in Kensington. A meeting of their political brethren was called in the City Hall Park, to give them a suitable reception, and escort them through the streets. Bishop Hughes felt that the crisis of the excitement was at hand; if this meeting were held, he believed that nothing could save New York from the disorder which had disgraced Philadelphia. An extra *Freeman's Journal* was immediately issued, warning the Irish to keep away from all public meetings, and especially the proposed meeting in the Park. The bishop also called upon the mayor, Robert H. Morris, and advised him to prevent this demonstration.

"Are you afraid," asked the mayor, "that some of your churches will be burned?"

"No, sir; but I am afraid that some of *yours* will be burned. We can protect our own. I come to warn you for your own good."

"Do you think, bishop, that your people would attack the procession?"

"I do not; but the Native Americans want to provoke a Catholic riot, and if they can do it in no other way, I believe they would not scruple to attack the procession themselves, for the sake of making it appear that the Catholics had assailed them."

"What, then, would you have me do?"

"I did not come to tell you what to do. I am a churchman, not the mayor of New York; but if I were the mayor, I would examine the laws of the State, and see if there were not attached to the police force a battery of artillery, and a company or so of infantry, and a squadron of horse; and I think I should find that there were; and if so, I should call them out. Moreover, I should send to Mr. Harper, the mayor-elect, who has been chosen by the votes of this party. I should remind him that these men are his supporters; I should warn him that if they carry out their design, there will be a riot; and I should urge him to use his influence in preventing this public reception of the delegates."

How far the mayor may have been influenced by this conversation I do not pretend to say, but there was no demonstration on the arrival of the Philadelphia Native Americans, and no disturbance in New York either at this time or when the riots broke out again in Philadelphia in July. The bishop publicly claimed the merit of having prevented an outbreak.

He had received a letter, purporting to be signed by a

brother* of the George Shiffler who was killed at the beginning of the Kensington riot, and threatening him with assassination. He made this the text of a public letter to the Hon. James Harper, who had just entered into office as mayor. It was dated May 17th, 1844, and printed in *The Courier and Enquirer*. In it he sketched his early history, reviewed his whole public course, explained such of his actions as had been most severely condemned by the public press, refuted the popular charges that he had " entered into collusion with politicians," "organized a political party in New York," "attempted to drive the Bible from the public schools," and "disfigured the public school books with expurgations." He assailed *The New York Herald*, as well as the private character of its editor, Mr. Bennett, with a bitterness of invective almost unparalleled in newspaper controversy; for he believed that, if a riot had taken place in New York, the *Herald* would have been chiefly responsible for it. Before the echoes of this terrific assault had died away, he attacked the *Herald* again with redoubled fierceness, in a letter to Colonel William L. Stone, editor of the *Commercial Advertiser*, dated the 27th of May, and entitled "A Second Letter on the Moral Causes that have produced the Evil Spirit of the Times; including a further Vindication of the Author from the infamous Charges made against him by James Gordon Bennett, William L. Stone, and others." This was almost wholly devoted to Mr. Bennett, and in very great measure to his character as a man. Colonel Stone replied to it, and the bishop addressed two more letters to him, intended principally as a defence of his public course. Certain of his friends were anxious that he should write something on the relations of Catholics to the civil government and the existing state of political parties, less personal and less ephemeral than these philippics. His reasons for not doing so will be seen from the following letter:

* The public authorities searched for this person, and found that the signature was a fiction.

TO MR. FRENAYE.

June 21, 1844.

DEAR SIR:

I suppose I need hardly apologize to you for not having answered sooner your letter of the 11th. I have myself had some idea of writing an essay on the subject to which you refer, but I have hitherto been so much engaged that I have not had leisure to attend to any thing which could bear to be postponed. Another thing is, that I do not think it right that the other bishops should be silent in a matter in which all are equally interested, and that I know not how far even it might be agreeable to them that I should write on any matter which might implicitly involve them in the responsibility of my production. Bishop O'Connor has written to me, suggesting the propriety of an official exposition of Catholic principles; but there is one reason which I mentioned to him against this, which is, that at this moment the malignity of the opposition will construe it into an evidence of that species of understanding among ourselves and combination for ulterior purposes of which they already accuse us. I should be glad if you would present my best respects to Bishop Kenrick, to whom I should have written before, with the offer of such sympathy as I can afford in my own situation, had I not been prevented by the causes already assigned. Here there is much under-talk, and much abuse in one or two of the lowest papers; but, generally speaking, the tone of the respectable portion of the press is decidedly in our favor. I should be glad to know whether Bishop Kenrick would think it advisable that I should write such an essay as you suggest—whether [he would] conceive it likely to be beneficial, or the contrary, in reference to the more troubled state of things in your city.

I remain sincerely yours in Christ,

✠ JOHN HUGHES, *Bp. N. Y.*

The question of the Bible in the public schools assumed prominence soon after this. The deputy-superintendent of public schools in New York city—the same Dr. Reese who took part in the discussion before the Common Council in 1840—wished to compel all the teachers to read a portion of the Bible daily to the children. In those schools which contained a preponderance of Catholic children he was willing that the Douay version should be used. The Board of Education would not consent to the compulsory use of any version, denying that the superintendent had any authority to make such an order. Bishop Hughes remained passive throughout the long and animated discussion which ensued; and I allude to the quarrel only because, in the course of it, the often-repeated falsehood that he had endeavored to exclude the Bible from the schools was emphatically contradicted by Dr. Reese himself. The bishop's silence was perhaps partly owing to a feeling that it would be imprudent for him to interfere while the public were still excited by the Native American movement, and partly because he had made up his mind to have nothing more to do with State schools, but to get schools of his own without further delay. He determined to go to Europe and make another effort to obtain Brothers of the Christian Doctrine. He wanted also to introduce into the diocese some community of religious persons to take charge of an orphan asylum and hospitals; for he was not altogether satisfied with the Sisters of Charity, for reasons which will be explained hereafter. He took with him the Rev. John Harley, an estimable young clergyman, who was then President of St. John's College, and afterward for a short time the bishop's secretary. The bishop was warmly attached to Father Harley, and he said that one of the chief reasons which induced him to make this voyage was the hope of its restoring the failing health of this "dear and esteemed young priest." On the eve of his departure he wrote to his sister Ellen:

> I shall bear your relic on my person. I hope to sail "homeward bound" on the 19th of March. I have arranged every thing for my absence, and I shall go light and free as the wintry winds by which I shall be buffeted—but I trust *not so cold*. *N'importe.* Pray for me, dear sister. I have much to write. I shall drop you a line from Boston. God bless you, dear sister.
>
> ✠ JOHN, *Bp. N. Y.*

He wrote again to the same sister a few days afterward, in pencil:

TO SISTER ANGELA.

(*This will be posted in Halifax.*)

At Sea, *Wednesday, Dec. 3, 1845.*

Dear Sister :

I wrote you a last line from Boston on the moment of our departure, but I fear the note was mislaid. In that case, it will be some amends to receive this from Halifax. We are at this time—Wednesday noon—passing Seal Island, in sight of the spot where the steamer Columbia was lost a few years ago. We are going as fast as steam can drag, and fresh, fair winds waft us along. Poor Mr. Harley is rather sick at this moment, as indeed are most of the passengers, not excepting some old sea-travellers who tell me they never were sick before. According to this rule I too may feel what sickness at sea is. So far, it is as usual with me ; the sea-air makes me light of heart ; and if it be necessary for any kind of sickness which may be conducive to health, I must have recourse to medicines, which I have not neglected. The weather is clear, cold, and delightful—blowing from the northwest what the sailors call a stiff breeze, in the which a pencil is the best pen to write with. Besides the usual exhilarating effect of the sea on my feelings, I have to *play* the hero a little on this occasion, to keep my *compagnon de voyage* in good tune. We shall arrive at Halifax to-morrow morning at 4 o'clock, and leave about 8 or 9.

The sea was a never-failing source of delight to Bishop Hughes. The only rest that he obtained during this trip, was, as he said, " on the always glorious ocean, with its untiring monotony and ceaseless change." While on shore, he was almost all the time unwell, though, either in travelling or in preaching, he was in constant activity. His journey was confined to Ireland, England, and France. He seems to have had no very keen sense of the beauties of nature—except, as I have said, the beauties of the ocean. His letters from abroad show that his mind was occupied rather with the social and moral condition of the people, than with features of landscape or the wonders of art which commonly attract travellers. "The first thing that strikes a stranger in Europe," said he, "is the contrast between the poverty and feebleness of the laboring population, and the power, derived from hereditary wealth, with its vast capacity for self-increase, of the more favored classes. This produces almost inevitably a tendency to crouching and servility on the one hand, and a disposition to domineer on the other. The separation is so wide, in fact, that it seems hard to realize at times that the two classes belong to the same country, or even to the same race."

Ireland was unquestionably the most depressed physically of the countries which he visited. "But after all," he said, "the distress there is not so great as it seems. In the first place, the Irish have become accustomed to suffering. And then again, they have discovered that the amount of exactions and rents levied upon them is always in proportion to their apparent comforts, so they conceal as much as possible the better part of their condition. As an illustration of this, being requested to dedicate a church in a very poor neighborhood, I consented on condition that I should not be expected to make any appeal to the charitable feelings of the congregation, as they seemed to be rather objects of charity than persons who could give money. Yet, when a collection was taken up at the close of the service, the amount received was no less than £50 or £60 sterling; and among the poor of Ireland that was a very large sum of money."

He was much struck by the evidences of religious improvement which he noticed on every side. It was a period of revival and activity in the moral and intellectual world. Piety was generally on the increase; churches and charitable institutions were rapidly multiplying. Ireland was yet in the first flush of the temperance excitement, and the bishop recorded with delight the remarkable fact that he did not see one intoxicated man in the kingdom. England had recently been aroused by the Puseyite movement. The bishop obtained an introduction to the principal Oxford converts. "I found them," he says, "eminently meek, simple, God-like men, who could not appreciate the surprise which had been so widely manifested at their renunciation of worldly honors and luxuries, in obedience to the dictates of conscience." In France he observed a great change for the better, especially among the laboring classes. The reaction had set in, after the reign of the infidel philosophy, and the churches were now crowded by men who, a few years ago, had been scoffers at all sacred things. He did not find Paris the sink of iniquity which many travellers described; "although he who should say that Paris is a metropolis of impiety, irreligion, and immorality would say true; so would he speak the truth who should say that it is a city of faith, charity, zeal, and holiness. The view depends a good deal upon the character of the observer."

Before he left Ireland he visited his birthplace, as the guest of Dr. McNally, Bishop of Clogher. He used to describe with great feeling the delight with which he saw again every familiar spot of his childhood, and the kindness with which he was welcomed by his old neighbors and schoolfellows, Protestants as well as Catholics. There were many yet living who remembered him as a poor farmer's boy; and among the foremost to show him attention was Mr. Moutray, in whose garden he used to work. He found many of his relations alive, and took pleasure in settling upon some of them such annuities as their necessities called for, or his own means warranted. On the feast of the Epiphany a great number of his relatives and early friends were collected to hear him preach in the cathedral of Clogher.

He succeeded in obtaining in Ireland a community of Brothers of the Christian Doctrine, and another of Sisters of Mercy, whose principal duties are to visit the sick and prisoners, and protect destitute but virtuous women.

TO SISTER ANGELA.

PARIS, "MARDI GRAS" [*Feb.* 24], 1846.

DEAR SISTER:

I will not write you more than a few words, for I have nothing to say but what you will hear from other quarters; still a few words will not be unwelcome to you. I have succeeded in all the objects of my visit to Europe, even beyond my hopes at starting: details for another time. I have had three bad colds, but my health is good, for all that. Mr. Harley is better, but only better.* I hope to embark in the steamer of April 4, and to be in New York about the 20th.

I wrote Mag a shorter letter than this, if possible; still I wrote to her to say, if nothing more, that I am her and your

Affectionate brother,

✠ JOHN, *Bp. N. Y.*

He reached home on the 21st of April, and Mr. Harley soon followed with the Sisters of Mercy. The Brothers of the Christian Doctrine arrived in October, but, owing to various circumstances, they did not succeed in establishing themselves permanently in New York. A more valuable acquisition was made, however, in the form of a community of Jesuits from Kentucky, to whom, in July, the bishop committed the care and ownership of the college. He had invited them to take charge of this institution before his departure for Europe. Through his efforts a charter had been secured for the college from the Legislature in April, 1846, and it now enjoyed all the privileges of a university. It had in July, 1846, one hundred and forty-six students. There was still a debt upon it of $40,000, due principally to depositors of small sums. St. Joseph's seminary was not sold with the college, but remained under the control of the bishop, though the Jesuits were employed in it as teachers of theology until 1855.

At the sixth council of Baltimore, which opened in May,

---

* Mr. Harley died at the bishop's house, December 8th, 1846.

1846, the bishop asked for a division of his diocese and the erection of two new sees, one at Albany for the northern part of the State, and the other at Buffalo for the western. The Holy Father issued the necessary briefs, at the recommendation of the council, and the Rev. John Timon was appointed bishop of Buffalo, and the Right Rev. John McCloskey bishop of Albany (July, 1847).

While Bishop Hughes was attending the sessions of this council, he received a communication from the Honorable James Buchanan, secretary of state, inviting him to visit Washington in order to advise with the Government "on public affairs of importance." It was rumored in Baltimore that the bishop was to be appointed a special peace envoy to Mexico. The war with that country had just begun, and the news of the commencement of hostilities reached Washington on the very day the council opened. The bishop seems to have had some intimation that Mr. Polk intended to offer such a mission to him. He asked the advice of the council as to accepting it. They recommended him to refuse it, unless the Government would give him the full rank and title of a diplomatic representative.

The ostensible purpose for which he was summoned to the capital was nothing more than to give his advice respecting the appointment of Catholic chaplains for the troops in Mexico; but this business transacted, the subject of the embassy was broached. "It occurred to the president," says Mr. Buchanan, to whom I am indebted for the particulars of this affair, "whilst the bishop was in Washington, and most probably at an earlier period, that, should he consent to visit Mexico, he might render essential services in removing the violent prejudices of the Mexicans, and especially of their influential clergy, which then prevailed against the United States, and thus prepare the way for peace between the two republics. In this I heartily concurred. Independently of his exalted character as a dignitary of the Church, I believed him to be one of the ablest and most accomplished and energetic men I had ever known, and that he possessed all the prudence and firmness necessary to render such a mission successful." The matter was discussed in several private interviews between the president and the bishop, but the bishop finally refused the proposed mission. "The president," says Mr. Buchanan, "much as he desired to avail himself of the bishop's services, could not, at that time, offer him any thing more acceptable. He could not appoint a new envoy to the Mexican government so soon after they had refused, in an insulting manner, to receive our former minister. Paredes was at that time the revolutionary president of Mexico. He owed his elevation to his extreme and violent hostility to the Government and people of the United States."

The bishop often alluded darkly to this affair, but he would not tell the whole story; because he thought "it would not be proper for him to repeat any thing of what transpired in a confidential interview with the chief officer of the Government." Even with his most intimate friends he used to make a little mystery of it; and when he was directly questioned as to the correctness of an account of this offer published by an English lady, Mrs. Maury, in a book called "*Statesmen of America*," he answered that he "did not feel at liberty to affirm or deny, or explain her statements."

The bishop was on terms of intimacy with many prominent statesmen. He seemed perfectly at his ease in political circles. Although he was no politician himself, never voted but once, and never influenced the vote of any man except on the occasion during the school controversy already mentioned, he was fond of discussing public affairs in conversations with his friends, and often showed remarkable acuteness and foresight in his comments upon political movements. It has been said that had he lived in old times he might have been such a cardinal statesman as Wolsey or Ximenes. He would have made a better prince-bishop of the middle ages, with a little temporal sovereignty of his own, recognizing no master but the Pope, ruling his subjects absolutely, and venting his pugnacity with the sword instead of the pen. He would have resisted to the death any encroachment upon his dominion; but he would not have been aggressive. In his polemical wars he always stood upon the defensive—never beginning a controversy except in reply to some attack. He had a talent for government; but he was too independent and too keenly sensible of the supremacy of the spiritual over the temporal order to make a good prime minister. He would have quarrelled with his sovereign about the rights of the Church, and instead of rising, like Wolsey, to a place only a little lower than the throne, would probably have died like Thomas à Becket at the foot of the altar. He never courted the great. Indeed, except the Pope and his cardinals, he believed there was no dignitary in the world whose rank was so much higher than his own that it would be worth his while to bend to it. The office of a Christian bishop was far beyond any that men could bestow. There was no vanity in this feeling; it was something quite apart from his estimate of the merits of the individual who filled the office. Had it not been so, his manners would have lacked that quiet dignity which so generally charmed those with whom he came in contact.

The only vote he ever cast was for Henry Clay for president, in 1832; and he says that one of his principal reasons for voting then, was that his congregation "almost threatened him," on account of his good opinion of Mr. Clay. When Mr. Clay visited New York, the bishop, accompanied by his secretary, called upon him at his hotel. The room was full of politicians and distinguished persons; but Mr. Clay turned them all out, and chatted with the bishop alone for more than an hour. The venerable statesman showed unfeigned delight at seeing Dr. Hughes, and parted from him with evident regret.

CHAPTER XVII.

1846.

Division of the Sisterhood of Charity—Correspondence with the Very Rev. Mr. Deluol.

The Sisters of Charity in the diocese of New York were offshoots of the house founded by Mrs. Seton at Emmitsburg. They were under the control of the general superior at the mother-house, who had full authority to regulate their conduct and appoint and remove all the local superiors. The bishop made no secret of his opinion that it would be better for all parties if the sisterhood could be organized as a separate community in each diocese, and thus brought more immediately under the jurisdiction of the bishop. In fact, he was in general no very cordial friend to religious congregations subject to the rule of a distant superior. It is not likely, however, that he would have attempted any change in the constitution of the Sisters of Charity, had it not been for certain regulations determined upon by the authorities at Emmitsburg in 1846. The pressing wants of the diocese of New York had induced the Sisters, contrary to their usual practice, to take charge of orphan boys as well as orphan girls. Their superior in Maryland now gave notice that they must withdraw from all the male orphan asylums hitherto under their charge. The bishop remonstrated; and after a long correspondence it was at last agreed that such of the Sisters in the diocese of New York as chose to do so, should organize themselves as a separate community, under the control of the bishop. Out of fifty sisters, thirty-one joined the new congregation, and on the 8th of December they were constituted an independent body, under the title of Sisters of Charity of St. Vincent of Paul. As the conduct of Bishop Hughes in this matter was greatly misrepresented, I have thought it only just to give the substance of correspondence with the Very Rev. Mr. Deluol, superior general of the sisterhood in Maryland. Apart from its historical importance, it illustrates forcibly the bishop's character.

TO THE VERY REV. MR. DELUOL.

NEW YORK, *June* 7, 1846.

VERY REV. DEAR SIR:

The report that the male orphans are to be ejected from the Asylum, is heard with consternation by the Catholics of this city, and in case it be carried into effect will produce results which I look forward to as deplorable. The boys in the Asylum are mere infants. They number some 130 or 140. It is impossible for me to make any provision for them. If removed, they must be taken by the cold law as the abandoned offcasts of charity. Yet I do not intend to interfere. I shall leave matters to take their course, for I see no remedy within my reach at present. Neither do I oppose it, as there may, and indeed must be sufficient reasons for the proceeding. But I could not convince the multitude of this, nor should I if I could. But I must say that, if carried out, it will "break us up."

I suppose Mother Étienne* may have mentioned to you a proposition which I made, half in jest, half in earnest, of retaining the sisters now in this diocese (who choose to remain), with the consent of their superiors to a transfer of their obedience to the ordinary. I will not enter into any detail of reasons for recommending this course. It will suffice to say, that in amount they would be the same as those which have induced me to divide the diocese, viz., that those who owe obedience *shall be more immediately under the supervision of those to whom it is due.* That this supervision can extend from Emmitsburg to New York in any practical or efficient sense, is im-

---

* The mother superior of the sisterhood at Emmitsburg.

possible; and in the present state of things it is equally so that it should come from any other quarter. I am not, indeed, indifferent; but unauthorized interference, even when the object is a sound one in other respects, often does more harm than good, and at best anomalies and anarchy are its natural results.

Now, what I would propose—to be accomplished, however, only so far as the present superiors of the sisters approve and agree—is that—

1. It should be made lawful for the sisters now in the diocese, or who may come, until the next festival of St. Joseph, to be responsible to me, and under my direction in so far as relates to the vow of obedience; the other vows remaining, as well as the rules in general, as they now are.

2. That by the authority of the same superiors, and, if necessary, of the Holy See, the Bishop of New York shall be, after said festival, the lawful superior of such of said sisters as choose to remain in the diocese.

3. I do not propose to change a single rule or canon of the original constitutions except what is implied in the above, or *necessarily* resulting from it.

4. In case this should be agreed to, I shall open a mother-house for the supply of new members, and, of course, hold St. Joseph's acquitted of all temporal responsibility for those who may remain.

Those four sections contain the general principle of what I propose. Details could easily be arranged if the principle be agreed to. I am about securing from the Corporation *for the Orphans* a lot of about seven acres in what will be the heart of the city. But if *even the report* of excluding the male orphans get abroad generally, I shall be defeated. These seven acres join five others which we already own; and on the twelve acres which both would make, I intend to build all our charitable establishments, as time and circumstances will allow.

Do not, I pray you, suppose that in this I am going to do or authorize any thing without the previous consent of those whom God has placed, *hic et nunc*, superiors over the Sisters of Charity. It is for you to reflect on it, and decide as I trust God will direct.

It was my intention, in going to the council, to have had a long and frank, as well as confidential communication with you on this whole subject. But I felt myself at every leisure moment entrapped by the hospitality of the Baltimoreans, and as you are of them so I found you surrounded by the consequences of the common attribute of your city.

I have not as yet been able to find a suitable house for my hospital. But I see no reason why the sisters for Rev'd Mr. Conroy's Asylum should not be sent on. I shall insist on his fulfilling the conditions required by the mother-house. I am at the end of my letter, and have only room to say that whatever you may decide, I am with sincere respect and affection,

Your devoted friend and servant in Christ,

✠ J. HUGHES, *Bp. of New York.*

MR. DELUOL TO BISHOP HUGHES.

BALTIMORE, *June* 17, 1846.

RIGHT REV. AND DEAR SIR:

Your favor of 7th instant came to hand on the 9th. And as you begin your letter by the male orphans, I will begin my answer by the same topic.

The male orphans could be taken care of by the Sisters of Charity here as they are in France, but not otherwise. In France the duty of the Sisters of Charity is to see that the orphans are properly taken care of, viz., that they are comfortably nursed, fed, clothed, etc. But they do not live in the same part of the house; their apartments are distinct from each other. A matron dresses and undresses them, cleans them, feeds them, warms them, puts them to bed, and sees that during night they are comfortable and behave themselves, etc. The Sisters of Charity have nothing to do with these details; moreover it is only foundlings (and not boys 7, 8, 9, 10, 11 years old) who come under their charge, and who whilst suckling have wet-nurses, and when weaned have matrons. We are willing to adopt the same system where the persons concerned are willing to coöperate.

But, Right Rev'd and dear Sir, as far as your diocese is concerned, this question seems an idle one, because you take a higher ground, which precludes this altogether, as well as the reëstablishment at Albany. You have come to the decision that the Sisters of Charity in your diocese cannot be governed from St. Joseph's, and of course that they must be exclusively under the control of the ordinary. This, for the two last years, I had heard from the Sisters of Charity living in New York; this I had heard from the lips of bishops, priests, and lay people; but I could not believe it until Mother Étienne and Sr. Rosalia assured me that they had it from your own lips, and I myself have seen it in black and white from your own pen. This brings the matter to an end at once.

I regret only that neither I nor those who are associated with me in the government of the community can agree with you on this subject. Whilst from Paris, in France, the central government of the Sisters of Charity governs not only the six thousand members disseminated over the kingdom, but also the colonies planted in Switzerland, in Piedmont, in Algiers, in Africa, in Constantinople, and Smyrna in Lesser Asia, in Alexandria in Egypt, in Mexico, etc., we cannot understand why the central government of St. Joseph's could not do the same in the United States. To say that it cannot, is (it appears to us) to pay a poor compliment either to the central government or to the sisters under its jurisdiction, or to their respective directors abroad.

We may be mistaken, but we consider this step of yours as calculated to inflict a deep and dangerous wound on the community; and if the example be imitated (every bishop in the Union has the same right), we would consider it as mortal.

Appointed as we are to watch over the conservation and to promote the welfare of the community, we can neither approve of nor even connive at the measure. Therefore we consider it our bounden duty to recall to the mother-house *all* the Sisters of Charity who are actually in your diocese, in order that none of them may, at least in this case, complain that without her consent she finds herself in a community different from that in which she has made her vows.

We have neither the right nor the inclination of using compulsion in their regard. Therefore those who come back of their own free will shall be welcome; those, on the contrary, who choose to remain will use their own pleasure, and take upon themselves the responsibility of their step. But it must be well understood that the separation is to be *complete* and *forever*.

Neither can we wait until the 19th of March, 1847, as you suggest, to settle the matter definitively. The business must be brought to a final and practical conclusion at latest by the 20th of next month, July 20th, 1846.

I am going to notify forthwith all the Sisters of Charity actually in your diocese, in order that they may make up their minds, and be ready, one way or the other, by the time mentioned above.

I trust, Right Rev'd and dear Sir, that in this our decision you will see no hostile feeling, but only a deep sense of duty which compels us to do all in our powers to transmit to our successors unmutilated an establishment dear to religion such as we have received it from our venerable predecessors.

Personally, I will always take great pleasure, Right Rev'd and dear Sir, in subscribing myself,

Your very respectful obedient servant and friend,

L. R. DELUOL.

Mr. Deluol's course, it will be seen, would throw upon the bishop the responsibility of dissevering the Society, if the proposed separation should take place. But he had no idea of accepting any responsibility which he did not assume of his own accord. He wrote a pretty sharp reply to the letter just quoted:

. . . . .

I may have said that the Sisters of Charity in this diocese "cannot be governed from St. Joseph's;" but unless I have been dreaming I could not have said that they "*must be*" "exclusively under the control of the ordinary here." Pray, have I said so? Or is it you that ascribe the words to my pen?

I repeat, with great respect, that for the local circumstances of the different establishments in this diocese, and the interests of religion and charity in the same, the Sisters of Charity cannot be governed, *i. e.* to the best advantage, from St. Joseph's. But I disavow an inference from this statement as if I made *this* the result of incapacity on the part of the Superiors. That was not, is not, my meaning.

I used, and use, the expression just in the same sense in which I say that three bishops are necessary to govern the diocese of New York, and that I alone, so remote from important portions of it, am incompetent to the task and responsibility.

The statement in your third paragraph, respecting the unity of government in France, is in my opinion irrelevant. It comes under the head of a general proposition that "many things can be done in Europe which cannot be done here." And I fear much that time will show this to be one of them.

* * * *

You tell me that "those who choose to come back of their own free will shall be welcome; those, on the contrary, who choose to remain will use their own pleasure, and take upon themselves the responsibility of their step. But it must be understood that the separation is to be complete and forever." Very Rev. and dear Sir, you mistake me if you suppose me, as would appear from this extract, capable of putting myself at the head of the *children of disobedience.* My letter, I trust, gave you no authority for such an unworthy inference. At all events, I have only to say that to "those who choose to remain" *under such circumstances I shall never speak.*

Lastly, you have fixed the 20th of July, 1846, for the term. On this limitation, as on all the rest, you shall be the judge. But I state to you solemnly that I do not consent to your decision; that I *am opposed to it;* that I *protest against it publicly and privately;* that I shall have nothing to do with it; that I consider the sisters bound to go on whatever day you appoint, and that I shall take no measure in anticipation of their departure; that after they are gone I shall apply myself to reconstruct, as best I can, the wreck and ruins of the charities of this diocese for the last thirty years, destroyed in an hour by the dash of a pen.

In short, I shall admit *no participation* of responsibility. The sisters are bound by their vows to obey you. Let them follow their obligation. The breaking up of so many and such establishments shall be *your* work ALONE. I do not consent to it, I protest against it; but you mistake my character if you suppose that I will place the obstruction of a straw in the way of its execution. Religious obedience is too sacred and too delicate a matter for that.

But you can easily understand that the Catholics of this diocese who have contributed no less than half a million for charities under the sisters either expended or invested, will interfere in spite of us. To *them* I shall be able to prove myself acquitted. I could say much more. But perhaps I have already said too much, and have only to add that I remain your faithful and obedient servant in Christ,

✠ John, *Bp. of N.Y.*

TO SISTER ANGELA.

New York, *June* 21, 1846.

Dear Sister :

As an appeal to the sisters has been made to ascertain whether they are faithful to their religious obligations, it becomes me to make the following declaration, which I beg of you to have the goodness to copy for each of the other Sister-Servants, and send to be read to her sisters, if she think proper.

The very Rev. Father Deluol writes to me that "we [the Superiors of the Sisters of Charity] have neither the right nor the inclination of using compulsion in their [the Sisters'] regard. Therefore those who come back of their own free will shall be welcome. Those, on the contrary, who shall choose to remain will use their own pleasure, and take upon themselves the responsibility of their step. But it must be well understood that the separation is *complete* and *forever*.

"Neither can we wait till the 19th of March, 1847, as you suggest, to settle the matter definitively. The business must be brought to a final and practical conclusion, at latest by the 20th of next month, 20th July, 1846."

This is the decision of the letter. I am not a promoter of anarchy, and of course I could have nothing to do with those who, *under such circumstances*, should "choose to remain." It is the duty of all the sisters therefore to obey their superiors, and to go on the day they may appoint. I can have nothing to do with this decision. All I know is that their vow of obedience obliges the sisters to obey their superiors, and that if any sister disobeys in such circumstances, it will be reason enough for me to conclude that she has lost the spirit of her vocation. I could not, of course, have any thing to with her. This I have written to Father Deluol. And on this point, the duty of the sisters is clear. Let schools and asylums fall to the ground. That is not their business. *Their* business is to redeem in every act their vow of obedience, and leave consequences to God.

But I have written to Father Deluol also that whilst I will not oppose the obstruction of a straw in the way of his decision, I not only *do not* consent to it, but *I protest against it solemnly, publicly, and privately.*

Mr. Deluol's next letter is dated June 26. After informing the bishop that the subjects of their correspondence had been maturely considered by the council of the Sisterhood at St. Joseph's, he concludes as follows:

Since by your last letter of the 20th instant you express regret that the sisters should be removed from the asylums which they have hitherto occupied, and are willing that they should continue to preside over them under the regulations by which they have hitherto been governed, the council are happy to say that since the cause of objection has been removed they make no difficulty in replacing the sisters in the same condition in which they were before my letter of the 17th.

As long as these regulations shall be observed, there will be no disposition on their part to withdraw the sisters from the good works in which they have been engaged.

It is very likely that Mother Étienne will be in New York toward the beginning of next week.

I remain, Right Rev. and dear Sir,
Your most humble, faithful servant,
L. R. DELUOL.

TO THE VERY REV. MR. DELUOL.

NEW YORK, *July* 7, 1846.

VERY REV. AND DEAR SIR:

I have to acknowledge the receipt of your letter of the 26th ult. enclosing a copy of mine dated the 7th. I have little to say on the contents of your last letter. There is one remark, however, of yours which I must beg leave to correct. It is that in which you impute to me the "expression of regret at the sisters' leaving my diocese," and use it as a reason for revoking your ordinance of the 17th. I assure you I felt no regret in the sense in which you used the term. My regret, if I expressed any, was for the injury you were about to inflict on religion and on charity, by your hasty decree. The perusal of it gave me to understand to what an extent the peace and the prosperity of my diocese depended on your good will and pleasure. I could not help regarding it as a rod uplifted to frighten or coerce me; and viewing it in this light you will agree with me that I could not, consistently with the dignity and authority of my office, become a pleader in any sense at your tribunal for a mitigation of the threatened punishment. If any well-meaning peace-maker has given you such an idea of my feelings, or offered any explanation on my behalf, I wish you to know that it was unauthorized, as it is now disavowed by me. . . . . .

The council at St. Joseph's, however, showed no disposition to rescind their resolution for the removal of the sisters from the male orphan asylums; and they moreover steadily refused to be governed by the wishes of the bishop with regard to the appointment and removal of local superiors within his diocese.

MOTHER ÉTIENNE TO BISHOP HUGHES.

St. Joseph's, *Aug.* 8, 1846.

RIGHT REV. AND RESPECTED FRIEND :

We rejoice to hear of your having succeeded in procuring the ground you so much desired to obtain for your future charitable institutions.

We frequently experience with yourself the force of this truth, "that we sometimes meet with success in quarters from which we should have least to expect."

Be assured we have no disposition to remove our sisters from their present exercise of charity in behalf of the *female* orphans of your diocese, and we fully rely upon your assurance of doing all in your power to provide persons to replace our sisters in taking charge of the orphan boys by the 1st of October next.

On *this* point we are *decided*.

Since the sisters have continued for thirty years "depending on a spring moved by persons at a distance," we see no reason why they cannot continue thirty, or even sixty, or a hundred years more, to be governed by the same spring.

The changes we contemplated, and of which I gave you some notice during our conversation at Mount Hope, and which we have had in view since you urged the necessity of such a measure, some three years since, were already made when your letter (bearing postmark August 1st) reached us; and the same mail which conveys this to you will carry to some of our Sister-Servants and Visitatrix of New York the late decisions of the council in their regards.

As it is not in accordance with the spirit of our rules and constitutions to consult the several bishops under whom our sisters may be placed when we deem it necessary to remove them, and since it has never been the practice, I hope you will pardon us for adhering to the spirit of our holy founder; and we feel perfectly satisfied that you will appreciate our motives—the more so as you assure us you "have no disposition to thwart our arrangements."

I remain, with great esteem,

Very respectfully your friend in Christ,

S. M. ÉTIENNE.

The bishop's reply to this letter was the following straightforward note to the Sister Visitatrix:

TO SISTER ROSALIA.

NEW YORK, FEAST OF ST. BARTHOLOMEW [*Aug.* 24], 1846.

DEAR SISTER:

I believe all the changes have been made among the Sisters of Charity under my jurisdiction, which it was the purpose of the council to make, on the principle that in such matters the bishop of a diocese is not to be consulted.

This kind of business has gone far enough.

Be assured then that I mean no personal disrespect when I communicate to you a message which must seem rude, addressed to a Christian and religious lady, viz.: that I wish, and request, and require that you shall leave the diocese of New York with as little delay as possible. I shall tolerate no officer of a religious community, male or female, exercising without my previous advisement and consent, powers of disturbance and embarrassment, such as have been exercised, conscientiously no doubt, in my diocese of late.

Your obedient servant in Christ,

✠ JOHN HUGHES,
Bp. of New York.

P. S. If for this the sisters are to be recalled, let them go; I shall look for others to take their place.

The same day on which this note was written, the bishop summoned all the clergy of New York and Brooklyn to meet him at Transfiguration church on the 26th. He explained and read the whole correspondence to them, and with the exception perhaps of one priest they all approved of what he had done.

The superiors of the Sisterhood at Emmitsburg at last consented to the plan of separation proposed by the bishop. The members of the community in the diocese of New York were offered their choice, either to return to St. Joseph's, or to receive a dispensation from their vows in order that they might organize an independent community.

CIRCULAR TO THE SISTERS OF CHARITY THROUGHOUT THE DIOCESE.

December 6, 1846.

DEAR SISTER-SERVANT :

I have received this day a letter from the Rev. Father Deluol, dated the 4th instant, advising me of the conclusion to which your superiors have come as regards the Sisters of Charity in my diocese.

It is known to you already that the circumstances of our principal orphan asylum were such as to render it impossible for me to comply with the requirements of your superiors in regard to male orphan children. The termination of this matter is that your superiors have recalled such of the sisters as wish to adhere to your Mother-House at Emmettsburg, and offered a dispensation from their vows of obedience to such other sisters as might be disposed to remain for the purpose of aiding to carry on the charitable institutions already begun.

These institutions, with the blessing of God, cannot, must not, be allowed to go down. In order to sustain them I shall form a community of my own for the wants of this diocese, with as little change as possible in the rules and constitutions of your community.

Since your Rev. Superior supposes that some of you will be disposed to remain, and since he has made it lawful for you to do so by the dispensation which he has offered, it is proper for me to state that I will receive as Religious all those sisters now in the diocese who are disposed to join me, as soon as they shall have obtained each the written dispensation aforesaid from their present superior.

Your friend and servant in Christ,

✠ JOHN, *Bp. of N. Y.*

P. S. You may read this to the sisters under your charge, if you think proper; and let such sisters as wish to join my community send me word as soon as possible.

TO THE VERY REV. MR. DELUOL.

NEW YORK [MIDNIGHT], 1846—'47.

VERY REV. DEAR SIR:

In the hours of deep night, during the silent interregnum between the going out of one year and the coming in of another, I write to acknowledge the receipt of your two last letters, to which I will add a very few words. The most painful controversy of my life has just been that closed, as I hope (painfully or otherwise), in which you, according to your sense of duty, were or seemed to be my opponent, not merely on your account or on mine, but still more on account of innocent, and in some measure, of helpless parties. That is now all past; on reviewing my share of it, I regret that I have used expressions, and a certain pungency of style toward you, which at the time seemed not only justifiable, but almost expedient. I regret them. They must have given you pain. They gave no comfort to me. At all events they were unnecessary, and I regret, I retract them. . . . . After what I have said, the object of this is to advise you of our purpose, present and future. 1. There were three sisters who were in this diocese when your first letter was read in July, and who, it appears, expressed themselves to some others as wishing to remain. If these should come within three months, with the dispensations granted to the others, I shall feel bound to receive them as *Sisters*. 2. As to any others now in your community, I shall not receive them *except as novices*, without—what I do not anticipate—a direct recommendation from their superiors for that purpose. My object is not to raise standard against standard, altar against altar. Even in seeming disorder I am for order and subordination.

I thought one page—the only one at hand—would be sufficient for all I had to say, but I would add still a few words. If all the sisters had gone, as I told them yesterday, I had taken precautions by which they might have left the keys under the doors; and, with God's blessing, on the same day the orphans should not have gone without their dinner.   .   .   .   .

One other wish, of which the sounding midnight reminds me, as it does of the *nugæ fugaces* that fly with time, is to you that of a Happy New Year, which I trust you will not reject *quand même* from

    Your sincere servant in Christ,
        ✠ JOHN, *Bp. of N. Y.*

A few years after the separation thus effected the Sisterhood at Emmitsburg became affiliated to the community founded in France by St. Vincent of Paul, adopted the French dress, and placed itself under the direction of the French general superior. The mother-house of the sisters in New York was fixed at Mt. St. Vincent's near Harlem, where they established a female seminary. Their estate was afterward purchased by the city, and included in the Central Park, and the sisters removed to Font Hill on the Hudson River. In course of time they sent out colonies to various parts of New York and New Jersey, and even to Halifax. They adhered to the old constitutions and dress adopted by Mother Seton, and consequently form, with their offshoots, the true representatives of the original Sisters of Charity of St. Joseph's.

CHAPTER XVIII.

1847–1850.

Young Ireland—The Irish insurrection of 1848—The Bishop's speech at Vauxhall Garden—Letter to Mr. Emmet—Letters against Mr. McGee—The temporal power of the Pope

BISHOP HUGHES seldom acted from impulse. There was a coolness, a far-sightedness, an absence of passion—often even a lack of enthusiasm—in his conduct which one is accustomed to notice not so much in Irishmen as in natives of the other side of the North Channel. There was one subject, however, which rarely failed to excite him; and that was the condition of his native country. "My feelings, my habits, my thoughts," he used to say, "have been so much identified with all that is American, that I have almost forgotten I am a foreigner." Yet with all this, let but a word be spoken about Ireland's wrongs and wretchedness, and the hidden fire of his Irish nature blazed up. The famine of 1847 affected him as a great personal grief. In February of that year he had published a pastoral letter ordering a collection to be taken up in all the churches of the diocese for the support of the theological seminary; but when the distressing news of starvation in Ireland reached this country, he announced that the collection would be devoted to the relief of the sufferers. "It is better that seminaries should be suspended than that so large a portion of our fellow-beings should be exposed to death by starvation." He had the happiness of transmitting to the Irish bishops about fourteen thousand dollars as the result of this collection. In March he delivered, for the benefit of the same starving people, a lecture "On the Antecedent Causes of the Irish Famine." A good idea of the drift of this address may be gathered from the title affixed to it when it was first published—"The Tyrant and his Famine; or, the Irish Tragedy of six hundred Years."

He understood the secrets and windings of Irish politics as well as if he had passed his life in the study of them. O'Connell and the Repeal Association enlisted, as we have seen, his deepest sympathies. For the Young Ireland party he had a hearty contempt. He lost no opportunity of warning his flock against their "spurious patriotism," as he called it, "fomented by big words and small deeds." He held them guilty of the overthrow of O'Connell, and, with him, of the best hopes of the country. "The Gulliver of Ireland," said he, "was overthrown by her Lilliputians." The dissensions which they introduced among the Irish patriots did the work which England had not been able to do with her army. The government cunningly allowed them the widest liberty of treasonable speech, well knowing that the only effect of their harangues would be the destruction of O'Connell's influence and the disorganization of his followers. "The curse of Young Ireland," said the bishop, "is more calamitous than the potato famine." It need hardly be said that for revolutionary schemes in general he cherished a holy aversion. But he believed that Ireland was in a different case from any other country in Europe, with the single exception perhaps of Poland, and that any effort of her people to achieve their independence would be justifiable provided there was a fair prospect of its succeeding. Speaking of the insurrection of 1848, he said: "I did not approve of the attempt to emancipate that country by violent measures against such fearful odds. If there ever was a country that could be justified for such an attempt in the sight of heaven and man, it would be Ireland at that period. But there could be no rational prospect of success, and on that account alone I opposed it with all my might." By the exaggerated statements of the Irish journals he was at last led to believe, in common with the rest of the world, that an organized conspiracy was afoot for a general rising of the people. Meetings of the friends of Irish independence were held twice a week in New York, during the summer of 1848, and the bishop was somewhat infected by the popular enthusiasm. He felt little or no confidence in the success of the insurrection, but he could not deny that the dearest wishes of his heart were with the insurgents. The news of the actual outbreak reached this country in August, and on the 14th of that month an immense meeting was held at Vauxhall Garden for the purpose of raising funds to help the patriot party. The bishop yielded to the entreaties of the managers of the meeting, and promised to attend it. "Liberty, Ireland, and humanity," said he, "are at stake; and if liberty, Ireland, and humanity have friends on this side of the water, now is the time for them to come forward." He had no sooner given the promise than he was half sorry for it. When the evening came he went into the office of his secretary the Rev. Mr. Bayley, which opened upon his own sitting-room. He walked back and forth for a few moments without speaking. There was evidently something on his mind that he hesitated to tell. At last Father Bayley inquired what troubled him.

"I am going to that meeting to-night," said he.

"You, monseigneur! What has induced you to do such a thing? I beg you not to go."

"Well, they have been after me so many times that at last I have consented. I think it will do no harm."

Father Bayley persisted in his remonstrances. "Do, monseigneur, send an apology."

"Oh, no; I can't do that; it is too late. Mr. Greeley is to call for me."

He seemed on the point of yielding to repeated arguments and entreaties, when the arrival of Mr. Greeley put a stop to the discussion. The bishop appeared at the meeting. Once on the platform all evidence of irresolution vanished. He spoke with his usual directness and energy. "There may be a crisis," he said, "in the history of a nation which will authorize and almost require one in my station to depart from what may be considered the ordinary and legitimate routine of his official duties. I think that such a crisis and such a period has arrived in the history of Ireland. By the last news it appears that the oppressor and his victim stand face to face. I come among you, gentlemen, not as an advocate of war—it would ill accord with my profession. My office is properly to be a peace-maker, when it is possible. But I come in the name of sacred humanity, not, if you will, to put arms into the hands of men by which they may destroy the lives of others, but to give my voice and my mite to shield the unprotected bosoms of the sons of Ireland. It is not for me to say any thing calculated to excite your feelings, when, as you perceive, I can scarcely repress my own. . . . My object in coming here was to show you that in my conscience I have no scruples in aiding the cause in every way worthy a patriot and a Christian." Alluding to the neutrality laws, he continued: "I am a citizen of the United States, and I would do nothing contrary to the laws of the country which protects me; but whatever those laws may be in the abstract, and however statesmen may define limits, there is a something in the human breast which knows nothing of their codifications; and whenever it sees reluctant men bowed in slavery, then that sentiment, which never studied international law, is waked. . . Let Ireland once go to housekeeping for herself, and then answer me if the American people will not come up to the work, as though they had all been born within gunshot of Tara's Hall?" He seemed unwilling to go to the point of directly contributing to aid the insurrection; he professed to draw a distinction between helping the insurgents and helping their cause. "My contribution," said he, "shall be for a *shield*, not for a *sword;* but you can contribute for what you choose." When he left the stand he laid on the table five hundred dollars, "to purchase a shield to interpose between the oppressor and his victim." This money was intended, as he afterward said in a letter to Horace Greeley, " to mitigate the sufferings that must result from so unequal a contest." " I am a friend," said he, " of Ireland and of freedom; but I could not and did not encourage so foolish an undertaking as that was. As well might it be said that if I were to throw a plank within the reach of a man that was struggling with the waves for his life, I had therefore encouraged the unfortunate individual to jump overboard."

He was intensely mortified at the failure of the movement, and especially at the ignominious manner of its ending. That this formidable insurrection—as he had been led to believe it—should have been put down before a blow had been struck—should have been put down " not by the British army, but by a squad of policemen,"—was an unspeakable humiliation to him. "Every Irishman," said he, "from Maine to Texas, who has taken the slightest interest in the cause, must blush and hang down his head for shame. Even in this city professional gentlemen and merchants are afraid to meet their American neighbors, lest they may be jeered at for having sympathized with such a set of gasconaders." He was unsparing in his denunciations of Young Ireland. He loaded that party with ridicule. He accused them of deception and poltroonery. " The armies of Young Ireland, routed at Slievenamon, of course had to run away. And this running away they afterward attempted to immortalize under the name of 'Felons' tracks;'[*] so that the awful revolutionary movements of Young Ireland in 1848, terminated precisely where the revolution of Hungary had begun —namely, in a war of *races*." [†]

[*] After Smith O'Brien, Meagher, Doheny, and other leaders had been convicted as felons, many a patriotic scribbler in the Irish newspapers took pride in signing himself A FELON OF '48. Michael Doheny published a book called " *The Felons' Tracks*."

[†] Letters of "Philo Veritas" to the "N. Y. Daily Times," Aug. 12, 1854.

He published an article on "The Question of Ireland" in *The Freeman's Journal*, September 9th, 1848, blaming the insurgents for their lack of organization, recommending Catholics to give them no more money, and intimating that little of what was given reached its destination. He urged that inflammatory meetings, passionate appeals to the feelings of the people, societies, rifle-clubs, etc., should be discontinued. They could do no good, and were not only foolish, but dangerous and wicked. He determined that his own contribution to the fund in aid of the rebellion should be devoted to some more useful purpose. He accordingly wrote the following letter to the president of the Directory, to which the disposition of the fund had been entrusted:

TO ROBERT EMMET.

Nov. 1848.

DEAR SIR:

About the middle of August it became evident to all men accustomed to place ordinary reliance on human testimony that a fearful and instant struggle was about to take place between the remnant of the Irish nation in Ireland and their foreign oppressors. So far, I had not the slightest doubt; neither had I any hope of the success which, it was announced, would attend that patriotic effort on the part of the Irish. Division, the evil genius that has dogged the path of Irish patriotism for 700 years, was still on its track; and with the view to effect something like union in this country at least, I took sides for the first time in my life, publicly, and I may add, against my own convictions, with that side in whose judgment I had but little trust, but in whose devotion, chivalry, and courage I had unbounded confidence. Under these circumstances, and with the view to enable *union* to repair the faults of sanguine anticipation and (to my mind at least) doubtful policy, I threw myself with all the influence that I might possess into the scale of a desperate experiment. This I have not regretted, and this I do not now regret. But besides what influence might attach to my humble name as an individual, or even to my office as a Catholic bishop, I deposited on the altar of my native country an amount of contribution which I could but ill afford for an occasion less powerful in its appeals to religion and to humanity.

The foregoing remarks will explain the peculiar emphasis with which I then urged the absolute necessity of unbounded confidence in your Directory. I was not ignorant that kindred motives had caused the names of persons in whom I have no confidence to be enrolled in the list. But your own name, that of Charles O'Conor, James White, Felix Ingoldsby, and some others whom I do not now call to mind, were a sufficient guarantee that the confidence which I had urged and demanded, whilst it was absolutely necessary for the cause, would not be misplaced.

It appears, however, that the mountains of Irish patriotism had already labored, and the mouse of physical exertion had gone forth, to be the sport of Ireland's enemies. My friend Mr. Charles O'Conor played on a word which I used in my remarks, and announced my contribution as for the purpose of a Shield. Events had already proved that the *men* of Ireland, on their own soil, had rendered the protection of a shield unnecessary. This, unhappily, is not the case of the *women* of Ireland arriving in this city, young, pure, innocent, unacquainted with the snares of the world and the dangers to which poverty and inexperience would expose them in a foreign land. To carry out, then, the spirit of my remarks and the letter of Mr. O'Conor's kind interpretation of them, I have to request that the Directory will transfer to the Sisters of Mercy the $500 subscribed by me for the purchase of a shield to protect the purity and innocence of the poor, virtuous, and destitute daughters of Ireland arriving in this city, toward whom, as far as their means will allow, the Sisters of Mercy fulfil the office of guiding and guardian angels in every respect.

I have the honor to be, dear Sir,

With sincere respect,

✠ JOHN, *Bp. of New York.*

Upon the failure of the insurrection, many of the defeated patriots came to the United States. If their conduct at home had aroused the bishop's indignation, he was ten times more incensed at their conduct in this country. They attempted to throw the blame for their disastrous failure upon the Catholic clergy of Ireland; they stigmatized the priests as traitors, the bishops as pusillanimous fawners upon the men in power. Mr. Thomas Darcy McGee, the editor of the New York *Nation*, made himself conspicuous by such attacks upon the clergy, and in January, 1849, the bishop began a series of letters to *The Freeman's Journal*, in which he handled *The Nation* with great severity. He did not wish to fight this little battle in his episcopal character, so he signed himself "An Irish Catholic;" but inasmuch as a sort of chivalrous feeling restrained him from making a personal attack anonymously, he took care that Mr. McGee should be privately informed that he was the writer. "Mr. McGee attempts to throw the responsibility of this humiliating result," says letter Number One, "on the Catholic clergy of Ireland. Impudent falsehood! He knows well that the Irish clergy never gave him or his colleagues any reason to suppose that they would join them. . . . . He knows very well that the confederation repudiated the influence of the Catholic clergy in the silly hope of thereby inducing the Protestants and Orangemen of the north to fraternize with them. He knows very well that the interference of the priests was proscribed and denounced in the policy of the confederation and the clubs. . . . . The priests of Ireland had no more idea of committing themselves and their flocks to the issue of a bloody struggle with the overwhelming power of the British empire than the people of England had." Elsewhere the bishop said: "The clergy would have been faithless to their obligations of religion and of humanity if they had not interposed, seeing, as they must have seen, the certain and inevitable consequences of a movement so nobly conceived but so miserably conducted."

Injustice to the clergy was not the worst of *The Nation's* offences. The bishop charged that it was infidel in its tone —that it was "anti-Catholic, directly in some instances, indirectly in all;" and he urged therefore that "every diocese, every parish, every Catholic door" should be closed against it. Infidelity was a charge to which he regarded the Young Ireland press in America as generally amenable. In a sermon on the occasion of a collection for the Pope in 1849, he used the following strong language in reference to the journalists of this party:

Let us get priests and religion out of the way; they make cowards of men; let priests be removed; let popes be removed; let everything that tends to create a conscience be abolished forever. These are their ideas, and you, dear brethren, have found among you recently this new school of liberal teaching; you have found among you editors and newspapers trafficking upon the ruins of a country which they have helped to degrade, and making their pages eloquent by a stupid imitation of Tom Paine and Voltaire. These are the political confectioners who seal up the poison of their infidelity in sugar-plums of flattery to popular prejudices, that they may sell them to the children of folly. They call themselves Catholics, too, even as Voltaire said he was a Catholic. . . . . They say that they are Irishmen; and they may be Irishmen, but not Irishmen of the legitimate stamp. They are not of those Irishmen who have preserved the nationality and honor of their country by preserving their faith in the midst of every persecution.

In another place he spoke of them as "an Irish tribe whose hearts have apostatized from the honored creed of their country, but whose lips have not yet mustered the bad courage to disavow the faith of their forefathers."

Apart from more serious objections, the bishop found great fault with the red-hot *Irishism* of Mr. McGee. "The Irish do not require the strong doses of patriotism which he administers. . . . . His countrymen here should mind first their duty to God, to their families, and to the country in which they live. If their native land should be in a situation to profit by their devotion to it, they will not be found wanting when the hour arrives." No one could accuse Bishop Hughes of forgetting the land of his birth; but he wished the naturalized Irishman of the United States to regard themselves as American citizens—not as exiles; and he deprecated every thing that tended to separate them from the rest of the people. He was no friend to Irish "military societies," "trade societies," "clubs," "institutes," and similar organizations—among other reasons, because they were apt to prevent their members from coalescing with their native-born fellow citizens. "Never forget your country," was his advice to the emigrant; "love her, defend her when the time comes; but let this love of old Ireland affect you only individually. In your social and political relations you must become merged in the country of your adoption."

While he was scourging the revolutionists of Ireland, he had also a few blows to bestow upon the red republicans of the continent. The news of the Pope's flight from Rome reached New York about the middle of December, 1848. On the first Sunday of January following he preached a vigorous sermon in the cathedral on "The present position of Pius IX." To a gentleman in Paris, who had proposed to him a plan for the reëstablishment of the Holy Father, he wrote the following letter:

NEW YORK, *March* 29, 1849.
DEAR SIR:

My delay in answering your letter of December last has not arisen from any want of appreciation of the generous motives under which it was written. In common with every faithful member of God's Church, I had heard with sorrow and indignation of the assault upon the Quirinal Palace, and the flight of his Holiness from the Eternal City; and gladly would I make use of any means in my power to aid in protecting him against the wolves that have broken into the fold, and to restore him to his just rights and necessary independence. It would be impossible for me, however, to take any steps in furtherance of the particular design you have meditated for that purpose, without an express wish from his Holiness that such efforts should be made, and also more particular immformation in regard to the nature and circumstances of the general plan. Even then it would be much more difficult than you imagine to take any concerted action in his favor in the manner which you suggest. The Catholic population of the United States, though numerous, is scattered and comparatively poor; and though if on the spot they would be willing to shed their blood to defend the Pope from violence, they could with difficulty be roused to engage in a crusade against the demagogues of Rome. The late news, however, though scanty and contradictory, would lead us to infer that our assistance will not be needed to restore him to the throne of his predecessors. From these distant shores all that we can offer, unless the necessity seems more urgent and the benefit of our attempting any thing in that way more evident, is our fervent prayers and sympathies, and, if needed, our money.

The provincial council of the bishops of the United States will meet at Baltimore in May, and by that time events will have shown what action will be necessary in defence of the rights of the Holy See on the part of this portion of the Church. Some measure will then undoubtedly be taken, if not to assist him in regaining his see (for I trust that by that time this will be no longer necessary), at any rate to aid in securing his personal independence, by the establishment of regular collections throughout all parts of the United States, in the way of Peter-pence, to enable him with more freedom to carry on the necessary business of the Church.

I remain, with sincere regard and respect, your obedient servant,

✠ JOHN HUGHES,
Bishop of New York.

On the first of July, in accordance with the recommendation of the council, he caused a collection for the Holy Father to be taken up in all the churches of the diocese. The sum raised by this means was between six and seven thousand dollars. In reply to *The Tribune* and other secular newspapers, which affected to consider this money as a fund to be used for the overthrow of the Roman republic, he addressed two letters to *The Courier and Enquirer* which impressed the public at the time very strongly in his favor. When the collection was made in the cathedral, he preached again upon the Roman question, and cautioned his flock earnestly against "that spirit of the world, that diabolical spirit, which clothes itself with the robes of liberty, forsooth, and whether out of the Church or in the Church, attempts to bring down every thing—even from the very throne of God—to its own level; that spirit which overthrows order and precipitates society into confusion; that spirit which becomes desperate when it finds there are other worlds and another life at the termination of the present, and that there is an antagonism in the conscience of man which prevents them from succeeding as they would wish."

One of the Young Ireland papers advised the bishop to be very cautious of offending American ideas of republicanism, and to send this money to the Pope secretly. "As if," he indignantly replied, "we were guilty of an act we should conceal! The American people are wise and sensible, and just; and they despise the man who does not appreciate the first principles of the country in which he lives." He made the collection, and the result of it, as public as possible.

He spoke upon the Roman question again in January, 1850, when he delivered a lecture in Philadelphia upon "The Church and the world since the accession of Pius IX." This was for the benefit of St. John's Orphan Asylum. On the 12th of May he held a solemn thanksgiving service in his cathedral in gratitude to Almighty God for the Pope's return to Rome, and preached a sermon with which the Protestant newspapers found a great deal of fault. In consequence of their strictures, he published in the form of a letter to *The Courier and Enquirer* a defence of the Holy Father's temporal administration. His position in this matter was wholly consistent with his principle that revolution is justifiable only as an escape from the gravest oppression. In the condition of the Papal States he could see no parallel to the wrongs which afflicted Ireland. "It is by a special direction and providence of God," said he, at a later period, "that the States of the Church have been reserved, amidst the strifes of nations, as a sacred and exceptional soil for the liberty and independence of the head of the Church, and for the happiness of their inhabitants. It is not yet a century since the temporal subjects of the Holy See might be numbered among the most contented, the most prosperous, the most happy, and the least burthened of any subjects of any sovereign in Europe. Their government was paternal, kind, and considerate; their taxes were light; their fidelity to their sovereign unquestioned." This fidelity had been destroyed, not by misgovernment, but by "the lava of infidelity which poured itself forth over Europe." In all the troubles of the Church and the sovereign Pontiffs, it was an instinct with him to range himself at once upon the side of the Pope. Loyalty and deference to his chief bishop seemed to be a part of his nature. With the most exalted ideas of the sacredness and dignity of the episcopal office, he exacted profound respect and obedience from his clergy to himself, and took pride and delight in paying the same homage on his own part to the Pope. He was not given to drawing distinctions between the temporal and spiritual functions of the sovereign Pontiffs. His veneration for the Holy See took the form of intense veneration for the person of the Holy Father. In his intercourse with the world he never affected humility; he conscientiously believed it his duty to assert his own dignity by way of upholding the dignity of the Church; but in his relations to the common father of the faithful he was the humblest and most dutiful of sons. That a Catholic should advise the Pope to "yield to the current of events," and give up his temporal possessions, seemed to him most horrible and unnatural. It is hardly too much to say that he looked upon some of the doctrines of the modern liberal school of Catholics as only a little way removed from heresy.

CHAPTER XIX.

1847–1848.

Sermon before Congress—Letters to Kirwan—Multitude of calls upon the Bishop's time—Letters of religious advice—Government of the clergy—Characteristics of his preaching—Personal appearance—Manners—Pride in his humble origin—His friends—Social qualities—Failing health—Daily occupations—Fondness for children—Kindness of heart—Generosity—Ignorance of money affairs—Income—Residence.

THE labors just recorded by no means fully represent the bishop's activity during the two or three past years. In December, 1847, he visited Washington in company with Bishop Walsh of Halifax, and at the invitation of John Quincy Adams, Mr. Douglas, Mr. Calhoun, Mr. Benton, and other distinguished members of Congress, preached one Sunday in the hall of the House of Representatives, on "Christianity, the only source of moral, social, and political regeneration," choosing a text certainly pertinent to his audience: "Then came to him the mother of the sons of Zebedee, with her sons, adoring and asking something of him. Who said to her: What wilt thou ? She said to him: Say that these my two sons may sit the one on thy right hand and the other on thy left in thy kingdom."—Matt. xx. 20, 21.

Soon after his return to New York he began a series of letters in *The Freeman's Journal*, on "The Importance of being in Communion with Christ's one, holy, Catholic, and Apostolic Church." His object was to counteract the effect of "Kirwan's Letters to Bishop Hughes," which had just appeared. He barely alludes to "Kirwan." He did not choose to have a personal controversy with any writer who made use of an assumed name. His tone is consequently calm and expository, rather than polemical; but in July, 1848, after nine letters had appeared, the Rev. Nicholas Murray avowed himself as "Kirwan," and Bishop Hughes, leaving the series of Letters on the Church unfinished, began his six letters entitled "Kirwan Unmasked." They were almost wholly personal, for he peremptorily refused to engage in a dogmatical controversy with his opponent; reserving the discussion of any theological points which he might find worthy of notice in Dr. Murray's book for the sequel to the interrupted letters in *The Freeman's Journal*. But this sequel he never found time or inclination to write. The personal part of this controversy is the only part which the bishop seems to have thought worthy of preservation. The effective portions of Kirwan's letters were the bits of calumny and scandal against priests, and the scraps of autobiography with which he had illustrated his recollections of his early life in Ireland. After exposing the falsehood or irrelevancy of these passages, the bishop felt that he might rest. Kirwan's arguments against the Church were too threadbare to need elaborate refutation.

In the course of the summer he obtained a little recreation by a trip to northern New York. The following letter to his secretary was written during the journey:

TO THE REV. J. R. BAYLEY.

BUFFALO, *June* 6, 1848.

REV. DEAR SIR:

I have just arrived. The bishop is absent, and I shall push on up the lake. I have heard of you at Oswego and here. Your travels remind me of Telemachus in search of his lost father. I suppose the object was my signature to some document. But the world must take care of itself till I return, which will be, I trust, "in all" of ten days. Until which time, do as well as you can. Respects to all the Rev. gentlemen of the palace. I feel strong and hearty.

Sincerely yours in Christ.

✠ JOHN HUGHES,

Bp. of N.Y.

During Lent of this year and the next, he preached every Thursday evening in the cathedral. The amount of labor which he performed seems enormous. Almost every week there was confirmation to be administered, a corner-stone to be laid, a church to be dedicated, or a grave-yard to be blessed in some distant part of the diocese. On occasions of this sort he generally preached. Sometimes he performed dedication services in two different parishes, with the addition of a sermon, on the same Sunday. Being anxious to provide a new convent for the Sisters of Mercy, he went about begging for it in person. If he made a journey of pleasure, he found little respite from fatigue; wherever he went he must officiate, preach, and receive a throng of admirers. At home, besides the ordinary duties of his ministry—the instruction of neophytes, the supervision of the affairs of all the churches, the regulation of the finances of the diocese, the satisfaction of heavy debts upon the ecclesiastical property—and for these last two duties, it must be remembered, he had no natural aptitude—the devising of means for building new churches, the establishment of Catholic schools, the foundation of charitable and religious institutions, he was obliged to carry a load of worry and perplexity which was not entailed upon him by his office, but imposed by the selfishness, or egotism, or ignorance of persons who had no claim upon his attention. His letter book from the year 1848 down to a period when, from the very multitude of unwarrantable calls upon his time, and from the weight of gathering years, he felt obliged to disregard many of those who addressed him, presents an amusing study. Young men in Ireland, whom he never heard of, ask his advice about coming over to America. One wants a situation in a bank. Another inquires about the prospects of business in general. All sorts of people send him boxes and packages to be forwarded to their relations in all sorts of out-of-the-way towns in America. Priests in Europe send him restitution-money that has been given them in the confessional by penitent thieves, and beg him to find out (mostly with the vaguest of directions) the persons to whom it rightfully belongs. Emigrants send him money, and request him to buy drafts to transmit to their friends in the old country. Poor people in the old country, on the other hand, ask him to find out their emigrant friends, whose address they do not know. A little army of office-seekers besiege him for letters of introduction. Pious souls write him letters of eight pages about their worldly and spiritual troubles. Protestant clergymen preparing themselves for a terrible assault upon the abominations of popery, request him to state, as clearly as possible, the Catholic doctrine on this or that question. One gentleman consults him about the Broadway railroad. A great many gentlemen ask for loans of fifty dollars. Suspicious, quarrelsome, or malicious persons trouble him with every kind of absurd charge against their parish priests. Most of these are promptly and politely answered; and in the great majority of cases, an effort is made to comply with their unreasonable demands.

There was another class of persons who occupied a great deal of his time, but to whom he was always glad to surrender himself. I mean honest inquirers after Catholic truth. He thought no labor thrown away which was bestowed in explaining to them the doctrines of the Church or answering their objections. A very great number of persons were led into the Church through his influence, or under his instructions. A conversion which made considerable excitement for a time, was that of Dr. William E. Horner, a distinguished physician of Philadelphia. He had been a particular friend of the bishop's when Dr. Hughes was a simple priest, and he corresponded with him on religious subjects for a long while before he finally professed himself a Catholic. He always retained a warm affection for the bishop, and as often as once a year used to come to New York to see him.

As an example of the bishop's mode of dealing with those who consulted him on the subject of religion, let us take the following letters—the first to an inquirer, the second to a recent convert:

TO MR. ———.

NEW YORK, May 15, 1848.

SIR :

I owe you many apologies for not having acknowledged sooner your letter of the 17th ult. The admirable sentiments which it contains, and the frank and straightforward manner in which they are expressed, were quite sufficient to interest me deeply in the matter which you have at heart. But as it was marked "private," and as you gave no special instructions as to your address, I hesitated, under the impression that there are several, or at least more than one, of the same name as yours in ———, and that something awkward and unpleasant might result from my letter's falling into the hands of some one for whom it is not intended. Even now I take precautions.

I should be glad to converse with you on the subject of your letter. In such matters, writing, though useful, is but a poor substitute for the living voice, to which our Lord committed the preaching and teaching of the word of life.

I do not think that such a mind as yours, if you preserve the uprightness of heart and purpose of which your letter gives evidence, will ever find a solid resting place in any phase, form, or system of Protestantism. Each of these contains some truth, but there is one deficiency common to them all—and that is vital, viz. : a divine basis for divine *faith*.

The only work which I would recommend to you at present is the Catechism of the Council of Trent. It is not controversial, nor yet intended for Protestants. But it is an exposition of the Catholic doctrines for the guidance of the parochial clergy in the instruction of their flocks, more especially in reference to the erroneous opinions which were promulgated against the Church at the period in which it was written. It supposes in the reader the knowledge of many principles of Catholic faith with which you can hardly be acquainted, and which it does not treat of. Bossuet's Exposition of the Doctrines of the Church is another short tract which you might read with advantage.

But *faith* is the gift of God, imparted to those who with true desire seek it from the Father of light. Books without prayer, will be to your soul as earth without water. Pray to God, with a mind simple and resolved to do whatever God will make known to you as His will; and in that frame of disposition enter on the question. You need not be solicitous about the result. Put God and the safety of your own soul *above all* beside.

I should be glad to hear from you again, and any thing which it may be in my power to do, shall be done cheerfully, not only from a sense of duty, but also with pleasure. The tone and spirit of your letter have inspired me with that personal respect for you with which I beg leave to subscribe myself your obedient servant in Christ,

✠ JOHN HUGHES, *Bishop of N. Y.*

TO MISS ———.

NEW YORK, *Oct.* 4, 1848.

DEAR MISS ———:

I have just received your letter of the 3d instant, the one of last week not having reached me in time to answer it within the period prescribed. Do not be anxious about the result of your interview with Dr. ———. Almighty God, who sees the sincerity of your heart, will come to your aid, even if all external help should be placed beyond your reach. I regret that I shall not have an opportunity of conversing with you previous to the interview, as what I may say in writing must necessarily be brief and imperfect. I will suggest, however, a few rules which may assist you on the occasion. First, I would confine Dr. ——— to the duties of his profession as a *Protestant* clergyman, reserving the exposition of the Catholic side of the question to those who understand and profess it. Secondly, I would require of him to prove the divine origin and character of the Church of which he is a clergyman, and to which he will labor to bring you over. Thirdly, I would insist on the proofs of his doctrine, or the views to which he would convert you; and these proofs, recollect, should be something more than his opinion with regard to the meaning of the Bible. Fourth, as to the corruptions which he will allege against the Catholic Church, waving all discussion of them, and supposing them to be as he will state, let him point out the true Church which existed before Protestantism was introduced. These general views, improved by your own reflection, will tend to abridge the discussion, and I have no doubt that the inconsistencies of his attempts to answer these questions will tend to strengthen your convictions. But let him particularly confine himself to the Protestant side of the question; inasmuch as, if you wish to know the Catholic doctrine, you must seek the explanation of it from Catholics themselves. It would be a queer proceeding to ask the explanation of the Westminster confession of faith from Quakers.

You will also keep clearly in view the great outlines of the Catholic faith, which, with the grace of God, has already won the assent of your understanding and heart: namely, its divine mysteries and internal spiritual life; its unbroken history from the days of our Redeemer; its triumph in converting all nations from paganism to Christianity; its holy martyrs and saints in all ages; its conformity to the Holy Scripture, as a Church existing at all times—as a Church whose ministers are sent in perpetual succession—as a Church which *teaches*, instead of giving out the private opinions of its members— as a Church which, without coercion, unites all believers by the same faith, the same Lord, and the same sacraments—as a Church which seems to be, as it really is, supported by God himself, so that it has triumphed over every obstacle which persecution and impiety and heresy have raised to impede its progress and to accomplish its overthrow. By reflection on these general hints as to what the true Church is, you will easily fill your mind with those striking points of difference which distinguish the Church of God from the sects founded by men, which, under one form of error or another, have not ceased to rise and rail against her from the beginning of Christianity even to the present day. Now this Church of God is to be entered by all those to whom he vouchsafes the light of divine faith, and this too, as the Scriptures remark, at every sacrifice of an earthly and temporal character. If, then, Mr. —— would lead you away from this, let him show some other Church of God having superior, or at least equal, claims to be the one holy Catholic Church. Let him not pretend to satisfy you with the chaff of opinions about the meaning of the Scriptures which Protestants call religion, and in which no two sects, and hardly two individuals of any one sect, are found to agree. Can God be the author of contradiction? Can the Holy Scriptures sanction even two opposite creeds? Can Mr. —— do more than give his opinion on any question of Christian doctrine? And what security attaches to his opinion more than that of a Methodist, a Unitarian, or a Universalist? To what, then, would he convert you from the faith which God has enabled you to believe and embrace! What pledge can he give you, more than any other speculator on the sacred text, that in following his opinion you are not renouncing the truth which Christ revealed! He would detach you from the rock of faith, and leave you afloat on the sea of doubt and uncertainty.

But you will be particularly careful to let Mr. —— state distinctly the doctrines which he would have you believe, and then give proof, better than his own opinions, that such doctrines constitute the belief of what he calls the Church, and then that there is a Church which really hold such doctrines. In short, there is a Church, or there is not. If there be no Church, then Christianity is a failure, for Christ declared that there would be a *teaching Church* until the end of the world, and that that Church should teach all truth. If there be a Church, it must be the Catholic. If Mr. —— says not, then let him point out any other having the marks of divine origin, and coming down uninterruptedly from our blessed Saviour. His objections against the mysteries of the Church are essentially the same which infidels urge against the Trinity, the incarnation, and other doctrines which Mr. —— professes to believe.

These are the general views which I suggest to you as a preparation for the painful interview that is before you. If you have some Catholic books, you will do well to make yourself familiar with the great principles on which all Christian and Catholic faith reposes. Then, above all things, appeal to God in fervent prayer, that he may direct and support you. If you have an opportunity after returning to the city, I shall be happy to see you at any time that you will designate, and to be ready to explain to you any point of Catholic doctrine, the knowledge of which may be essential to you in listening to Mr. ——. In the mean time, believe me

Very sincerely your friend and servant in Christ,

✠ JOHN HUGHES,
Bp. of New York.

A great many persons used to go to him with their domestic troubles. As a family peace-maker the world had little idea, said one who knew him intimately, of the scandals and quarrels that were avoided through his influence, and the vast amount of good that he effected by preventing evil.

In the government of his clergy he was not strict. He never inquired very closely into their conduct; and when delinquencies were brought to his notice he often forgave in cases wherein forgiveness was a weakness, not a virtue. But having once convinced himself that it was his duty to punish, he was inexorable. The penalty of suspension came swiftly and surely, and the rebuke that accompanied it was scathing in its severity. He wrote as follows to an unworthy priest who had petitioned for restoration to the ministry:

REV. SIR:

It is my duty to acknowledge the receipt of your letter of the 26th instant. I ought to rejoice at your resolution to make your peace with God. You will soon have to appear in His presence, and you ought to think of your poor soul without a moment's delay. If you had some wise and truly sincere friend to advise you, he would counsel you to retire and do penance. This is the only reparation you can now make to the Church of God for your past but unforgotten scandals. When by the fervor of your penitence you shall have built up a new foundation of character, you may perhaps be allowed to exercise to some extent the functions of your abused ministry. But not among the people who have known you. If God should give you grace to labor for the salvation of *your own soul*, it will be happy for you.

✠ JOHN HUGHES,
Bp. of N. Y.

He demanded exact obedience from his priests, and it was cheerfully given him. He was but little troubled with the insubordination which had occasionally disturbed other prelates. He was fortunate in having to rule over an exemplary body of clergymen; but we cannot doubt that had he been less happily situated he would soon have set matters in order. In Bishop Conwell's place, for instance, he would have made short work of Messrs. Harold and Hogan. It needed a brave man to face him when he was displeased. His rebukes were terrible. He had the power of expressing scorn to a greater degree than any other man I ever saw. On a certain occasion a student in his seminary was charged with a venial infraction of discipline. In attempting to excuse himself before the bishop, he told a lie. Bishop Hughes detected him at once, and in the presence of some thirty other persons administered a verbal castigation which no one who heard it will ever forget. It was short: but in bitter sarcasm and crushing invective, Junius hardly equalled it. He drove the unfortunate offender from the house, and never would consent to see him again.

I have alluded several times to the effectiveness of his preaching. Only a very faint idea can be obtained of it by reading his sermons. Charles James Fox used to say, "Did my speech read well when reported? If so, it was a bad one." It was the case with the bishop also, that his most successful efforts in the pulpit are not those that appear best in print. For more than thirty years he rarely wrote a sermon, except upon some great occasion when he was anxious that what he said should be correctly published. His printed discourses, as they now appear, were nearly all taken down by short-hand writers. Sometimes he corrected them before they were published; but a great proportion of them are very inaccurate reports. Many of his most eloquent sermons were never reported at all. It was no uncommon thing for him, at the dedication of some little country-church, or after confirmation in some obscure parish, to deliver on the spur of the moment a magnificent discourse to which his more elaborate sermons were not worthy to be compared. As these read, they are discursive; sometimes, but not always, impassioned; faulty in arrangement, and now and then slovenly in style: but as they came from his lips, with the added effect of his dignified manner, his commanding and expressive features, his graceful movements, his clear enunciation and agreeable voice, they possessed a charm which the pen can hardly describe. His favorite gesture was an impressive motion with the right hand, the thumb and forefinger joined, and the other fingers extended. He had just enough of the Irish accent to give a mellowness to his tones, and an occasional piquancy to his inflections; it was not by any means a brogue, and a careless observer would not have discovered his nationality from it. He seldom raised his voice very loud or high, but he now and then dropped it, when he aimed at solemnity, until it was scarcely audible. Perhaps there never was a popular preacher so utterly free from rant. "For more than a third of a century," said he, a few years before his death, "it has been my duty to preach the Word of God; but it was almost always to the willing ears and fervent hearts of the humble and simple-minded, who, in their own fervor, were prepared to hear and be edified at whatever might be said. In speaking to them I have acquired the habit of imitating the simplicity of the gospel itself, caring little for ornaments of style, provided I could find terms calculated to convey ideas. If the ideas should be retained by my hearers, the language which had been used as their vehicle was of the slightest consequence." It must be admitted that he did not always succeed in bringing down his language to the level of an unlettered audience, neither was he always very practical in his sermons. His preaching consisted more frequently in explaining and proving Catholic doctrine than inculcating Catholic morality. He used often, before he went into the pulpit, to read a homily or extract from one of the Fathers, and taking a single suggestion from that, he would amplify and illustrate it in the most admirable manner. He made very happy use of his various reading; but his best and most striking thoughts were those which, without premeditation, were struck out of his own brain.

He excelled as a preacher of Charity sermons, wielding an influence over his audience quite disproportionate to the intrinsic eloquence of his language, and only to be accounted for by that personal magnetism to which, in other relations of life, he owed so much of his power over his fellow-men.

When he preached in St. John's Church in Philadelphia in behalf of the Polish exiles in 1834, the enthusiasm of his hearers rose to such a pitch that, it is said, many of them not only gave all the money in their purses, but threw their jewelry into the plates. His discourse at the laying of the corner-stone of the new St. Patrick's Cathedral in 1858 reads as one of the least happy of his efforts; yet it was in reality a very effective sermon. The preacher was often interrupted by the emotions of his audience. As the services were held in the open air, the people did not scruple to applaud, and cry "Good!" and "Hurrah!" at passages which especially pleased them.

His personal appearance was striking and agreeable. He was about five feet nine inches in height, well formed, with a powerful frame, and, in early and middle life, an erect carriage. He had a remarkably large head, prominent features, a large but well-shaped Roman nose, keen gray eyes, a sharp resolute mouth, and brown hair. He became bald long before he was an old man, and from the time of his consecration as bishop he always wore a scratch-wig. Until age and disease had set their mark upon him he was a handsome man; and he never lost a graceful and prepossessing demeanor, which is far more attractive than mere personal beauty. His voice was clear and musical. His movements were dignified, yet unconstrained. He was neat but not finical in his dress and personal habits. His ordinary apparel at home, as well as at lectures and on all public occasions not of an ecclesiastical character, was the purple cassock with red buttons appropriate for a bishop. The golden episcopal cross usually hung from his neck on a gold chain. His purple barreta, or square cap, was generally on his head or within reach. In the street he dressed in plain black clothes, with no distinguishing mark except the purple Roman stock around his neck.

His dignity of manner was free from every thing like pompousness or affectation. He never laid it aside, for it was a part of his nature. He had not one manner for his chamber and another for his parlor. Of course, like all other men, he would unbend at times; but even in his most careless moments he seemed to bear a recollection of the sacredness of his episcopal character. "Never forget that you are a bishop," said he to a prelate just consecrated. He was jealous of his dignity. Fond as he was of a joke, he suffered no one to joke at his expense: the rash man who might try to do so would be certain to repent his temerity. He never seemed embarrassed. He had an instinctive perception of the requirements of etiquette, and appeared equally at home in a laborer's cabin and in the palace of the Tuileries. As a general thing his bearing to strangers was exceedingly kind and assuring. But when he was not favorably impressed by a visitor his politeness was rather chilling. The keen, searching glance of his eye, the occasional curl of his lip, the clear, subdued tones of his well-modulated voice, the quiet attention with which he listened to every word that was uttered—seeming to weigh it, and criticize it, and judge from it of the character of the speaker—often covered timid people with confusion, and sent them away from his presence in a very uncomfortable state of mind.

He loved to refer to his own early life. He had no false shame about his humble origin. He was rather proud of the poverty of his ancestors, "because," he said, "it was a proof that they had always been faithful to their religion." A gentleman whom he had known in Philadelphia, and who had just been appointed to an honorable position in the diplomatic service, came to call upon him in New York. After chatting for a few moments on various topics, the bishop looked around as if to be sure that the door was shut, drew up his chair close to that of his friend, and said: "Now, C——, let us talk about ourselves? What a change in both of us since you and I first became friends!"

One Sunday a man who had worked with him in the stone-quarries at Chambersburg, and had since risen a few steps higher in the world, being on a visit to New York, went to the cathedral, but could not find a seat. He was leaving the church by the sacristy door, when he met the bishop coming in to preach. The bishop recognized him, gave him a warm welcome, ordered the sexton to show him a good seat, invited him to dinner, and spent a long time chatting with him about old friends.

Though he had many acquaintances to whom he was warmly attached, there were few to whom he opened his heart, or with whom he could be said to live on terms of familiarity. He entertained a very warm regard for Mr. Peter A. Hargous, a well-known merchant of New York, and a devout Catholic, who was perhaps as near to being his confidential companion as anybody was. His most intimate friends were by no means all clergymen, and not even all Catholics. A somewhat celebrated Protestant gentleman of New York with whom he associated a great deal, was the late Jacob Harvey; "such a nice man," said the bishop, "that I cannot help hoping he will get to heaven some how or another." Many of his old Philadelphia friends used to visit him or write to him after his removal to New York. Clement C. Biddle of Philadelphia was one of his best correspondents. Some of the bishop's most valuable and interesting letters were written to this gentleman, and it is a matter of deep regret that no trace of them can now be found. Matthew Carey, the well-known bookseller, printer, and philanthropist was another of his special associates; but he died the year after Dr. Hughes was consecrated bishop. He seems to have imbued the bishop at one time with a good share of his own enthusiasm for prison-reform and kindred subjects. He used to send copies of all his numerous pamphlets on such topics to the bishop, and the latter not only read them, but sometimes added marginal notes to them—a practice to which he was not generally addicted.*

---

* He did not always agree with Mr. Carey. On the fly-leaf of a copy of that gentleman's "*Thoughts on Penitentiaries and Prison Discipline*" (a defence of the Auburn and Weathersfield systems), he wrote:

"I have read this pamphlet through: and whatever theory may be adopted,

In the company of his chosen friends he was one of the most genial of men. Wit and philosophy, fun and good sense, flowed together from his lips; although, as Bishop Bayley expressed it, there was a *snap* to every thing he said, his conversation had none of the caustic tone which was so characteristic of his writings. He always spoke kindly of those with whom he had sustained his sharpest controversies. He was charitable in his judgments, and tender of others' reputations. His strong religious convictions never interfered with the amenities of social intercourse. He would have received any one of his old opponents with sincere cordiality.

Admirably as he was fitted to adorn society, he mingled very little with the world. The Rev. Mr. Bayley made a great many efforts to bring him more into company, believing that his health required the stimulant of variety in his daily life. At Mr. B.'s suggestion, some of the principal Catholic gentlemen of the city gave occasional dinner parties, at which Protestants of distinction, authors, scholars, officials, and others, were invited to meet the bishop. On such occasions Dr. Hughes always appeared to great advantage. He had the gift of adapting his conversation to his company; he appreciated the agreeable qualities of the other guests; his spirits rose with the excitement of genial intercourse;* he illustrated every topic that was broached with some apposite bit of knowledge, or some original and striking thought—

---

it seems to me that the well-known principles of human nature will be its soundest *basis*. Facts here quoted are far from sufficient to prove the great superiority of modern improvement in prison discipline. It seems to me that the fear of punishment is the strongest restraint on the depraved; and this barrier will be entirely broken down if prisons be changed from places of punishment into houses of correction, where the wolf and the tiger, after having preyed upon humanity, are to be wheedled out of their ferocity and soothed into kindness by the influence of an ill-timed, sickly affectation of humanity. The difference of punishment between murder and robbery has saved many a life, when otherwise the life and purse would be taken together."

* I must not be misunderstood—I do not mean convivial intercourse; for he was very abstemious.

astonishing everybody by the retentiveness of his memory, and the native vigor of his intellect. He joked; he told stories; and, by a rare combination of social gifts, he was a good listener. Strangers were almost invariably delighted with him; but he never could be induced to take the trouble of leaving cards or calling upon the acquaintances whom he made at these parties.

He very seldom entertained company himself, although other bishops and priests were often his guests in an informal way. Every year, on St. Patrick's day, he invited the priests of the city to dine with him; and always after any grand ceremonial at the cathedral, a party of clergymen sat down at his table. He also entertained now and then distinguished foreign visitors. He not only seldom dined out, but he rarely made visits of friendship or ceremony.

The robust bodily health which he had enjoyed in early life, already began to forsake him by the time he was fifty years old. His friend, Bishop Walsh, of Halifax, writes in April, 1848, to remonstrate with him upon his carelessness of his own health:

It seems to me that you have no moments of repose, that you are always swallowed up in a whirlpool of multifarious occupations, and that no one appears to have the slightest pity or compassion for your incessant drudgery. This is cruel. Your close confinement in your room would break down the most powerful constitution, and to do yourself common justice, you should have a good walk, ride, or drive every day in the week, and I would add, an entire day's relaxation in each week, on the sound principle of the "*fugit opes strepitumque Romæ.*" I have seen you so exhausted after some of your sermons that I have been alarmed. But I knew well it was not the sermon alone that did this, but the previous toil and incessant occupation of mind and body.

His way of life was fast destroying his constitution. He rose late in the morning and breakfasted in his room, taking very little except a cup of coffee. He seldom or never appeared at breakfast with the other clergymen of the house. This meal over, he read his office, received visitors—rarely refusing to see any respectable person; attended to whatever business might be laid before him by his secretary, and gave a little time to his correspondence. From about the year 1843 he used to dictate his letters, at first occasionally, and during the latter part of his life altogether. Sometimes he made use of the Rev. Mr. Bayley's pen, but after a while, when his fingers had become so much distorted by rheumatism that he could not write without pain, he kept an amanuensis.

When not otherwise occupied, he spent much time in reading newspapers. At this period of his life he rarely took up a book; he did not often look at even reviews or magazines; but he received nearly all the leading daily and weekly papers, and perused them attentively. Of course this habit was a stimulant of his appetite for controversy.

He took no exercise unless business obliged him to do so. Dinner was served in his house at two o'clock, but he was not often at table, except when his secretary persuaded—I might almost say forced him to come. But even when seated at table he ate very little. He was not fond of good living; and eating a regular meal was a duty which he neglected whenever he could. At table when he felt well, or when company was present, his conversation was charming. But he needed some one to draw him out. When left to himself, he listened more than he talked, and sometimes he listened with a closeness of attention which to a timid person was embarrassing. When he did not dine with the rest of his household, he sometimes took no dinner at all, sometimes called for a morsel of whatever might be in the house whenever he felt hungry.

He sat up very late at night writing, or dictating, or preparing his controversies. He composed rapidly, and seldom revised what he had once put upon paper; but he now and then submitted his writings to his friend Mr. Hargous, or some other person whom he trusted, before sending them to the press; and he was ready to take advice about them, to modify them, or even to suppress them altogether. His sitting-room, or study, communicated with the office of his secretary; and when he was tired writing, he often perched himself upon a high stool by Mr. Bayley's table, and chatted, discussed public affairs, and told stories by the hour. His genial qualities never shone forth more brightly than on these occasions; "most of the conversation," says Bishop Bayley, "as you may well suppose, was on one side."

He had no fixed time for any thing. He lacked all idea of order or system. He never followed a regular plan of action, and never laid out his work in advance. All his great achievements, such as the overthrow of the trustee system and the destruction of the Public School Society, originated by accident. He was not persevering; but he threw himself into difficult enterprises with a resolution which generally insured success. If matters went according to his wish, his application soon flagged; if he met with opposition, his energy was aroused, and he never rested until he had accomplished his purpose; but when the victory was gained he very often neglected to pursue it to its legitimate consequences. He had a far-reaching, comprehensive mind, but no head for details. Had there only been some practical, hard working, clear-headed man whom he could have called to his assistance, he would have accomplished much more than he actually did; but his clergy were all busy with their own duties, and as for laymen he never would let them interfere in church matters if he could help it.

His lack of order was partly the consequence of his irregular education, and partly the cause why he never fully repaired the defects of his early training. He had great natural aptitude for learning, a remarkable memory, and a clear, logical mind.* But in his youth he had to pick up knowl-

* This is very strikingly manifest in many of his controversies—in the Letters to Kirwan, for example, and to a less degree in those to Senator Brooks. His skill at a cross-examination was admirable.

edge here and there during the intervals of manual labor; and after he entered upon the active duties of the ministry, he was obliged to study in a hurried and desultory way, to prepare himself for his great public efforts. Thus he contracted a habit of trusting to superficial scholarship, and collecting knowledge only as he had immediate use for it.

Though he furnished his brain in such a disorderly manner, he had a wonderful knack of making the most effective use of his information. He often astonished people in conversation by his acquaintance with minute historical details to which nobody supposed that his attention had ever been directed.

I have said that he had naturally a logical mind; but in time his defective mode of study injured his style of reasoning, and during the latter part of his life his writings showed very plainly that discursiveness and want of system which was his principal mental defect. His books and papers were always in disorder. Every now and then he would engage somebody to set his library in order, make a catalogue of it, number the books, and give each volume its proper place on the shelves. But when he had taken down a book he never remembered to put it back, and the confusion was soon as bad as ever. "It is very strange," he would say; "I don't know how this library is arranged: I never can find any thing in it." Then some one would be called in to do the work over again. He lent books freely, and almost always forgot who had borrowed them. He consequently lost a great many valuable works. His amanuensis was instructed to docket all his letters and papers, and file them away in a large case with pigeon holes made for the purpose, which he kept in his study. If he had occasion, however, to refer to one of these papers, he was almost certain to put it into the wrong hole when he had done with it, or to fold it up with any thing else that might happen to be at hand. So the filing and docketing soon became of little use to him. Occasionally he would devote a day to examining his papers and burning such as he did not wish to keep. His principle of selection appeared inexplicable. Many a letter of historical value was devoted to the flames, while the most insignificant notes and invitations to dinners were carefully preserved. He generally kept the rough copies of letters and newspaper articles that he dictated, no matter upon what subject, but he was not particular about his printed works; there are many of them of which he had no copy. In 1855 he began to keep a scrap-book, in which his amanuensis pasted newspaper-articles referring to or written by him; but it was by no means complete.

He was fond of young people, and generally noticed and petted children. Orphans were always the objects of his tenderest solicitude. The children from the asylums sometimes waited upon him in a body to present addresses of welcome on his return from a long journey; he seemed very much gratified by such visits. He had one of the kindest hearts that ever beat in a human breast; although from the sharp tone of his writing he was generally considered a severe man by those who did not know him. A tale of distress always moved him. He gave away money lavishly—almost foolishly. He was not fond of parading his name as a contributor to public charities; but privately he exercised all the proverbial generosity of his race, and he did it with a delicacy which doubled the value of the gift.

He had no idea of accounts. For many years he carried neither a purse nor a pocket-book. When he was going on a journey his secretary used to put up in two little parcels as much gold and silver as he supposed the bishop would need; and no matter how large the amount or how short the journey, Dr. Hughes never brought a penny home with him. Sanguine friends sometimes induced him to invest money in enterprises with which they were connected, and as a general rule he lost it. He kept a bank account, but did not know how to manage it. If he wanted money, he asked his secretary for it, and he was almost always in debt to the diocesan fund. He made no minute of his deposits in bank, and even his memoranda on the margin of his check book were generally unintelligible. Sometimes he set down only the amount of the checks he had drawn, sometimes only the name of the payee, sometimes only the date or the number. He never knew how much money he had. Whenever Mr. Bayley wanted to adjust his accounts he had to go to the bank. The bishop would sign a check in blank, and if there proved to be a balance to his credit, Mr. Bayley would then draw enough to cover the advances he had made. The bishop seldom remembered these small loans. "See here," he would say to Mr. B. every now and then, in a jocose manner, "you have been robbing me."

"I know I have, monseigneur; but you robbed me first. You owe me money now."

"Well, well; let me have an exact account of my affairs; I must be more careful and economical for the future."

The account was often drawn up; but he never could understand it, and things went on again in the old way.

His income was chiefly in the form of a salary paid by the trustees of the cathedral. It varied at different periods of his life. When he first came to New York it was quite small; it was afterward increased until it became ample to support him in comfort, though it never was extravagant, and was less than is now paid to some Protestant ministers. He saved none of it, and spent but very little upon himself. Almost the only expensive gratification he allowed himself was, in the latter years of his life, a carriage and a pair of horses, of which he made very little use—though he had been very fond of horses in his youth.

His residence in Mulberry street was a plain brick double-house, simply and even sparely furnished. On the first floor were his library, secretary's office, and parlor. His bedroom was in the second story. The rest of the house was occupied by the vicar-general, the secretary, and one or two priests attached to the cathedral. He kept for several years a confidential man-servant; he had no other domestics except the women necessary to do the work of the household.

CHAPTER XX.

1850-1852.

Dr. Hughes appointed an Archbishop—Visit to Rome—Project for making him a Cardinal—Letter on Toleration—Letter about Kossuth—Lecture on the Catholic Chapter in the History of the United States—Letter from Clement C. Biddle—Catholicism and the American people—The Auxiliary Church Building Association—Settlement of the affairs of St. Peter's church, and end of the trustee system.

THE seventh council of Baltimore was held in May, 1849. One of its most important acts was the passing of a recommendation that three new archbishoprics should be erected in the United States, namely, at New Orleans, Cincinnati, and New York. The only sees which then enjoyed metropolitan dignity, were Baltimore, Oregon City, and St. Louis. The consideration of the subject by the Sovereign Pontiff was delayed by the political troubles in Italy, and it was not until the 3d of October, 1850, that the papal brief was received by Dr. Hughes, advancing him to the dignity of an archbishop, with the bishops of Boston, Hartford, Albany, and Buffalo for his suffragans.

He announced his promotion the next Sunday to the congregation of St. Patrick's, expressed his intention of going to Rome to be invested with the pallium—the insignia of his new dignity—by the Pope himself, and alluded to the necessity of preparing to build a new cathedral. At the beginning of November he made a hurried farewell visit to his friends in Philadelphia and Washington, where he dined *en famille* with President Fillmore. On the 10th he delivered a lecture in the cathedral, for the benefit of the Sisters of Mercy, on "The Decline of Protestantism and its Causes." It provoked a great many replies from "Kirwan" and other Protestant clergymen; but before they appeared Archbishop Hughes was out of hearing, for he sailed in the Baltic for Liverpool on the 16th. On the eve of his departure he published a pastoral letter, in which, after alluding to his new dignity, he referred to the subject of education:

I think the time has almost come when it will be necessary to build the school-house first, and the church afterward. Our fellow-citizens have adopted a system of education, which I fear will result in consequences to a great extent the reverse of those which are anticipated. They have attempted to divorce religion, under the plea of excluding sectarianism from elementary education and literature. There are some who seem to apprehend great mischief to the state, if the children in our public schools should have an opportunity of learning the first elements of the Christian doctrine in connection with their daily lessons. Happily they require of us only to contribute our portion of the expense necessary for the support of this system. This, as good citizens, we are bound to do, especially as we are not compelled to send our children to such schools to receive the doubtful equivalent which is given for the taxes collected. I hope that the friends of education may not be disappointed in their expectations of benefit from this system, whilst for myself I may be allowed to say that I do not regard it as suited to a Christian land, whether Catholic or Protestant, however admirably it might be adapted to the social condition of an enlightened pagan.

After a short stay in England, where he was treated with great honor, the archbishop proceeded to Rome, and arrived there Christmas eve. He was one of a distinguished company of bishops and cardinals who celebrated the festival of St. Thomas à Becket at the English college on the 28th of December. In the month of January he began a course of controversial sermons in English, before large congregations of English, Irish, and American residents, in the church of

S. Andrea delle Fratte. On the feast of St. Agatha, February 5th, which is kept in Rome with great magnificence, he was chosen to pronounce the panegyric of the saint. His lecture on the "Decline of Protestantism and its Causes" was translated into Italian and published in the principal journals. "Our archbishop's rooms," writes a priest who bore him company on this journey, "are daily crowded with lords, knights, secretaries, masters of ceremonies, princes, priests, and friars, black, blue, red, violet, scarlet, etc." The Pope showed him particular regard, and sent him choice dishes from his own table. The archbishop spoke as follows of the Holy Father's situation:

He feels secure in his position, in the midst of all the agitations around him; and if it had been your privilege, as it has been mine, to have so recently and so intimately communed with him and with the venerable members of the sacred college, who sympathize with him in all his joys and sorrows, you would perceive that they are the only tranquil, calm, and self-possessed public men in Europe. . . . It would be impossible for you to behold without veneration the peace that is manifested by these holy men, and especially the Holy Father himself, in whom is blended the highest majesty with the profoundest humility.

Oh, how blessed in the midst of these things for one from a remote part of the world to spend a few days or a few months in that Eternal City, surrounded by such men, interested by such associations that he cannot turn round, even on material objects, without being reminded of so much; but principally how glorious and consoling it is to find himself coming into communion with men from the opposite side of the globe during the ceremonies of holy week, when he witnesses whatever is touching and edifying, during the time in which the sorrows of the Saviour, and His passion, are commemorated by the Head of the Church himself, and those round him! How grand is the contemplation, when you behold, partly by accident, men from all parts of the globe—all finding themselves at home, all in the presence of their parent! If you read books about holy week in Rome, they will tell you that the spectacles are rather a kind of public pageant. It is true that when these holy things are presented to the spectator, every feeling of sanctity is taked away from them by the mob of strangers who go there at that perion, to gratify the eye and their curiosity by their wild and unmannerly staring. But it is the mob who do this.

The archbishop had not been long in Rome before it was reported, on what seemed to be good authority, that he was about to be advanced to the rank of cardinal. The matter was certainly discussed unofficially among the dignitaries of the papal court. It originated, however, not at Rome, but at Washington. It had not escaped the notice of the American government that Pius IX. was disposed to make the college of cardinals more catholic than it had lately been, and it was thought by some of the cabinet that certain personal and political interests might be subserved by having an American prelate presented for this dignity. The United States minister at Rome actively promoted the scheme, though perhaps not strictly in his official character. It was generally understood that if it should be carried into effect, Archbishop Hughes would be the nominee most acceptable to all parties. So certain seemed his appointment that the Leopoldine society in Vienna actually offered to present him with a suitable outfit. Another American prelate, who was in Rome at this time, introduced the subject during an audience with the Holy Father.

"I will tell you," said the Pope, smiling, "what there is of that. It is true that your government did ask me for a cardinal—*non pas celui la, mais un cardinal*" (emphasizing the indefinite article); "and I told them, which was true, that there was no place of cardinal priest vacant."

In the mean time the archbishop of Baltimore had written to Rome to say that in his judgment it was inexpedient to create an American cardinal, and it is understood that other bishops of the United States, as well as the Pope himself, were of the same opinion.

The ceremony of conferring the pallium was performed on the 3d of April, not, as was customary, by the cardinal vicar of Rome, but by the Holy Father himself. The archbishop was very sensible of this mark of kindness, and spoke of it after his return to America with no little gratification. On the 3d of May he left Rome for a short visit to Vienna, having first on the morning of his departure celebrated mass in the ancient subterranean chapel of Santa Croce in Gierusalemme. From Germany he passed over to England, and on the 11th of June sailed from Liverpool, homeward bound. On the eve of his departure, the Catholics of Liverpool entertained him at dinner.

He landed in New York on the 22d, and spent the next two or three days in visiting the schools, colleges, and religious institutions of the city and vicinity, and receiving addresses of welcome and congratulation. On the 1st of July he preached in the cathedral, and gave an interesting account of his visit to Rome. On the 21st the Catholics of New York gave a grand banquet in his honor at the Astor House.

An effort was making at this time to raise money in the United States for the establishment of a Catholic University in Ireland. Two Irish clergymen came over to this country on a tour of collection, and several public meetings were held for the purpose of explaining and promoting their enterprise. The archbishop's patriotism, as well as his interest in the cause of education, forbade his remaining a passive spectator of the movement. He freely gave permission to the collectors to appeal to the Catholics of his diocese from any pulpit which the parish clergymen might see fit to put at their disposal; and on the 18th of November he attended a public meeting at Stuyvesant Institute, New York, where he proposed a resolution, and commended the Irish university to the liberality of his people. In the course of his address, he made some disparaging remarks about revolutionists in general, and Kossuth in particular, which involved him in a short controversy with *The New York Tribune*. The following extract from his letter to Mr. Greeley, dated Nov. 21st, gives his opinion on the question of religious toleration:

I deny, with the Catholic Church, any right of one man, by physical coercion, to compel the conscience of another man. Hence, therefore, I am opposed to all penal laws having the coercion of conscience for their object. In countries which are already divided and broken up into religious sects, mutual toleration, kindness, and goodwill, in all the civil and social relations of life, constitute at once, in my opinion, the duties and the rights of all. But I am not aware that a Protestant State, such as Sweden, is bound, by way of granting religious liberty, to place atheism on the same footing as Lutheranism. Neither am I of opinion that the Sovereign Pontiff, whose subjects are entirely Catholic and united in belief, is bound to throw his States open for the preaching of every form of Protestantism and infidelity. As spiritual head of the Catholic Church on earth, he is bound to preserve the revelation which has Christ for its author. To encourage opposition to that religion would be to take sides with the father of lies, and I am sure, sir, that you would hardly expect the Pope to go so far. Besides, as a temporal prince, he knows the horrors of civil war which have desolated other countries, springing out of the ambitions of religious sects, each struggling for political ascendency in the state. But, besides all this, he knows that it is a fundamental article of the Protestant religion to believe that he is Antichrist. Liberty of conscience, therefore, in your sense, would require that the Pope should become directly a party to the introduction of every species of error and impiety, and the overthrow of his own authority both as temporal prince and sovereign pontiff.

Kossuth arrived in America on the 5th of December. The Catholics of New York, warned by the archbishop, took no part in the demonstrations of welcome which greeted him. The archbishop looked upon the ex-governor of Hungary as little better than a demagogue, and what was more, as an enemy of the Catholic Church. He expressed his opinion of him very clearly in the following letter to the Austrian minister at Washington:

TO THE CHEVALIER HULSEMANN.

NEW YORK, *Dec.* 11, 1851.

DEAR SIR:

I had the honor to receive your letter of the 5th instant, with the interesting document by which it was accompanied, and which I have sent to the consul here to be returned to you.

As I remarked before, it would not become me to regard the question of Kossuth's arrival in this country as it might affect the special politics of Austria and Hungary. I regard him and all that I have known of his class, as arch-enemies of the Catholic Church and of the peace of mankind; and, therefore, I take it for granted, that no blessing can attend their efforts, and that it is a charity which we owe to Christian faith and the tranquillity of nations, to use every just and honorable means for the extinguishment of their efforts with as little delay as possible. I have very little doubt myself, that the cause of Austria, as against Kossuth and his band of conspirators, is a just and true cause; but my state of life forbids me to view the question according to its specific merits under this light. I have been in both Austria and Hungary; my recollections of the treatment I received in both are of the most pleasant kind. To both I owe gratitude, charity, and truth. Nor is it necessary that, even to you, I should pronounce an opinion with regard to the merits of any controversy which may have arisen between them. The immediate occasion of my allusion to Kossuth in my speech, was his vile flattery of English bigotry and English persecution against the Church of God, proclaimed by himself in his speech at Southampton. But besides that he took occasion to praise your infidel emperor Joseph II., who signalized his reign, not by putting iron fetters on the Church as a whole, but by tying her down to the earth with a multiplicity of small cords. Kossuth praised him, and Kossuth denounced your present young Catholic emperor, who of his own accord, and without instructions from his cabinet, cut those small cords, and set the Catholic Church free in the Austrian dominions. Again, Kossuth denounced the French nation bitterly, and its president in particular, for having restored to the See of St. Peter our then exiled Holy Father Pius IX. The uncle of that president had reduced Pius VII. to captivity; and thus the nephew of Napoleon, like the present Emperor of Austria, has reversed in favor of religion, the policy which his predecessor had employed against it. Now I have faith enough to believe that Almighty God will ward off, both from France and Austria, many of the dangers with which both are threatened, in consideration of these two noble acts which he has inspired their present rulers to execute in favor of his Church.

As regards Kossuth himself, my feelings toward him now are rather those of pity than of resentment. He is suffering in health; he is broken or breaking in spirit; he is disappointed in his mission to this country; he is by this time disgusted, in his inmost soul, at the loud, hollow, deceptive acclamations which greeted his arrival. A great appearance of respect is still exhibited in his regard, but even when it is sincere, under the shock of rebuke and disappointment it brings him nor comfort nor confidence. One thing I am happy to know, that the Catholics of this city, whether American, Irish, German, or French, have treated him with the utmost indifference; and in doing so have placed themselves in a most honorable position, since it appears by the newspapers that the public men who are supposed to have invited him, are utterly at a loss to know what to do with him now that he has arrived. As for yourself, I think you may be quite satisfied with the result of your able and successful efforts to neutralize his influence against the country which you represent near Washington with so much tact and ability. I think that for the future, as regards the diplomacy of this question, your sailing will be on a smooth sea. In the mean time, although it will give me at all times great pleasure to hear from you on any other topic, I think it will be expedient to avoid any correspondence on these political matters of which I am so incompetent a judge, and which, so far as the interests of your country are concerned, are entirely safe in your hands.

In a lecture on "The Catholic Chapter in the History of the United States," which he delivered in New York in March, 1852, for the benefit of the House of Protection of the Sisters of Mercy,* he has a more explicit statement of his views respecting revolutions:

* "The object of this lecture," he says, "will be to show that Catholics, as such, are by no means strangers and foreigners in this land. . . The

The Catholic Church has no recognized theory on the subject of forms of civil government. The little republic of San Marino has preserved its independence and its republican forms for fourteen hundred years in the very heart of the Papal States. The Church, however, is not an approver of revolutions, except when they are clearly justifiable. Having experienced singular protection in all the vicissitudes and revolutions of the social and political world during eighteen centuries, she has the consciousness that she lives by an inherent vitality within herself, of more than human origin. This has sufficed her during the past; it is sufficient for the present; and she is never troubled with doubts or misgivings in regard to her position in the future, which God has in His own hands and can dispose of as He will. The first impression which the influence of her doctrine in regard to the principle of revolution would produce, I think, would be a presumption in favor of existing authority, until cause to the contrary should appear. Yet the principle of passive obedience on the part of subjects, or of absolute and irresponsible authority on that of sovereigns, never was, and certainly never will be, an approved principle of hers. She seems to have little confidence in theoretical systems which assume that great or enduring benefit is to result from those sudden and unexpected excitements, even of a religious kind—those enthusiasms in favor of new schemes—those irregular starts, and leaps, and bounds of popular ardor—now in one direction, now in another, and not unfrequently in different and even opposite directions at the same time—by which the pace of society is to be preternaturally quickened in the path of universal progress. In short, having witnessed so many experiments tried on poor credulous humanity by new doctors who turned out to have been only quacks, panaceas are not by her highly valued. She has had long and universal experience, and such opportunities of studying her subject, that she knows what is in the heart of man,

---

Catholics have been here from the earliest dawn of the morning. They have shared in your sufferings, taken part in your labors, contributed to the common glory and prosperity of your country and theirs; and neither the first page, nor the last page, nor the middle page of your history would have been where and what it is without them." This lecture was one of the most successful and effective that he ever wrote. The receipts from the sale of tickets amounted to $1,600.

the bad as well as the good, much better than he knows it himself. She is inclined to suspect or distrust all those creedly conceived political changes which disturb the peace of communities and nations, without improving their condition. Oh, how many of these abortive and disastrous changes has she not witnessed throughout the whole world during her life of eighteen hundred years!

He sent a copy of his lecture to his old friend, Mr. Biddle, and received a long letter from him in return, a portion of which I subjoin:

MR. BIDDLE TO ARCHBISHOP HUGHES.

PHILADELPHIA, *March* 11, 1852.

In thus recurring to American revolutionary annals, and imbibing some small portion of the spirit of your eloquent address, I have spontaneously brought to my recollection a remark made by my late father, who served as an officer of rank on the staff of General Washington during the revolutionary contest, that the rank and file of the best disciplined and most effective continental regiments of the Pennsylvania line were chiefly Irish Catholics; and three of these very religious regiments were commanded by the sons of Irishmen, namely, Wayne, Irvine, and Shea; the former the distinguished favorite of Washington, and all three afterward general officers. And when Wayne, by the selection and orders of Washington, led a handful of men to the difficult and bloody conquest of Stony Point, most of these gallant men were Irishmen, and a number of whom fell in forcing their way into the enemy's works.

I have a perfect recollection of General Wayne, for on his last visit to Philadelphia, in the year 1795, after his successful campaign against the Indians on our then Northwestern frontier, the General stayed with his old friend, the late Colonel Sharp Delaney, an Irish gentleman, whose residence was next door to my father's house, and we were all quite intimate with his family. Colonel Delaney, I may moreover mention, then held the important appointment of collector of the port of Philadelphia, given to him under the administration of Washington, as some return for his gallant services during the revolutionary war.

At the same period, and residing in the same family, I well remember a handsome and accomplished young aide-de-camp, Major De Butts, a native of Dublin, who had been serving with distinction under General Wayne, and had been wounded in these Indian wars—the delight and admiration of our gay and fashionable circles, "the observed of all observers," and great star of attraction wherever he went.

And about the same period, in Philadelphia, lived another gentleman, the late General Stephen Moylan, a brother of the then bishop of Cork. General Moylan was a very dear friend of my father's, and our two families saw each other every day. My father, indeed, was one of General Moylan's groomsmen or attendants at his wedding, which took place before the close of the war. General Moylan, from his military education in France, had become an excellent cavalry officer, and accordingly was selected by General Washington to command the continental dragoons when these cavalry regiments were formed. After the war, General Moylan had assigned to him, under the Federal government, one of the most important posts in the United States Treasury, namely, that of Commissioner of Loans, which he held to the time of his decease. The General was a most excellent and estimable man, a high-bred soldier, of the old *bien poudré* school, and his house in Philadelphia was the abode of elegant and refined hospitality. The general had three other brothers, one of whom, the late Counsellor Jasper Moylan, was the father of the first Mrs. Robert Walsh, [wife of] our late consul at Paris; all these brothers, except the bishop of Cork, left Ireland during the revolutionary war, and settled and died in the United States. I knew them all.

And now, whilst indulging in these reminiscences of distinguished Irish gentlemen whose hearts and souls were embarked in the American revolutionary cause, and who had won the respect, esteem, and affection of all who were earnest and ardent in supporting it, I must not forget another venerable gentleman still left among us, as a model and standard of the class of men of whom I have been speaking. I allude to our distinguished friend, John Keating, now, as he only told me ten days ago, in his ninety-third year, having been born in the month of January, 1760! Where, I will ask, can you produce a more polished or accomplished gentleman, a more pious or devout Christian, a more excellent or estimable man! Who, during a long and well-spent life, has enjoyed more the respect, confidence, and esteem, as well as affection, of all his contemporaries high and low, rich and poor, exalted and humble, than John Keating! And he too is a soldier, and a distinguished officer of the Irish Brigade, and is the last gentleman now living who had conferred upon him the cross of St. Louis by Louis XVI. Although brought up in one of the military schools in France, Mr. Keating was of an ancient Irish Catholic family, and was born at Gastle Keating in the county of Limerick. He has told me that he was a lieutenant before the Emperor Napoleon was a cadet at the military school. In the year 1778, on his way with his regiment to the Isle of France, he was shipwrecked at the Cape of Good Hope. He served in the West Indies, before the close of the revolutionary contest, and was present at the capture of the Island of St. Eustatia. In 1792, at the evacuation of Cape Française by the royalists, he was the colonel commanding the troops and the governor *ad interim* of the Cape. Such was Mr. Keating's popularity with the troops he commanded, although he was a firm and decided supporter of the king's government, that on the arrival of the Republican commissioner to take the command of the Island of St. Domingo, at the solicitation of the troops, he was invited to remain in their command. This, however, he has told me, he at once refused, and removed thence to Philadelphia, where he has ever since resided—sixty years—enjoying the respect, confidence, and esteem of all his fellow-citizens.

Mr. Keating, whom I see almost every week or two, and [who] is one of the managers of the Savings Bank of which I have been so long the president, still enjoys tolerable health, with all his former vigor of mind. He almost regularly attends the meetings of our managers, and takes his full share in the transaction of the office-business. He very often gives me the pleasure of his society, and from his own lips I have gathered the particulars of his life I have given you. Mr. Keating, in my opinion, is quite remarkable for not only the coolness and calmness, but for the soundness of judgment he still *always* displays on all the various topics which from time to time are brought under our notice; and within a year I have had occasion to see letters of business written by him with all the clearness, vigor, and conciseness that characterize the strongest periods of our life.

You must, my dear Archbishop Hughes, excuse me for occupying, as I have done, too much of your valuable time. But I have been desirous of proving, from my own recollections, how essential a feature the Irish gentleman and lady constituted in the best and most polished circles of our metropolitan society at a time (the close of the last century) when Philadelphia was the residence of the General Government, and not only filled by its own distinguished citizens in Congress and office, from the Northern and Southern States, but was also visited by the greatest celebrities from Europe, namely, King Louis Philippe, then Duke of Orleans, with a younger brother, the Prince Talleyrand, Count Volney, Viscount de Noailles, etc., etc.

With this apology for weighing you down with revolutionary and other reminiscences—altogether subordinate, it is true, to your important and most interesting address, "The Catholic Chapter," but which may in some minor points of view illustrate still further the Catholic and Irish character in its connection with the revolutionary history and our American annals—I will no further trespass upon your time.

With the warmest and truest regard and respect, believe me, my dear archbishop,

Most faithfully yours,
CLEMENT C. BIDDLE.

The archbishop was far from admitting that there was any thing in the spirit of the Church hostile to republican institutions. He says in another place:

In the annals of Church history, there has never been a country which in its civil and social relations has exhibited so fair an opportunity for developing the practical harmonies of Catholic faith and of Catholic charity as the United States.*

The great elements of our institutions, namely, representative government, electoral franchise, trial by jury, municipal polity, were all the inventions of Catholics alone. They come in part from the period of Alfred the Great. They had acquired a very high development already under Edward the Confessor, and it was only after

* "Reflections and Suggestions on what is called the Catholic Press," in *The Metropolitan Magazine*, December, 1856.

royal power had attempted to make encroachments on the rights secured by them, that the barons at Runnymede extorted from King John a written pledge, not to secure new privileges, but to confirm those which were understood as the hereditary birthright of English Catholic freemen.*

But with certain American Catholics who believed " that the predispositions of their countrymen were especially adapted to the reception of the Catholic religion," he had no patience. He regarded them as being under a mischievous error. He admitted that the American people were willing to give the Church fair play, and that having once established the principle of religious toleration, they were generally ready to act up to its legitimate consequences:

Although you may quiz them on many peculiarities, they are too strict in their logic to admit a principle, and then cut off the consequences. They are not a people to tell you, "Here we have opened a fountain," and then say, "But the water must not flow." Therefore, admitting the universal right of man in this country to serve and worship God according to the dictates of his conscience, they are too logical and too just to quarrel with the consequences, however much some of them may, in their own way, deplore them, as evidence of the progress of that awful thing to so many—the spread of popery.†

Still he believed that when Catholicism was in question, the sense of justice was very apt to be obscured by old prejudices:

Convents have been burned down, and no compensation offered to their scattered inmates; Catholic churches have been burned down, while whole neighborhoods have been, under the eye of public officers, reduced to ashes. People have been burned to death in their own dwellings; or if they attempted to escape, have been shot down by the deadly messenger of the unerring rifle. Crosses have

---

* "The Catholic Chapter."
† Speech at the banquet in Liverpool, June 10, 1851.

been pulled down from the summit of God's sanctuary. Priests have been tarred and feathered. Ladies have been insulted for no crime except that of having devoted themselves to the service of their divine Master in a religious state, in the hope of conferring aid or consolation on their fellow-beings. . . . . These things were the work of what is called mobs; but we confess our disappointment at not having witnessed a prompt and healthy, true American sentiment in the heart of the community at large in rebuke of such proceedings, and so far as reparation was possible, in making it to the injured parties whom they had failed to protect.

He was sternly opposed to drawing any comparison or making any distinction between native and foreign Catholics; but privately he was convinced that Irish emigrants would long continue to be, as they always had been, the main stay of the Church in this country.

In the spring of 1852 he made another attempt to consolidate the faithful of the whole city in an organization for defraying the cost of building churches. At the close of his sermon one Sunday morning in February, he invited the congregation to attend at Vespers, that he might have " an opportunity of addressing them on matters essential to the progress of religion in this city." The cathedral was crowded in the afternoon to its utmost capacity. At the close of the service he explained the object for which he had called the people together. After giving a brief sketch of the progress of religion in New York since he took charge of the diocese, and the struggle to pay off the church debts, notwithstanding the heaviness of which the number of churches had increased from seven to twenty-two—he described the urgent necessity of new places of worship to accommodate the two hundred thousand persons whom he supposed to form the Catholic population of New York city. He had intended to build a new cathedral, but he would postpone that undertaking until eight or ten smaller churches should have been put up. "Now," said he, "why should not all the congregations in the city unite in an effort to create a general fund to be employed in aiding, partly by donations and partly by temporary loans in the erection of these new churches?" At another meeting, held in April, he explained more fully his plan for this "Auxiliary Church Building Association." There was to be a central council, composed of the pastor and one lay member of each congregation in the city, to advise the archbishop in all cases touching loans or appropriations to aid in constructing new churches; there was to be a treasury board, consisting of the vicar-general and three prominent laymen; and there was to be an organization in each parish for the purpose of receiving weekly, monthly, or yearly contributions from the faithful. The plan was popular for a little while, but like other measures for uniting all the Catholics of the city or diocese in one homogeneous body, it failed. The archbishop never could persuade one congregation, for any long time, to help another.

The affairs of the bankrupt churches, to which I have before alluded, had meanwhile been in a most deplorable state, but, except in the case of St. Peter's, they had all gradually been righted. In some instances the trustees resigned; in others they passed over the property to assignees, by whom it was sold or conveyed to the archbishop—the archbishop satisfying the demands of all the creditors, which he was not legally bound to do. Two churches, those of St. Nicholas and St. Patrick (the cathedral), still continue under lay management.

The case of St. Peter's was such a flagrant example of the evils of lay trusteeship, and gave the archbishop so much trouble, and caused so many scandals and heart-burnings, that it may as well be told in full. When the church and the pastoral residence were completed in 1838, the debt amounted to nearly $116,500; under the administration of incompetent trustees it had increased in 1844 to $135,000. In that year the trustees became bankrupt, and made an assignment. Most of the funds which they had so unaccountably wasted had been obtained by the issue of interest-bearing notes—principally to poor people who entrusted their little savings to the officers of the church, with more confidence than they would have felt in putting them into a savings bank. At the time of the assignment, about $100,000 of the debt consisted of these notes. When the assignees were about to sell the church under foreclosure of mortgage, these poor note-holders, foreseeing that such a sale would leave them little hope of recovering their deposits, obtained an injunction, and brought suits to test the validity of the assignment. The matter was five years before the courts. In the mean time no interest could legally be paid on the notes; and in addition to the worry and trouble of the long litigation, the bishop had to bear the daily annoyance of the entreaties, complaints, and recriminations of these poor creditors, whose just demands he had no power to satisfy. At last in 1849 the assignment was confirmed by the Court of Appeals, and the bishop took measures to have the notes paid off.* Still it was not easy for him to do any thing. He had no legal control over the property. The affairs of the church were in the hands of a layman, properly appointed, between whom and the bishop there was no good will. The bishop honestly believed that this gentleman had grossly mismanaged the business; and when Bishop Hughes felt called upon to rebuke an evil-doer he did it without much regard to the feelings of the offender. He invited the principal members of the congregation to meet him in the sacristy of the church. "The bishop is coming here this evening," said the agent to one of the parishioners. "I hope he will behave well. If he does, we shall treat him with respect; but if he does not, I shall say to him, 'Bishop, there's the door for you.'" Dr. Hughes tells this incident himself, and adds that "the bishop did behave well;" but he entered into such an unmerciful analysis of the recent administration of the church, that the agent virtually gave up his office.

In consequence of arrangements made at this meeting

---

* The debt had now increased to about $140,000.

the property was soon afterward bought at sheriff's sale by a gentleman of the congregation, and transferred by him to the bishop. Some lots on the Fifth Avenue and Fiftieth street (the same on which the new cathedral is to be built) were purchased of the church by the trustees of St. Patrick's. Collections were made throughout the parish; a church-debt society was organized; a pastor was appointed who had a good head for finance; and in the course of three years a large part of the notes was paid off, and the treasury brought into such a prosperous condition that the extinction of the entire debt within a very short period became assured. The note-holders could not have recovered at law the whole face of their claims. The assignees, after paying off the mortgage which had been foreclosed, and dividing among the creditors the balance of the money realized by the sale of the church and of the Fiftieth street lots, were relieved of all further legal responsibility. The note-holders would then have received only about sixty-five cents on the dollar; but the bishop declared that whatever the law might say, justice demanded that they should be paid in full. The faith of the church was pledged to them, and he would see that it should not be broken. Protestants who had invested their savings in the notes, should be paid both principal and interest; but it was only fair that Catholic depositors should forego interest, when their brethren were making such efforts and such sacrifices for their benefit. Speculators who had bought up notes at a heavy discount ought to receive no interest, and only the legal percentage of the principal.

On the 26th of December, 1852, a service of thanksgiving was held at St. Peter's, in gratitude for the extrication of the church from its long-standing difficulties. The building was elaborately decorated; the altar blazed with lights; a vast crowd of people, whose faces testified to the joy which filled every heart, occupied all the seats and aisles; and after the archbishop, in a powerful address, had described the evils of lay trusteeism in general, and given a history of the affairs of St. Peter's, a *Te Deum* was sung, the congregation all standing. Good cause was there for singing it; for in the year just closing had passed away from the Church in New York not only "a long desolation and a shame grown old," but with them, let us hope forever, the abominable trustee system which had been so prolific of mischief.*

* With regard to the one or two boards of trustees that were left in New York, it ought to be mentioned that the archbishop bore ready witness to their uprightness and capacity. But these were exceptions. He liked the system none the better for the merits of individual trustees.

CHAPTER XXI.

1853–1855.

Arrival of a Papal Nuncio in the United States—Project of a permanent nunciature at Washington—Voyage to Cuba—Letter on the Madiai case—Controversy with Gen. Cass—Letters of Philo Veritas—First provincial council of New York—Visit to Rome—Definition of the dogma of the Immaculate Conception—Controversy with Senator Brooks—Letters to Terence Donnelly and Cassius M. Clay on political alliances.

IN the spring of 1853 the papal government despatched Monsignore Bedini, Archbishop of Thebes, as Apostolic Nuncio to the court of the Brazils, and charged him with delivering, on his way to his mission, a complimentary autograph letter from the Pope to the President of the United States. He was also to confer with some of the American bishops on matters touching the interests of religion, and to make a report to the Holy See of the condition, prospects, and wants of the Church in this country. The nuncio arrived in New York on the 30th of June, and became the guest of the archbishop, with whom, after a gratifying interview with President Pierce, he made a journey to the West. They visited Milwaukee, where the archbishop preached at the consecration of the cathedral; made an excursion on Lake Michigan and Green Bay; passed a few days at Saratoga; and then went to Montreal. The archbishop returned to New York at the end of August, after a month's absence. The nuncio followed him about the close of October, and remained with him until the beginning of winter, receiving the hospitalities of the city, officiating occasionally on great ceremonial days, and consecrating the bishops of the new sees of Brooklyn, Newark, and Burlington (Vt.). The creation of the first two of these, while it lessened the archbishop's labors by dividing his diocese, deprived him of his vicar-general, to whom fell the mitre of Brooklyn, and his secretary, who was honored with that of Newark.

The archbishop was keenly sensible of the advantage which might result to the American Church from a prolonged stay of the nuncio in the United States. He was pleased with whatever tended to strengthen the union between Rome and her distant children; and in a letter to a correspondent in the papal capital, describing the favorable manner in which the nuncio had been received by the president and people, he urged the propriety of Monsignore Bedini's being commissioned to visit the principal parts of of the Union. The answer was as follows:

ROME, *Dec.* 29, 1853.

. . . . .

With regard to Monsig. Bedini, I considered it better to have your letter all translated by an Italian. I gave a copy of it to the *sostituto di stato*, Monsignore Berardi, who is a particular friend of mine; he read it to the Pope, who was delighted beyond measure at the news about Monsig. Bedini. I made a second copy, and gave it to Cardinal Antonelli. His Eminence feels very much obliged to your Grace for the active and prudent part you have taken in promoting both the dignity of the Holy See and the good of religion. He desired me also to thank you in his name for your beautiful report of the mission of Monsig. Bedini to the United States. Though Monsig. Bedini be already destined for another mission, yet I think they will allow him time to visit the principal parts of America, as your Grace suggested; so I understand from Monsig. Berardi and from his Eminence.

Since I sent your report to the Holy Father I have not seen him; but shortly before, I had the pleasure of speaking to him. He seemed to be well satisfied with the reception of Monsig. Bedini in the

United States. He gave a grand reception to Mr. Van Buren, your ex-president, who is here. Mr. Van Buren told me he made him sit down at his table for half an hour, while in England he was *bowed* in to see the queen, and immediately *bowed* out.

About the same time he wrote as follows, at the nuncio's request, to the Hon. James Campbell, postmaster general, with whom he was personally acquainted :

> There is another matter on which, if there be no impropriety in calling your attention to it, I should like to know your opinion or that of your colleagues. It is in reference to the establishment of a nunciature representing the Holy See near the Government at Washington. So far, the Pope, though he has been urged to appoint a nuncio, has constantly refused. Yet I foresee the probability of this matter being urged upon him again; and I should take it as a great favor if, with your knowledge of the opinions of the President and cabinet, such an appointment on the part of his Holiness would be favorably entertained.

Mr. Campbell's answer disappointed him :

> In relation to the establishment of a nunciature in this country, the President will receive a chargé or minister from the Pope, but he can only of course be received as his political representative. If his Holiness were to appoint a layman, there would be no difficulty in receiving him in the same manner as the representative of every other sovereign power is now received—charged of course only with the public affairs of the Pontifical States.

Before this answer was received the nuncio had left New York on another visit to the western States, and during his absence Archbishop Hughes was obliged, by the alarming state of his health, to make a voyage to Cuba. He did not see the nuncio again until he met him some years afterward in Europe.

TO THE VERY REV. DR. KIRBY, RECTOR OF THE IRISH COLLEGE, ROME.

NEW YORK, *Aug* 10, 1854.

During the visit of Monsignore Bedini, he was desirous to know what might be the sentiments of our Government at Washington in regard to the establishment of a nunciature in this country. I took occasion to sound the cabinet, in an indirect manner however, and as connected with other matters in relation to this one. This was intended for the information of my esteemed friend the archbishop of Thebes. You will see by my letter to Mr. Campbell, Postmaster General and a member of the cabinet (and also a Catholic), under date of the 25th of November, what object I had in view. Unfortunately, his reply to me reached New York only at the very last hour before my departure to Havana in consequence of ill health. From that time, things took so unfavorable a course in this country toward the nuncio, that I did not know where to address him; and besides, the answer of Mr. Campbell was, in my judgment, so unsatisfactory, that I did not attach much importance to it. I enclose copies of both these letters to you, requesting that you will show them to Monsignore Bedini, as a proof that I did not forget the fulfilment of a promise which I made to him. And also, if you should think it advisable, you might communicate the information contained to the proper quarter in the government of the Holy See. It may give them an idea of the feelings which prevail at Washington.

The hint that a lay representative of the Holy See would be most acceptable at Washington, is merely a phrase *ad cautelam*, whilst I have every reason to think that if Archbishop Bedini had been commissioned directly to this Government, without any previous consultation on the subject, he would have been well received. Of course as to the expediency of such a measure, there is some difference of opinion, even among the Catholic bishops of this country. Inasmuch as our Government is prohibited by the constitution from any direct interference with questions of religion, a nuncio would have very little to do at Washington; and yet there have been already, and there are likely to be henceforward, many questions in which some authorized person should represent the temporal interests of the Church in relation to territories which have heretofore been under Catholic governments, and have been absorbed, or annexed, or conquered, or purchased by ours. I remember distinctly, that both in the case of the acquisition of Texas and of Upper California, the Secretary of State wrote to me that in the pending treaties, before they should be finally concluded, the rights of Catholic ecclesiastical property should be willingly and scrupulously provided for by the cabinet at Washington, if such rights should be made known to them. I advised the late archbishop of Baltimore, in whose diocese the city of Washington is, of such communication; but I have reason to fear that the matter was never attended to, and that the bishop and archbishop, who are now in California, are under the necessity of losing great part, and almost begging for other portions of ecclesiastical property, which would have been secured by the articles of treaty, if the matter had been attended to in time. The almost certain prospect is at present, that the entire island of Cuba will come under the jurisdiction of this Government. Its population is entirely Catholic; but notwithstanding the apostolic zeal of its devoted archbishop, religion itself is not in the most flourishing condition. I have expressed to his excellency the nuncio, that I thought questions of this kind arising, or likely to arise, would make it desirable that some quasi-representative of the Holy See should be on the spot to see after the rights and interests of the Church as far as possible.

I have never known any prelate who would have made a more favorable impression, not only on the members of the Government, but in fact on all classes, than Monsignore Bedini, had it not been for the infamous slanders which were put in circulation against him by Gavazzi and his bad associates. Those slanders have left no bad impression on the minds of Catholics nor intelligent Protestants, by whom the nuncio is remembered with respect and affection. In reality his wicked enemies, by using not only the post from one town to another, but also by turning the telegraph-wires to purposes of falsehood, have created an appearance of hostility against him which was altogether fictitious, or very much exaggerated. Please, my dear Father Kirby, to present him the expression of my respect and attachment.

The insults to which Monsignore Bedini was exposed by European republicans in Cincinnati, Wheeling, and elsewhere, were poorly atoned for by a complimentary reception given him afterward in the Senate at Washington. But when he returned to New York, in order to take the steamer for Europe, crowds of foreign radicals gathered on the wharves to watch every departure; and indications of a riot were so threatening, that, at the suggestion of the mayor, the nuncio went secretly to Staten Island, and boarded the steamer in a tug boat as she went down the harbor. Archbishop Hughes was intensely mortified when he heard of these disgraceful occurrences. He wrote thus to the nuncio:

. . . . .

The part that afflicted me most was the mode of your leaving New York; and it is perhaps a presumptuous thought of mine which prompts me to say, that if I had been at home, you never should have been allowed to depart as you did. I know that it was a great trial to you, as it is a deep humiliation to us. And on reflection, I think that God may have ordained that I should be absent, in order that some greater evil might thereby be prevented; for be assured, that if I had been in New York, we should have taken a carriage at my door, even an open one if the day had been fine enough, and gone by the ordinary streets to the steamboat on which you were to embark. You will perhaps be astonished when I add, that in such an event, notwithstanding the lying clamors of the telegraph wires and the newspapers, I do not believe that either violence or insult would have been offered either to you, or to me, or to any of our party. . . . . .

The archbishop had sailed for Havana just after Christmas, in company with the Rev. Mr. Martin, of St. Bridget's church, N. Y.

TO SISTER ANGELA.

HAVANA, *Jan.* 23, 1854.

MY DEAR SISTER:

I received your letter and Margaret's yesterday. My visit here, and the sea voyage, have wrought a most wonderful change in my health and spirits. I have no cough worth notice. My appetite is excellent, and I sleep well. The order of time is, rise at six, say mass at seven, breakfast at nine, dine at three, drive out with the bishop at five, a walk in the country of an hour, home at eight, retire at ten or half past. I am now able to converse in Spanish. It would be impossible to give you any idea of the delightfulness of this climate.

Father Martin is well, but he does not thrive as much as I do. We go to-morrow to Matanzas for a week or so. The good bishop is recovering from an attack which, if you heard him describe it, you would say was as like my own as possible. It commenced on the 16th of August with a slight attack of cholera. This was followed by a general prostration of strength both of mind and body, loss of appetite, repugnance to going out or receiving visits at home, with an unconquerable tendency to weep all the while. He speaks of the remedies prescribed by the physicians, viz.: that he should go out, take exercise, amuse himself, etc., and ridicules the whole by saying that if he had been able to do so, he would not need the physician. His friends say that he is much better since I came, and so he says himself. He is one of the kindest and most amiable prelates I ever met with. I celebrated pontifical mass yesterday in one of the churches. The governor general, the bishop, and all the notables of the city were present. I intend to sail for New Orleans about the middle of February. All letters, after you receive this, had better be directed to me at that place, care of Archbishop Blanc.

I had letters for the return of the Crescent City, but she came into port and passed out again without my knowledge. I have sent them by the Charleston steamer. I cannot say when I shall reach New York, but it will not be sooner than the middle of March. Kind love to Margaret and all friends.

Your affectionate brother,

✠ JOHN, *Abp. of New York.*

In a letter of the same date to Sister Angela, Father Martin, speaking of the pontifical mass celebrated by the archbishop on the occasion above referred to, says:

But when leaving the church, you would be very much amused to see the crowds that flocked about him to get his blessing. The most affecting of all, was the jostling and driving of a few Irish girls, making their way through blacks and whites, and saying they had more right to be there than the Havanians. We leave here to-morrow for the country; a gentleman has invited the archbishop to see his plantation. .... Letters and papers received yesterday have given him great satisfaction, as he was very anxious to hear from home. .... He has been able to read all the time since his arrival here, though I have remonstrated with him on that head; but he tells me it has had no bad effect on him. ...... The excellent bishop of this place has done every thing to make him happy.

The archbishop spoke in warm terms of gratitude of the kindness shown him during this visit. "Nothing," said he, in a sermon on his return home, " could be more soothing to an invalid at any time, although to me so unexpected, than the attention and kindness which I everywhere received. I was not among strangers, but among friends; and a friendship so delicate, so studious to anticipate every wish, I never experienced, nor did I suppose possible."

He went from Cuba to New Orleans, and, after a trip through the Southern States, reached New York on the 25th of May, in excellent health, but not with his old power of supporting fatigue; that he never regained. The improvement was only temporary. In the course of the summer we find him once more travelling in search of health, and once more indulging in deceptive hopes of a lasting benefit.

It almost always happened that his return from a journey was the signal for a newspaper controversy. When he came back from Cuba, his first care was to publish in *The Courier and Enquirer* a reply to a speech delivered in the United States Senate, on the 15th of May, by General Cass, senator from Michigan. The anti-Catholic feeling which seems to break out every now and then in this country, and which in 1854 was assuming definite shape and purpose under the designation of the Know-Nothing movement, had found vent in January of the previous year, in a meeting at Metropolitan

Hall, New York, held to express sympathy with the Madiai family at Florence, who had recently been imprisoned "for reading the Bible," as their sympathizers said, but in reality for holding private conventicles. Archbishop Hughes attended this meeting *incognito*, and afterward published a letter in *The Freeman's Journal*, vindicating the Grand Duke of Tuscany from the charge of religious persecution, and making some remarks upon a report presented by the Committee on Foreign Affairs of the United States Senate, on the subject of the claim of American citizens abroad to be protected in the freedom of religious worship. He believed that the report and the Madiai meeting had a common parentage. General Cass's speech was in reply to this letter. Both the senator's speech and the archbishop's rejoinder were temperate and dignified. The archbishop gives the following account of the controversy in a letter to the nuncio, dated July 2d:

You can easily conceive, my dear lord, what an accumulation of business there would be waiting my return to New York, to which it would be my first duty to attend. I had scarcely got through with that, when Gen. Cass delivered a speech in the United States Senate which it took three hours to pronounce, having, for pretence of basis, the refutation of a letter written by me some sixteen months ago, on the occasion of the Madiai meeting here in New York. The General was pleased to mention my name probably a hundred times in the course of his speech. The intention of the speech was to authorize our ministers abroad to interfere in behalf of American citizens in sustaining them in regard to what they call "liberty of conscience." The bearing of the speech was to insinuate, if not to assert directly, that Catholic governments are inimical to the rights of conscience, and place me in a position by which I should either be compelled to take sides with General Cass in condemning such governments, or else become odious to the American people as sustaining their right to practise the tyranny over conscience which he had imputed. Under these circumstances, I was obliged to reply to the senator from Michigan, which I was fortunate enough to do in a manner which has not rendered me odious, and has effectually broken up the conspiracy of the Evangelical Alliance, for the carrying out of which General Cass has been selected as the fittest tool in Congress.

While the archbishop was at Saratoga this summer, *The New York Times* published, on the 31st of July and the 1st of August, two articles purporting to disclose certain schisms, heartburnings, and hard feelings between the native and foreign-born bishops of the Catholic Church in this country. The archbishop reached home on the 3d, and wrote the same day a long letter to the *Times*, signed "Philo-Veritas," in which he stoutly repelled the injurious charges. The *Times* replied, and three more letters appeared from "Philo-Veritas," in the last of which the archbishop made a virtual acknowledgment that he was the writer of them. He never felt comfortable under an anonymous controversy. In the first letter he made some sharp allusions to the Young Ireland party, which called forth an answer from Mr. John Mitchel, addressed "To the Most Reverend 'Philo-Veritas,' Catholic Archbishop of New York." The archbishop took no notice of this communication. Mr. Mitchel abused him in his paper *The Citizen*, from the 11th of August to the 23d of September, without provoking a reply. Once, indeed, the archbishop was on the point of answering. He began a letter to the *Times*, of almost unexampled severity, but on second thoughts he threw it aside, wisely thinking that silence would wound the editor of *The Citizen* far more deeply than any thing he could say. "A controversy of a personal character between us," he remarked, "is of course out of the question."

With respect to the Know-Nothing excitement the archbishop's course was extremely prudent. He neither wrote nor spoke much against it, for he thought it would die out all the sooner for being let alone. He was only careful to warn his flock to keep away from all public meetings in which their nationality or their religion was to be discussed; and especially to avoid the street-preachers, who earned a little cheap notoriety about this time by abusing Catholics from the top of a barrel. Although churches were sacked and burned by the fanatics in neighboring cities, there was no disturbance in New York.

On the last day of September, a council of all the bishops of the province of New York assembled at the archbishop's house. It was the first ecclesiastical council ever held in New York, and the archbishop resolved to celebrate it with all possible magnificence. His seven suffragans were present, besides their consulting theologians, and the superior of several religious orders. Their first meeting was an informal one, and the only business transacted was the appointment of secretaries, chanters, and other officers, and the settlement of their rules of proceeding. The bishops of Boston and Albany were named a committee for the consideration of matters pertaining to ecclesiastical discipline and jurisdiction. Questions touching church property were committed to the bishops of Hartford and Newark; and the subjects of Catholic education and the Catholic press were referred to the bishops of Albany, Buffalo, and Brooklyn. The first solemn session was held the next day, being the seventh Sunday after Pentecost. The prelates assembled at the archbishop's house, and thence moved in procession through the streets to the cathedral. A clerk led the way, bearing aloft the processional cross; then followed a long file of acolytes in red cassocks, the chanters in their black robes and surplices, priests in chasubles of many colors, the theologians, the crosier bearers and other attendants, and lastly the archbishop and his seven bishops, wearing mitres and copes and other rich insignia of their sacred office. The Mass of the Holy Ghost was celebrated by the bishop of Albany. The archbishop preached; the appropriate decrees of the Council of Trent were read; the profession of faith of Pope Pius IV. was solemnly repeated; and after a benediction by the archbishop, the procession returned to his house. The council sat for a week, during which period there were two solemn sessions like that at the opening. The bishops and secretaries met privately at ten o'clock every morning, in the sacristy of the cathedral, for the discussion of business. There was comparatively little ceremony at these private meetings, and the only ecclesiastical vestments worn by the bishops were the rochet and mozetta. Questions for the decision of the consulting theologians were now prepared. At one o'clock the bishops, theologians, and officers of the council dined with the archbishop, and during the repast some one read aloud, after the custom in religious communities, a chapter of the Bible and a passage from the Roman Martyrology. At three o'clock a public meeting, or "congregation," was held in the church. The laity were not admitted; it was called public only because the theologians and other priests who held any appointment in the council were present. The questions referred for the examination of the theologians were now brought forward, and decrees proposed in the private congregation were discussed. At the third solemn session, after a mass celebrated by the archbishop, and an eloquent sermon by the bishop of Albany, the decrees were laid upon the altar, and each bishop in his turn signed them there. They were six in number. The first was a profession of obedience and devotion to the Holy Father. The second promulgated anew the decrees of the seven provincial councils of Baltimore. The third forbade priests to mortgage church property without the permission of the bishop. The fourth repeated the injunctions of the national council of Baltimore respecting Catholic education, and exhorted clergymen to labor zealously for the establishment of schools. The fifth admonished priests that it was unlawful for them to exercise functions of the ministry requiring "faculties," except within their own diocese, or with the permission of the bishop in whose diocese they might be sojourning. The sixth enjoined upon all parish clergymen the duty of providing as soon as possible a pastoral residence adjacent to the church, the title of which, as well as of all other church property, was to be in the name of the bishop. A letter was written to the Pope, submitting the decrees to his approval, and one to the Society for the Propagation of the Faith, thanking them for their past liberality to the American Church, and praying a continuation of their favors. A pastoral letter, in the name of all the prelates of the province, was written by the archbishop. ·It touched lightly upon the prevailing hostility to the Church, and urged the faithful to let their refutation of the calumnies of their enemies be "less in writings and in words than in deeds and actions." It gave notice that, "according to the general law and custom of the Church, the banns of holy matrimony were henceforward to be published in the appropriate places, previous to the administration of that holy sacrament," and it encouraged the clergy to "renewed efforts for providing means of education to the flock with which they were charged." "Two other subjects," it continues, "have engaged the attention of the Fathers in the council which has just been brought to a close. One is, the indiscriminate reception into your families of journals not at all calculated to impart, either to you or to those committed to your care, those solid maxims of public instruction which would tend to edification. We do not here intend to speak of merely secular papers; but we do speak rather of those which, taking advantage of certain feelings supposed to be alive in your breasts, whether in reference to kindred, country, or religion, involve you in political relations which it would be expedient for you to avoid; except, indeed, in the sense in which it is the right of every free man to give his vote freely, conscientiously, individually, as often as the laws of the country call upon and authorize him to do so. There appears to be abroad an ignorance or prejudice on this subject, which it would be our desire and your interest to have removed. It is to the effect that every paper which advocates, or professes to advocate, the Catholic religion, or which advocates some imaginary foreign interest in this country, is, as a matter of course, under the direction of the priests and bishops in the locality where it is published, and consequently authorized to speak for and in the name of the Catholic Church. Hence, when the editors of such papers publish their own sentiments by virtue of their indisputable right to exercise the liberty of the press, it is assumed by persons outside of our communion that they speak in the name of the Church, and under direction of her pastors. Nothing could be more false than this inference, and we exhort you, venerable and beloved brethren, to leave nothing unsaid or undone to remove every shadow of foundation for this inference, so absurd in itself, but yet so injurious to us."

The other subject to which allusion is made above, was the establishment in this country of the "association which is known in Europe as the Propagation of the Faith. The originators of this society proposed that its members should contribute one cent a week for the support of foreign missions. It has already spread over a large portion of Christendom. We exhort you, then, venerable brethren of the clergy," continues the pastoral, "to institute, with as little delay as possible, this great work of Catholic charity."

The publication of the banns of marriage was only one of several measures adopted by the council for the purpose of making the mode of administering the sacrament of matrimony more conformable to the time-honored discipline of the Church. In the previous December the archbishop had established a diocesan chancery, from which all dispensations for marriage within the forbidden degrees of relationship, marriages between Catholics and non-Catholics, and marriages without publication of the banns, were to emanate. The Rev. Thomas S. Preston, the archbishop's secretary, was appointed chancellor.

An informal council was to be held at Rome during the winter of 1854, at which it was expected that the doctrine of the immaculate conception of the Blessed Virgin would be defined as an article of faith. The Pope desired that all the bishops of the world who could conveniently make the journey, should be present on the solemn occasion. Archbishop Hughes accordingly sailed from New York on the 18th of October, in company with his chaplain, the Rev. Mr. McNeirny, and with the Right Rev. Bishop Timon, of Buffalo. He passed the night before his departure in writing a pastoral letter, in which he announced a jubilee, commended the Sisters of Mercy to the liberality of the faithful, and alluded to the Sisters of the Good Shepherd—an order designed for the protection of female penitents—whom the zeal and indefatigable exertions of a pious lady of New York soon afterward established in the diocese.

Arrived in Rome, he lodged, together with the archbishop of Baltimore and the bishop of Pittsburg, in the Canouica Palace attached to the sacristy of St. Peter's. He expressed a purpose, before he left home, to preserve notes of the proceedings of the council, which he called "the most important since that of Trent." He seems to have neglected doing this; but in a sermon which he preached in the cathedral upon his return, he gave an interesting account of some of what he had witnessed:

For the last three hundred years, but particularly since the beginning of this century, those who were most nearly in communion with God—bishops, priests, and holy persons devoted to religion—expressed outwardly their great desire that the Sovereign Pontiff should define, as an article of faith, that belief which had been floating from the beginning on the sea of Catholic tradition, and abiding in the Catholic heart, with reference to the Immaculate Conception. The Holy Father entertained with favor the expression of this sentiment; and during the period of his exile from beside the tomb of the apostles, when at Gaeta, he issued an encyclical letter to all the bishops of Christendom, requiring or requesting them to furnish him with a declaration of the sentiment which prevailed among their clergy and people on the subject. Of course, it required a long time to receive answers to such a letter, sent to the various parts of the earth; but, little by little, one after another, these responses came in, to the number of, I think, five hundred and sixty-four, from so many bishops scattered throughout the world; and of these, there were less than fifty whose writers considered that, although the doctrine was true, and was believed by them and by their people, it was not expedient to define it at that moment. There were only four out of that immense number whose writers were not prepared for the definition. These letters are published, and constitute an aggregate of nine octavo volumes. And still, owing to the difficulty of access in such remote and pagan lands as some of the bishops dwell in, they have not yet received the encyclical letter, or had not been able to forward their answer. These letters having been received, the Holy Father, even then, while yet at Gaeta, appointed a commission of twenty of the most learned theologians, for the purpose of investigating every thing which history has recorded on this subject. These, again, after their return, were aided by others in Rome; and finally, after much prayer and fasting, and supplication of God, both by himself and by others whom he required to unite with him, the Holy Father determined—no doubt under Divine inspiration—to make that solemn declaration of the doctrine. For this purpose he invited a certain number of bishops, so that the episcopacy of each country might be more or less represented, to assemble at Rome. He did not invite many, because he was aware that to some bishops it would be a matter of great inconvenience to go, and he knew that any thing like an invitation or formal request would be corresponded with, no matter at what sacrifice. Notwithstanding even this, for some days previous to the 8th of December, there were assembled, from day to day, some one hundred and fifty-four bishops of the Catholic Church, representing every nation, and, I may say, every tongue and tribe under the sky. These had come together, and the question was submitted to them, not, indeed, as to the doctrine, for they had already been foremost to profess; nor as to the appropriateness or fitness of the time—these two points were withheld; but as to the framework and words, or what is called BULL—the form or article of the proclamation—in which this doctrine was to be defined, as it had been drawn up by the theologians. It was this which was submitted to them. This it was their duty to canvass, paragraph by paragraph, line by line; and they did so, having for the purpose simply to sift out and examine, and probe whether any authority had been quoted in support of the doctrine, which authority could be questioned. It was their province to see that no slight error of the theologians should introduce a doubtful testimony in support of such a doctrine. O dearly beloved brethren, what a spectacle was the meeting of these bishops! All were kindly received by the Holy Father. All assembled in a public hall adjoining the great St. Peter's. There was no introduction necessary. On the second, third, and fourth days, there came in other bishops, travel-worn, who had come from the distant East, or from the far-off South. These men, who had journeyed thousands and thousands of miles, had but just time to refresh themselves and put on their episcopal robes before they walked into the assembly; they took part in the discussion of the matter before the body in the very hour within which they had arrived. There was no comparing of notes as to what each one believed; there was no question of high doctrine or low doctrine; there was no interrogation as to what school one belonged, or as to what had been the influence which the sentiments of the government, or the effect of the climate, or of the Church, North or South, or East or West, had had upon the minds of those who came to take part in the proceedings of that august assembly. There was the oneness, the universality of truth—one heart, one faith and language. If every bishop had spoken his mother tongue, what a jargon would have been there! What an imitation of the scene at the Tower of Babel! But there was one language used—the language of the Church; and a faithful and a truthful one is that language, by which every bishop understood the other, and read his thoughts without ambiguity. There was no time, I say, for introductions or making acquaintances; but they were able to read each other's countenances. And. thus, after they had transacted the business for which they came, they returned home, each to the fold they had left behind, without—with a few exceptions—having made the acquaintance of even the brethren whom they had met in that assembly. Finally came the day for the promulgation of the dogma. That 8th of December deserves to be celebrated in the annals of the Church for all time to come, as a day of joy to every Christian heart. The Holy Pontiff himself—the supreme Pontiff—officiated; and at the proper time received, in the name of the whole Catholic Church —including the Greek and Armenian—received, in the name of the whole Catholic world, from the lips of the Dean of the Sacred College of Cardinals, supported by the bishops, the supplication that, by the authoritative and infallible decision of the Church, he might declare the prerogative of the Mother of God. That scene cannot be described; and no one ought to attempt to describe it. I shall not attempt to delineate to you the picture which that scene has left still fresh and glowing in my memory. I do not speak of the wonders of art, architecture, painting, and music by which that scene was rendered so impressive. Let those things pass. They became insignificant on that occasion.

* * * * *

There sat the august successor of St. Peter, the head of that Church which had endured persecution, and still triumphs; while the tempests now agitating the world, and the waves of persecution, were wasting their harmless fury around the base of the rock. Around him knelt venerable bishops, his brethren in the episcopacy; and at the proper time, that document which had been prepared for the promulgation of this doctrine, was read by him in a clear, distinct, audible voice, but amid a silence which was, I may say, awful, in such a multitude of people. When he came to that part which is purely doctrinal, which is the definition—namely, that God, by a special prerogative, had, through the merits of Jesus Christ, preserved the Virgin Mary from every stain of original guilt—when he came, I say, to that point, his voice grew tremulous with emotion, and then you might have seen every cheek present bedewed with tears of emotion and of tenderness. And at the proper time, after having announced it, the music of the special choir was forgotten— that choir so peculiar and so cultivated in its power of execution, was forgotten—and the great hymn of praise and thankfulness, *Te Deum Laudamus*, was raised under the mighty dome of St. Peter's, and sustained by forty thousand voices. Such was the spectacle witnessed on that occasion. But, in the mean time, the bells from the towers of three hundred churches announced the joyful tidings to the expectant population; and from town to town, and from village to village, went forth the news that at last, by the supreme authority of the Church, it was no longer a belief of individual choice or affection, but a doctrine of the Catholic Church, that Mary, the Virgin Mother of the Son of God, among other prerogatives of divine grace, had been conceived without a stain of sin.*

---

* The sermon from which this extract is taken, was translated into Italian for

After a short visit to England, where he was the guest of Viscount Campden in Gloucestershire, he sailed for America in the steamer Atlantic, and arrived in New York March 27th, after a passage of nearly sixteen days. As usual, he immediately began a controversy.

A bill had been introduced into the State Legislature, at the instigation of the trustees of the church of St. Louis in Buffalo, the purpose of which—to state it briefly—was to necessitate the transfer of all ecclesiastical property to trustees. Of course, it affected only Catholics, as it was the custom of all other denominations to vest their church property in corporate bodies. In the course of a speech in support of this bill, the Hon. Erastus Brooks, senator from New York, and one of the editors of the New York *Express*, made the following statements:

> I have had occasion, during a visit of a day in New York, to secure references, taken from the register's office there, of the amount of property held by John Hughes in that city. I suppose its value to be, in New York alone, not much short of five millions of dollars. So far from this property being held, when in churches, by trustees, there are numerous transfers from trustees to John Hughes! Beginning with February, 1842, and continuing through 1854, a friend of mine copied fifty-eight entries of as many distinct parcels of property made in the name of land for John Hughes, all in the space of twelve years!—not to John Hughes, Bishop, nor to John Hughes, Arch-bishop, nor to John Hughes, as trustee for the great Roman Catholic Church, but to plain John Hughes, in his own *propria persona*. Some of these parcels cover whole squares of land, and nearly all of them are of great value. The rule of that Church is never to part with property, and to receive all that can be purchased.

After a little preliminary skirmishing, through *The New York Times* and *The Freeman's Journal*, with the Buffalo trustees and the general demerits of the bill before the senate,

the cardinal prefect of the Propaganda, and the Pope ordered it to be published in a collection of sermons on the Immaculate Conception.

the archbishop addressed himself to Mr. Brooks, pronounced the statements contained in the extract just quoted to be false, and called upon the senator either to prove or retract them. A long and acrimonious controversy ensued. Mr. Brooks cited all the entries found in the register's office. The number was not fifty-eight, but forty-six. Of the deeds registered several were duplicates; one or two were leases; one conveyed a strip of land *two inches wide;* one conveyed the half of a burial vault, and seven related to property which had some time ago passed out of the archbishop's possession, either by transfer to the trustees of the cathedral or to religious communities, or by sale to outside parties. The whole number of actual deeds of real estate recorded in the archbishop's name, including one lease for nine hundred and ninety-nine years at a nominal rent, was finally proved to be thirty-three. Other statements of Mr. Brooks were also shown to be inaccurate. The value of this property, instead of being only "a little short of $5,000,000," was estimated by the archbishop at $385,000, and there were mortgages on it to the amount of $245,000.

And this property, he said,

Is in equity and truth, though not in its legal form, the property of the several congregations to be enumerated hereafter. Its management has been, by a rule of the diocese dating as far back as 1843, in the hands of the respective pastors of each congregation, who are required to associate with them one or two respectable and competent laymen, to assist them in the administration of the temporalities of their church; to keep regular accounts of its income, its expenditures, etc.; to make and publish from time to time, at least once a year, a report of the condition of the church, to be distributed among their pew-holders, and a copy of the same to be forwarded to the archiepiscopal residence, in order to have it inserted in a diocesan register kept for that purpose. The title of their church lots was vested nominally in the bishop. But he never considered this as giving him any more right to the ownership, in the sense of Mr. Brooks, than he would have to regard as his own an offering of charity handed to him for the benefit of the orphan asylum. Neither has he ever received so much as one farthing of revenue or income from this property in consequence of his nominal ownership. Neither has he troubled himself with the management of the temporalities of these congregations, except in so far as to prevent the church property from being mortgaged or exposed to alienation, as had been the case under the irresponsible management of lay trustees.

In a subsequent letter he dismisses his antagonist with the following contemptuous language:

Mr. Brooks .... is utterly unworthy of notice. I take him, consequently, with covered hands to the nearest open sash of a window, with the single mental observation, "Go hence, wretched and vile insect; the world has space for you as well as for me."

The archbishop afterwards collected the letters on both sides, and published them in a little volume, which he called "*Brooksiana*" (12mo, New York, 1855), with an introduction reviewing the trustee system. Mr. Brooks also published the controversy, with two or three letters of his which the archbishop had omitted as being irrelevant to the main issue.

The church-property bill passed the Legislature, but its provisions never were enforced, and in 1862 it was repealed.

During the election in the autumn of 1855, a report was put in circulation that the archbishop was using all his influence in behalf of the Soft-shell Democratic ticket; and at the same time he was blamed for failing to support a certain senator who, in spite of strong Protestant associations, had earnestly opposed the church-property bill. He wrote as follows to a friend who had called his attention to these matters:

TO MR. TERENCE DONNELLY.

NEW YORK, *Oct.* 29, 1855.

DEAR SIR:

I have just read the note enclosed in yours of this morning.

It appears to me impossible to prevent interested parties from making use of my name in politics, in which I take but very little interest. I may say to you, however, that Mr. John Van Buren has had no authority from me, directly or indirectly, to use my name in connection with the subject of politics. I may say in one word, that whatever my partialities may be as a citizen in regard to political questions, they are strictly confined to my own breast, but that I have not directly or indirectly expressed any opinion with regard to the respective merits of the rival parties and candidates who are now presenting their claims for the votes of the country. I hold, and have ever held, that the position of a clergyman forbids him from taking any active part in such questions, and that he could not be a partisan without at once endangering and degrading his influence as a priest. I give you entire liberty to make known, in any way you think proper, that I have never been, that I never intend to be a partisan in any political contest; that if persons make use of my name as in favor of one side or opposed to another, such persons take an unwarrantable liberty, which I have, in ordinary circumstances, no opportunity to resent.

The allusion to the case of Senator Crosby presents, of course, a feature which one might regret, but for which, according to my principles, I see no remedy. The wonder to me, in regard to the church-property bill, which violates our civil and religious rights as well as our rights of property, is not that one should have voted for and another against it, but that it should have been enacted in the Legislature, which, it seems to me, had the power to prevent its enactment. Since Catholics were admitted to equal rights with their Protestant fellow citizens in this State, nothing has occurred so insulting to Catholic feeling, or so ominous of what they may anticipate under the outcry of adverse fanaticism, as the enactment and confirmation of that iniquitous bill by the Legislature and Executive of the State of New York. All this, however, is not a reason why those who have been insulted and injured by it should turn round to forsake those who stood by them in the hour of trial, or to elevate into power their undisguised and open enemies.

I remain, very respectfully

Your obedient servant,

✠ JOHN, *Abp. of New York.*

Some time afterward he received a letter from Cassius

M. Clay, on the subject of "the Catholic vote." Mr. Clay seemed to assume that the archbishop had the keeping of the political consciences of his flock, and he labored to convince him that the Republicans were the natural allies of the Catholics, and the Democrats their natural foes. "I pray you," he wrote, "to change your alliances. Whilst we [the Republicans] are not the advocates of 'Religion and State,' we are the fast friends of religious freedom. . . . . I do not speak singly my own sentiments (they are known to all the world), but the sentiments of my leading friends who have conversed freely with me on this subject, and who join me in, I may almost say, astonishment, that our friendly and essentially unchangeable feelings are not reciprocated by the Catholic Church." The following is the archbishop's answer:

TO CASSIUS M. CLAY.

NEW YORK, *Feb.* 6, 1858.
DEAR SIR:

Absence and incessant occupation have combined to prevent my acknowledgment of your letter dated Dec. 28th, 1857. If it had been on business requiring immediate attention, I should have attended to it sooner. It refers to a subject in regard to which I have made it a rule to avoid any expression of opinion. My own principles are, that the American people are able in their own way to manage their affairs of state, without any guidance or instruction toward any class or religious denomination, by either priests or parsons.

The Catholics are liable to commit mistakes either in their selection of parties, or of candidates for office; but in all such cases they are in the wise company of the great controlling native American people of this country. They initiate nothing, but, by various influences, their votes are coaxed or driven to and fro in the rivalship of the great parties who have assumed the government of the country, and to whom it rightfully belongs.

As for myself, I never influenced a human being, Catholic or Protestant, as to the party to which he might think proper to attach himself in his capacity of a voting citizen. I never voted but once in my life, and that vote was cast nearly thirty years ago, in favor of your illustrious namesake, and I believe relative, "Harry of the West." He was, in my estimation, a statesman as well as an orator, and I voted the more [readily] because my congregation were in the main opposed to him, and some of them had almost threatened me on account of my good opinion of him, as a man much calumniated, but of whom, as a statesman and orator, his country might well be proud.

You can easily perceive by all this, that the Catholics vote, as individuals, in the proper exercise of their franchise; but without any direction from their clergy—so far at least as has ever come under my knowledge, and certainly so far as the clergy under my own jurisdiction is concerned.

I have the honor to be, with great respect,

Your obedient servant,

✠ JOHN, *Abp. of New York.*

CHAPTER XXII.

1855-1858.

Visit to Newfoundland—Lectures in Baltimore and Pittsburg—Essay on the Catholic Press—Attack upon the Archbishop in the *Times*—Report to the Propaganda on his administration of the diocese—Curious scene at the Tabernacle—Letter on the death of an old friend—Letter on the consecration of two bishops—Alleged rivalship between the sees of New York and Baltimore—Primacy of honor conferred upon Baltimore at the request of Archbishop Hughes—Letter to Bishop McNally.

IN September, 1855, the archbishop visited St. John's, Newfoundland, where he had been invited by Bishop Mullock to preach at the consecration of the cathedral. The occasion was celebrated with extraordinary impressiveness, and during the two or three weeks which the archbishop spent in the province, he received many a flattering evidence that his fame had travelled beyond his own country. The steamer in which he arrived at St. John's carried also the bishops of Toronto, Arichat, and St. John's, New Brunswick. As soon as their arrival was signalled, an immense crowd of people, besides the bishop and all the Catholic societies of the city, collected on the wharf, and as the vessel came up the harbor, peals of rejoicing were rung by the bells of the churches and convents. It was eight o'clock in the evening, when, amid the hurrahs of the crowd and salvos of artillery, the visitors landed. A torch-light procession was then formed, Bishop Mullock and Archbishop Hughes at the head, the other prelates following—all in open carriages—and a band of music, the societies, and the people at large, taking up places behind them. In this manner they passed to the cathedral; the houses were illuminated along the way; bonfires blazed on the acclivity upon which the city is built; the ships in the harbor sent up signal rockets; and the air resounded with the discharge of cannon and small arms. Entering the cathedral, the prelates knelt a few moments in silent prayer, the archbishop gave his benediction, and Bishop Mullock then dismissed the people with a few pertinent words. The bishops and the clergymen who accompanied them were entertained during their visit at Bishop Mullock's house.

Archbishop Hughes journeyed about the province a good deal, preaching at several places, laying the corner-stone of a new church at River Head, receiving addresses, making speeches at banquets, and submitting to be lionized with the best possible grace. Though somewhat fatigued by carrying all his honors, he was upon the whole delighted with his visit, and in a sermon in his own cathedral, the day after his return home, he spoke enthusiastically of the faith, piety, and heroism of the Newfoundland fishermen.

With the exception of two lectures—one in January, 1856, before the Young Catholic's Friend Society of Baltimore, on "The Present Condition and Prospects of the Catholic Church in the United States," and the other in June, before the St. Paul's Institute of Pittsburg, on "The Relation between the Civil and Religious Duties of the Catholic Citizen"—he did little to bring himself before the public for the space of a year or more after this. As his health failed, his mental energies seemed to slumber. Not that his mind was weakened, but things that would have roused him to battle in the days of his strength, now made little or no impression upon him. Once in a while the old powers would awake in all their former majesty, but only for a little time. He passed almost entire days in his room, reading newspapers chiefly, chatting with any one who happened to call upon him, dictating letters, or perhaps beginning an article for some of the journals, and throwing it aside unfinished. For a while he tried exercise on horseback, but he soon tired of it. At the instigation of some of his friends, the trustees of the cathedral purchased for him a country house at Manhattanville; but he made scarcely any use of it. It was consequently sold, and a handsome house bought on the corner of Madison avenue and Thirty-sixth street, where he continued to reside until his death. He made occasional trips to the country—either to watering places, like Long Branch and Saratoga, or to Lafargeville, where he had bought on his own account the old college property, on which the family of his brother Michael were now living. He had no taste for country life, and never took very long summer vacations; but his excursions were almost always of benefit to him, because his impaired vitality needed the stimulus of change of scene and society. By long disregard of the commonest laws of health, carelessness and irregularity about eating, want of exercise, and overtasking his brain, he had entirely destroyed his constitution. The current of his blood flowed sluggishly, and naturally his mind at the same time lost much of its activity, so that he was indisposed or unfit for bodily exertion which might have strengthened him. Besides this, he had suffered much for several years past from rheumatism and other complaints, which made exercise painful to him and sometimes impossible.

In *The Metropolitan* magazine for December, 1856, there was a remarkable article from his pen, entitled "Reflections and Suggestions in regard to what is called the Catholic Press in the United States." Probably many who read it did not understand its full meaning, and yet it was very well adapted to the purpose which he had in view in writing it. It will be remembered that the influence of the religious press had been a matter of discussion in the provincial council in 1854, and whatever his suffragans may have thought about it, the archbishop was far from believing that influence to be altogether beneficial to the Church. There were three classes of Catholic periodicals which he considered mischievous. The first were those of the Young Ireland stamp; the second, those which spoke, perhaps unconsciously, as if they looked upon the Catholic Church in this country substantially as an Irish Church, or a German Church, according to the nationality which they professed to represent; and the third, as he supposed, were trying to Americanize the Church by conforming Catholic practices—so far as they could do so consistently with sound doctrine and good discipline—to the character of the American people. I think he disliked this third class the most of the three. They were the spokesmen of what has been not very aptly called "the party of progress and adaptation in the Catholic Church"—"a new school," as the archbishop said in a letter to a friend, "which, without noise, I had been obliged to counteract since the last outbreak of Know-Nothingism." He made a curious manifestation of his disapproval of them at the annual commencement of St. John's college in 1856. In an address to the graduating class, Dr. Orestes A. Brownson remarked, in substance, that if the Catholic religion could be presented to the American people through mediums and under auspices more congenial to their feelings and habits, the progress of the Church would be far greater than it had been. The archbishop was present as a guest. At the close of Dr. Brownson's address, he went upon the platform, and, vastly to the entertainment of the audience, kindly but decidedly controverted the doctor's opinions.

It was against this "new school" that the essay on the Catholic Press was principally directed, though at first sight the Irish journals appear to be the offenders whom he most desired to castigate. He rebuked all parties pretty soundly, with a view to composing their differences, or at least "stifling the growing elements of discord and controversy;" and, near the close of the article, penned the following paragraph:

The heading of our article implied that we should offer suggestions as well as reflections in regard to what is called the Catholic press. This we shall do with great diffidence; but, so far as depends on us, *with a determination that they shall not be disregarded*, at least in reference to the spiritual interests of our own diocese, and of the people committed to our care. We advise that Catholic periodicals abstain from every thing having even a tendency to infringe on the regular ecclesiastical authority by which God has been pleased to appoint that his Church should be governed; that they shall not presume to draw odious comparisons, and publish them, between the clergy of one section of the country and those of another; that they shall not arrogate to themselves the position of oracles or umpires, to decide where is merit and where is demerit; that they shall not single out a clergyman for premature panegyric, simply because he is a patron of this or that journal, whilst they pass over in silence other clergymen, oftentimes of more than equal worth.

Alluding to this essay in a letter to a friend in Rome, intended for the eye of the Propaganda, he speaks as follows of the conductors of the American section of the Catholic press:

As they became more numerous and more acquainted with Catholics, especially young men born in this country, they imagined themselves an auxiliary corps to aid the bishops and clergy in propagating the Catholic doctrine among the Protestants of the United States, whom *they* professed to know by heart. Their general idea for the accomplishment of this, was a combination of lay elements, to aid indirectly in the work of the ministry. Their reliance was principally on "the press;" but, in connection with it, on "associations," which they have tried and which have all failed, viz.: "Catholic library associations," "Catholic lecture associations," and, last of all and least profitable, "Catholic clubs." I did not especially approve of any of these; but I gave permission for the several experiments from which they anticipated so much benefit to religion. They were encouraged to make these experiments by the example of what has been called "Young Catholic England." They were encouraged farther by the kind words which the Pope had addressed from time to time to learned laymen who were laboring for the defence of religion against the rising surges of infidelity and of heresy in different old Catholic countries of Europe. All these encouragements of the Holy Father they *appropriated to themselves*, inasmuch as they were all directly or indirectly connected with the "Catholic press." They made no discrimination between the circumstances of the Church in the old countries of Europe, and those which surround her in the United States. As regards her past career in this country, her enemies have nothing to assail; and, consequently, these young and injudicious friends had no opportunity to refute the writings or assaults of her adversaries. However, as in America the past is little thought of, but the future every thing, so these writers would take, to some extent, what I might call the *prospective engineering* of the Church into their hands, as knowing, if not the doctrines of religion, at least the genius of the American people, much better than the bishops. They have been disposed, if not to find fault with every thing that has been done, at least to point out how much more might have been accomplished. But especially they take pleasure in suggesting to the prelates and clergy what is to be done for the present and for the coming time. Of course, they leave it to the bishops to carry out what they had projected; and if this be neglected, it is the fault of the clergy, and not of the zealous conductors of the "Catholic press." Appropriating to themselves the words of encouragement which the supreme head of the Church addressed, under peculiar circumstances, to certain eminent lay editors of Europe, they have been disposed to look upon themselves as an unofficial but approved portion of the Catholic hierarchy.

I have set my face strongly against the exceptionable part of all this. There are many wants which no bishop can supply for lack of means. There are many other wants which they point out, but which it would be inexpedient to supply as they propose, even if the bishop had the means. As for themselves, few of them have either the will or the ability to take any serious part in supporting the burden which, in their immature zeal, they are so ready to see the bishops and clergy impose on others.

These remarks will explain to you the necessity which prompted me to publish "*Reflections and Suggestions on what is called the Catholic Press in the United States.*" But I had another object, which was to prevent these papers from sowing divisions, or creating factions among the Catholics of my diocese. In this I have been successful. They indulge still in their little theories, but nobody minds them any more.

He believed that some one who felt aggrieved by this essay, was the author of a communication signed "Equitas," which appeared in the *Times* in January, 1857, reviewing with severity his administration of the diocese. He took no public notice of it, but he demanded of the editor the name of his assailant, and threatened him with legal proceedings in case he refused to give it. It appeared, however, that the writer had imposed upon Mr. Raymond, the editor of the *Times*, by affixing to his letter the name of a worthy and venerable priest of Boston, who was one of the archbishop's best friends. Nobody that knew this reverend gentleman could doubt for a moment that the signature was a forgery. Mr. Raymond made an apology in his paper; but while he was in Europe the following summer, a scurrilous article, evidently from the same pen which wrote "Equitas," appeared editorially in the *Times*, under the heading "Rome and New York." It charged the archbishop with "maladministration, nepotism, indolence, arrogance, and a meddling and petty spirit;" more absurdly still, it accused him of "indifference to the Virgin Mary," inasmuch as he had "omitted to notice, with due solemnities, the declaration of the dogma of the Immaculate Conception;" and of "disrespect to the representative of the vicar of Christ on earth," because he "turned his back and fled to Cuba, when the nuncio of Pius IX., assailed by the press, hooted and stoned by the mob, and burned in effigy in a hundred cities and villages, most needed his support." The archbishop answered this in a very effective public letter, of which he writes as follows, in the communication to a friend in Rome, from which I have just quoted:

My answer is more severe than it is possible for you to understand from reading it. The editor of *The New York Times* has not recovered from it, but neither he, nor any of the other papers, has attacked me since the date of its publication. The Protestant, as well as the Catholic public, were indignant at his unprovoked and malicious attack. The newspapers denounced him for it, and whilst my refutation was published in more than twenty-five journals, his assault was not copied into a single one. The attack of "Equitas," in accordance with the intrinsic malice of its author, was cut from the paper in which it had been published, and a copy of it sent to every bishop in the United States, without either name, or note, or comment. I have reason to think that it was also sent to many of the bishops of Europe, and even to some of the cardinals at Rome, if not to the Holy Father himself. Several of the prelates in this country, on seeing it, threw it into the fire; but, anonymous as it was, it would be almost natural that bishops unacquainted with the circumstances of New York, should think that, although it was malicious, still it could never have been written and published here under my eyes if it were not founded upon truth of some kind; and hence I have no doubt that my reputation has been shaken in the minds of some, at least, of my episcopal brethren. It is true that each of them has his own troubles to encounter; and it is equally true, that at all times there have been discontented individuals both among the clergy and the laity of my diocese, as well as of others. But they have never been numerous enough to manifest any open opposition to my administration. The clergy and laity are as united with me at the present time as they ever have been.

This last remark was certainly true. There never was any thing like an "opposition-party" during his administration. And he might have felt perfectly easy about the effect of "Equitas's" articles. The archbishop was too well known, both in Italy and at home, to be injured by an anonymous newspaper writer whose personal animosity betrayed itself in every line. He was always sensitive, however, to public criticism, and particularly jealous of his good name at Rome. It was probably in consequence of these attacks in the *Times*, that he wrote the letter or report above referred to, a document of some seventy-five or eighty foolscap pages, giving a complete history of his episcopal administration. He sent it to a friend in Rome, with the following letter:

> NEW YORK, *March* 30, 1858.
>
> I enclose you a draft for $300 on Packenham, Hooker & Co., in Rome, for the purpose of defraying the expenses of translating into Italian the long documents which I have already forwarded to your address by the American-European express company—or at least so much of them as the Cardinal-Prefect may wish to have translated. I confide in you to have it done as respectably as possible. You will find the English text very plain and simple, and it must acquire its elegance, if any, from the translation.
>
> The topics alluded to by me are treated of in the briefest possible terms. They are the mere skeleton of events and circumstances, which, with their consequences, would spread out into a work of large size. I may remark also that the circumstances by which I have been surrounded, and the character of the country and people with whom I had to deal, did not allow me to use at all times that meek and apostolic style which is so appropriate and beautiful, and for which Roman writers are so especially distinguished. The people of this country, and especially those among whom I have lived, have great respect for a manly, straightforward, and outspoken vindication of any rights, whether civil or ecclesiastical, which men deem worthy of being defended at all. The gentle language of meekness and forbearance which, in ordinary circumstances, should flow from the lips and the pen of a Christian bishop, would have no effect upon the class of adversaries that I have had to deal with. They are a class who have very little respect for those who submit tamely to aggression of any kind, when the assailed party has truth and justice and reason on his side. They look upon tame submission to wrong of any kind, not as a virtue, but as an encouragement to the evil-doer—nay, as a scandal, inviting oppression and even persecution.
>
> You will be pleased to explain this to his Eminence the Cardinal-Prefect; in all other respects, the documents, I trust, will sufficiently explain themselves.

I quote a few paragraphs from the concluding portion of this interesting manuscript:

Allow me, in conclusion, to make some general remarks in relation both to the past and the present condition of the Catholic Church in this country, and more especially the diocese of New York, with which I am most familiar.

The increase of the Catholic people in the United States has been very great indeed. But I think an exaggerated idea of the Catholic population would result from the assumption that it was in proportion to the increase of the hierarchy. We have forty-six bishops. The Catholic population throughout the whole United States can scarcely exceed three millions and a half. These are very unequally distributed. In many dioceses the Catholics are very few. The bishops throughout the interior, residing in their quiet towns or villages, are anxious to propagate the kingdom of Christ in all simplicity and mildness, without saying or doing any thing that would excite the enmities or opposition of the Protestants among whom they live. The same remark would apply to several of the episcopal sees established in cities of a populous and prosperous character. Now my lot was cast in the great metropolis of the whole country. My people were composed of representatives from almost all nations. They came under episcopal government in a new country, and in circumstances such as they had not been accustomed to in their own. It was necessary that they should be brought to coalesce as one Catholic flock. They were surrounded by many inducements to diverge from the unity of the Church, both in profession and in practice. Many snares were laid for them; and, under these circumstances, I found it expedient to adopt a mode of government resulting almost by necessity from the peculiarity of my position. I had to stand up among them as their bishop and chief; to warn them against the dangers that surrounded them; to contend for their rights as a religious community; to repel the spirit of faction among them; to convince their judgment by frequent explanations in regard to public and mixed questions; to encourage the timid, and sometimes to restrain the impetuous; in short, to knead them up into one dough, to be leavened by the spirit of Catholic faith and of Catholic union. Hardly any thing of this kind was either expedient or necessary in any other episcopal see within the United States.

I will remark here, that in all this I never thought of speaking, or writing, or legislating, except for the special flock which the

Church had committed to my episcopal care. But in a country like ours, so teeming with newspapers, and in which every thing goes forth (especially from the metropolis) on what are called the "wings of the press," the questions agitated in New York were carried away into every village and hamlet, and there discussed in the local newspapers and in society, very much as they would be in New York itself. Many a quiet episcopal see has been agitated; many an annoyance brought upon both clergy and laity of those remote localities, from the struggles which had to be sustained in this place alone. . . . . This result was inevitable, in the circumstances of the country, but was never intended by me; since I only looked, as my first duty, to the welfare of the diocese committed to my charge.

As time went on, however, and the solution of different disputed questions here became public, and as it was always found in favor of the position I had taken, New York acquired a certain kind of general predominancy in the minds of the Catholics. What was done at New York, or said by me, was taken to be the true course for every place else as well as this. And thus, through the medium of the newspapers, rather than from any direct instruction or guidance on the part of the local ecclesiastical authority, a certain tone of action and feeling became prevalent among the Catholics. . . . . Even this it was not in my power either to prevent or avoid. I wished to do my duty toward my own diocese; and beyond that I desired neither praise, nor censure, nor responsibility.

. . . . . .

There never was a composition containing so much egotism as this; and I make no apology; for, even if I were disposed, I could not separate myself from the events which I have narrated, or the circumstances of the times and places in which they occurred. It is not to be supposed that at my present period of life, and with a constitution far from being as robust and vigorous as it has been heretofore, I could again go through the labors and trials to which I have briefly called your attention. The last act by which I now could attest my devotion to the Holy See would be, whenever it is pleasing to our Holy Father, to resign, and transfer to younger shoulders the burden which I have endeavored to bear, and the honor of which I never was worthy, as first archbishop of New York.

This paper made a very happy impression at Rome. "The cardinal Barnabo," writes the archbishop's correspondent, "told me he had read a great portion of your report. He said he was delighted with it; that he admired greatly its order and luminous descriptions; but, above all, he admires your penetrating grasp of mind, in judging not only the past, but also the future of the American Church. His Eminence directed me to tell your Grace the impression your report has made on him. 'I will answer,' said he, 'the good archbishop as soon as I have time to read over all the report. But in an official letter I cannot say all I would like on this subject.'"

The archbishop was particularly annoyed by the charge of the writer in the *Times* that he had been wanting in respect for the nuncio:

I beg you also to present my sincere respects to Monsignore Bedini, and to say that nothing has occurred to alienate from him the personal affection, I might call it, with which our earlier and later acquaintance had inspired me. I cannot, however, deny that those who have been attempting to lessen me in the estimation both of the bishops of this country, by their anonymous writings, and, as I have said before, in the estimation of Rome itself, have made a use of his name which I am sure was never authorized, or even suspected by him. And although this was at all times my interior and heartfelt conviction, still I could not help feeling wounded and mortified, as well for his sake as my own, that his name should have been introduced at all in such a hidden and unchristian manner of proceeding.

I will say, however, now, once for all, that so far as I am concerned, he occupies in my respect and in my esteem the same place which he did when I took leave of him in Vienna in 1840, and when, at a more recent period, we both witnessed the lofty and ground tumbling of the Chinese paupers on Blackwell's Island in 1853.

I shall refer no more to this subject, and shall only remark, that during all this period, the movement of my administration of the diocese has never been ruffled or obstructed for a moment in consequence of all these things, in regard to which I have already written to you. In fact, there are not ten Catholics in the city of New York who have even the slightest idea of the efforts that have been made to injure me at a distance; and so let the matter drop.

He gave rather an odd exemplification, in the spring of 1857, of that anxiety of which he speaks on a preceding page, to unite as one flock the people of various nations who compose the Catholic population of this country. A priest from a western diocese was attempting to induce the Irish of New York to emigrate to Nebraska, where he proposed to found an Irish colony. It was to be called the town of St. Patrick's. The streets were to be named after the cities of the old country, as Dublin street, Limerick street, Kilkenny street. The reverend gentleman called a meeting in the Tabernacle on the 26th of March, and made an address in support of his project, in the course of which he declared that he had called upon the archbishop, and found that he was not opposed to it, but, on the contrary, had once entertained a similar plan himself. The clergyman and the archbishop, however, seem to have misunderstood each other. A little while before the meeting, Bishop Bayley had spoken to the archbishop upon the subject, and told him that it was reported he was in favor of the colonization scheme. "On the contrary," said Dr. Hughes, "I am strongly opposed to it." It was agreed that he should explain his sentiments in a public letter to Bishop Bayley. But after the bishop had left him he thought over the matter, and the end of it was, that, without telling any one what he was going to do, he put on his hat and walked quietly to the Tabernacle.

As soon as the Reverend Mr. —— had finished his address, a gentleman in overcoat and muffler rose in the gallery, and exclaimed: "Wait a moment; I have a word to say."

"Come on the stand, then," shouted one of the audience.

"No, I shall not," was the answer; "I would rather be by myself."

He took off his muffler, and was recognized as the archbishop.

He expressed his disapprobation of the colonization scheme in the most emphatic manner. He reprimanded the reverend speaker, first for concealing the object of his visit to New York when he called upon him; secondly, for representing him as favorable to a plan which was impracticable and unwise; and thirdly, for degrading the sacred office of the priesthood by stooping to become the tool of land speculators. He then continued :

Talk not to me about an Irish town! Five and thirty years ago I heard some of my countrymen buying and selling in the streets of Pittsburg in the Irish tongue, and I was glad to hear it, for it revived the memory of the few words of that language which I learned in childhood. But suppose they succeed in forming settlements exclusively Irish and speaking Irish? why, by-and-by they will become as distinct as the Mormons. . . . . Theories are good for nothing. Every man who would settle in this country must trust to his own good conduct, his own sobriety, morality, and rectitude. The gentleman alluded to a remark of mine referring to one of my early dreams, in which I imagined that I might associate a number of worthy gentlemen in an undertaking from motives of pure philanthropy—motives of Irish patriotism, I may call it, or at least a love of my country—to buy ten or twenty thousand acres of land in what is now called Wisconsin, and that they should dispose of those acres in small lots to emigrants, that is, to those who should know how to use the axe and even the plough in this country; to have always cabins in advance for those who might come, and still to keep it working regularly, so as to bear its own expenses. That was the theory; but when I spoke of it to gentlemen of means and intelligence, they said it was all nonsense.

The priest attempted to excuse himself. The archbishop catechized him sharply, and finished by declaring that the apology was worse than the original offence. The audience, as if awe-struck, withdrew in profound silence.

TO MR. FRENAYE.

February 18, 1857.

MY DEAR MR. FRENAYE:

I received your letter of the 2d instant, announcing the death of my old and honored friend Dr. Nancrede. I am happy and rejoice at the evidences of religion and piety which preceded and accompanied his departure from this life. Had I known of his illness, I certainly should have had the melancholy satisfaction of seeing him once again before his death. May God be merciful to his soul! With all his peculiarities, he clung nobly to the faith of his fathers from childhood to old age, and this amidst many temptations to abandon it. During the period of our difficulties in the erection of St. John's church, the doctor stood by us with great constancy and great fidelity.

Week by week I hear of the death of one or another of the prominent Catholics whom I numbered among my friends five-and-twenty years ago. In a little time you will be the last—"*ultimus filiorum Job*"—that is, if I shall not die before you, which is by no means improbable. In the mean time, it is a great source of consolation to me to know that your kindness toward myself is as constant and warm as it was from the first days of our acquaintance. I assure you that that feeling toward you is most sincerely reciprocated. The position which you now occupy, and have occupied since 1833, is in my estimation of too sacred an order to be ascribed to any human being, either as to its commencement or as to its continuation. You have been the servant of God, and in His service you have been honored and happy. May that happiness continue until its full reward shall be realized in heaven, is the sincere wish of your ever devoted friend and servant in Christ,

✠ JOHN, *Abp. of N. Y.*

TO THE REV. BERNARD SMITH, ROME.

NEW YORK, *March* 30, 1858.

Two bishops were consecrated on the fourth Sunday of Lent—the 14th instant. The one was Dr. Lynch, bishop of Charleston, consecrated by the archbishop of Baltimore; the other, the bishop of Hartford, Dr. McFarland, consecrated by myself, in the pro-cathedral of Providence, Rhode Island. The ceremony was exceedingly grand, and as it was the first consecration of a bishop in Yankee-land, properly so called—that is, in New England, the home of the Puritans—it produced a very deep impression. All the bishops of the province were present, wearing their copes and mitres. We were nine bishops, including the one to be consecrated, and about sixty priests. We proceeded in solemn procession from the episcopal residence, through the public streets, to the front door of the church. The crowd was immense, and among them very large numbers of the most influential Protestants of the city. Many a Catholic heart sympathized with the solemn Te Deum, in thanking Almighty God, and in grateful reverence to the vicar of Christ, who had at length appointed over them a bishop so universally revered for his piety, prudence, and learning.

He wrote to Rome, in April, 1858, with regard to a rumor that had obtained currency, of jealousy between the sees of Baltimore and New York:

As to any rivalship between Baltimore and New York in connection with the idea of metropolitan superiority, that, I think, is quite out of the question. Baltimore was the first bishopric, the first archbishopric, and continued quite long enough as the sole metropolitan see of the United States. When the proper time came, other metropolitan sees were instituted by the wisdom of the Supreme Pontiff of the Catholic Church. This did not occur too soon. But I am persuaded that, out of Baltimore itself, it has never entered into the mind of any priest or any prelate to think of a rivalship between any other metropolitan see and the early but feeble, yet faithful mother of the provincial hierarchy in the United States.

. . . . .

If, however, I might express my own convictions, I would recommend that Baltimore should be erected into a primatial see, just for the sake of form and proportions. It is true that this idea has been suggested to the Holy See on two several occasions in our provincial councils. Rome, for reasons which are satisfactory to us, because they are *hers*, has decided otherwise for the present; and yet I will take the liberty of saying that I think it would be well if Baltimore should enjoy the honor of the title at least. Neither primate nor archbishop, it is well known, is authorized to exercise the powers which, in the earlier ages of the Church, were recognized, or at least tolerated, as inherent in these titles. And certainly I should not desire much that Baltimore should be erected into a primatial see, at least for the present time, with any privileges beyond the mere title and the mere honors connected with it. But it would give the hierarchy in this country a form; and even forms, in a new country like ours, have their influence for good, but have very little influence for evil. All Catholics in America look back to the memory of Baltimore with respect and gratitude. As a city, it is, of course, becoming insignificant and fading in comparison with some others. But this is not a reason why its ancient distinctions or honors should be either taken away or overshadowed. And as to any rivalship between New York and Baltimore on that score, the idea seems to me almost childish—as if we were to go through once again the immense troubles recorded in ecclesiastical history, as between York and Canterbury, in England, or as between Armagh and Dublin, in Ireland.

The new dignity, however, was not conferred upon Baltimore, in accordance with these suggestions, but merely a "prerogative of place," by which precedence is given to the Archbishop of Baltimore in councils or assemblies of the Hierarchy of the United States.

TO BISHOP McNALLY, CLOGHER, IRELAND.

May 26, 1858.

My desire to visit Ireland, when I was last in Europe, was more of a wish than an intention. I was anxious to be at home for the festival of Easter, and besides, at the period of embarking at Liverpool, a most violent snow-storm was raging in the harbor. In passing up the Channel, the mountains and hills of Ireland were deeply covered with snow, and apart from private and personal feelings, what attraction could Ireland have for me, unless I could see "the green"!

Having been present at the definition of the Immaculate Conception by our Holy Father, I resolved to erect in this city a memorial church both in honor of the immaculate Mother of God, and commemorative of the definition which establishes two points of doctrine—one, the last undefined prerogative of the Blessed Virgin, and the other, by implication, the infallibility of St. Peter's successor, with or without the aid of the general council.

The church to which I refer was begun immediately on my return from Rome. It is exceedingly beautiful in its way, and I had the consolation of consecrating it in the solemn manner prescribed by the Pontifical on Sunday, the 15th of this month. You will be perhaps surprised when I mention that this is the ninety-ninth church that has been erected and dedicated under my personal guidance and responsibility since the period of my appointment as Bishop of New York; and from this simple fact you will easily infer, that what remains of mind and body to one who has gone through so much, must be henceforward of little advantage to the Church or the people committed to my care.

CHAPTER XXIII.

1858–1859.

The Archbishop talks about resigning—Applies for a coadjutor—Foundation of the American College in Rome—Letter on Ecclesiastical Education—The new St. Patrick's Cathedral begun—The Atlantic Telegraph—Death of Archbishop Walsh—Miscellaneous letters.

THE idea of resigning his episcopal office, to which he alludes in the Report quoted a little ways back, frequently presented itself to his mind during the last six or seven years of his life. He wrote on that subject to one of his correspondents in Rome, in December, 1857, with a request that his feelings should be made known to the cardinal-prefect of the Propaganda. "His Eminence was very much afflicted," says this gentleman, in reply, "and desired me to tell you in his name not to think of resignation. For twenty years you have been able to make religion triumph. That there is no person so qualified as you are for the present difficulties is certain; will you then make way for some one *less* qualified to take your place? 'Tell his Grace,' continued his Eminence, 'that I will oppose the project. But should he require a coadjutor, perhaps there would be no objection.'"

The archbishop signified his readiness to accept an assistant, and the matter was again brought to the notice of Cardinal Barnabo. He sent word to Dr. Hughes, that if he made a formal application for a coadjutor, he would in person present it to the Holy Father. "But to show what esteem I have for the archbishop," he added, "I will never consent to his resignation." It is a painful evidence of the rapidity with which he had broken down, that he should have been so ready to accept the assistance of a coadjutor. It was not long since he had said to Mr. Hargous: "They may do what they will with the diocese when I am under the ground, but so long as I live there shall be no coadjutor bishop of New York." But now he felt the cares of his office too severely to object to sharing his authority with another. He selected one of his suffragans for the proposed office, and submitted his choice to the other bishops of the province. He writes of the matter as follows, in September, 1858:

They [the other bishops] admit that I am overburthened with labor. They are willing to recommend any thing that could relieve me; but as I knew only one whom I am prepared to select and approve, and as I made my choice known to them, they manifested a good deal of sorrow, and turned the question on my weak point, viz., "Was I going to deprive an important diocese of its bishop, when they could not think of one fit to succeed him?" An argument of this kind was well calculated to break me down. But I think that they suspected an ulterior intention on my part, viz., that I wished to resign as soon as some one should be prepared and fitted to take my place.

This, my dear S., is still my intention. I do not wish to die out in the same turmoil in which God has so far appointed that I should live. I wish this to be understood at Rome; but for the rest, I will not desert my post until the permission of the Holy Father and a provision for this diocese shall have been obtained.

Before any further steps had been taken in this matter, the archbishop received an intimation that it would be more agreeable to the Holy See if he would not urge his application for the present. He wrote in reply:

Please make my profound respects to his eminence, Cardinal Barnabo, and say that I have not any disposition to ask for a coadjutor at the present moment; but that my knowledge of the condition of things in this diocese impresses me with a sense of the expediency of my having a coadjutor—and you know whom it is that I would select. In case of my death, I fear there might be much confusion—not indeed as to the selection of my successor, for that will depend on the Holy See, but in reference to the many institutions that now exist, but which are not thoroughly consolidated; still more, however, in reference to the ecclesiastical property of this diocese, which for the most part is legally invested in my name. One advantage of a coadjutor would be, that perhaps during my life he would become familiar with the state of the diocese in all respects, and that I could secure all ecclesiastical property against the contingencies of wills by means of a conveyance to him directly, as *inter vivos*, to take effect on my decease.

However, for the present I will not insist on this; although, as I have before made known to you, the matter was discussed in a full assembly of the Fathers of this province in our cathedral; and on that occasion the prelate whom I would choose, when appealed to, stated that "he would never decline or refuse any thing which the Holy See might approve in his regard."

In the summer of 1860 he wrote again :

My health is poor and declining, and I think that if I could get a coadjutor, more than once mentioned, it would prolong my days, if not years. I intend to write directly to his eminence, Cardinal Barnabo, for the inspection of his Holiness, the reasons which prompt me to this desire. Otherwise, I shall be obliged, for the interests of religion in this diocese, to solicit a resignation of my office.

The matter, however, was allowed to drop. He was really in great need of a coadjutor. His health was very feeble, and daily growing worse. He became continually less and less active both in body and in mind. He seemed to live more and more in his sitting-room and chamber, to shut himself out more and more completely from society. Besides, there were several weighty undertakings on his hands at this time, the principal of which were the establishment of an American college at Rome, and the building of a new cathedral. The idea of a college for American ecclesiastical students in the holy city originated with Pope Pius IX. He proposed it to the bishops of this country in 1855, in his answer to the letter of the prelates composing the first provincial council of New York. Archbishop Hughes entered warmly into his views, and was from the first the most ardent advocate of them in the United States. He addressed circulars to his suffragans and to the other archbishops, urging them to take the matter up, and to say how much they were able to contribute toward the support of the college. The Pope purchased, in 1857, the ancient convent of the *Umilta* for 42,000 scudi, and gave it to the American Church for the proposed institution. The American bishops were expected only to furnish it and provide for the current expenses. These would not be heavy. The students would attend the classes of the Propaganda, like the young men of the other national colleges in Rome. The only officers to be paid and supported would therefore be a rector and vice-rector. The rector was to be selected by the Pope from three candidates nominated by the prelates of the United States.

The *Umilta* was occupied by French troops, and much vexation and delay were caused by their unwillingness to leave it. Matters at last were arranged, and the American bishops ordered a general collection in their dioceses to defray the preliminary expenses. In New York and several other bishoprics it took place on the 12th of December, 1858. The archbishop advanced $5,000 to the college, on the faith of this collection. "For myself and my own diocese," he wrote, "apart from this collection, I hope to be able within two years to invest, either here or in Rome, a fund which will support seven ecclesiastics, although that number may not be at all times in the college."

TO THE REV. BERNARD SMITH, ROME.

Feb. 21, 1859.

. . . . . I fear I did not succeed to make myself understood in regard to the local direction of the future American college in Rome. This I infer from your remark that "the dread of promoting those who study in Roman colleges has no foundation." It would be very strange if I thought otherwise, or so expressed myself. But certain imprudent reports had gone abroad in this country that, *as a matter of course*, whoever should have received his education in the American college in Rome, would and should, independent of other considerations, be found in the line of promotion. This idea I considered unauthorized and imprudent, and, so far as it might prevail among the priests of this country, by no means likely to interest their zeal in favor of the new college.

As for myself, I had no such fears or such feelings. I suppose that at all times merit in the sight of God will be the ruling principle of the bishops of this country in selecting the fittest clergyman for any vacant place. I would take the liberty, however, of remarking that there is no common ground of comparison between the missions in Ireland or England, and the missions in the United States. In both the former countries there is a well-established tradition of Catholic hierarchical government. In the United States, however, there is no tradition of the kind, or but of a very recent origin. For a missionary in this country, but still more for a bishop, the great point is to adapt the strictest rules of the Catholic religion with judgment, discretion, and prudence, to the circumstances in which he is placed, and to those of the people who are committed to his care. If he insists on too much, he will be sure to fail; he must wait patiently until it may be possible to bring in gradually the full spirit, not only of Catholic faith, which indeed exists strongly, but also of Catholic discipline, which may best assimilate the Church in this country to the highest standard of canonical form, as set forth in the authorized teachings of Rome itself. But this must necessarily be a work of time. Much, indeed, has already been done in the United States in this direction; and there is no reason to doubt but that the rest can be accomplished by those who are to succeed us, if they will only blend the best application of ecclesiastical science and administration with the actual circumstances of the country.

It would be on this account that I should wish the theological students of the new college to be under the domestic training of superiors who should keep before their minds, in the way of private instruction, of spiritual reading, even of devotional exercises, the peculiarly novel condition of the Catholic people among whom they are to labor afterward in the United States. This should be no hindrance to their highest progress in the study of those branches which of course are best taught at Rome.

As for myself, I have no theory on the subject. Rome does not disdain to receive even the human and solitary opinions of the prelates in different countries in reference to matters in regard to which she alone is divinely appointed to decide. And even in regard to matters of expediency, I have lived long enough to learn from experience itself that, whatever may be the opinion of even wise men in regard to the expediency of this or that other measure, the decision of Rome will ultimately be found to be the wisest of all.

It was characteristic of the archbishop, who never seemed terrified at the magnitude of any task which he had once resolved to accomplish, that he should enter so warmly into this Roman project just at the time when he was about building a new cathedral, which he intended to make the most magnificent church on the western continent. In the following letter he describes his plan for raising money to begin it:

TO MR. FRENAYE.

May 18, 1858.

MY VERY DEAR FRIEND:
I have just received yours of yesterday's date. . . . . I am sorry indeed to learn, by your letter, that your sight and hearing are so much affected; but notwithstanding all that, I will expect you to pay your long-promised visit to New York on a very important occasion, which I hope is not remote. I am now grading the site for the new St. Patrick's Cathedral, on the corner of Fiftieth street and Fifth Avenue. I hope to be able to lay the corner-stone

on the feast of the Assumption, which will be Sunday, the 15th of next August. The ceremony will take place at four o'clock in the afternoon; and I confidently trust that, even at some inconvenience, you will come and take a room in my house for a week or two before and after.

The block of ground on which the cathedral is to be built is two hundred feet on Fifth Avenue on the west, two hundred feet on Madison Avenue on the east, by four hundred and twenty feet on Fifty-first street, north, and Fiftieth street, south. The building is to be three hundred and twenty-two feet long, ninety-seven feet wide, the transept a hundred and seventy-two feet, the height from floor to ceiling at the summit of the clere-story, one hundred feet. There will be fourteen chapels, besides the grand altar.

Now for the means of accomplishing all this. First: time is a great agent in such undertakings, and I allow five years for the completion of the building. The budget for the first year is founded on the calculation of obtaining from one hundred subscribers in New York one thousand dollars each. This may not be so easily accomplished now, as it would have been before the last money crisis; but still I think it will not be an unsuccessful attempt. The second year, another hundred thousand can be obtained in subscriptions, each of a hundred dollars or upward. The third year, the churches of the city will take it up, and after that the people of New York will not allow it to lag until it is finally completed; and if I should live so long, I shall not suffer it to be opened for Divine service until it is finished according to the plan, from the foundation-stone to the cross on the spires. It will cost at least three-quarters of a million; but as we own another block of the same dimensions on the eastern side of Madison Avenue, it is our intention to lease that block for private dwellings of a choice character, and thus make provision for the support of the cathedral in all future times. This, together with the income which the cathedral already enjoys, will enable us to cope successfully with a debt of two or three hundred thousand dollars when the structure shall be completed. There will be no other building on the ground except the archiepiscopal palace.

You will, I presume, be surprised that I should talk in this style, considering that I have not as yet received one dollar for the undertaking. But I trust, with the blessing of God, and under the patronage of the most blessed and immaculate Virgin Mother, all that I have said will be accomplished, either by myself, or those who have to come after me. It is for me to begin the work, and let it be finished by those who can. One thing, however, is certain: that it shall be, as far as possible, worthy of God, worthy of the Catholic religion, and an honor to this great and growing city, Babylon though it be.

Recommending myself and this great work to your fervent prayers, and relying on your visit at the time before mentioned, I remain, as ever,

Your devoted friend and servant in Christ,

✠ JOHN, *Abp. of New York.*

TO THE REV. BERNARD SMITH.

August 12, 1858.

MY DEAR FATHER SMITH:

I have just received yours of the 19th ultimo, in reference to the American College, and the honors to be conferred on Baltimore. When the time shall come for the publication of these measures, I am sure that it will gladden the hearts of the Catholics throughout these United States. I am particularly glad that the Catholic Church in the United States will no longer have the appearance, in a local sense, of being acephalous, but will have for its local head a primacy of honor at least.

I rejoice equally in the prospect of the American College, and I would write to you very fully on that subject, even for the information of the cardinals, so far as it might seem useful, were it not that I am at this moment over head and ears in preparing to lay the corner-stone of our new grand cathedral on next Sunday, at 4 o'clock, as I mentioned in a former letter. . . . . I shall send you an account of the ceremony immediately after it shall have taken place; and if I am not disappointed, I hope to be able to announce it to our Holy Father by the medium of the Atlantic Telegraph, on Monday or Tuesday of next week. We are waiting to hear every moment the announcement by that medium of the Queen's salutation to our President, and of his reply. It is stated, however, that, immediately after, there will be a pause of several days, to allow the electricians in charge of the cable at Valencia Bay, in Ireland, and Trinity Bay, in Newfoundland, to make experiments testing or improving the power of their respective batteries. Still, if the gentleman, a portion of whose speech I reported to you a few years ago, and whose persevering energy has brought this daring and almost impudent enterprise to a successful issue, and who is the president of the whole concern in this city, should return in time, I shall call upon him to fulfil his promise and prediction about my "sending a message to the Pope of Rome, and receiving an acknowledgment of it on the same day."

We shall soon, no doubt, be called on by circumstances to fulfil our pledges toward the American College. Please say to his eminence Cardinal Barnabo, that neither myself nor the bishops of this province shall be wanting in the fulfilment of our pledges. At the same time, so far as regards myself, it would be inopportune for me to advance the money at the present moment. This you will understand the more clearly, when I mention that I have just been raising funds for carrying on the new cathedral during the first year of its progress. On the 14th of June last I had a circular letter lithographed (of which I send you a copy), and had it addressed through the city post-office to about one hundred and fifty of the most pious, zealous, and (what is essential) wealthy Catholics of the city and diocese of New York. As promised in the circular, it was a matter of form that I should call upon them individually. This I have done—at least to a great extent—and I know you will be pleased when I tell you that I met no refusal; that some, more wealthy and zealous than others, offered me more than the sum mentioned in the circular, which I declined for good reasons; that others, owing to the depression of the times, regretted their inability to advance within the first year the sum prescribed, but were willing to give $500, which I likewise declined, for the same reasons. I have not been more than twenty hours altogether in making these visits, and I think it will speak well for the Catholics of New York, that more than a hundred have given $1,000 each for the first year, as laid down in the circular.

The bishops and myself will confer, on Monday or Tuesday next, on the subjects which I alluded to in my last letter. I shall immediately write the result. As soon after as possible I shall write out my reflections in regard to the American College, which, I think, is by all odds the most important measure that has been adopted since the appointment of the first Catholic bishop in the United States. And I think that its importance in all its bearings will require a good deal of foresight and caution in its organization. There is, so far as religion is concerned, but a slight and sometimes a deceptive analogy between the countries with which Rome is best acquainted and these United States of America. But I perceive that I am gliding into the subject which I had reserved for another occasion.

I am, as ever, my dear Father Smith,

Your devoted friend and servant in Christ,

✠ JOHN, *Abp. N. Y.*

TO THE SAME.

Sept. 10, 1858.

. . . . .

The corner-stone of our new cathedral was laid on the 15th ultimo. We had seven bishops, one hundred and thirty priests, one hundred and twenty boys in cassock and surplice, well trained to chant alternately with the clergy the psalms. The multitude of the faithful, with a very large number of Protestants, could not have been less than 100,000. There was no disorder among the people; no accident occurred; and the secular papers, without exception, have spoken of the ceremony with kindest feelings of praise and admiration. I will send two or three of these papers, which represent fairly the average of the whole class.

Since then I have been called on by the municipal authorities of the city to take a prominent part in celebrating what they call the great event of the age, the laying of the telegraphic cable under the Atlantic Ocean between Europe and America. The authorities requested me officially to write one of their addresses, which I did. They invited me, as one of their special guests, to take a seat in the same carriage with the British minister near this government (Lord Napier), Hon. Mr. Everett, and an old Presbyterian parson named Dr. Nott, now eighty-six years of age, and for the last fifty-four years president of Union College. They invited me also to their municipal banquet. To all which I submitted, at the expense of some inconvenience and much fatigue. But I thought that for religion's sake I should correspond with their polite attentions.

The telegraph will scarcely be in working order before the beginning of the next month. But I have a right to the first message next after those between Queen Victoria and President Buchanan, which have already passed along the wires. I first intended to address it to the Holy Father; but now I think it more becoming, out of respect for his supreme office and his sacred person, to address it to the Cardinal-Prefect of the Propaganda; and I hope soon after the first of October next to give his Eminence a gentle surprise.

Work was prosecuted vigorously on the cathedral until about the 1st of August, 1860, at which time the walls were twelve or fourteen feet high. The whole amount collected—seventy-three thousand dollars—had been spent, and, in accordance with his original determination to incur no debt until the building was nearly finished, the archbishop thereupon suspended operations. For various reasons he thought it expedient to defer his second collection for the cathedral, and the work still remains as he then left it.

Dr. Hughes was deeply afflicted by the death of his friend, Archbishop Walsh, of Halifax, which took place in the summer of 1858. He was invited to preach his funeral sermon, but he felt altogether unequal to the task. "The archbishop and myself," said he, "lived so much together during our last visit at Rome, and I became so much more intimately acquainted with him, that I could not even be present without being overcome by the recollections of his friendship and the goodness of his nature."

TO BISHOP CONNOLLY, ST. JOHN'S, N. B.

Sept. 8, 1858.

MY DEAR LORD:
I received your letter of the 16th, in which you allude so feelingly to the death of our much-beloved friend, the late archbishop of Halifax. . . . . . Nothing would give me greater consolation than to be able to pronounce the funeral oration of my departed and most cherished friend. But even if I were on the spot I could not undertake a duty which would, in discharging it properly, be so op-

pressive to my feelings. I would have much in mind, suitable, perhaps, for such an occasion; but I know myself too well to imagine that I could utter my sentiments without being choked with emotion. But I shall be with you that day at the altar of God, and in the fulness of an affectionate heart, toward the spiritual repose and the just commemoration of our departed friend.

The most reverend Dr. Walsh, first archbishop of Halifax, was a man of rare endowments and of excellent qualities of heart. Through life, from the first infusion of the divine grace that suggested to him his vocation to the holy ministry of the Church, he proved faithful to the lights which Heaven imparted from day to day in his chosen career. He was not less faithful to the voice of God, as made known to him through his superiors. His episcopacy would have adorned the Church of any metropolis in Christendom. God appointed him to labor among the humble and faithful people of the diocese of Halifax, in which, however, there were not wanting those, either among the clergy or among the laity, who could and did appreciate his rare and select erudition, his untiring zeal, his social qualities—in which he always stood forth, not less conspicuous in the fitting attributes of a Catholic prelate, than in the accomplishments and education which distinguished him as a Christian gentleman.

God, in His mysterious providence, has called him, we trust, to the recompense of the good servant who has been faithful over a few things. I sympathize deeply with the clergy and people of the diocese of Halifax, and I pray God that He will mercifully provide, in His own time and in His own way, a successor who shall carry on the high work of the episcopal office, not only in a manner worthy of his vocation, but in continuance of the example bequeathed for imitation by his illustrious predecessor.

I beg of you, as occasion may offer, to convey to the clergy and laity of the diocese of Halifax my deep sympathy with them in the privation with which it has pleased God to test their patience and their fidelity, in being bereft of the good chief pastor, who, to my knowledge, cherished them as if they were perpetually clustering round his heart.

As to the future, we can only say that God will not leave any portion of His Church to entire orphanage. The Church must go on, as it ever has done, renewing its own divine life in the manifestation of its power among men, from generation to generation. And it will, no doubt, be recommended that prayers should be offered constantly by the clergy and the faithful, that a good pastor be appointed by the Holy See to occupy the vacant archiepiscopal throne of Halifax.

I must conclude, for I know not where I should stop if I continued to give expression to all the feelings which the death of the most reverend archbishop of Halifax has awakened in my heart.

Ever your devoted brother and servant in Christ,

✠ JOHN, *Archbishop of New York.*

TO THE REV. BERNARD SMITH.

February, 1859.

You ask me if I have any intention of visiting the Holy City this spring; and my answer is, that I have not. It would, indeed, be very agreeable for me to visit Rome, since every Catholic heart naturally gravitates to the centre of unity and of supremacy. But even if I were disposed, I could not frame a pretext for such a journey that would warrant me, in conscience, to absent myself from this diocese for so long a time as the voyage would require. I am exceedingly fond of the ocean; first, because I am never sea-sick; second, because, from the moment I leave port, I give up that solicitude of mind which is so wearing upon me when I am at home; and thirdly, because, if I am sick or worn out on shore, I immediately begin to get better as soon as I embark, and launch out in the pure air of the great waters. I know you will be glad to learn that my health is better this winter than it has been for several years past. I suffer a little from rheumatism and from dyspepsia, by which I have been afflicted for a long time past, without actually knowing the name of the maladies under which I was laboring.

Every thing goes on in this diocese and throughout the country, as far as I know, as usual. "Know-Nothingism" is dying out, and the public feeling of the country, from the President downwards, is apparently under the influence of a reaction in favor of the Catholic Church. I do not think that any anti-Catholic party will attempt to rise into power on our ruins for the next fifteen or twenty years. But the country itself is threatened on all sides by what croakers might call the incipient symptoms of dissolution. This cry, however, is not novel, nor is it alarming. At the same time, the wisest men begin to be apprehensive.

I remain, reverend and dear Father Smith,
    Your sincere friend and servant in Christ.

TO THE REV. J. O'CALLAGHAN.

March 8, 1859.

REV. DEAR SIR:

I have received and read your letter of the 22d instant. Of course I take to myself, so far as I think just, the admonition which it contains. I would observe, however, that a thousand things, such as you refer to, pass and must pass unheeded by the Catholic people to whom God has given the gift of faith, if not of theological education. This is God's protection, in spite of our blunders with regard either to ecclesiastical decisions or philosophical systems. Their practice is but little influenced by our theories. And if every statement put forth by would-be or real teachers should be reduced *ad normam ecclesiæ*, the episcopal authority would be promptly confounded in vague, useless, schismatical, and, no doubt, heretical discussions, terminating in an appeal to public opinion; and you can imagine what the sentence of public opinion would be on all these subjects.

It only remains for us, during our brief day, to work together under all the embarrassments of our position, or rather of circumstances in which the Church is placed in this country, provided we do not betray the faith; provided we fight a good fight.

    Yours faithfully in Christ,
    ✠ JOHN, *Archbishop of N. Y.*

TO THE REV. CHARLES STONESTREET, S. J., WASHINGTON CITY.

Sept. 8, 1859.

REV. AND DEAR FATHER:

I have made it a rule to decline all invitations either to preach or lecture outside of my own diocese for the last many years. Your invitation, however, shall be an exception; and if the third Sunday of October will suit for the blessing of your church of St. Aloysius, I shall be on hand, and preach as well as I can.

The President's invitation to be his guest is, as you may suppose, very flattering to me; nor could there be the slightest hesitation on my part to accept it—the less because Miss Lane is a great friend of mine, as well as her estimable and honored uncle. If they still lived at Wheatlands, in Pennsylvania, I would throw myself on President Buchanan's hospitality, with or without an invitation, knowing well that the generous feeling of his Irish ancestors is by no means worn out in his breast. As it is, I shall stop with the rector of St. Patrick's, who replaces good old Father Matthews. But, of course, my first duty will be to pay my respects to the President and his amiable niece, whom I saw as a school-girl, at that time the princess of the academy, as I thought and still believe.

Very faithfully yours.

TO MISS C——.

NEW YORK, *September*, 1859.

DEAR MISS C——:

I received in due course your very pleasant and kind letter of May 19th; but I have been absent from the city and very much engaged during the interval, and it is only now that I can have the pleasure of acknowledging the receipt of it. Your sister's hasty call I number among the most agreeable surprises of my life, for I had imagined you all at the Cape of Good Hope, since the time when I had the pleasure of seeing your parents and yourself. I told your sister that if I could see you now, I would give you another ring for your finger; but as I cannot expect that pleasure, I send you a little memorial of my recollection, which is to be common to yourself, in the first place, and to your father and mother, your brothers and sisters, next; but through you, to signify that I have not forgotten our tour on the Lakes of Killarney.

. . . . .

And now I must tell you a little about scenery in this country. My health was not robust toward the end of May, and, by advice of the doctors, I took an excursion of about fifteen or sixteen hundred miles into the country. I varied the route in returning, and though I was but twenty-one days absent, I had an opportunity of employing six days in recreation. The principal part of the time was spent at the house of my late brother's widow, on the borders of the St. Lawrence, in the State of New York. Her sons invited me to go with them on the river itself for a fishing excursion, and I was not sorry at having the opportunity for doing so; for during four days our boat glided on the tranquil waters of that river, among what is called the Thousand Islands, although it is well known that the real number is more than 1,900. Some of these islands are about as large as Phœbe's Island, or O'Donaghoe's Bible, in the waters of Killarney; and your father and mother can give you from memory an idea of their dimensions.

Now, you talk about scenes in Ireland, and although they are exquisitely beautiful, they are not to be compared with any thing of the kind in this country. Suppose I should see you some day in one of the boats on the St. Lawrence, among the Thousand Islands, inhaling the purest air that ever passed over the surface of this globe —this will be your position: there will be two oarsmen propelling the little boat; two passengers, one at the bow and the other at the stern; you, of course, in such a canoe will be in the stern, sitting in an arm-chair, as I have done during four days of piscatory amusement. You will see all the islands through which the boat passes— for it neverrests. You will have two fishing-rods transversely placed, and fixed just before you. Formerly you would have to look to the bend of your rod when a prize had taken hold of the hook. But now, owing to Yankee ingenuity, you need not fatigue your eye in looking to the rod on the right hand or on the left, for we have so arranged it that when a fish catches the hook, he will ring a bell about the size of a thimble at the extreme end of the rod, to give you notice that he is about to pay you a visit and to lay himself at your feet.

I was not in time for the best fishing on the St. Lawrence, nor did I care so much about that as for any thing that might give me strength, through the means of retirement from duty, and fresh pure air, combined with scenery unsurpassed in the whole world. Still, in obedience to the order of the place, I had my two fishing-rods transversely posed, and I sat in my arm-chair, before referred to, with a sense of admiration as to the sceuery, and breathing at the same time deep draughts of the purest air. In fishing, our boat was successful. My friend who was with me caught a species of fish called muscalonge, which weighed thirty-one pounds. The rascally newspapers ascribed this catch to me, and they published it over the country; but it was not mine.

What I have said about the St. Lawrence, as to the large scale on which Almighty God has graded the things of this country, would be true of its mountains, its valleys, its lakes, and every thing appertaining to it.

But, my dear Miss C——, what does all this amount to? A little amusement during the brief life of an individual, and eternity is coming upon us all. Try, my good child, faithful as I have believed you to have been to your parents, true to yourself in every thing, to look out for the main chance, which is your immortal soul. I do not despair of seeing you in this country, although you will have to announce to me who you are, just as your good sister did, whose visit, as I said before, was to me a most agreeable surprise.

I cannot have the measure of your finger to send you a ring that might suit; but I send you a little memorial in the way of a cross and a chain to be placed on your neck, and by which, in case you should ever come to New York during my life, I will be able to recognize you at once.

This letter has not been written with my hand, but it is dictated from my heart. For some years my thumb-joint has been dislocated, and I am obliged to depend on others for the manual labor of writing my sentiments.

· · · · ·

CHAPTER XXIV.

1859–1860.

Letters on the Roman question—Provincial council—Address to the Pope—Pastoral letter on the Pope's temporal power—Its reception in Rome—Trip to Florida—Apostasy of Dr. Forbes—Proposed mass meeting to express sympathy with the Holy Father—Letter to Bishop Dupanloup—Collection for the Pope—The Archbishop and the City Inspector—Sermon at Chapel Hill University, North Carolina—Letters to the Rev. Bernard Smith.

TO THE REV. BERNARD SMITH.

Sept. 24, 1859.

MY DEAR FATHER SMITH:

I received, two days ago, your kind favor of the 13th of September. I am especially bound to thank you for the attention which, on your part, was given to my worthy Protestant friend, Senator Seward. His eminence, Cardinal Antonelli, has also deigned to write me a most esteemed letter, acknowledging my letter of introduction for the Hon. Senator. I must thank his Eminence in a special letter for his kindness on this occasion; but I may say to you, what I could not write with the same regard to delicate propriety on all sides, and that is, that Gov. Seward wished to know Cardinal Antonelli above all the statesmen of Europe. You are not ignorant that the Red Republican papers have painted his Eminence in colors the opposite of what would be flattery, but what I and others believe to be the opposite of truth. And yet, so far as this country is concerned, newspapers are becoming a perfect drug, and nobody pays the least attention to what they publish, unless the same should be confirmed by other testimony or circumstances. You need not be surprised then, that there is no statesman in Europe who catches the eye of this American people so powerfully as your cardinal Secretary of State. Mr. Seward must have been fully impressed with this idea when he desired especially an introduction to his Eminence.

I regret deeply the turn that affairs seem to have taken in the States of the Church. Your letter, reporting the observations of the Holy Father when he admitted Senator Seward to an audience, has made me quite sad. To say that "the whole world is against him," is a melancholy thought to be entertained in the breast of the Vicar of Christ. It cannot be so. On the contrary, if I were to multiply proofs, I could make it clear enough, in a small volume, that the whole world—in its substantial character—of Catholic faith, is with him more than with any of his predecessors for the last three hundred years. There is, however, this difference—that his circle of communication with the revolutionary, turbulent, and destructive world is limited to the walls of Rome; and I can easily imagine how his great heart has been inebriated from day to day with the ingredients of bitterness presented to him from the east and the north, the south and the west. This has been the chalice in his Garden of Gethsemane. But yet his glorious reign will stand out in ecclesiastical history as one of those in which God will have most manifested His near presence with His supreme vicar on earth.

. . . . . .

TO THE SAME.

Dec. 11, 1859.

My dear Father Smith:

I have just received yours of the 16th of November. The Cardinal-Prefect, in his last letter to me, mentioned that you were at that time in France. I am glad you have returned to your post, to share in the trials, and, I hope, the triumphs of the Eternal City. There is a feeling here that we should do something to give expression to our sentiments with regard to the situation in which the evils of this time have placed our most revered and most beloved Holy Father. As yet, no one has come forward to propose any course; and as for myself, although I should have no hesitation as to the course really to be pursued, still I hesitate lest it might turn out to be injudicious, if not premature.

My idea would be that the Catholic hierarchy of this country should proclaim with unanimous voice the indefeasible right as well as title by which our Holy Father governs, as a temporal prince, the States of the Church. Secondly, our approval and admiration of the apostolic firmness and courage with which the Pope and his most eminent advisers cling to the maintenance of that indefeasible right. Of course, neither justice nor reason avail much against armies. Still the expression of Catholic Christendom in declaring favorably to what is right and what is just, might have some effect on the conscience of sovereigns, commanders, and soldiers, if they attempted any sacrilegious violation of the rights that belong to the successor of St. Peter in the government of the Papal States. Thirdly, against physical violence of the powers of this earth, there does not appear to be any means of resistance, except the same moral, religious, and apostolic courage which has so often distinguished, in different periods, the occupants of the Holy See.

In that melancholy alternative, God will not withdraw or leave unfulfilled his promises to the Church. And then it will be time for the Catholics throughout the world to unite in creating a treasury sufficient for the supreme dignity of the Sovereign Pontiff, and the expenses to be incurred in maintaining it.

I observe that in England they have broached the topic of Peter-pence. In my own humble judgment, I think this is premature, and may give apparent sanction to that unsound and fallacious idea which the enemies of religion would wish to see propagated, viz.: that the Pope could be sustained on what is called the voluntary principle, by the Catholics of the world; that it would be better for religion if he should have nothing to do with temporal affairs; that in this latter event he would cease to be a butt for the enmities of modern nations, whether Catholic or Protestant; that he would become an object of universal respect and reverence to Protestants as well as Catholics; that, in fine, he would be more honorably sustained by the free offerings of his spiritual subjects all over the globe.

For myself, I not only do not believe, but I detest these bad and vulgar principles. Yet every thing is in the hands of God. Prayers are offered up here daily for the Holy Father; and we must leave the rest to the direction of Divine Providence. I am convinced that if the Pope were deprived of his sovereignty, his faithful children throughout the world would provide an income for the maintenance of his dignity, and that of those by whom he should be necessarily surrounded. But the touchstone of this question is, Shall he be a *subject* or a *sovereign?* And it would be an awful blow to Catholics everywhere, if he should be reduced to the necessity of exercising the high and universal functions of his most sacred office under the patronage or by the permission of any sovereign on the earth. Of course, I have not the slightest apprehension that this, or any thing like this, is about to occur. Nevertheless, looking at the unsettled condition of Italy, rendered more unsettled by the interference of two nominally Catholic empires, it is difficult to foresee what may or what may not happen.

I am inclined to convoke the bishops of this province for the purpose of deliberating and preparing an address to his Holiness. In it I would take occasion to pay a just compliment to those bishops of France and of Europe who have expressed themselves conscientiously and fearlessly on this subject, without giving any reasonable offence to the temporal governments under which they live. . . . .

There is nothing new in this country, except a small insurrection on the borders between what are called the free States and the slave States. This, though insignificant in itself, threatens to become, if not the beginning of the end, at least the end of the beginning, in our federal system. . . . .

TO THE SAME.

Jan. 20, 1860.

MY DEAR FATHER SMITH:

I write you to-day a brief and hurried letter, that it may go by the steamer of to-morrow.

We have just had our provincial council, in regard to the more solemn parts of which I shall give you an explanation by the next subsequent steamer. We have drawn up, however, a pastoral letter, which will make about ten columns of *The Metropolitan Record.* It is to be published in the *Record* next week, signed with all our names, giving not only the sees to which we respectively belong, but also the States in which they are severally placed. It takes very strong ground indeed with regard to the position of our Holy Father. It maintains his right to the temporal sovereignty which has descended to him, and which cannot be legitimately taken away from him by either rebellious subjects or secular princes. At all events, we have spoken out in a language on this subject which cannot be mistaken either here or in Europe. I shall enclose you several copies of the *Record*, or at least of the pastoral letter, the moment it is published here. I trust that it will reach you before the middle of February, and very soon after, if not before the meeting of the much talked-of congress. And I am sure it will furnish its members with matter for reflection.   .   .   .

TO THE SAME.

Jan. 30, 1860.

MY DEAR FATHER SMITH:

The steamer which will take this, will also carry the brief acts of our late council, so called. The Latin address, expressive of our perpetual fidelity to the See of Peter, and of our deep sympathy with the sufferings and afflictions of our Holy Father, has been already forwarded from this place. Our pastoral letter will have come to hand probably before this shall reach you. In that pastoral we have taken strong grounds on the question of the integrity of the Papal States, or, as we preferred to designate them, the States of the Church. If our language should appear too strong for European latitudes, you will bear in mind that a tamer style would produce very little impression here; and that probably very many bishops in Europe would expect from us plain, out-spoken language, which it might not be considered either lawful or expedient for them to utter. We know that they must speak under a certain amount of restraint, or of prudent reserve. They, on the other hand, know that our Government, taking no part in the affairs of religion, leaves us at perfect liberty to speak the whole truth on the subject of the Pope's temporal sovereignty.

Our Catholic laity needed such a document to brace them up, since all manner of evil has been said and published in Protestant journals against the government of the Holy See.

The Fathers assembled considered it inexpedient to convoke popular meetings for the purpose of giving expression to the sympathies which are universally felt for the Sovereign Pontiff. In this I could not but agree with them. *First*, because we have no titled nobility whose presence could give a species of dignity to such meetings. *Second*, because, though we have eminent professional men, such as judges, lawyers, physicians, etc., still they are so few in comparison, and so dependent upon the good-will of the Protestant community for their position and their prospects, that it would be a trial which might be too strong for their nerve to attend such meetings or sign the proper documents attesting their proceedings. Then it would be said that the meetings were a failure; that the educated portion of the Catholics would have nothing to do with them. We did not wish to run this risk. But, at the same time, we know that these same persons go hand in hand with the doctrine of the pastoral letter of their prelates, which has been already published. *Third*, our Catholics are so scattered, except in the large cities, that no meeting, respectable even for numbers, could be successfully convened. This you will understand when I mention that the area of the different dioceses governed by the prelates assembled in the late council is larger by 8,000 square miles than that of England, Ireland, and Scotland taken together. Some of the prelates reside at a distance of over five hundred miles from New York. Now, over this immense surface there are Catholics to be found almost everywhere, but they are

" . . . rari nantes in gurgite vasto."

To my utter astonishment, the pastoral letter has been received by the Protestants with very great indulgence. Many of the secular papers criticise one portion or another, but not one has attempted to grapple with the whole document. On the other hand, some of them have not only adopted its whole doctrine, but have also recommended it in special articles to the consideration of their readers.

A copy of it has been sent to every sovereign in Europe except Queen Victoria and Victor Emmanuel. It has been sent also to several of the bishops of France, and to all the bishops of Great Britain and Ireland. It is now being published in a pamphlet form. I trust you have already received your copy of *The Metropolitan Record*.

I have written to his eminence the Cardinal-Prefect, explaining how it happened that our council was not celebrated with all the solemnities prescribed in the ritual. In my letter of the 19th of December I mentioned that the season was entirely inopportune, on account of the approaching festivals of Christmas and the Epiphany. I received several letters from prelates on your side of the Atlantic, urging me to write on the subject, even in my own name;

and I gave you my reasons for preferring that all the bishops of this province should unite with me in the public expression of our sentiments and convictions on the present state of affairs in Italy. I convoked my suffragans for the 10th of January. In our first session it was discussed whether we should describe our convention simply as a meeting for the purpose of presenting an address to the Holy Father, or whether we should consider it as a provincial synod, with a view to give our document more weight and authority. This latter course was agreed to at my suggestion, with the understanding, however, that I should explain to his eminence the Cardinal-Prefect the reasons why some of the forms required in the *Pontifical* were omitted. These reasons were, that scarcely any preparation had been made for the celebration of the council, but more especially with the view that our pastoral letter should reach Europe with as little delay as possible, and especially before the opening of the congress in Paris. At the same time, such business as the Fathers brought before us was transacted in the ordinary way. . . . .

The Pope and the cardinals were very much pleased with this pastoral letter. A friend writes to the archbishop as follows:

The best proof of the reception your pastoral got in Rome is, that it has been printed at the Propaganda both in English and Italian. This was done by orders of the Holy Father—the only pastoral yet published in Rome by orders of the Pope.

And two or three months afterward the same friend writes:

You will be glad to hear that the Propaganda has received letters from many parts of Italy, calling for a new edition of your pastoral.

The rigor of the winter aggravated his old complaints so much, that his physicians recommended him to make a trip to the South. In the latter part of February, 1860, accompanied by his chaplain and another priest, he sailed for Charleston; and being there joined by Bishop Lynch, travelled overland to St. Augustine's, in Florida. He visited the grave of his old schoolmate, Mr. Mayne, who had been twenty-five years dead, but for whose memory he always retained a tender affection. After an absence of four weeks he reached home again, much better for the change of air and scene; "but yet I feel a cold and stiffness in my limbs," he writes, "which, I fear, means something more than physicians have accounted for." He was suffering, in fact, from the malady which at last killed him—Bright's Disease of the Kidneys.

He saw reason to change his opinion about the expediency of calling popular meetings to express sympathy with the Pope. He writes thus to Father Smith, on the 26th of March:

I intend that the Catholic clergy and laity of my diocese shall have an opportunity of presenting their personal devotion in an address to the Holy Father. This cannot be done, however, sooner than the second or third week after Easter. I have already intimated in former letters that a public meeting of our people at an earlier period might not be so honorable to themselves as, with their improved knowledge of the real merits of the case, we may now hope it will be.

. . . . . .

The present confusion of Italian affairs cannot be cleared up or adjusted without a congress, in which at least all the great powers will be represented. The position of the Pope is so clear and strong, it is so just in itself, its principle so essential to all permanent governments, that the five great powers of Europe, even for their own sakes, will be slow to assail it. Three of them, certainly, will be on the side of legitimacy—Austria, Russia, and Prussia. France will reflect also; and England, in my opinion, will prove herself rather indifferent. Her policy at present is to stand well with Louis Napoleon. But she has no affection for the man; she would be very glad to see him tripped up in his ambitious career.

. . . . . .

Before closing this letter, I am impelled to request of you to present, on the first fitting occasion, my respectful sentiments of admiration at the masterly manner in which, it appears to us at this distance, Cardinal Antonelli conducts the delicate questions that must necessarily come under his notice. Of course, in all these affairs, we speak of the Sovereign Pontiff, supreme head of the States of the Church, and supreme head of the Catholic world. But by his side we recognize the Cardinal Secretary of State as having had no superior in the responsible position in which he is placed, since the days of Consalvi. I make this remark the more willingly, because the newspapers, until within a recent period, have treated his Eminence with contumely, pretending at the same time that they reported only the sentiments of the Roman people proper, and of the Italians in general. Now, however, the tone is changed; and even Lord John Russell is looked upon as a pigmy statesman if compared with Cardinal Antonelli.

I am, my dear Father Smith,
Your devoted friend and servant in Christ,
✠ JOHN, *Abp. of New York.*

TO DR. KIRBY, IRISH COLLEGE, ROME.

March 27, 1860.

RIGHT REV. AND DEAR FATHER KIRBY:

I received your welcome letter of the 4th ultimo, but having been absent from the 22d of the same month until the 23d of March, it was only within a few days that I had the pleasure of seeing it. The parcel, in the mean time, has been received from the hand to which it had been intrusted, but the name of the bearer has not been left.

We are all much afflicted at the second edition of trouble that is falling on the heart of our Holy Father. Yet the example of his apostolic courage and firmness, even in the temporal order, has been well calculated to confirm his brethren even to the ends of the earth. I have great hopes of better things for the security and tranquillity of the Holy See, as likely to result from the present imbroglio. The Holy Father has the protection of God and the support of the Catholic world on his side. Napoleon, for the first time in what the world would call his prosperous career, has exhibited, or rather is exhibiting, as events succeed each other, a certain indecision and shakiness of purpose, which, up to this date, has not amounted to any thing like a consistent and cohesive policy.

All these things are in the hands of Almighty God, but, so far as we can understand the progress of events, our fears are diminishing and our hopes rising. One thing is certain—that the Holy Father, whether under the tempest or furious outbreak which succeeded his elevation to the chair of St. Peter, or now under the pressure of strategical diplomacy, in the face of emperors, and kings, and armies on the boundaries of the States of the Church, has been equal to every vicissitude; and that he is to be ranked and is already ranked in the affections of his spiritual children throughout the world as one of the most illustrious Sovereign Pontiffs that have ever governed the Church since the days when its occupant was, *ipso facto*, a predestined martyr under the cruelty of the Pagan emperors of Rome.

The opening of the American College in Rome, and the presence of the excellent bishop of Portland to speak in a very happy manner of the sentiments universally entertained by the hierarchy of this country, have given us great consolation. Of course, nothing could be more gratifying, than the tender feeling and most generous liberality manifested by the Holy Father for the encouragement of this new and important ecclesiastical establishment. Future ages will do justice to the boundless charity of its real founder. It has been planted by the most sacred hands; it will be, I trust, watered by the bishops of America; and of its taking root and increasing from year to year in usefulness to the Church in this country, there cannot be entertained the shadow of a doubt.

As to poor Dr. Forbes, his fall has produced as little sensation here, as if he had been a leaden shot dropped quietly into the Red Sea. Many Catholics feel deeply on account of his own soul, and the dignity which had been conferred upon him by the reception of priesthood. I was absent when he wrote the brief acknowledgment of his apostasy. When I returned, I observed to the priests and people who called on me in regard to him, that for seven days I held myself free to speak of him and his conduct; but after the expiration of that term I did not wish any one to mention his name in my presence. And so it has been—not a word in the papers, not a word in private conversation, not a word even from Protestant journals, except in censure of his fickleness and humiliation at his fall. I know, however, that many secret prayers are offered up both here and in Europe for his salvation. His fall has been to me a blow of chastisement; for I had rashly blamed other prelates for having ordained, too hastily, converted persons. My own turn of humiliation has arrived in the case of Dr. Forbes. But I have this consolation, that there was no impediment with regard to the means of supporting his children which had not been arranged, on his own testimony, even before I allowed him to think of the Catholic priesthood. Notwithstanding this, as time went on after his ordination, I discovered by personal and intimate observation that he was influenced by the desire of honors, ease, emolument, and distinction, which it was impossible to afford him. This discovery of his character, besides other influences, prevented me from treating him at any time except with a forbearance, and I might add affection, the same as if he had been my son. All the details connected with his career would make a small volume; but they are unnecessary. There is one thing, however, I must say—that he has left no reproach either against his character, or on his exercise of the ministry, which could create a scandal, or cause him to be ranked among the degraded apostates who have from time to time forsaken our Holy Mother.

I entertain still grateful recollections of the kindness experienced by me in the Irish College. I do not know that I shall ever visit the Eternal City again : I never went except from a sense of duty to the Sovereign Pontiff, or for some purpose connected with the prospective interests of my diocese. On this latter score I would have no inducement. The establishments of education and religion that have already been made appear to me sufficient for the wants of the diocese during my life. They work by their own machinery, so to speak; but they require occasional inspection and general supervision. Then, on the other hand, my health is not so robust as it was twenty-five years ago. Travelling has lost many of its charms for me, although there is no reasonable amount of fatigue which I am not still strong enough to bear and improve by, in case the necessities of my diocese or the interests of religion require me to do so.

TO MR. CHARLES O'CONOR.

April 4, 1860.

MY DEAR MR. O'CONOR:

As to our Catholic movement in sympathy with the Holy Father, I do not yet see my way very clear. But there is no hurry. It will be months, if not years, before the troubles of Italy shall have reached any settled form. I trust that the result will be a permanent reëstablishment of the Pope, the visible head of our Church on earth, in a position such as his predecessors for many ages have occupied. So far as reforms in the temporal administration are concerned, he is and ought to be the first to promote them. If the people clamored for a republic, or what we call [one], in our sense of free government, which, in their actual condition, would be very unsuitable for them, it would be, in our regard, a quasi *argumentum ad hominem*. But, admitting abuses, what are they to gain by transferring themselves from allegiance to one sovereign, with a view to be more cruelly treated by another of the same class, but in a lower degree? It will be only a change from larger freedom to smaller; from smaller taxation to larger. But these matters should not come under our consideration. The main thing is, that the spiritual Father of more than 200,000,000 of Catholics all over the globe shall not be a subject of the King of Sardinia or the Emperor of France, or any other emperor or king on the globe. Private individuals may enjoy freedom, in a moderate sense, under any sovereign, or even despot. But not so the Pope. He has been invested by the Son of God with a trust, the discharge of which is limited only to the ends of the earth. For this he is not indebted to sovereigns. But it is clear that, as mankind are constituted, there is no condition for him left in the world for the free apostolic exercise of his divinely appointed office, except that of a sovereign or that of a subject. Oh! he would be a precious subject of even the Catholic kinglings of Europe. But he would not be free. We want the vicar of Christ to be free; and this implies that there must be some portion of the earth of which he shall be recognized the sovereign. God knows it might be better if he could exercise the plenitude of freedom without any care of state; but as the world is constituted, this is impossible. He would be a prisoner of some temporal state in Europe.

His decisions on great questions affecting the spiritual interests of his children throughout every land would lose much of their dignity and force, in consequence of a universal suspicion that would arise to the effect that his decision had not been entirely free.

The deep feeling which now pervades every Catholic breast, is that the Sovereign Pontiff may not be deprived of his freedom and independence. There is no civil government, whether Catholic or Protestant, that is fit to be his guardian or his keeper in the condition of a subject. The calamities which press upon him from all sides have awakened the Catholic sentiment in every breast. Addresses of sympathy are pouring in upon him from every nation and from every point of the compass. These addresses have not the immediate force of the aggregate of the armies that met at Solferino. But time is a great agent in working out justice; and the period is hastening on, in which enlightened public opinion, manfully expressed, will either prevent or counteract the effects of such bloody collisions. Meanwhile, it must be consoling to the Pope, and indirectly a rebuke to his enemies, that they have not such nor so numerous friends as he has. We stand by our Holy Father, we stand for justice, and right, and truth. The Pope, except in ameliorating the condition of his subjects by concessions immediately after his election, has done nothing to warrant the rebellion of a few—and indeed they are a very few—of the northern subjects of the States of the Church against his authority. Neither has he done any thing to warrant the insolent interference of foreign powers, in their encroachments upon the patrimony of St. Peter.

Excuse me for this long and unnecessary outline of the case.

I remain, etc.

TO MGR. DUPANLOUP, BISHOP OF ORLEANS, FRANCE.

April 18, 1860.

MY DEAR LORD:

I cannot any longer do violence to my own feelings, by withholding the deep, heartfelt expression of the sentiments with which I have witnessed and admired the noble stand which your lordship has taken in reference to the rights of the Holy See and the integrity of the States of the Church. The hierarchy of France have been, as ever, true to the hopes of the Church as well as to their own exalted dignity. But your lordship has furnished them—nor will I say furnished them alone, but all Christendom—with a brilliant example of episcopal energy and apostolic fortitude, at a crisis in the condition of the holy Catholic religion and of its supreme head on earth. We are all determined in this country to follow such a magnificent leadership in the episcopacy. We admire your principles; we admire your courage; we admire your perseverance in a right cause; and even at this distance from Europe we shall endeavor to imitate them all.

I have the honor to remain, dear lord, your obedient servant and brother in Christ,

✠ JOHN, *Abp. of New York.*

Instead of holding a public meeting, he finally resolved to make a collection and present it to the Pope with addresses from the clergy and laity. Even the children in the schools and orphan asylums, he determined, should be called upon to contribute their mite and add their signatures to the long list of names which he hoped to send with the money. He declared his intention in the cathedral on Sunday, the 24th of June, 1860, and at the same time gave notice that on the following Sunday he would preach a sermon, "which he had no objection to see in print," and in which he would explain at length his views on the whole question of the temporal power of the Pope. Contrary to his custom, he wrote this sermon, and furnished copies of it to the newspapers. It need hardly be said that he took very decided ground in support of the Pope's right to govern his own States. He was severely criticised by the secular press, and on the 14th of July published anonymously, in *The Metropolitan Record*, an answer to his assailants generally. The collection amounted to about $53,000. It was presented to his Holiness by Cardinal Barnabo; and on receiving the money, together with the letter of sympathy that accompanied it, the Holy Father literally wept. He sent to the archbishop "a first-class medal, for his zeal for religion, and singular and devoted attachment to the chair of Peter."

In the spring and summer of this year an attempt was made by the city inspector to induce the archbishop to comply with the requirements of a law of the State, which, according to his interpretation of it, made it the duty of every clergyman to keep a registry of the marriages celebrated by him, with the names and surnames of the parties married, and the residence, age, and condition of each, and report the same every month to the city inspector. The archbishop refused; first, because cases sometimes occurred "in which it was for the Catholic priest to remedy privately the evils which corruption of morals may have entailed;" and secondly, because he was not a servant of the State, and therefore not bound to render to the State officers an account of his stewardship. The matter was freely discussed in the newspapers; but although the city inspector threatened to enforce the legal penalties for violation of the law, the matter was allowed, after a time, to sleep. In fact, it was by no means certain that the statute, rightly interpreted, would oblige clergymen to do more than keep a registry of marriages; and this the Catholic priests all did, in accordance with a regulation of the diocese. Once before, namely in 1858, a similar demand had been made of the archbishop, and had been met with a similar answer.

TO BISHOP MULLOCK, ST. JOHN'S, N. F.

June 16, 1860.

MY DEAR LORD:

I have just received your favor of the 2d instant. I am sorry to say that my health, which was poor enough when you left, has not improved much since. An engagement of eight months and more bound me to go to the University of North Carolina, to deliver a sermon before the graduating class of that institution at their commencement in the beginning of this month. It is a very large and entirely a Protestant university; but the graduating class have the privilege of inviting their own preacher, and no doubt intended it as an evidence of their liberality and of their respect for me, to select me for this occasion. I had no reason to regret my acceptance, for I was treated with very marked attention by the faculty and by the students. But owing to change of climate or food, or fatigue of the journey, I returned much worse than when I left home. I have been confined, by the doctor's orders, not merely to my room but to my bed, for the last seven or eight days, with something like inflammation of the bowels. I suffer less at present than I did at the commencement of the attack, but I am told that my convalescence will depend much on prudence in diet, and in occupying a recumbent position as much as possible. I have given up all idea of having the pleasure of a visit to your lordship during the present summer.

. . . . .

A correspondent of a North Carolina paper gave this description of the archbishop's appearance at Chapel Hill: "One saw in the preacher an elderly man in infirm health, of bowed form, yet of striking appearance. He wore a tight-fitting cassock, ornamented with a row of red buttons down the front and down the sleeves, and surmounted by a doctor's cape. On his breast there lay a carved cross of gold suspended by a heavy golden chain, and on his finger appeared the episcopal ring, which flashed strange light into the wondering eyes of poor Protestants. The style of the preacher and the services for devotion were simple even unto plainness. He and Father McNeirny pulled aside the desk which held King James's Bible, so that no screen separated him from his audience. . . He pulled out his big red bandanna handkerchief, or his spotless one of linen, with utter indifference. He would spit and scrape with his foot, as if he had never preached in the loftiest cathedrals of the world. He would call on Bishop Lynch for water, as if in too big a hurry to get it for himself. But then, from the reply of our Saviour to the question of the tempting lawyer, as it is recorded in the 22d chapter of Matthew, he discoursed on love to God and love to man, as is not often heard in a college chapel. The densely packed audience listened with scarcely a stir for an hour and three quarters."

TO THE REV. BERNARD SMITH.

September 9, 1860.

MY DEAR FATHER SMITH:

Yours of the 18th ultimo reached me on the 6th instant, together with one from his eminence Cardinal Barnabo. Both gave me very great pleasure, particularly a statement in yours to the effect that the position of our Holy Father is becoming reassured, notwithstanding the reported success of Garibaldi and his hordes.

I had written to you in answer to your former letter, and had just posted mine, when your last reached me. With regard to the administration of my diocese, there is no complaint here that I know of, on the part of either clergy or laity. You can easily understand that among both there may be criticisms and conversations which never reach my ears. But this is universal, and does not amount to much. The true test is, that when any great undertaking is commenced or recommended by me, they all coöperate and aid me in carrying it through, without a single murmur.

. . . .

I am very much consoled by the kind words which our Holy Father was pleased to speak in regard to me at your last audience. As long as I have his confidence and his apostolic blessing, I have no dread of public or private enemies. . . .

The letter of his eminence the Cardinal-Prefect, in reference to the appointment of a coadjutor for New York, is entirely satisfactory; but I will write to his Eminence by this mail.

. . . .

You have heard of the temporary breaking up of my seminary here.* I could not make you understand how deep a sacrifice it has been to me. But I think that the good of religion here required it. I shall proceed immediately to the erection of another, but not in a way to be of the slightest umbrage or annoyance to the Jesuit Fathers. And I will say more, that if I had been a Jesuit at Fordham, I could not have helped wishing the diocesan seminary to be removed from the grounds of that beautiful location. They know this themselves, for I told them. Every thing has been transacted

---

* He had lately sold the seminary ground and buildings at Fordham to the faculty of St. John's College.

between us in an amicable and charitable manner. My little family of seminarians are distributed—I had almost said scattered—into different directions, according to the stage of their advancement in ecclesiastical learning. One band I have sent to Rome, another to Baltimore, and a third to Montreal, in Canada. I have not allowed them to travel, except under the protection of a priest; and this is the reason why Dr. Morrogh accompanies those sent to Rome.

. . . . .

As to what friends or enemies may say for or against me in Rome, it does not trouble me at all. We do not mind what Rome *hears;* but what Rome *says* is law. Still, I do think that very bad priests and bad people are allowed too much facility in representing their real or supposed grievances in the Eternal City. The conduct of bishops who only do their duty, with intimate knowledge of all the circumstances, becomes harsh and cruel compared with the charity which the complainants are sure to experience in Rome. In one sense this is a most touching and a most glorious truth; for, to the loving Catholic world, what can be more consoling than the knowledge that the fountains of hope for the unfortunate, and of charity for all, gush forth hard by the well-spring of faith, which is perennially distributing the principle of spiritual life all through the mystical body of Christ on earth; and in another sense, this can be sadly perverted against the authority of bishops who only endeavor—with a great mixture of human imperfection, no doubt—to do their duty.

As for myself, my dear Father Smith, I have been praised, I have been censured, I have been cut up in the newspapers in every way; I have become familiar with the world and with its ways, its caprices, and its ingratitudes; and of course it would require something extraordinary to make an impression on me now. From the beginning of my ministry as a priest up till the present day, I have been on my guard against friends, or those who wished to be considered as such. Enemies, if any, I never wished to know any thing about; and even when I did know, I have always treated them the same as others. This has been the rule of my life, and on this subject I should like to "die in my simplicity." Nevertheless, if any thing should be said against me in Rome, I should like to know it, and even the source from which it comes; not indeed to preserve any memory of resentment against its author, but to enable me to forward immediately an explanation of the facts, in view of which the Sacred Congregation would form their own just conclusion.

．　　　．　　　．　　　．　　　．

CHAPTER XXV.

1861.

Sentiments on the slavery question—Review of Brownson on Emancipation—Letter to Mr. Seward—Letters to Southern bishops—Advice to the Government on the conduct of the war—Interview with a Southern lady—Letter from President Lincoln.

IN the early part of his life, Archbishop Hughes, though he never was an abolitionist, had a great horror of negro slavery. We have seen how, in one of his lyrical moods while at college, he invoked Columbia to

"—— chase foul bondage from her Southern plain."

In his discussions with Breckinridge there were several allusions to the same subject. In the written controversy he says (Letter XIX.): "When you wish to pay a compliment to 'our memorable Declaration of Independence,' were you not rather unfortunate in coupling it with an allusion to slavery? It reminds me of the negro slave who, on his way to Georgia through Washington, shook his manacled hands at the capitol, and began to sing 'Hail Columbia, happy land!'" But there is evidence that he was opposed to Northern interference with slavery; for in the oral debate he made it a reproach to the Presbyterian doctrines of civil liberty, that they made "the master a criminal against God for holding slaves, and the slaves criminal against God for submitting to their condition." Some years afterward, an address signed by Daniel O'Connell, Father Matthew, and other Irish anti-slavery men, was circulated among the naturalized voters of this country for the purpose of influencing them in favor of the abolition movement. Bishop Hughes wrote concerning it to the *Courier and Enquirer*, in March, 1842:

> My first and decided impression is, that, as it appears, it is not authentic. . . . . . . Should it prove to be authentic, then I have no hesitation in declaring my opinion that it is the duty of every naturalized Irishman to resist and repudiate the address with indignation. Not precisely because of the doctrines it contains, but because of their having emanated from a foreign source, and of their tendency to operate on questions of domestic and national policy. I am no friend to slavery, but I am still less friendly to any attempt of *foreign origin* to abolish it.

But later in life, after he had made several visits to the South, and especially after his trip to Cuba in 1853, he was far less decided in his condemnation of slavery. He believed that emancipation would be a very bad thing for the negroes as well as for the planters. In his sermon in the cathedral on the Sunday after his return from Havana, he spoke of the condition of the Cuban slaves in a way which showed that his recollections of their physical well-being were more vivid than his impressions of their social and intellectual abasement. He did not apologize for the institution of slavery; but it did not shock him as it had done of old. When Dr. Brownson, in the number of his *Review* for October, 1861, recommended the emancipation of the slaves as a measure for the more effectual prosecution of the war against the rebellious South, the archbishop published a severe article in his official organ, *The Metropolitan Record*, satirizing the abolitionists, and declaring that they had committed the very crime of attempting to overthrow the Constitution and Government of the United States, which was charged against "the adherents of what is called the Southern Confederacy." He went to such lengths in extenuation of slavery, that he was accused of favoring the slave trade. It is hardly necessary to say that it was far from his intention to do any thing of this kind; but it cannot be denied that, in the excitement and haste of composition, he said more than he meant, and much that he afterward regretted.* In a letter to Mr. Cameron, Secretary of War, in October, 1861, he says:

* The passage to which most objection was made is the following:
"Now, suppose that the savage king of Dahomey sent his subjects or prisoners to some of the factories on the coast, and sold them as slaves; would he be more guilty than if he had cut their heads off? Suppose the slavers at the dock should buy them off at $1.25 a head from the massacre of their barbarous tyrant; would they be doing wrong? They would only have to choose between leaving those wretches to be butchered, or transporting them to some of the slave colonies of America. We of course believe that no genuine Christian—no decent man—would be engaged in this kind of business; still, we cannot discover the crime, even of the slaver, in snatching them from the butcheries prepared for them in their native land. When they arrive in those colonies, would it be a crime for humane masters to purchase them at a sum which prospectively might cover the annual or semi-annual wages given to laborers in other parts of the world? Those purchasers should be bound, and, if they are men of conscience, they would be bound, to take care of these unfortunate people. Under the circumstances, it is very difficult to discover in the purchasers any moral transgression of the law of God, or of the law of man where that traffic is authorized. The terrific part of the question is, that not only the individuals brought to the American continent or islands are themselves to be slaves, but their posterity, in like manner, for all time to come. This is the only terrific feature about American slavery. And yet it is not alien from the condition of mankind in general. Original sin has entailed upon the human race its consequences for time and eternity. And yet the men who are living now had no part in the commission of original sin."

It is evident from a preceding part of this article, that the archbishop had no intention of apologizing for the slave trade. That the Catholic Church is opposed to slavery, he says, "is true, but only in the sense that she is opposed even to the calamities of human life, which she has no power to reverse. Her doctrine on that subject is, that it is *a crime* to reduce men naturally free to a condition of servitude and bondage, as slaves."

While he was in Paris, in 1861-'62, this article was quoted to his disadvantage by the French journals, and Mr. Augustin Cochin suggested to him the propriety of making some explanation. It has been said that, in a letter to the editor of the *Journal des Débats*, he denied the authorship of the article. This is a mistake: what he did write to that periodical was that, as the article in question had appeared editorially in *The Metropolitan Record*, the editor of the *Record* was the proper person to be made responsible for it. At the same time he declared that, although opposed to abolitionism, he was not, never had been, never could be an

There is being insinuated in this part of the country an idea to the effect that the purpose of this war is the abolition of slavery in the South. If that idea should prevail among a certain class, it would make the business of recruiting slack indeed. The Catholics, so far as I know, whether of native or foreign birth, are willing to fight to the death for the support of the constitution, the Government, and the laws of the country. But if it should be understood that, with or without knowing it, they are to fight for the abolition of slavery, then, indeed, they will turn away in disgust from the discharge of what would otherwise be a patriotic duty.

He writes to Mr. Seward about the same time:

Oct. 10, 1861.

MY DEAR GOVERNOR:

You may have seen, in *The Metropolitan Record*, a criticism of mine on what I regarded as an untimely article in *Brownson's Quarterly Review*, entitled "Slavery and the War." If you have seen, or have had time to read it, it has explained itself. It contains my sincere convictions on the subject. If I had not corrected the reviewer's position, he would have done vast mischief, without, I think, intending it, to the struggle in which the country is now engaged. Some of our editors are exceedingly thoughtless in discussing abolitionism of slavery through the instrumentality of the Government and of the army. Not a few of our Protestant clergymen avail themselves of the privilege which the pulpit affords for promoting the same unreasonable purpose.

It will be time enough to regulate this unhappy question of slavery when the war shall have terminated, on the merits of its own basis, whether in the North or in the South. And I regret exceedingly that these intemperate advocates have no real friends by them who might whisper in their ears, at this critical moment, the prudence of not casting any new firebrands of division into that portion of the country which is loyal and still united. I think further, that on this subject (delicate as it may be to interfere) the Government has a responsibility which ought not to be too long procrastinated.

---

advocate of slavery. Among his friends he made no secret of his being the writer of the article in the *Record*.

When the rebellion first broke out in 1861, he hoped and prayed for peace until all room for hope was gone. He was not carried away by the warlike enthusiasm which broke out all through the North after the capture of Fort Sumter; though he was by no means a believer either in the doctrine of State sovereignty or the right of secession. In a remarkably calm and temperate letter to Bishop Lynch, of Charleston, in August, 1861, he used the following language:

> I am an advocate for the sovereignty of every State in the Union within the limits recognized and approved of by its own representative authority when the constitution was agreed upon. As a consequence, I hold that South Carolina has no State right to interfere with the internal affairs of Massachusetts; and, as a further consequence, that Massachusetts has no right to interfere with South Carolina, or its domestic and civil affairs, as one of the sovereign States of this now threatened Union. But the constitution having been formed by the common consent of all the parties engaged in the framework and approval thereof, I maintain that no State has a right to secede, except in the manner provided for in the document itself.

To another Southern bishop he wrote as follows:

NEW YORK, *May* 7, 1861.

RIGHT REVEREND DEAR SIR:

I have just received your letter of the 3d instant. I fear that your apprehensions in regard to the future, both North and South, are not exaggerated. As to myself, it is very well known here that I am for peace; and further, that on many points I have sympathized with the South, in view of complaints which I thought to be too well founded. At the same time, I cannot help thinking that they have gone too fast and too far for any hope of peace until the issues of war shall have been tried. For several months back they have proclaimed that any concession from the Federal Government was already too late to be accepted.

With regard to the Catholics, North and South, I can have but little to say. I myself have never recommended any man to go to the war, unless circumstances rendered it either expedient or necessary. . . . . Deprecating the assumed necessity for this war, I have not interfered by giving encouragement to Catholics to take part in it, or by giving them advice not to do so. It is the same with the South, I presume; but certainly there is a great difference in principle between the two sections of the country. The North have not been required to do any thing new, to take any oath, to support any new flag; they have kept on the even tenor of their way. The South, on the contrary, has taken upon itself to be judge in its own cause, to be witnesses in its own cause, and to execute, if necessary, by force of arms, its own decision. In a constitutional country this means either revolution or rebellion, since there are tribunals agreed upon by North and South, and supported by both for a period of more than seventy years. When these tribunals are set aside, and men appeal to the sword, the Federal Government has only to abdicate, or meet sword with sword. . . . .

The flag on the cathedral was erected with my permission and approval. It was at the same time an act of expediency going before a necessity likely to be urged upon me by the dictation of enthusiasm in this city. I preferred that no such necessity of dictation should overtake us; because, if it had, the press would have sounded the report that the Catholics were disloyal, and no act of ours afterward could successfully vindicate us from the imputation. On the whole, however, I think, my dear Bishop, that the Catholics of the North have behaved themselves with great prudence, moderation, and a dignity which has, for the moment at least, inspired, among the high and the low, great respect for them as a religious body in this Union. I regret that I cannot say as much for the Catholics, and for some of their clergy, in the South. In their periodicals in New Orleans, and in Charleston, they have justified the attitude taken by the South on principles of Catholic theology, which I think was an unnecessary, inexpedient, and, for that matter, a doubtful if not a dangerous position, at the commencement of so unnatural and so lamentable a struggle. . . . . .

I could write much more on this subject, but I think it is unnecessary. My respect and affection for the people of the South are the same as they ever have been. And I look forward with hope to a reconciliation between the contending parties, to be effected, perhaps, at no very distant day. You may be sure that if, directly or indirectly, it should be in my power to exercise the slightest influence toward the attainment of this desirable end, there is no sacrifice which I should not be prepared to make, if my influence could have the slightest effect in bringing it about.

When President Lincoln finally issued the emancipation proclamation, an Episcopal minister of New York proposed that a number of prominent clergymen of different denominations should unite in writing public letters of disapproval to the President, for the purpose of "bringing the conservative sentiment of this city to bear" upon him. Archbishop Hughes consented to take part in the movement, but most of the Protestant clergymen, whose coöperation was expected, thought it imprudent to speak their sentiments openly; so nothing was done.

As soon as the Government, however, was fairly committed to the great contest, the archbishop declared himself boldly in favor of the most energetic measures for the support of the national authority. He wrote every few days to the Secretary of State, Mr. Seward, giving advice as to the best method of prosecuting the war, and keeping him informed of the state of feeling among the people. At a very early period he foresaw the necessity of concentrating a large force between Washington and Richmond, and pointed out the strategic importance of Cairo on the Mississippi. As far back as April, 1861, he urged upon the Government, through Mr. Seward, the necessity of collecting at least one hundred thousand men about Washington—a force which most persons at that time would have thought extravagantly large. It is better economy, he said, to incur vast expense at the proper time, "in order to save greater in the feeble drag of a contest wherein the forces are entirely or nearly balanced."

Let the question of the rights of the Federal Government over the whole country be settled once and forever. Let there be no compromise until the States shall be disposed to return to their allegiance to the Federal Government, which they themselves contributed to create, and from which nothing new in the legislation of the Federal Government has given them the slightest pretext for seceding; no recognition of the pretended Government of the Confederate States; no negotiation with them as such; but ample kindness toward the States, taken one by one.

June 18, 1861.

More attention should be paid to the forces at Cairo. If they can stand for a while, very well. But there should be, for that matter, a camp on higher ground, ... in which, during the sickly season, vigorous troops could be always on hand at Cairo. The sickly of the army at that post might be transferred to the other locality, from which able-bodied men could be called to replace them at the great point of strategy on our Western waters. Then Fort Pickens ought to be gradually strengthened until, as by way of an outlet, its troops should be able to retake Pensacola and the navy-yard. Norfolk to be secured from the land side is a small question. The battle, if any should take place, will be, as I think now, about Richmond. I pray you, for Heaven's sake, not to allow it to be a half battle, but one in which, whatever the consequences may be, the South will be taught that it is incapable of coping with the North.

The rebel privateers, he declared, were "essentially pirates," and American cruisers ought to sink them whenever they encountered them upon the high seas.

TO THE ARCHBISHOP OF BALTIMORE.

May 9, 1861.

MOST REVEREND AND DEAR SIR:

The superior of the Jesuits here called on me more than a week ago, to state that their Society would be prepared to furnish for the spiritual necessities of the army, North and South, as many as ten chaplains, speaking all the civilized languages of Europe or America. I heard him, but did not make any reply. For myself, I have sent but one chaplain, with the Sixty-Ninth regiment, and to him I have already given the faculties which you had the kindness to confer upon me for such an occasion.

There is also another question growing up, and it is about nurses for the sick and wounded. Our Sisters of Mercy have volunteered, after the example of their sisters toiling in the Crimean war. I have signified to them, not harshly, that they had better mind their own affairs until their services are needed. I am now informed indirectly, that the Sisters of Charity in this diocese would be willing to volunteer a force of from fifty to one hundred nurses. To this last proposition I have very strong objections. They have as much on hand as they can accomplish. Besides, it would seem to me natural and proper, that the Sisters of Charity in Emmitsburg should occupy the very honorable post of nursing the sick and wounded. But, on the other hand, Maryland is a divided community at this moment, whereas New York is understood to be all on one side. In fact, as the question now stands, Maryland is, in America, for the moment, as Belgium has been, the battle-field of Europe. As I mentioned several days ago, Baltimore must be destroyed, or it must succumb to Northern determination.

On these several points, I should like much to know what your grace thinks and would advise.

Sincerely your devoted brother and servant in Christ,

✠ JOHN, *Abp. of New York.*

He does not seem to have been at all discouraged by the result of the first battle of Bull Run.

TO SECRETARY SEWARD.

July 21, 1861.

MY DEAR GOVERNOR:

Serious military reverses are reported here in all the newspapers. I do not attach much importance to them. They have just intensified the contest, and by so much have abridged the period of its duration. . . . . . Let an appeal be made to the loyal citizens and loyal States of this country, under the auspices of the stars and stripes, and you will have a practical echo quite sufficient to clear out nuisances from Virginia, North Carolina, Kentucky, and Tennessee—leaving rebels further South to live on water-melons for the next six months. Your flag of appeal to the loyal States should be, in my opinion, an appeal to the *pluck* and *perseverance* of men who wish to support the Government.

This is no time to hesitate; what is to be done should be done quickly and promptly; and if the Government be at once wise and true toward the people, the people will be true and brave toward the Government.

I remain, very sincerely, your obedient servant,

✠ JOHN, *Abp. of New York.*

TO THE SAME.

LONG BRANCH, *Aug.* 18, 1861.

With regard to Colonel Corcoran, I would advise his appointment as brigadier-general, even if he should never return from his honorable captivity. I have discovered symptoms of wounded feelings among his countrymen, arising from the fact that in the different official reports, the Sixty-Ninth has scarcely been alluded to. A slight is for them worse than a blow. Corcoran's appointment as brigadier-general, even though a prisoner, would heal the wounds of their *amour propre.*

. . . . . .

I think I suggested, at your table, that delay in hazarding a battle, until there should be a moral certainty of its terminating favorably for the Government, was a safe and wise policy. There should have been no hasty battle. Still, its teaching may be useful for the time to come. Skirmishing must be encountered as it comes; but a deliberately planned battle ought to have in its programme the almost if not absolute certainty of victory.

. . . . . .

TO THE SAME.

Sept. 12, 1861.

MY DEAR GOVERNOR:

Our papers have paragraphs every day about what is called the "Irish Brigade," intended for military service during the war. The thing itself may be all correct; but I would respectfully suggest that the name is not indicative of good. I think regiments and brigades ought to be distinguished by numbers, and companies by alphabetical distinction. I am of the opinion that if there be Irish brigades, German brigades, Scotch brigades, Garibaldian brigades in our army, there will be trouble among the troops even before the enemy comes in sight.

I am aware that it will require a good deal of management and delicacy to put aside these distinctions of foreign nationalities; still, I think that it can be accomplished.

TO THE SAME.

NEW YORK, *Oct.* 12, 1861.

MY DEAR GOVERNOR:

I have had a queer visit this morning. A lady, aged, I suppose, about 47 years, called on me, requesting that I should allow her to take refuge as a boarder, or even nominally as a pupil, in one of our religious female academies. Of course I was surprised, but her story removed that feeling, and won for her another.

She is Madame ———, a sister of General ———. She has lived in the North for 13 years, but yet is so much a creole, that our conversation was in French. She has a son, aged 22 years, who has sailed for Europe, but who, she fears, is bent on joining the Southern cause as soon as he can accomplish his purpose. Her relatives in the South, perhaps her brother, although she did not say so, have been smuggling to her address letters, as she says, on private affairs. These have been, in some instances, detected and opened, and, as she says, a policeman named Jones or Johnson has been sent from Washington to find her out. She keeps her room. She has a married daughter who is quite as nervous as herself; and between them, this respectable lady, of diminutive size, pale countenance, and weak nerves, is almost dying of apprehension. She imagines, if she walks out of her room, that everybody is looking at her, and she does not know among them who is the officer that is in pursuit to make her a prisoner.

This has affected my own feelings not a little, and though I mentioned at an early period that you need not answer any of my letters, now I must plead an exception, and I must tell you what I said to Madame ———. I said in substance:

"My good lady, it is your nerves, and not your peril, that have made you so unhappy. I will go your security, and nothing shall be done to you in consequence of letters addressed to you from the South, provided you write no letter to the South that would be, in these melancholy times, improper. But I will be your security to any reasonable amount—and now I pray you not to trouble yourself about the matter. Be quiet. Go out when your health or your inclination may require; and fling away that silly imagination that, because you are General ———'s sister, people gaze at you and spies are on your track."

Now, my dear Governor, the winding up of this tedious communication is a request that you would, if it can be done with propriety, signify in a private letter to me that unless some act of her own, by writing, or otherwise, should compromise this lady, she need have no anxiety or apprehension in consequence of her being the sister of General ———.

PRESIDENT LINCOLN TO ARCHBISHOP HUGHES.

WASHINGTON, D. C., *Oct.* 21, 1861.

ARCHBISHOP HUGHES,

RT. REV. SIR: I am sure you will pardon me if, in my ignorance, I do not address you with technical correctness.

I find no law authorizing the appointment of chaplains for our *hospitals;* and yet the services of chaplains are more needed, perhaps, in the hospitals than with the healthy soldiers in the field. With this view, I have given a sort of *quasi* appointment (a copy of which I enclose) to each of three Protestant ministers, who have accepted, and entered upon the duties.

If you perceive no objection, I will thank you to give me the name, or names, of one or more suitable persons of the Catholic Church to whom I may with propriety tender the same service.

Many thanks for your kind and judicious letters to Gov. Seward, and which he regularly allows me the pleasure and the profit of perusing.

With the highest respect, your obedient servant,

A. LINCOLN.

TO SECRETARY SEWARD.

NEW YORK, *Oct.* 15, 1861.

* * * * *

I take it that the President is the responsible man of this nation. No President has ever been so severely tested as he. A great conspiracy, of which he knew nothing, was in existence when he was elected. It burst forth almost immediately after his inauguration. There was no preparation to meet its extravagance, for it was a foolish enterprise, and a snare sprung upon him before he could be aware of it. Things are changed, however, and the country begins to know, if it did not know before, that Mr. Lincoln is not less than equal to the emergency which had been prepared for the first months of his administration. He has been fortunate in surrounding himself with advisers competent from their understanding of the whole case, from their ability in their several departments, from their unity as a cabinet, and their loyal devotion to the interests of the country, to strengthen and sustain its chief magistrate during the unexpected events that have occurred since his election.

. . . . .

For myself, I am rejoiced to see the success of the blockade, and especially what the papers have lately announced, that the outlets of the Mississippi are being taken care of. But the headwaters of that great river should also be looked after. Old Cato used to say *Delenda est Carthago;* I would say *Augenda est Cairo.*

I would request you to present my most respectful compliments to the President for his condescension and patience in reading or hearing my ideas on the crisis. To you, also, I offer the same testimony of grateful feeling in regard to the subject. . .

There is only one word I would add, and that is, that in your effort to bring back the Southern States to their condition before the war, you would, as far as it could be consistent with the high principles of supreme government, be as patient and as considerate toward the State authorities of this so-called Confederacy as possible. Conquest is not altogether by the sword. Statesmanship, and especially in our circumstances, may have much to do with it. But no backing down of the Federal Government.

I think it unlikely that I shall venture to encroach on your precious time by any further communications on this great national crisis. I am getting old, and it is time for me to begin to gather myself up for a transition from this world to another, and I hope, a better. I know that this world would have gone on just as well as it has done if I had never lived. At the same time, as I mentioned in my first letter, I have not been able to sever my thoughts and feelings from what has occurred, almost under my own eyes, in the only country which I call mine, and to which I am devoted by every prompting of my understanding, and every loyal sentiment of my heart.

I remain, as ever, my dear Governor, your devoted servant,
☨ JOHN, *Abp. of New York.*

"I submit your letters to the President," says Mr. Seward, "who reads all you write to me with deep interest." Mr. Lincoln was so well pleased with the letter last quoted, that he caused a copy of it to be made for his own use.

CHAPTER XXVI.

1861-1862.

The Archbishop accepts from the Government a special mission to Europe—Letters to Cardinal Barnabo—Correspondence with Mr. Seward—Arrival in Paris—Interview with the Emperor and Empress—Embarrassment of the American minister—Visit to Rome—Letters to Mr. Seward—Letters to his sisters—Canonization of the martyrs of Japan—Visit to Ireland—Sermon at the laying of the corner-stone of the Irish University—Speeches in Dublin—Enthusiastic reception—Address from Irish Nationalists—Letters to the Mayor of Cork, the Archbishop of Dublin, and the Bishop of Clogher—Return home—Visit to Mr. Seward—Promotion suggested to the Holy See.

ON the 21st of October Mr. Seward invited the archbishop to come to Washington, as he was very desirous of having a personal conference with him on matters of grave public concern. This was a few days after Messrs. Mason and Slidell, Confederate commissioners to England and France, had succeeded in running the blockade from Charleston, with the intention of taking passage for Europe at Havana. The administration believed that the influence of these gentlemen abroad could be better counteracted by special envoys who would be free from the restraints of official etiquette, than by the regular diplomatic representatives of the United States. They believed likewise that envoys of this description might render valuable service by informing public opinion in Europe, mingling freely in society, correcting popular misapprehensions, and so working to prevent what men were beginning to fear, a war between the United States and some of the great European powers. They determined to send Archbishop Hughes to France, and Mr. Thurlow Weed to

England. The archbishop proceeded to Washington immediately upon the receipt of Mr. Seward's letter. He gives the following account of what passed between him and the cabinet, in a letter to Cardinal Barnabo, Prefect of the sacred congregation of the Propaganda, written immediately after his arrival in Liverpool:

It was proposed by the cabinet that I should accept a special mission to England and France, in connection with very important national questions between the United States and these powers. I declined, until it was made known to me that the President of the United States made it a special request that I should accept, and if possible render some service to the United States in the present condition of public affairs. I could not refuse his request, and at the same time I imagined if any success should attend my mission, it would redound to the benefit of the Catholics, and to the promotion of the interests of the Church. The nature of my mission is such that, in the best days of the Church, a bishop would have no reason to decline it. My first business is with the Government of France, and I shall have to remain in Paris perhaps for a month or two. I have not, at the present moment, any idea of going to any other country, except that on my way homeward it may be necessary for me to spend some time in London, after the Parliament shall have been opened.

Please lay the testimony of my profound veneration and fidelity at the feet of the Holy Father, and obtain his apostolical benediction for me, even in this matter, so apparently foreign to my sacred vocation, as a prelate of the Catholic Church.

I shall remain, at least for the first two or three weeks, in Paris, at the hotel Meurice, where any communication from your Eminence will be sure to reach me.

In a subsequent letter to the same person, he says:

My mission was, and is, a mission of peace between France and England on the one side, and the United States on the other. . . The time was so brief between my visit to Washington and my departure from New York, that I had no opportunity of writing to your Eminence on the subject, or of consulting any of the other bishops in regard to it. I made known to the President that if I should come to Europe, it would not be as a partisan of the North more than of the South; that I should represent the interests of the South as well as of the North—in short, the interests of all the United States, just the same as if they had never been distracted by the present civil war. The people of the South know that I am not opposed to their interests. They have even published that in their papers, and some say that my coming to Europe is with a view to bring about a reconciliation between the two sections of the country. But, in fact, no one but myself, either North or South, knows the entire object of my visit to Europe. . . . . . I made known to the ministers in Washington that I could accept no official appointment from them; that it was not in their power to bestow any distinction upon me equal to that which the Church had already conferred; that I could not undertake to fulfil any written instructions; but that if I came I should be left to my own discretion, to say and do what would be most likely to accomplish good, or at least to prevent evil. Then they said that I should go with a *carte blanche*—do and say for the interests of the country, prevention of war, and interests of humanity, any thing that I should think proper.

This much, your Eminence, I think proper to communicate, so that your Eminence may have a clearer view of the circumstances under which I have acted, not doubting that your Eminence would have approved of my course, if I had had an opportunity of consulting you before my departure. I would take it as a great favor if you would explain briefly these circumstances to our most Holy Father the Pope.

And now permit me to make some remarks on the motives which prompted the Government of the United States to request of me the sacrifice necessarily involved in a tempestuous voyage across the Atlantic.

1st. The Government knows that the people of America, both of the North and of the South, whether Catholics or Protestants, have great confidence in me, as one who will never say any thing but what he knows or believes to be true; that although loyal to the only legitimate government in America, I am regarded as no enemy of the South; that, as the cabinet at Washington believe, more reliance would be placed on my statements, on account of my being a Catholic prelate, than would be placed on the words of any official minister of the United States, either in Paris, or London, or elsewhere.

2d. The Government at Washington were pleased to think that, in requesting me to accept this mission, they were paying a great compliment to the whole Catholic people of the United States; and they wished to give me also a mark of their confidence which might go far, as an example for future administrations to be well disposed toward the Catholics, and by this act to condemn that spurious faction who, but a few years ago, under the name of Know-Nothings, attempted to treat the Catholics of America as disloyal citizens, unworthy of the equal privileges which the laws of the country extend to all its inhabitants.

They may have had other reasons of their own with which I am less acquainted.

TO MR. THURLOW WEED.

NEW YORK, *October* 29, 1861.

MY DEAR MR. WEED:

I cannot "condescend" to appoint you to any of the offices which you so humbly solicited in a whisper the other evening in Washington. But I do hereby appoint you, *with* or *without* the consent of the Senate, to be my friend (as you always have been), and my companion in our brief visit to Europe.

The more I reflect upon the subject, the more I am convinced that, whether successful or not, the purpose is marked, in actual circumstances, by large, enlightened, and very wise statesmanship.

I have engaged a state-room for you next to my own, on the Africa, which sails on the 6th proximo.

We shall have time enough to talk, on the way, about matters and things.

The archbishop was accompanied on the voyage by the Rev. Francis McNeirny (his private secretary and chaplain), and a young man who acted as his amanuensis, and attended to his personal wants.

TO SECRETARY SEWARD.

On board the "AFRICA," *Nov.* 13, 1861.

MY DEAR GOVERNOR:

This is our eighth day out. First two days boisterous—since then fine weather, with light head winds. Few passengers, but very agreeable. English, Irish, Scotch, and Americans.

They settle the questions of your cabinet and of the war, about once a day. On the next day, however, they have to be resettled. The Irish and Americans among us—you know what they are. The Scotch have little to say; the few Englishmen are those who take the deepest interest in the whole matter. They speak freely, but with apparent good feeling; and I have discovered one of their greatest troubles to be, in addition to the other embarrassments of the situation, that, having visited America for the purpose of seeing with their own eyes and hearing with their own ears, they are obliged to return to Old "Hengland" without knowing well what to say to the British people on this important topic. Among them I find that the sympathetic needle points to the South. But after making allowances for its variations, they generally come round to the acknowledgment that the South has had no real ground for its hasty and unwise measures.

I have had very little to say, and yet I could not help sometimes correcting their misconceptions, and sometimes suggesting that if the English people, with or without the approval of the Government, will stand by their good feelings, as exhibited during the last fifty years, it will be vastly better for us and for themselves; that America is as proud of its rights as England can be of hers, and as able, as well as willing, to defend them at every hazard; that even friendly interference, provided it should be a real interference, on their part, would be very damaging to the interests of both countries.

I hope to be able to have this letter forwarded by the steamer which we expect to meet at Queenstown. This is my note for to-day. I shall add to it as we progress further, if any thing interesting should occur.

LIVERPOOL, *Nov.* 20, 1861.

Nothing occurred on board, since the date of the preceding note, that would be worthy of special remark. A lively discussion sprang up a few nights before our landing, in which all hands took part. It turned upon the word "belligerents" used by Lord John Russell. The English tried hard to apologize for, rather than to defend, that uncivil expression. Our Americans sustained the cause nobly, but became more or less excited, whilst the phlegmatic Britons remained very cool, and I had almost said, apparently callous.

I was in the centre of the circle, and thought myself obliged, at this stage of the debate, to have a word to say. The remarks on both sides had been rather of an irrelevant and wandering character. I brought the question to a focus by inquiring of a very intelligent Englishman, who was the chief speaker on that side, "whether, since the foundation of modern civilized nations, any government or any member of any government in Europe or America, at any time, or under any circumstances, raised rebellion within the limits of a friendly State to an equality with the legitimate government which they attempted to overthrow!" I quoted the instance of Ireland in 1798: America could have called the rebels "belligerents" against England, but they [sic] did not. The French, indeed, sympathized with them, but France was engaged in war with England at the time, and did not pretend to have any sympathies except with England's enemies. I quoted the Scotch rebellion of 1706, and again of 1715; did any power at peace with England proclaim the Scotch "belligerents"! Other kindred instances were brought forward, and my good English friend had no answer, except a reference to the case of Greece against Turkey. That was easily disposed of, and it was shown at once that there is no parity between the two cases. Finally, I brought the gentleman down to a response to one single question, and that was, "whether any official statesman, in the history of modern nations, ever used an expression, especially in his official capacity, equivalent to that which Lord John Russell had employed toward the Southern people of the United States by calling them "belligerents"! I wished a clear answer to that simple question, but no answer was or could be given. Then, deducing a principle from *this* first instance, I showed that Lord John Russell would pass in history as the first public man who inaugurated a word calculated to upset the peace and the government of the world.

But my friend had an auxiliary at hand who came to the rescue, and he said: "But, after all, archbishop, you must acknowledge that Lord John is friendly to the North, for you will remember that he enjoined, in the strictest manner, perfect neutrality on the part of the British people pending this lamentable contest."

I replied, that was well; but his proclamation of neutrality came too late. If he had not recognized the seceding States of the Union as "belligerents," and thus lowered the North, or elevated the South to an equality, in theory at least, there would be no chance, no possibility of neutrality on the part of England.

The proper language for Lord John Russell to have employed would have been, "that the United States were unhappily disturbed by one of those domestic strifes with which few great nations are unacquainted within their own borders, and that it was the purpose and policy of the British people not to interfere either morally or physically."

By this time the "English members" became taciturn, and I suppose the house in general became fatigued, and an adjournment was unanimously agreed upon. Since that time, the question has not been touched by any one among our passengers. The utmost good feeling was manifested on all sides, and in our sentiments expressed, after the last dinner on board, I could hardly tell which side exceeded the other in expressions of mutual good will, and a desire and hope that the present troubles may come to an amicable and early termination.

Since our landing, the papers here have copied the speculations of the New York press, especially in regard to my presence in Europe on a supposed mission. I think this is not to be regretted, and the less so, that not one of them, not even my own secretary, has the slightest idea of any business that may have been intrusted to me. Several distinguished friends have called upon me, reporting what the papers say, as copied from New York journals. My answer has been, that it is hardly worth while to pay any attention to speculations of the press, especially in a country where there are so many journals published as there are in the United States; that every one who knows me will be assured that if I can do good and avert evil, whether at home or abroad, I shall not fail in attempting to do it.

I start to-morrow morning for London, where I shall stay one day, and hope to be in Paris to celebrate mass next Sunday.

TO MRS. RODRIGUE.

LIVERPOOL, *Nov.* 20, 1861.

Safely landed. Since setting out, the joints of my limbs have become more supple. A swelling still occasionally continues, without pain. Appetite good, and vigor of mind at least improving still.

TO SECRETARY SEWARD.

HOTEL DE L'EMPIRE, PARIS, *Nov.* 23, 1861.

MY DEAR GOVERNOR:

Since my last from Liverpool, nothing has occurred worthy of special mention. I left Liverpool on the 20th; spent one night in London; paid a hasty visit to Mr. Adams. But as he was kind enough to leave the dinner-table to see me, I remained about eight minutes—too short a time to converse with him on public matters, not too long to keep him from his company. Started next morning for Paris. It rained all day; but from Boulogne to Paris it was a small hurricane of wind and rain, and arriving at the Hotel Meurice, it became a perfect tornado; so that even in entering the hotel, my clothes became perfectly saturated. This would be about 1 o'clock on Saturday morning. In consequence, a cold and a lie-by. Sent for a doctor, took medicine; but now, thank God, I feel well and bright.

I have changed quarters, and am now staying at the hotel above mentioned, having my good friend Weed occupying adjoining apartments.

Though unwell at the time, I hastened about 10 o'clock Saturday morning to place the proper documents in the hands of Mr. Dayton. He received me with great politeness. After reading, or rather glancing over his papers, some general remarks were made about matters and things, during which time I could not help perceiving a certain amount of embarrassment on his part. I understood it at a glance, and it was nothing more than what might have been expected in the circumstances. He is the representative of our Government. So am I; but in a different order. For I would have been its representative under any possible circumstances, so far as concerns a right to think and speak on behalf of the only nation on the face of the earth to which I owe allegiance and loyalty.

Mr. Dayton took occasion to say, awkwardly a little in the manner of expressing it, that he did not feel disposed to introduce me to the Secretary of Foreign Affairs in this country. I replied that I comprehended the delicacy of his position as regarded myself; that if I should have occasion to call on M. Thouvenel, I could find abundant means to have an interview with him.

Mr. Dayton invited me to dine on the following Monday, which I did. The company was exceedingly agreeable. In the mean time Mr. Dayton had thrown off any momentary reserve, like that of our first interview. "He had seen M. Thouvenel and communicated your despatch. But he was quite surprised that M. Thouvenel was perfectly conversant with my movements; that, except what was sealed up, under your signature, he knew every thing about me." "How long was I going to remain in Paris?"—"Did I intend to visit the provinces?"—"Was I going to Rome?" etc., etc.

Mr. Dayton, in repeating the conversation, did not seem to have the slightest idea of the real drift of these questions. But I caught their meaning, which is this:

You know the relation now existing between the noble episcopacy of France and this Government on the one side, and between that same episcopacy and the Holy See on the other. Thouvenel, being informed in advance, as it appears, of my probable movements, did not like an American bishop, whose own Government leaves him at liberty to discharge freely the duties of his office, within the common law of the country, but without any interference on the part of the civil and supreme authority of the United States, to communicate his ideas to the prelates of this country. But let that topic pass for the present.

In travelling through England, I found generally my fellow-travellers apparently well-disposed toward the United States; but by a generally foregone conclusion convinced that the country was divided, and that henceforward there would be two nations instead of one within the former boundaries of the Union. "To conquer the South was impossible."—"To reconcile them to return to their allegiance was equally so."—"Was it not, on the part of the North, a fight against destiny to protract a war that would be bootless under any circumstances!"—"That in this civilized and enlightened age it was distressing to every feeling of humanity to witness any protraction of a sanguinary strife, and especially between brethren of the same country," etc., etc., etc. Just as if John Bull turned and talked Quaker in his old age. I found my French travellers on this side of the Channel much more reasonable. They did not seem to have made up their mind on the American question. In fact, for the most part, they acknowledged candidly that they did not understand it.

Having been indisposed nearly all the time since I arrived here, I can add, with regard to European sentiment, nothing to what I have just said.

Since my arrival, however, two events have occurred which have put all Paris on the *qui vive:* one, the arrival and reception of the Nashville in Southampton; the other, the seasonable capture of some representatives of what is called the Southern Confederacy, on their way to Europe, standing, as they are said to have been, on the oaken deck of a British vessel, with England's flag above their heads. To-day I have been visited by some Americans and some distinguished French gentlemen, by way of paying me tribute of respect. But invariably before retiring they have alluded to these late events. "Would they not lead to war between England and the United States?"—"Was the act warranted by the laws or usages of nations?"—"Would not England resent it as a national insult?" etc.

To all this I replied, in brief, that of all nations England should not resent it; it was not intended to provoke any controversy with England, but it was a measure of wisdom and necessity; that England's pretension and claim to exercise the right of search, especially on board American vessels, led to and caused the War of 1812; that when the parties were tired of war, peace was restored, the United States still clinging to its determination to resist the right of search, whilst England was not required to renounce officially her pretended right of search, although she has not since attempted to exercise that right on an American vessel. The position then would be that the United States, for the first time, have exercised a right which the British government had often practised, and has not, even to this day, renounced; that, in fine, England may do as she thinks proper, but that the United States, if assailed by Great Britain, will not hesitate to employ every means that God and Nature shall have put within her reach to defend herself against foreign and unjust assailants, whether they be England, France, or both combined; and that even now, if England should adopt the course so much at variance with the interests of commerce, of communities, and of nations that have no real ground for mutual hostilities, the Government at Washington will not be taken by surprise, nor will it shrink in the least from the ordeal through which it will have to pass.

This is all, or at least sufficient, for the present.

Believe me as ever, my dear Governor,

Your devoted friend and servant,

✠ JOHN, *Abp. of New York.*

TO THE SAME.

PARIS, *Dec.* 5, 1861.

I have been dining out almost every day, and every day I have an opportunity of enlightening a good many people on the whole state of our affairs. To-day, even, I had occasion to develop the condition of our country, in view of the new troubles which could hardly have been anticipated when I left New York. Three or four gentlemen clustered around me after dinner, and the conversation turned upon the actual condition of things between the United States and Great Britain. After an hour very pleasantly spent thus in chit-chat about grave matters, one of them, a member of the Emperor's household, a highly educated and intelligent gentleman, said: "The fact is, we, here in France—and the same may be the case in England—do not understand the power of that new people, nor do we appreciate their means of self-defence."

I hope to have an audience of the Emperor next week. The new troubles connected with the "Trent" are embarrassing for both sides of the question. So far, America has gained by the last news, according to which Commander Wilkes has taken upon himself, and exonerated the government from the responsibility of his act. This is a great advantage. But John Bull is not satisfied. He will have the traitors liberated, because they were found on the deck of his vessel. The tone of the English papers makes known, either by direct assertion or by implication, that for the continuance of peace between the United States and England, the release of the traitor-citizens is a condition *sine qua non.*

I know that the American people will never comply with this condition, especially dictated by a rival power that has played us false since the beginning of our domestic struggle; and if there be no escape from the dilemma in which the British cabinet would place us, I would say, let Uncle Sam put forth the plenitude of his strength at every point on which a country can be defended, and an enemy repelled and cast forth.

But two ways occur to me by which this dreadful alternative may be, if not absolutely averted, at least so modified in its conditions that America, ready to defend herself, shall at the same time show a willingness to make every concession consistent with the preservation of her honor, and at the same time with the hope of preserving the world's peace.

Two modes—or at least two efforts—present themselves to my mind. The one is, that the Emperor of the French should act as arbiter in the dispute, before the effusion of blood between the two nations shall have occurred, provided they would agree, on the one side and on the other, to submit the controversy to his friendly decision. This I shall propose to his Majesty, acting, as you know, on my own responsibility. He will unquestionably be reserved on the subject, but at all events I shall write you my interpretation of the result.

The other alternative would be, that whilst John Bull is getting on his seal-cap and military boots, the prisoners should be tried according to the laws of the land. They would be, no doubt, condemned to death; but I presume that it would be competent for the President, in the exercise of his constitutional privileges, to commute the sentence of the culprits, and allow them, under that commutation, to go on board any neutral vessel, and forsake the United States forever, except at the peril of their lives, or by virtue of an Act of Congress permitting them to return to the country which they have left nothing undone to betray.

. . . . .

Keep up the forces, both by land and sea. They constitute a strong argument in favor of the cause of a nation which may be called upon to maintain its high sovereignty, its independence, its honor, and its interests. Surely 23,000,000 or 24,000,000 of freemen, of patriots, of skilful and determined men, will not consent to be subjugated or reduced, or conquered back into subservient colonies, no matter whether the national life is attempted by France, or England, or both combined.

You would be surprised if you could have witnessed the wide opening of eyes among those to whom I made this known after dinner to-day, developing much more than I do now the reasons on which my conclusion was founded; and it was then that my distinguished friend acknowledged that Europe was very ignorant of the power and resources of the United States.

I make no apology for the tax imposed on your time, if indeed you should find leisure to read this letter; to which I shall add nothing except the assurance that I am as ever your devoted friend and servant,

✠ JOHN, *Abp. of New York.*

TO THE VERY REV. DR. McCLOSKEY, RECTOR OF THE AMERICAN COLLEGE IN ROME.

PARIS, *Dec.* 4, 1861.

VERY REV. DEAR SIR:

You must have heard before this time that I am again unexpectedly on European soil.

I saw Mr. Hart, of New Haven, two or three days ago. He tells me that the American College stands well in Rome, especially in the *physical* treatment of its alumni. I was glad to hear this, although it refers to only one branch of a real ecclesiastical Seminary. We do not want in America sickly or weak missionaries as to the physique, nor tender and delicate clergymen to carry on the work of God in your native and my adopted country. Let your Seminarians know that they should be rugged enough both in mind and body to meet and bear their part in the struggle of the Church which must be carried on during my life and after my death, and possibly yours, so far as the diocese of New York is concerned. Out of New York, this struggle will require, even more, right preparation and energy to carry on the missions.

If I can accomplish it, I hope to have the consolation of spending a few days, during the approaching Christmas holidays, in the

Eternal City. During my stay I hope to be the guest of the American College in Rome. . . . . . . I intend to test your accommodations for an American bishop, and to look sharply into your administration of the college, but without saying a word on that subject except to yourself.

But at any rate I wish you to believe me very faithfully,
Your friend and servant,
✠ JOHN, *Abp. of New York.*

TO MR. THURLOW WEED, LONDON.

PARIS, *Dec.* 10, 1861.

MY DEAR MR. WEED:

I received your letter of yesterday, but since your departure I have found myself a little lonely. I have heard within an hour past that General Scott is on his way to Havre, intending to sail by the Arago to New York. He does not wish his friends here to speak of his departure, until after he shall have embarked. He said to my informant: "War is inevitable, as I now think. I am old, and not strong; but I trust I have yet energy enough of both mind and body to be of service to my country. I shall devote my talents and my experience to work out a military plan of defence for the city of New York." These were in substance the remarks of the gallant old soldier.

I expect within a few days to have an audience with the Emperor, and I shall urge him, on my own responsibility, to step in as arbitrator between England and America. I am willing that every reasonable and honorable apology be made, if indeed any apology is needed, for the actual cause which has excited John Bull so much. But after having played us false in our domestic troubles, and when he now mounts his high horse, pleads his own cause, judges and decides without having even heard the other party, and when he lays down a condition of peace, *sine qua non*, for the American people, which, if I am not mistaken, they will never accept—then I say let the Americans prepare for the worst, and prepare in the best manner they can.

I am writing a public letter to the Hon. Mr. Bright, for which his excellent and rational speech at Rochdale has given me a pretext. I hope you will be here again before it is finally committed to the press. I shall publish a couple of thousand copies. Of course it will be written and printed in English, but I have very little doubt that it will be translated and published also in French.*

. . . . . You may be sure that I should prefer to be in New York, attending to the duties of my sacred office; but I consider that the citizen should not be forgotten in the title of archbishop.

Please present my respects to Mr. Adams (at the same time apologize for my intrusion at an hour when he was so engaged), as well as my thanks for his kindness in leaving his guests to receive me. Kindest respects to your good daughter. Mr. McNeirny enjoys himself occasionally in turning your excellent cigars into smoke and vanity, but the champagne has not been touched yet.

I remain, etc.

TO SECRETARY SEWARD.

PARIS, *December*, 1861.

In Ireland a war against the United States will be very unpopular among the classes that furnished troops for the Crimea, India, and China. Springs of communication have already been touched, which will render such a strife yet more odious in their estimation.

As to France, it does not seem to have any political parties at the present day. Heretofore, France, on questions of this kind, meant scarcely more than the city of Paris. At present, the politics of this gallant nation are neither France nor Paris, but the brain of the Emperor. He is wise in his generation. I have reason to think that whatever may be his entanglements of alliance with Great Britain, he is not hostile to the United States.

TO THE SAME.

PARIS, *December* 12, 1861.

I have not yet had my audience of the Emperor; but I expect it within a few days. Opportunities of much intercourse with distinguished and influential men, from different parts of France, have been afforded me by the private hospitality of this great capital. The Legislative Body is now convoked. His Eminence the Archbishop of Paris has invited me to dine with him on next Tuesday,

---

* This letter was not published.

to meet the other Cardinals of the Empire, who are *ex officio* members of the Senate. If I am not deceived, the feelings of what we would call "the people," are in this country far from being opposed to the attitude which the United States have taken in reference to pending difficulties. But the tone of the papers here does not indicate any warm national friendship. They half echo the sentiments of the London journals, and ours seldom reach them. There is a wide-spread ignorance of the state of affairs in our country, both among the journals and among the gentlemen whom I have had the pleasure of meeting. At the same time, so far as the latter are concerned, there appears to be a desire to know the real state of the case, whether as regards our domestic difficulties or the recent and threatening troubles with Great Britain.

TO THE SAME.

Paris, *Dec.* 27, 1861.

My dear Governor:

By appointment of the Emperor and Empress, I had an audience on last Tuesday, which lasted one hour and ten minutes, and during which I had an opportunity of saying all that I thought it expedient to say in connection with our domestic strife, and in relation to the apprehension of foreign interference on the part of England, as well as to make known the good dispositions and good intentions which the American people always entertained toward France. Memoranda of the conversation I have written down. But it will be time enough to show it to you when I return to America. I may say that nothing could be more kind and gracious than the manner of my reception, and the ease with which the conversation was supported on all sides. The result was entirely satisfactory and encouraging to me. I have no idea that France will unite with England in an assault upon the United States. Neither do I believe that she will interfere in the quarrel with the South, especially if the purpose of the Government when I left Washington can be carried out.

The whole of that purpose was suggested vaguely to his Majesty, who, by the by, must have been already acquainted with it through another channel. I took it upon myself to implore the Emperor to use his good offices in preventing a rupture between England and

America, by the interposition of his kind and potent offices as a mediator. To this he replied in a way which I had not thought of. He expressed his good wishes, but mentioned that in this matter he "could not act as arbitrator, because, whilst it would be competent for him, if invited by the parties, to assume that office on questions of a material kind, such as deciding upon disputed boundaries, yet as things now stand, it is not a question of boundaries or the like, but it would be determining a *point of honor*, arbitration on which between two such nations would not be perhaps satisfactory to either."

We conversed very freely on the whole question of our present difficulties, in all of which her Imperial Majesty the Empress took great interest, and no small part in the discussion. They brought in the young prince to see me. He is a charming child.

I have had every day, more or less, an opportunity of explaining our whole situation of affairs to gentlemen the most intimately acquainted with and most nearly related to the administration of this Government. It is quite difficult, in some cases, to make them understand the actual position of our affairs. Among these gentlemen were senators and secretaries of the Government. They seemed anxious to understand better than I could explain. I mentioned the admirable discourse of Mr. Everett, delivered in New York last Fourth of July. One of them suggested to me that it would be well received in this country if translated into French, and published. This I am more than half inclined to have done. I had written a general explanation to the same effect. I do not deem it expedient, however, to publish it at this time. But Mr. Everett's discourse is at once so accurate in its statements, so lucid in its argument, and so eloquent withal, that, published in classical French, it will be much sought after, and very generally read by the people of France, but especially by the Parisians.

I remain, &c.

P. S. I owe my introduction to the Emperor, not to any kind encouragement or patronage of our people on this side, but to determination that even their "cold shoulder" should not prevent me from a purpose which I had entertained; so I wrote to him, as one man would write to another, in a polite and brief note to the effect: "Sir, I wish to have the honor of a conversation with you."

The following is the memorandum of the interview with their Majesties to which the archbishop alludes above:

CONVERSATION BETWEEN ARCHBISHOP HUGHES AND THE EMPEROR AND EMPRESS OF THE FRENCH, AT THE TUILERIES, DEC. 24, 1861.

Emperor.—Monseigneur, you left America in a very unsettled condition; and now there are new troubles between England and America.

Archbishop.—Yes, Sire, America has its own domestic strife, and this that is now spoken of with England is much to be regretted. Your Majesty is the only man in Europe, or out of it, that could bring these difficulties, whether internal or foreign, to an end, without bloodshed. Being a bishop, it is not out of keeping with my character to pray and even plead for peace.

Emperor.—But how could I be useful in such a state of things?

Archbishop.—Your Majesty could employ your kind and potential influence as a mediator or arbitrator between two nations that ought to stand well toward each other, but are now apparently on the brink of a sanguinary struggle. If we can judge the purposes of the British cabinet, according to what we read in the English newspapers, the Americans are called upon, under unconditional menace, requiring them to give up two prisoners, now in their country, or else meet all the consequences and horrors of war. Your Majesty knows that the Americans are, or think they are, derived from an English, or rather Anglo-Saxon origin, and they are as proud as their British ancestors ever were.

Emperor.—But, Monseigneur, it is precisely on that account that my mediation would be useless and inexpedient. If the dispute turned on some material basis, such as determining boundaries, or the like, I might be able to effect something toward preserving peace. But the present difficulty seems to me to turn upon a *point of honor* between two nations equally proud, as you have said; and when nations find themselves in such a position relatively to each other, each usually judges of its own sense of duty; so that arbitration of a third party would not be acceptable to either.

Archbishop.—Still, Sire, the manifestation of your wish in favor of peace could not but be beneficial. And though I have no right to speak for America, I am still confident enough in regard to the

30

result, to believe that the American people would agree to any decision which your Majesty might come to, and not feel in the least humbled in abiding by it, although they will be disposed to resent from the British ministry any conditions that will be laid down in the form of a menace.

Empress.—Monseigneur, what kind of a passage had you across the ocean ! Travellers say that it is but a trifle now.

Archbishop.—Imperial lady, I am an old sailor. Considering the season of the year, the passage was very pleasant, but a little tedious —having been thirteen days, instead of eleven, the ordinary time.

Emperor.—Are you long in Europe, Monseigneur !

Archbishop.—Just four weeks. I spent two days in England, and have been here in Paris since then.

Emperor.—Did you see General Scott !

Archbishop.—Yes, Sire.

Emperor.—I should have been glad to see him, for I knew him in America many years ago.

Empress.—They say that he has returned to America to advise peace, but I fear that his arrival may be too late.

Archbishop.—Your Majesty, he will advise, no doubt, whatever he may think consistent with the honor of his native country, to which he has devoted successfully half a century of military service.

Emperor.—I cannot help thinking that the Northern portion of the United States have made a mistake in the high figure of their tariff on foreign importations; and that, it seems to me, is one of their causes of discontent in the South.

Archbishop.—Sire, the radical causes existed before the tariff; and, besides, it must have escaped your Majesty's memory that the South was the first to obtain protection from the Federal Government by the way of tariff.

Emperor.—How is that !

Archbishop.—The first cotton in the United States was introduced from the West India islands. As soon as it was found suitable, the South demanded and obtained a tariff of protection, amounting to three cents per pound on any further importations of cotton. As an American production, it was then very feeble; but in a short time it became important enough to authorize an export duty on American vessels, placing it on the same level with molasses, sugar, and cocoa.

Emperor.—How is it cultivated?

Archbishop.—Your Majesty, I am not an inhabitant of the South, but I know that, by the process of cleansing and separating the fibre from the seed, there is enough of the seed left for planting purposes; and, in addition to other material of the same kind, the surplus seed is found to be an excellent fertilizer of the cotton-fields. By the by, I have an idea of visiting Algeria, for the purpose of seeing how the new industry of raising cotton is carried on.

Emperor.—Oh, you will not see much in Algeria. Whatever may be the advantages of the climate, we have not the practical science among the cultivators which success would require.

Archbishop.—Still, Sire, the beginning of its cultivation in America was small, and for a time discouraging, as the tariff of protection would seem to indicate. And I think that, for the benefit of the world and for the peace of America, it would be well if both England and France should encourage the growth of cotton in their respective colonies, and contrive to blend it, for manufacturing purposes, with the superior samples of cotton grown in the United States.

(*A pause.*)

Emperor.—How has the civil war broken out so unexpectedly between the two sections of the country?

Archbishop.—Your Majesty, it would be impossible for me to even allude to all the causes or occasions of discontent in the South, without trespassing on time which is so precious to France and to the world.

Emperor.—Proceed.

Archbishop.— .   .   .   .

Empress.—How can that blockade be sustained along so extensive a coast? It cannot last. Napoleon I. had that topic in his mind during the war with England; and, with all his immense capacity, he gave it up as impracticable.

Archbishop.—Imperial lady, if Napoleon I. had been acquainted, for maritime purposes, with the power of steam and the velocity of electric communication by telegraph, his dynasty would not have suffered an interruption; and where England would be at this day, under such circumstances, it would be hazardous to say.

* * * * *

[About this time the Prince Imperial was introduced. He is an exceedingly interesting boy; his features composed of a blending of intelligence, with goodness and exceeding modesty. His imperial mother presented him to me, and asked my blessing for him. This I gave with a full and good heart, and its wishes found expression at my lips: "God bless you, my good boy, and preserve you; so that when you shall have grown up to be a man, you may be able, under the divine benediction, to realize the good hopes that are entertained in your regard, not only by your own country, but by many other nations."]

TO MRS. RODRIGUE.

Paris, *Dec.* 27, 1861.

MY DEAR SISTER:

My health, thank God, is better since I arrived here. Sulphur baths have done good. Rheumatism diminishing.—Much association with prelates, and with what the world would call great men in this city.—Audience of the Emperor on last Tuesday, during an hour and ten minutes.—Empress present and taking part in the conversation.—Brought in the Prince Imperial to receive my episcopal benediction.—Charming boy, reflecting the beautiful, and yet more sweet than beautiful countenance of his mother.—Shyness on the part of some to introduce me.—Wrote myself, although a stranger, for audience.—Immediately granted, in a note from the Emperor, and another from the Empress.—Must remain yet for some days in this capital.—Then Rome.—Then I know not whither.

* * * * *

TO SECRETARY SEWARD.

Paris, *Jan.* 3, 1862.

* * * *

The last news from America is very agreeable to me, and I think very surprising to the John Bulls and other people on this side.

They would seem to have imagined that on the reception of Palmerston's ultimatum all America would have been shaken up as by the heave of an earthquake. Now they find that America smokes its pipe calmly, disregards threats, and at the same time says: "We will do what is right, if you have common patience and common sense; but if you have neither, then we say, *Try it.*"

. . . . .

I pray, every night and morning, for peace between the two countries. . . . . But all with whom I have occasion to converse, know perfectly well that I have no fear or apprehension of the result even in case of war.

TO THE SAME.

PARIS, *Jan.* 11, 1862.

MY DEAR GOVERNOR:

The good news has just reached us that there is to be no war, at least for the present, between the United States and Great Britain.

I am also very proud in believing that the difficulty has been adjusted on terms that are rather honorable than otherwise to our country. The English press makes the most of the case in its own favor. But the tone here, except among the secessionists, is all that could be wished in connection with the result. The course of your Government has turned the scale of sympathy in your favor. The decision is not ascribed to any lowering of national dignity on the part of America, but rather to the quiet but conscious magnanimity of a people who could sustain their cause, but who prefer to economize human blood and turn aside the horrors of war by a generous and just decision. So far, I think, America has gained and England has lost the sympathy of reflecting men in this capital, in consequence of the news that has just been received.

But, my dear Governor, that awful war, between England and America, must come sooner or later. And in preparing for it, even now, there is not a moment to be lost. Our Government has enough on its hands for the present, but that very circumstance furnishes an occasion for strengthening all the defences and means of defence which will be found useful, perhaps necessary, in reference to contingent warfare against foreign assailants. Attention, in this capital, will be turned more to our domestic struggle than it has been since the affair of the "Trent" took place; and on that subject, I think the right of the North is becoming daily better understood.

There are some of our loyal men who are getting impatient that nothing greater or more decisive has as yet been accomplished. I am not one of that number; and even from this distance, I would say, that nothing should be left undone to make every contest *a certain victory* for the Union, whether the strife comes sooner or later.

Mr. Weed has been in England working like a beaver for the interests of his country. I have just placed in the hands of Mr. Bigelow a document which will be a preface to the arrival of Mr. Slidell. The subject of it I alluded to in my interview with the Emperor and Empress. It had reference to the forcible acquisition of the Island of Cuba, a subject on which her Imperial Majesty is naturally sensitive. Whether and how Mr. Bigelow can make a telling use of it, I do not know. But it has such a connection with the present secession, that it ought to be efficient for good.

TO THE SAME.

PARIS, *Feb.* 1, 1862.

I have had no encouragement from our officials. But, independent of their patronage, I have had, as you may suppose, the entrée to the best society in Paris, as an American bishop. At dinners and soirées, it has come up invariably, that the company, either before, or during, or after dinner, referred to me for an explanation of the civil war that is now existing between the two sections of our once United States. I did explain, as well as I could—perfectly satisfied that whatever I said would reach the ears of one or another of the ministers within twenty-four hours after its utterance. Besides, during my interview with the Emperor, I felt no hesitation in stating what none of his ministers would venture to say. I might almost add that, on the same occasion, I had the effrontery even to give advice. It is generally thought that certain men are above being influenced. This is a mistake. If there ever was a man of such a type, it would be General Jackson; and yet, whilst General Jackson would disregard, under certain circumstances, the opinion of his whole cabinet, General Jackson might take up and reflect upon a phrase uttered by the barber who shaved him.

At all events, I think we might have fared worse in France than we have done.

Several of the bishops from districts that are suffering, owing to the interruption of trade with America, called upon me as they successively arrived in Paris. To them also I had an opportunity of relating the state of the case. For the most part, they came to see the Emperor on the following day, and to expose to his Imperial Majesty the state of destitution in which their poor people were suffering. Whether they made known to the Emperor the views which I communicated or not, I have no means of ascertaining; but at all events, I thought it no harm to make them acquainted with the substance of the despatch, a copy of which you were kind enough to confide to me for private use.

I have just received your kind letter of January 9th. I am glad that the President does not deem it useful or necessary for me to execute the purpose which I had conceived only on the hypothesis that it might be useful to the country. By the by, in speaking of the President, I may be allowed to say, that in this country at least, he is winning golden opinions for his calm, unostentatious, mild, but firm and energetic administrative talents.

I intend to leave next Monday for a short visit to Rome. After that I shall have to visit Ireland in consequence of invitations from that country, and for reasons of my own. From Ireland I shall sail for home as soon as the severe winter months are over.

Believe me, etc.

On his arrival in Liverpool, in November, the archbishop had accepted an invitation to preach at the laying of the corner-stone of the Catholic University in Dublin during the coming summer. This was one of his reasons for wanting to visit Ireland; but the American Government had also hinted that it would be well for him to pass through that country on his way home. Probably the administration foresaw that he would be enthusiastically received in his native land, and that the Irish would manifest a sympathy toward the United States which would make the British cabinet especially careful to avoid a war with this country.

During his stay in Paris he preached several times before large congregations in the church of St. Roch. On the 30th of December he dined at the Irish College, with the Archbishops of Abyssinia and Peking, and a number of Irish bishops; and in the evening appeared in his episcopal garb at the American consul's, where he received great attention from a large and brilliant company.

TO SECRETARY SEWARD.

On board the "Visuvio," *Feb.* 11, 1862.

My dear Governor:

Just entering the harbor of Civita Vecchia—a terrible passage from Marseilles—sixty-four hours, instead of thirty-three. I write in order to post this time enough for next Saturday's steamer. Nothing new since I last wrote, except that the tone of intelligent Frenchmen is immensely changed in our favor. I have reason to think that the same has taken place to a great extent among English as well as Frenchmen. The Emperor has a small pique in his mind about the opportunity that has been afforded to the striplings of the Orleans branch, by which they may chance to distinguish themselves in the American army, and thus prevent their names from being forgotten in France and in England.

I think this has been, to some extent, at the bottom of the Emperor's thoughts in reference to our present difficulties. But he has got over even this, although he will not forget it.

How long I shall stay in Rome I cannot say. I will see the Spanish ambassador, and if the result of an interview should be the accomplishment of my purpose, I shall not proceed further. But if it should not be all that I wish, I will drop down in a week or two to Alicante and Madrid by steamer and railway. In Madrid I shall see "the O'Donnell," and leave nothing unexplained to advise him that any recognition of the would-be Southern republic in the United States could not but jeopard the interests of her Catholic Majesty's colonies in the West Indies.

．　　　．　　　．　　　．　　　．　　　．

TO THE SAME.

Rome, *Feb.* 21, 1862.

I have had a most cordial and flattering reception in this capital among the civil and ecclesiastical magnates, from the Pope downward. The Holy Father has been particularly kind. He and Antonelli both speak of you with kind remembrance and with great respect. By the by, I was on the point of getting into a little quarrel with another Cardinal, who praised you, I will not say too much, but apparently at the expense of the President. This did not suit me, and I remonstrated by saying that, in my opinion, there has been no President of the United States more capable, more honest, more moderate, more safe and reliable, than the actual incumbent who is now at the head of the country. I may have said this with some indications of warmth, as repelling what I considered a very unjust appreciation of our chief magistrate. But the difficulty grew out of a *mal entendu.* I heard, according to my English ears, "President," whilst the good Cardinal intended to say "*le précédent;*" and as soon as the equivoque was explained, we had a hearty laugh at each other.

The object which I hoped to accomplish if I went to Spain, can be as well accomplished here in Rome; and I shall see to it, with or without further instructions, for I consider that Spain has the deepest interest in supporting the United States as they were, and as in a short time I hope to see them again. Spain will not be ruined, perhaps, but extremely perplexed, if by any calamity the Southern portion of our country should be recognized as a separate and independent state. I have felt my way on this subject, and am satisfied that Spain at least will keep out of any such absurd recognition.

A new topic has come on the tapis here, unconnected with the political schemes of nations. It is that the Holy Father has appointed the 8th of June, the day of Pentecost, for the canonization of a number of glorious martyrs who, in the time of St. Francis Xavier, underwent cruel tortures and death itself for the profession of the Christian faith. The Pope has, by a circular letter to all the bishops of Christendom, invited them to be present on that solemn occasion. The invitation is qualified, and applies only to those who can absent themselves from their dioceses without great inconvenience, or injury to the interests of religion. Many will unquestionably be here from different countries. I have preferred, being now on this side of the Atlantic, to remain, rather than go home and return within so brief an interval. In the mean time, I have not forgotten that, being already on the spot, I shall have occasion, not even of my own seeking, to give a true explanation of the troubles in America, and imbue the minds of those who may listen to me, from different states, with at least correct notions.

* * * * *

TO THE SAME.

Rome, *March* 1, 1862.

* * * *

You will hardly be surprised to learn that, on my arrival here, I found communications from some of my episcopal brethren, not precisely censuring me, but yet complaining of my acceptance of any commission from the Government of our country, on the ground that it was, or might be, offensive or injurious to some of our Catholic brethren placed in circumstances of great embarrassment. I explained the whole matter to the Holy Father and to Cardinals Antonelli and Barnabo. I am happy to say that they all approved of my conduct, and, instead of censuring me, showed a disposition to confer additional honors.

* * * * *

TO THE SAME.

Rome, *March* 29, 1862.

* * * *

Yesterday I received the New York "World" of the 7th inst. I regard the President's message, which it contains, as the most wise, judicious, and I will add, political movement that has been elicited during the war up to this time. It is the combination of moderate and just policy with external evidence of military power, which must bring back reflection to the heated minds of Southern demagogues.

In my only conversation with Cardinal Antonelli, who understands the American system perfectly well, I spoke of your kind dispositions and words of good will toward the Pontifical Government. I mentioned an observation which you made to me in Washington, viz., that in the course of events resulting from the contest at home, it might be in the power of the American Government to be of service to the cause of the Holy See. He expressed himself much satisfied with your kindness, but remarked that he did not see how it would be possible. I said, in reply, that the only way in which it could be useful would be in directing our representatives abroad to be cautious of uttering speeches in favor of crude efforts at revolution in Europe. By the by, your predecessors in office I think encouraged the opposite system more than was expedient either for Europe or America. We have now on hand an experiment such as our people had too hastily recommended to other states, and this alone would be a sufficient reason for our foreign ministers and representatives to deal fairly with the courts or governments to which they may be accredited in Europe, without stimulating insurrection anywhere.

Nothing but the distance which separates me from New York and Washington could be an excuse for inflicting upon you so long and so uninteresting a letter as this. But it gives me another opportunity of saying that I am, at home and abroad,

Your devoted friend and servant,

✠ JOHN, *Abp. of New York.*

The archbishop lodged at the American College during his stay in Rome. He was visited by throngs of notables, and obtained a better insight into the society of the papal capital than he had ever enjoyed before. An American gentleman, who called upon him at the college, was ushered into the reception-room, and there found the archbishop being shaved. "To be sure," says this gentleman, "it was all very well to receive one of his countrymen in that democratic fashion: but if Cardinal Antonelli had called, his Eminence would have been introduced just as I was." The city contained an unusual number of strangers from all parts of Europe, many of whom had come to witness the approaching ceremony of canonization. The archbishop lost no opportunity of conversing with them upon the American war.

"With ladies," he writes, "either of the South or of the North, I do not discuss it; though one lady announced here that during a brief interview she had converted me to the Southern side. I pity them, ladies especially, and I do not discuss except to console them with the idea that their private interests will be honorably and conscientiously attended to." In another letter he says: "A Roman gentleman told me a few days ago that the Southern Catholics who happened to be here, hold me responsible for having prevented France and England from coming to the aid and support of their cause. My answer was, 'I hope the accusation is true.'"

He took part in a great many ecclesiastical ceremonies, and on one accasion officiated at the devotion of the stations of the cross in the Colosseum, when he was followed by no fewer than four or five thousand pilgrims.

TO SECRETARY SEWARD.

Rome, *April* 18, 1862.

My dear Governor:

This is, as you know, an exceptional week in the Eternal City. The functions are solemn and profoundly touching to those who understand them, in commemoration of the passion and various sufferings of Jesus Christ, undergone for the redemption of the world.

These offices of the Church I have attended during the whole week, almost by the side of the Holy Father, in my capacity of an archbishop assisting, as it is called, at the pontifical throne.

I have no particular observation to make with regard to the circumstances on account of which I find myself here at this time. But leaving wars and rumors of wars to regulate themselves as God will permit, *this hour* seems to me appropriate for expressing the deep sympathy which I have felt, since the news reached me, with the President and his amiable lady, in the death of their beloved son. Please convey to his Excellency this sincere tribute of my heart and feelings, and believe me, as ever, my dear Governor,

Your devoted friend and servant,

✠ John, *Abp. Bishop of New York.*

TO MRS. RODRIGUE.

Rome, *April* 4, 1862.

The physician of the house [the American College] has taken me in charge; and to-morrow I am to have a supply of sulphur-water from the baths of Tivoli, which, I think, together with the warm weather, will drive out the rheumatism, at least for the present season.

I do not like to describe, and I am sure you will not like to read, of the attentions that are paid to me by dukes, princes, cardinals, marquises, and I believe I mentioned before, by the Holy Father himself. These are as numerous and as distinguished as if I could trace back my genealogy to the fourteenth century, like her ladyship of Havana.* Castle Angelo is quite as great a lion as the Moro, and Pius IX. is more of a captain-general than Concha; so that, all things taken into consideration, Margaret has nothing to boast over me— except the masked balls, which I care nothing about.

TO THE SAME.

Rome, *April* 25, 1862.

For the last two or three weeks I have been taking sulphur baths occasionally, here in the college. The water is brought from Tivoli, about twenty miles distant, in small barrels, four of which make a comfortable bath. The water is heated in the bath by inserting a vessel of charcoal, with tubes to keep up a draught, and give vent to the gas. They have done me a great deal of good, but I find them, especially in this hot weather, weakening in their effect.

TO THE SAME.

Rome, *May* 9, 1862.

The time is now fast approaching for the canonization of the Japanese martyrs, twenty-six in all. There is great religious excitement in St. Peter's, and all through the city. It is now calculated that there will be over a hundred bishops from foreign countries present on the occasion of the solemnity. I never was present on

---

* An allusion to the character assumed by his niece at a masquerade in Havana.

such an occasion, but I suppose it will be one of the most solemn that has taken place in Rome within the last two hundred years. There will be a procession of the clergy, bishops, archbishops, and cardinals, around the whole piazza of St. Peter's, the procession closing with the Holy Father, bearing relics of those martyrs.

The Pope is well. I have met him by chance on several occasions, and he always recognizes me in the crowd, and has some kind word to say to me; but, as I have no special business, I have not intruded on his time after the first interview.

TO SISTER ANGELA.

Rome, *May* 16, 1862.

. . . . .

I have been out almost every day since I arrived in Rome, but always in a carriage. It is not that I would not be able to walk a reasonable distance on level ground; but to mount five to eight flights of stairs, in order to return a visit, would be more than I could accomplish, owing to that same rheumatism which, as you say, has not yet forsaken me. Happily, however, visits are usually returned here by leaving cards on the person to whom they are due. The warm weather has not brought the improvement that I had expected during the damp weather of the early spring months. In all other respects I may say I am perfectly well.

It would be idle for me to attempt any description of Rome or its population at the present time. Bishops of all the nations of the earth, I may say, have already arrived, and others are on their way, for the great solemnity of Pentecost. The Holy Father is in good health, and keeps up his heart and determination with immense fortitude and courage. What is now and is to be before the bishops separate, you must wait to see in the newspapers first, or in a deliberate volume afterward.

. . . . .

The canonization of the martyrs of Japan took place on the 10th of June, in the presence of two hundred and ninety and odd cardinals and bishops. Immediately afterward the archbishop made his preparations for departure.

TO SECRETARY SEWARD.

ROME, *June* 12, 1862.

MY DEAR GOVERNOR :

This will be my last letter from Rome. I have seen on the present occasion but little of this wonderful city, partly because I had seen much of it before, still more because I have been scarcely a day free from rheumatism since my arrival. Still I have not been disabled from having constant and general intercourse with the multitude of distinguished foreigners who have continued to arrive here during the last three months. I have lost no occasion (and indeed occasions were not wanting) to make known to them the true situation of our affairs. They begin to understand that there is no equality between the rights and the physical powers of the two contending parties, and that therefore the strife must soon come to an end. . . . . . .

I shall leave here on next Sunday for Marseilles. Thence, without stopping, to Lyons again. Thence to Aix-les-Bains, where I shall stay for a week or ten days, to ascertain whether the waters and treatment at that place may not help to drive out the rheumatism from my hip-joints, my knees, and ankles. From Aix-les-Bains I shall go to Paris. From Paris I am still tempted, even without instructions, to go to Madrid. The interests of Spain, connected with or likely to grow out of our civil war, I have made known to the Spanish minister here, and to the two newly-created Spanish cardinals. The minister thinks that the O'Donnell government would be much obliged if I would make known to them personally, and by documents in my possession, the real situation of affairs as regards Spanish interests in the Antilles. If I should go, my stay will be very short. I shall then go immediately to London, where (I have reason to believe) the premier and foreign secretary would like much to have a conversation with me.

From London I go to Dublin, by general invitation of the Irish bishops, to pronounce a discourse on occasion of laying the cornerstone of the new Catholic University. A large number of these bishops have been here for the last three weeks. They take a deep interest in our troubles. They look upon the United States as the benevolent friend of their country and of their countrymen, whether in the United States or in their own Ireland. At Dublin they will be present in large numbers, and, as opportunity offers, I shall have something to say in strengthening their sympathies and the sympathies of the people in our just cause.

From Ireland I shall steer directly for New York, hoping to be back again with my flock on the feast of the Assumption of the Blessed Virgin Mary—15th of August.

✠ JOHN, *Abp. of New York.*

P. S. Since the above was written, I have had the pleasure of knowing that both Cardinal Antonelli and the Holy Father himself have been much pleased, and so expressed themselves to me, with our new minister, Mr. Randall. The Pope particularly, recognizing me in the crowd among the bishops in the Pontifical garden, took occasion to turn aside and say that he was much pleased with the American minister. Mr. Randall's reception at the Roman court has been all that his friends could desire.

TO MRS. RODRIGUE.

AIX-LES-BAINS, SAVOY, June 25, 1862.

MY DEAR SISTER :

I arrived at this place on my return from Rome this day week. The waters have done me an immense good already, and I intend to remain ten days more. I cannot yet say, with any precision, whether I shall arrive before the middle or toward the end of August.

Kindest remembrance to all friends. Father McNeirny and John * are well.

Your affectionate brother,

✠ JOHN, *Abp. of New York.*

He did not go to Madrid. He spent a little while in England, and then proceeded to Dublin, to fulfil his promise of preaching on the occasion of the laying of the corner-stone of the Catholic University. The ceremony took place on Sunday, the 20th of July, in the presence of an enormous

---

* John Regan, his amanuensis.

concourse of people. The sermon was pronounced at high mass in the cathedral: it was from the text, "Woe to you, lawyers, for you have taken away the key of knowledge; you yourselves have not entered in, and those that were entering in you have hindered."—*St. Luke* xi. 52. After mass, a procession was formed and moved to the University grounds. Archbishop Hughes was assigned the place of honor, and at the close of the ceremony delivered a short address. In the evening a banquet was given by the University to the distinguished guests, the municipal authorities, and others. The archbishop was everywhere greeted with unbounded enthusiasm. He remained about a week in Dublin, receiving addresses and deputations, accepting public and private hospitalities, and making speeches, in which he alluded, with very little reserve, to the wrongs and sufferings of Ireland, and the tyranny of the British Government. Speaking of the conduct of England toward the United States, he made the following remark at a meeting in the Dublin Rotundo:

I tell you, gentlemen, that even if peace was restored to the whole country of America to-morrow, the people would scarcely unbelt themselves until they had put other questions right. They feel sore; they feel that their national dignity has been attacked; that in the moment of their trial and of their difficulty, an ungenerous attack was made on them, and they have unfortunately treasured up the memory of that attack with a feeling of revenge.

This was loudly cheered; but what follows was received with extraordinary manifestations of delight:

There is another thing. The Irish, besides discharging what they consider their duty to their own legitimate government—and they are ever loyal, if you give them the opportunity—besides that, the Irish have, in many instances, as I have the strongest reasons for knowing, entered into this war partly to make themselves apprentices, students as it were, finishing their education in this, the first

31

opportunity afforded them of becoming thoroughly acquainted with the implements of war.

A friend in Rome writes to him of the effect of his exertions:

Your work in Ireland can never be forgotten in America; and England can never pardon you. I know they are writing from every quarter against you; but you stand on the rock of truth and justice. I love you more than ever. You have nothing to dread. The Cardinal Barnabo gave a full account of the demonstration in Dublin to the Pope last Thursday. He was much pleased with it.

On the eve of his departure from Dublin a deputation of "Nationalists of Ireland" waited upon him with a complimentary address, to which he replied in a few patriotic words. He understood that his visitors represented the town of Nenagh, in Tipperary. He was afterward informed that the address emanated from a secret political society called the Brotherhood of St. Patrick—something akin to the Fenians. "They are boasting," said his informant, "of the great success they obtained in their interview with you. These Brothers are very few in Dublin, but they are now flushed with the hope of increasing their numbers, under the pretence of having obtained your approbation. Through the medium of the newspapers over which they have command, they will do a great deal of mischief among the poor people." Now the archbishop had always been a determined enemy of secret societies. He felt that he had been entrapped into a seeming departure from his long-cherished principles—that these Nationalists had endeavored to make a tool of him. He was indignant; and on his arrival at Cork, where he spent a day or two as the guest of Mr. John Francis Maguire, mayor of the city and editor of the *Cork Examiner*, he wrote a public letter, explaining the circumstances connected with the presentation of the address, and rebuking the authors of it very severely. Several members of the deputation replied to him; and after his return to New York, he prepared another letter on the subject, which he sent to Mr. Maguire, with the following note:

TO MR. MAGUIRE, CORK.

Nov. 24, 1862.

MY DEAR MR. MAGUIRE:

Had it not been for the *gaucherie* of what I call the Nenagh deputation in Dublin, I should have written to you long since in acknowledgment of your personal kindness and hospitality during my brief stay in Cork. I should have acknowledged the pleasure afforded me under your roof in meeting so many gentlemen of your city. I assure you I have forgotten nothing that eye or ear could have taken during my brief stay at your villa.

. . . . . .

I am about to send you for publication in the *Cork Examiner* an *exposé* of the un-Irish treatment which I received at the hands of the Nenagh deputation. I shall affix my name to the document in manuscript, and I request of you that it shall be published in your paper, without any change of phrase, or word, or sentence. I know that this precaution is unnecessary, for I am certain that you and your journal are upright and honorable in all matters affecting truth, justice, and a decent respect for personal character.

I read, partly on the voyage, and partly since my return home, the improved edition of your work on Rome.* I must confess that I have not been able to appreciate its improvement upon or over the first edition; but this I can say, that whilst I have a library of some 10,000 volumes, there is not one volume, especially emanating from a writer of the present generation, which I hold so precious as yours.

. . . . . .

TO ARCHBISHOP CULLEN, DUBLIN.

NEW YORK, Dec. 5, 1862.

MY DEAR LORD:

It is very late for me to acknowledge the receipt of your letter, dated August 9th; but after so long an absence, business of every

---

* "Rome; its Ruler and its Institutions. By John Francis Maguire."

description had accumulated to such an extent that I have been engaged in arranging matters that had fallen into arrears during my absence.

You will perceive by the *Cork Examiner* that I have analyzed and taken apart the whole fabric of that un-Irish cheat which was broached to me as the Nenagh deputation. I have no feeling on the subject, except that of regret that there should still survive in Ireland persons capable of playing me such a trick. But whilst I have not spared them, my object in writing has been to put myself right in the estimation of the good Catholics of Ireland. As for the persons who treated me so disrespectfully in Dublin, I have toward them neither respect nor resentment. They are indifferent to me. But though a bishop should be humble and forbearing, he is not bound to be trampled upon by virtue of his humility.

I bore with the insult offered to me in Dublin (although I do not think it was intended as an insult) long enough. You will see in the *Cork Examiner* that I have expressed myself fully on this subject, and henceforward I shall never allude to it in writing or otherwise.

I remain, my dear lord,
 Your grace's most obedient servant
  and brother in Christ,
   ✠ JOHN, *Abp. of New York.*

TO BISHOP McNALLY, CLOGHER.

NEW YORK, *March* 20, 1863.

MY DEAR LORD:

I received your favor of January 14th, 1863. I need not dilate on its contents. My little contribution of £50 sterling toward the wants of your diocese, and in the first place those of my own kindred who are most in need, is still in reserve, and may be relied upon. But the atrocities of exchange are such as I shall not submit to.

If I did not visit the north during my recent and probably final visit to Ireland, it was because time did not allow of it. If I had not been restricted by time to meet my engagements at Queenstown for the steamer, I should certainly have been with you. The little annoyance that occurred to me in Dublin by the midnight clique, calling themselves afterward "Nationalists of Ireland," would have been avoided if I had gone with you; but my position did not permit it, as I thought at the time, and so I must bear the consequences without repining. But my countrymen did not treat me well on that occasion. I forgive the country, but I can hardly overlook the misconduct of the fellows who attempted to utilize me.

I am afraid to inquire about those of my relatives who are probably still living, nor shall I now go into the subject. The only thing is, that if circumstances should permit me to place at your disposal the amount already specified, trifling as it is, you will have the kindness to think that among the poorest my relatives should not be overlooked.

I have the honor to be

Your most obedient servant,

✠ JOHN, *Abp. of New York.*

On the 31st of July the citizens of Cork entertained the archbishop at dinner. Two or three days afterward he sailed from Queenstown in the Scotia, and on the 12th of August he reached New York. His return home was celebrated by his fellow-citizens of all denominations. The municipal authorities presented him with congratulatory addresses. The week after his arrival he went to Washington:

I arrived on Thursday evening; saw Mr. Seward, and had a brief conversation with him. He invited me to dinner the next day. I reminded him that it was Friday, and not a good day for a banquet. He said: "Never mind; I shall see that you will be provided for." He invited his company to meet me—secretaries, generals, and other distinguished gentlemen: and, to my astonishment, there was not a particle of meat on the table for any one. This was in compliment to myself, and in fact what I consider the most delicate compliment I have ever received.

How much the archbishop may have done for the country by his voyage to Europe, can only be conjectured. The government at Washington seemed, at any rate, to have no mean idea of the importance of his services. An official intimation was conveyed to the Holy See that the President, unable to offer Dr. Hughes a reward that he could accept, would feel particular gratification in any honors which the Pope might have it in his power to confer upon him. It would appear, from a passage in one of the archbishop's letters from Rome, quoted a few pages back, that his Holiness did contemplate advancing him in dignity. Indeed, I believe that he was much nearer the cardinal's hat in 1862 than in 1851.

CHAPTER XXVII.

1862–1864.

Sermon on the war—Displeasure of the Archbishop's Southern friends—Controversy with *The Catholic Mirror*—Letters to Father Smith—New seminary at Troy—Declining health—Daily life—Meeting for the relief of Ireland—Last sermon—Death of Archbishop Kenrick—Draft riot in New York—The Archbishop's speech to the mob—Last sickness—Death—Funeral—Conclusion.

The next Sunday after his return from Washington the archbishop delivered a discourse before a crowded audience in the cathedral. He spoke of the object of his journey abroad, and described the state of feeling which prevailed in Europe toward the United States. He urged the people to put forth all their strength, and finish the war by one great effort. He commended the President's recent call and draft of six hundred thousand men. "If I had a voice in the councils of the country," said he, "I would say, let volunteering continue; if the three hundred thousand on your list be not enough this week, next week make a draft of three hundred thousand more. It is not cruel, this. This is mercy; this is humanity. Any thing that will put an end to this drenching with blood the whole surface of the country, that will be humanity. . . . . It is not necessary to hate our enemies. It is not necessary to be cruel in battle, nor to be cruel after its termination. It is necessary to be true, to be patriotic, to do for the country what the country needs, and the blessing of God will recompense those who discharge their duty without faltering, and without violating any of the laws of God or man."

It is hardly necessary to say that some of the half-loyal journals of New-York, and many of the archbishop's old friends in Baltimore and other slave cities, were intensely displeased with this address, as they were indeed with his whole course during the war. The next time he visited Baltimore, many persons who had formerly professed great regard for him, treated him with marked coolness. He felt the change in their sentiments deeply; not only was he always jealous of the good opinion of his friends, but he had a remarkably tender and affectionate heart. The world, which judged him only by his writings, would have been surprised to know how sensitive that apparently severe, sarcastic man, was to every thing like a slight. A Maryland priest, an old friend of the archbishop's, was expressing his feelings about secession and the war at a tea-table in New York, in the summer of 1862, when a distinguished Catholic layman, well known for his devotion to the Union, sprang to his feet, and exclaimed with great excitement: "By Heaven! if you say another word, I will have you sent to Fort Lafayette!" The story was told to the archbishop. Shortly afterward the archbishop, speaking in the presence of this same clergyman of his intention to visit Washington, alluded with feeling to the conduct of his Baltimore friends, and remarked that he felt a great deal of embarrassment about calling upon them as he passed through their city.

"The Archbishop of New York," replied Father ——, "will certainly be received in Baltimore with all respect and courtesy."

Dr. Hughes looked at his friend sharply for a moment, and inquired what he meant.

"I mean," was the answer, "that although I am confident that your station in the Church will be remembered by the people of Baltimore, I am not prepared to say how they will receive the semi-official envoy of Mr. Lincoln."

"Why," said the archbishop in a sad voice, "*you* do not disapprove, do you, of any thing that I have done?"

"Archbishop," rejoined Father ——, half in jest, half in earnest, "I do not see how you could find a confessor to give you absolution during your journey in Europe. I did hope that during this sad contest the Catholic clergy, at least, would have kept their skirts clean from blood."

"If you say another word," interrupted the archbishop, shaking his finger at his friend, with an indescribable expression of humor, "I will have you sent to Fort Lafayette!"

The Catholic Mirror, of Baltimore, attacked Archbishop Hughes with especial severity. He defended himself through *The Metropolitan Record;* and thus originated an acrimonious controversy which continued several months. The archbishop wrote a small volume in explanation and justification of his conduct, but never published it. He also wrote a letter to the Pope on the same subject, but did not send it. A great many letters, however, as well as newspaper articles, against him, were received at Rome. The following is his reply to a friend in that city, who had called his attention to the matter:

The recollections of the past, whether in America, Rome, France, Great Britain, or Ireland, so far as the Archbishop of New York is personally concerned, are quite fresh in my memory. It seems to me that I have been endowed with the almost undesirable faculty of forgetting nothing of importance that occurred during my whole life. Let me say then what I have to say in the following order:

1st. That so far as my conscience can be a guide, I have said, I have done nothing, in Europe or America, which a sense of duty and of zeal for the present and future interests of the Catholic Church in these United States would not warrant, almost demand.

2d. I have made known, by my letter from Liverpool, and by a still fuller letter written in Rome itself, the reasons and motives which induced me to visit Europe at a time when my health was not robust, and at a period of the year when travelling, whether by sea or land, would be rather a trial than a pleasure. In my intercourse with their Eminences the Cardinals, some, understanding all this, approved; others, who did not understand it, expressed no opinion.

3d. (And this part I would pray you to make known to his eminence Cardinal Barnabo, with the expression of my sincere respect.) I would beseech his Eminence and the other princes to do me one favor; and that is, if any charge or accusation, whether in speech or in writing, be made against me, it should be made known to me, that I might have an opportunity to offer an explanation; and if that explanation should prove unsatisfactory to them, then I should have nothing more to say.

4th. You tell me that the impression in Rome has become much more favorable to the cause of the South than of the North since my departure from the Eternal City. Unhappily, the impression in Rome can have very little to do with the ultimate decision of our melancholy civil strife. I have not a word to say which could bias their judgment in favor of the one side or of the other. Neither have I a word to say at the present time by way of vindicating myself from the gossip of more recent visitors, who certainly do not understand the subject upon which they either speak or write.

5th. I shall give an explanation of my sermon in the cathedral in a proximate number of *The Metropolitan Record*, on occasion of reviewing the insolent remarks of the *Courrier des États Unis*; but as no one officially authorized to do so in Rome has called my attention to that subject, it would be premature to enter on a vindication of myself against charges which have not been made known to me.

. . . . .

He defended himself, especially against the injurious comments which had been made upon his remarks in the cathedral respecting drafting, in a public letter to Secretary Seward, dated November 1st, 1862.

TO THE REV. BERNARD SMITH.

NEW YORK, *Oct* 16, 1862.

. . . . .

You can imagine the accumulation of business of every description that had taken place here during my absence, which no one but myself could dispose of. I have been able to get through with this to a very great extent; but still, neither can I enjoy for the present, nor even look forward to enjoying in the future, that kind of repose and leisure with which many bishops in Europe are familiar. As an instance, I gave confirmation, since the beginning of this week, to about fourteen hundred candidates. First, last Sunday, at the church of the Annunciation, in Manhattanville; yesterday, under a tent in Camp Scott, to about four hundred soldiers belonging to the Corcoran Legion. I had sent down ten or twelve zealous clergymen, who employed themselves devotedly for the previous three or four days in preparing those poor men for the sacrament of confirmation. A large proportion of the soldiers had been previously confirmed, and those who received the Holy Communion at early Mass in the same tent were twice as numerous as those who remained to be confirmed. And now I am writing within two hours of the close of what was to me a most consoling ministry—the confirmation of nearly seven hundred children in my own cathedral. The remote preparation was by the Christian Brothers for the boys, and the Sisters of Charity for the little girls. Both were attired in neat and perfectly clean costume—the girls in white, and the boys exhibiting an attitude of piety which twenty years ago it would have been vain to expect on such an occasion.

TO THE SAME.

Dec. 15, 1862.

MY DEAR FATHER SMITH:

I have had, from the middle of October, an attack more serious than usual. Its origin, I think, was from my preaching in the open air, and administering the sacrament of confirmation to some four or five hundred Catholic soldiers who were preparing, in Camp Scott, Staten Island, for the coming struggle of battle.

The war is going on indifferently, but on the whole quite in favor of what you would call the North. There is now in that same North a growing disposition more favorable to the hope of peace; but whether it will end in any thing serious, I am not prepared to say. In the mean time the war is to be continued with, if any thing, increased vigor and determination to conquer. It appears that the South, though quite unequal to maintain the contest, is animated by the same desperate spirit of determined resistance. What it will come to, God only knows. One thing, however, I may say; and that is, that both in the North and in the South, our holy religion has risen, and is still rising, to the first rank in the estimation of the American people.

Whilst all this has been going on, I have plunged into a new and serious enterprise for the promotion of religion in this ecclesiastical province of New York. You will understand it better if I make a few preliminary observations. The Methodist denomination in this country have been looked upon as rather an uneducated and illiterate class. Some twelve or fourteen years ago they determined to rival the other denominations, by founding a great university in the city of Troy, in this State. I am told that their subscription list amounted to half a million dollars. At all events, they purchased a piece of ground on a most beautiful site, called Mount Ida, consisting of thirty-seven acres of land, situated almost in the centre of Troy, and erected upon it an imposing educational building of three hundred and sixty feet front, four stories high, and sixty feet deep, with such architectural adornments of turrets, etc., as their crude notions enabled them to imagine. The building, independent of the ground, cost $197,000. It contains altogether about three hundred rooms for students. There are departments for philosophical experiments, museum, library, and a chapel already furnished, except merely the altar, for the accommodation of six hundred attendants, together with a very good organ, and the remnants of what they called a library, which, of course, if they do not think proper to remove, I shall commit to the flames. I purchased the whole property last week, including furniture, the organ, etc., for $60,000.

It is not in my diocese; it is in that of Bishop McCloskey, of Albany; but it is the central point of my ecclesiastical province, there being a railway from the home of each of my suffragans, as well as from my own, to that central point.

I intend to offer it and make it the provincial seminary of the metropolitan see of New York, to place it under the management of the Sulpitians of Paris, or some other priest-training association that will take charge of it, and maintain it as the ecclesiastical Seminary of the Province of New York, with all the advantages of purchase and prospects that have inured to me.

What will surprise you is, that amidst what in Rome are supposed to be gloomy and melancholy times in New York, trade, commerce, and apparent prosperity of all classes have never been more encouraging than they are to-day. Our colleges under the Jesuits are crammed with students; ditto the convents. The Sacred Hearts, the Sisters of Charity, the Ursulines, the Sisters of Notre Dame, the Sisters of Mercy—not to speak of the House of the Good Shepherds, which has one hundred and thirty inmates—are all, if I might use the expression, in a flourishing condition. The Good Shepherds have received a donation from the municipality of $5,000 a year. The orphan asylum of St. Joseph—an asylum for the Germans—also $5,000; and an appropriation by the same municipal authorities of $50,000 toward the erection of a new building to aid us in carrying on the work of charity, which, in proportion as our Catholic men fall in battle, becomes more and more necessary for the protection of their orphan children. In other respects, very little has been added in the way of church-building and the like since my return; but all my people and my clergy are still, I may say, perfectly united and willing to coöperate with me in any good work which I may undertake or recommend.

The new cathedral is in *statu quo*. Its average elevation above the surface of the ground is about fourteen feet. My contractors quarrelled more than a year ago between themselves, went to law, one against the other, and have been attempting to drag me into their controversy, which I have so far carefully avoided. Measures, however, have been taken to leave me free to go on with the work next spring, and I hope that during the year 1863 we shall be able to expend another hundred thousand dollars on its construction.

Two things I beg of you to do for me: One is, that you will have the goodness to have this letter translated into Italian, for the perusal of his eminence Cardinal Barnabo, and with the understanding also that it shall be deposited in the archives of the Propaganda, with other papers that have been forwarded by me in connection with the diocese and the province over which I am placed; this, together with the homage of my profound respect for his Eminence, and my eternal fidelity to the holy see of Peter. The other is, that you would read it to or leave it for reading with the very reverend Dr. McCloskey, rector of the American College. I intend to write to him on other topics, but it need not be necessary that I should repeat what I have said in this letter to you.

When in Rome I subscribed, but did not pay for the lottery of precious articles forwarded to aid the Pope. My subscription was the sum of $500. I received tickets to a very large amount; but, as the laws of this State attach a penalty to the offering or selling of any ticket in a lottery, I have not been able to dispose of those that were placed in my hands over and above the offer made by the Bishop of Albany that he will take $50 worth, which will make in all $550. But at present the rate of exchange is so enormous, that I must throw myself on the patience of those who have the management of the lottery; for it would cost me in exchange $250 more to have the original $500 forwarded. However, the money is set apart, and can be relied on. If this exchange were to accrue to the benefit of the lottery, I should not hesitate a moment; but if I sent it now, it would accrue to brokers and exchange dealers, and be a loss to me without being a benefit to the object of the charity. For the same reason and delay the $1,000 of my own which I intended to send even before Christmas in aid of the American College, and for the exchange, as it now runs, I would have to pay $420, or the rector of the college would have to find $420 less than $1,000. He too must give me time till our monetary affairs shall be in a better condition for remittance, from this side at least.

There was some difficulty in arranging the preliminaries for the establishment of the seminary at Troy. At one time the archbishop was on the point of selling the property, and founding a new institution at Fordham, about half a mile from the old St. Joseph's. He went so far as to request a gentleman to negotiate in his own name for the purchase of a certain piece of land which seemed to be especially well suited to his purpose; but before long the difficulties connected with the Troy scheme were overcome. This was Archbishop Hughes's last work.

His health had broken down during the last few months with astonishing rapidity. Very often for days together he did not leave his room. He spent a great deal of time lying on his couch, wrapped in great quantities of clothing: it was almost impossible for him to keep warm. Now and then, however, he rallied for a little while, and his friends flattered themselves that there was still a great deal of vitality in his frame. Very few understood how sick he really was until he took to his bed for the last time.

His household in Madison Avenue consisted of his sister Mrs. Rodrigue, with her husband and children. His secretary remained with the other clergy of the cathedral in Mulberry street. The archbishop's rooms comprised a chamber and study on the second floor. On the fourth floor was his library, extending the whole depth of the house. It contained some eight or ten thousand volumes, chiefly theological; though all departments of literature and science were represented in it. Many of the books were rare and valuable; but he never was a systematic collector of books, and consequently his library was defective in every branch. A part of it had belonged to Bishop Dubois. A few shelves in his study held the books to which he was most in the habit of referring.

His range of reading during the last few years of his life was more extensive than it used to be of old. He still spent a great deal of time over newspapers, but he also dipped into most of the current literature of the day. Numbers of books, of all sorts, were sent to him by authors and publishers, and he read them all.

His correspondence became more and more voluminous every day; but it is a mistake to suppose, as many have done, that he wrote for the mere pleasure of writing. In his apparently most trivial and needless letters, he generally had an ulterior object in view. He did nothing without a purpose.

The Metropolitan Record was established in January, 1859, as his official organ. For some time he exercised a direct influence over its columns, and contributed to it frequently. There was hardly any public affair of importance upon which he did not write for this paper. The course of the *Record*, however, in relation to the war, did not please him, and in March, 1863, he broke off his connection with it. He wrote little or nothing for newspapers after that.

For several years he was a diligent collector of paintings. His walls were covered with pictures, some of which were very good. During his stay in Rome in 1851, both the Pope and Cardinal Antonelli presented him with valuable works of art, and he also bought a great many during his travels.

He rose late in the morning—as he had long been accustomed to do. He had a private chapel in his house, where his chaplain, Father McNeirny, used often to celebrate mass. The archbishop himself, for many months before his death, was too weak to officiate. The last time he said mass was on Holy Thursday, the 2d of April, 1863—nine months before he died. He seldom ate a regular breakfast. He generally took a cup of coffee, and then, if he was well enough to go out, rode to Mulberry street, where he did all his writing, kept his papers, and attended to business. Very often he ate nothing until he went home again at five or six o'clock in the afternoon. Toward the close of his life he was sometimes seized with a morbid craving for particular dishes; but as a rule he did not care for his meals, and disliked to be consulted about them.

He seemed to have no domestic tastes; for although he was much attached to Mrs. Rodrigue and her family, he never sat with them in the evenings, and rarely alluded at home to his public actions. He spent the evening in his study, reading; and when there was any thing on his mind, he sometimes paced the floor all night. There was a billiard-table in the house, at which he used to play imaginary games without an adversary—an attendant meanwhile carefully keeping count. At one period he conceived a deep interest in the study of geography, and used to sit for hours poring over the globes. If visitors interrupted him at this pursuit, he was apt to take it for granted that they cared as much for the science as he did, and to discourse to them about it at great length. For awhile he had a similar passion for astronomy. On fine evenings he used to have his globes carried to the roof of his stable, which adjoined the house, and he would sit there for a long time studying the heavens. "I wish," said he one day to the Rev. Mr. Preston, "that you would buy me a set of the principal Greek and Latin classics. I must revive my acquaintance with them." He obtained the books, but read very little in them. As he grew old, the habit of devoting himself to a pursuit with avidity for a short time, and then dropping it to take up something else, increased upon him. His want of mental discipline became more than ever apparent when age and sickness prevented him from taking that active part in affairs to which he had been accustomed, and striking out from the rich ore of his brain, in the heat of conflict and discussion, the golden thoughts by which, far more than by the learning culled from books, he had built up his great reputation.

After his removal from Mulberry street to Madison Avenue, he made a slight effort to mingle more in general society than he had formerly done. Perhaps as often as once in three or four months, for five years, he entertained small parties of priests and laymen at dinner. But after his last voyage to Europe, he received no formal company. His exertions during that journey, in behalf of his adopted and dearly-loved country, were the final rally of his declining strength. As soon as the excitement of travel had passed away, he sank into a kind of mental and bodily languor, and never arose from it.

A mournful exhibition of his physical weakness was given at a meeting for the relief of the starving poor of Ireland, held under the auspices of the Knights of St. Patrick, in the New York Academy of Music, in April, 1863. He delivered a short address on that occasion. He seemed very feeble, and after he had been speaking for a few moments his voice became so weak that even persons near him on the stage could hardly hear him. He was very much affected at the thought of the misery of his countrymen. When he said, "It is but too well known that many of the Irish people are suffering for want of food and raiment"—his voice was choked with tears, and it appeared as if he would break down entirely. "I cannot bear it," he exclaimed; "we cannot think of it patiently; it is too bad!"

His last sermon was delivered in June, 1863, at the dedication of St. Theresa's Church, when he took occasion to impress upon his hearers the duty of all good Christians to labor and pray for the welfare of their country. He alluded to the peace-movement. "We must pray," he observed—"I do not say for peace, which appears at this moment ridiculous, since there is only one side can give peace, and the others won't have it. We may pray the Almighty to bring matters to a conclusion. One side can make war, but it requires two to make peace."

On the death of Archbishop Kenrick, he wrote as follows to the vicar-general of Baltimore:

TO THE VERY REV. HENRY B. COSKERY.

NEW YORK, *July 9*, 1863.

VERY REV. AND DEAR SIR:

I have received your letter of the 8th instant, confirming the sad intelligence communicated by a telegram from Father Foley. I have been suffering from exceeding weakness in my lower extremities, and for the last three days, *nolens volens*, I had to be present at distribution of honors in three of our highest literary institutions. On my return yesterday evening from the last of them, I was stunned with Mr. Foley's telegram. My mind became as much affected as the body was afflicted by physical debility. I gave up the hope of being able to go to Baltimore, for the obsequies of your late learned and saintly archbishop. Since then, I have made up my mind to go to Baltimore for the sad occasion, even if I should not be able to be present at the obsequies.

I shall be accompanied by Father McNeirny and John Regan; and as my state of health requires some kind attention on their part, I would prefer to take rooms in one of the hotels, rather than inconvenience any private family. Good Mrs. Spalding and Mrs. Gannendia have invited me, and I appreciate as ever their kindness But really I hardly feel that I should attempt to be a guest in a private family in my present state of health. Will you have the kindness to make known this feeling, lest there should be some misapprehension or some misunderstanding connected with it?

He went to Baltimore, and on the morning of the funeral attempted to say a low mass for the soul of the deceased prelate, at one of the side altars in the cathedral. But he had overrated his strength, and was on the point of falling, when some one ran to him with a chair. His attendants assisted him to disrobe, and he was led out of the church. Several times, during the last months of his life, he was obliged to leave the altar while endeavoring to say mass.

A day or two after his return from Baltimore the draft riots broke out in New York, when the rabble attempted to prevent the enforcement of the so-called conscription law, and for several days the city was given over to murder, robbery, and nameless outrages. There was little or no military force available at first. The Governor of the State called upon the archbishop to endeavor to restrain the rioters, most of whom were said to be Irishmen. "Will you exert your powerful influence," writes the Governor, July 14th, "to stop the disorders now reigning in this city? I do not wish to ask any thing inconsistent with your sacred duties; but if you can with propriety aid the civil authorities at this crisis, I hope you will do so."

In compliance with this request, the archbishop caused a notice to be posted about the city inviting the "rioters" to meet him at his residence:

"I am not able," he says, "owing to rheumatism in my limbs, to visit you, but that is no reason why you should not pay me a visit in your whole strength. I shall have a speech prepared for you. There is abundant space for the meeting around my house. I can address you from the corner of the balcony. If I should be unable to stand during its delivery, you will permit me to address you sitting; my voice is much stronger than my limbs."

Some three or four thousand persons assembled around his house at the appointed hour; but they were apparently decent, well-disposed working-men, not at all resembling the savage mob which had been burning, and pillaging, and killing for the previous three or four days. As soon as the archbishop appeared upon the balcony, accompanied by his vicar-general and one or two other clergymen, he was received with loud cheers. He sat down, and the people uncovered their heads, but at his request they put on their hats again.

The speech, which exhibited here and there some sparks of his old brilliancy and pointedness, was a long and rambling one, and indicated but too plainly that the disease which had destroyed his physical strength, had also weakened his mind, and that the archbishop's speaking days were over. When he had finished he retired, greatly exhausted; but he was compelled to return twice, in obedience to the calls of the multitude. He gave them his benediction, most of the men standing with uncovered heads, and crossing themselves as he pronounced it. Once more he exhorted them to repair peacefully to their homes, and with a lusty "We will," the assemblage broke up. This was the archbishop's last appearance in public.

It can hardly be supposed that the address had much effect in quelling the riot; for the rioters to whom it was addressed did not come to hear it. The disorders were suppressed very soon afterward by the military.

TO DR. McCLOSKEY, RECTOR OF THE AMERICAN COLLEGE, ROME.

NEW YORK, *July 22, 1863.*

. . .

For the last week this city has been under the violence of a mob, in which it is understood that nearly two hundred soldiers and civilians have been killed, besides a vast number wounded. I invited the rioters to meet me on Friday at my house in Madison Avenue, which they did to the number of six or seven thousand. It was understood that no police or military should interfere with their coming, or going home again. I harangued them for the better part of an hour, using all my powers of advice and persuasion to desist from violence. I amused them with anecdotes interspersed in my observations, to put them in good humor and make them laugh a little. They cheered me all the time, and went home in the most peaceable manner. Many of those who were Catholics lingered around to get my benediction; after which had been given, they soon dispersed. There has been no trouble since in the city; but still there is a very uneasy feeling among the citizens.

He travelled for a few weeks in August and September, "in search of health," he writes to the Archbishop of New Orleans, "which I have not found." The autumn he passed in a state of almost entire prostration. He attended to very little business, wrote very little, and hardly ever left the house. Early in December, or toward the middle of that month, he took to his bed. It was soon evident to the physicians that he was near his end, though neither the archbishop himself nor his immediate friends realized his position. He did not suffer severely, except occasionally; but he was very weak. A few days before Christmas the doctors informed some of the servants in the house that the archbishop could not recover. The sad intelligence was not communicated to his sisters and the clergy until Tuesday, the 29th. Mrs. Rodrigue and Sister Angela were first told. They sent word at once to the very Rev. Mr. Starrs, vicar-general of the diocese. He hastened to the house, accompanied by the Rev. Mr. McNeirny. When they had informed him of the opinion of the physicians, he looked intently from one to the other, and asked: "Did they say so?" Those were his last words, except his final confession, and an occasional faint intimation of some want that he could not express by signs. Although evidently surprised at his danger, he showed no trepidation, but prepared himself for death with perfect calmness and resignation. His old friend Father McElroy came to see him the same or the following day, and spoke to him again of his approaching end. On Wednesday he received the last sacraments from his confessor, the Rev. William Quinn. From that time no one spoke to him about worldly affairs. It was clear that he wished to keep his mind wholly fixed on God. If any one questioned him, he answered by signs. He gave tokens of recognition to many of the clergy who visited him, but did not speak to them. Sometimes it could not be determined whether he was conscious or not. From Friday (New Year's day) he had frequent spasms, followed by intervals of unconsciousness. On Sunday morning, January 3d, 1864, Father McElroy said mass in his room. In the forenoon his attendants succeeded in making him swallow a little nourishment, and it was then supposed that he might last two days longer. But about one o'clock he desired to be moved to another bed—thinking, as sick people are so apt to think, that he should rest more comfortably for the change. While he was being moved, a spasm came on. He did not recover consciousness after this. About seven o'clock in the evening he had another attack. When it was over, he laid his head back on the pillow, closed his eyes, breathed quickly and gently for a few minutes, and died with a smile about his lips, while Bishop McCloskey was reciting the prayers of the Church for a departing soul. His two sisters, Bishop Loughlin of Brooklyn, Father Starrs, Father McNeirny, and several other clergymen were present at the last moment. The causes of his death were general debility and Bright's Disease of the Kidneys.

At four o'clock in the morning of Tuesday, the 5th, the body was removed from Madison Avenue to the cathedral, followed by a number of the clergy, the trustees of the cathedral, and the managers of the orphan asylum. It was placed on a catafalque constructed in the middle aisle, near the sanctuary. The church was elaborately draped in black. The corpse was clothed in full episcopal vestments, the mitre on its head, and the crozier by its side. It lay in state for two days, during which it is estimated that no fewer than two hundred thousand persons went to visit it. The spot on which the coffin was placed was almost precisely that upon which the illustrious prelate had knelt, just twenty-six years before, to receive the episcopal consecration—for the cathedral had been enlarged since, and what was the sanctuary in 1838, is now part of the body of the church. The funeral took place on Thursday, January 7th, the anniversary of his consecration. It was perhaps the most imposing ceremony of the kind ever witnessed in New York. Eight bishops and nearly two hundred priests took part in the services. The neighboring streets were thronged with an excited crowd of people unable to get admission to the church. The funeral discourse was pronounced by Bishop McCloskey, and mass was celebrated by Bishop Timon. The body was deposited in the vault under the cathedral, by the side of the previous Bishops of New York. The courts and other public offices were closed on the day of the funeral, and resolutions of sorrow and condolence were passed by the State Legislature and the Common Council.

Archbishop Hughes was neither the most learned theologian, the best scholar, the most eloquent preacher, nor the most active missionary among the bishops of this country; but there was none of his episcopal brethren that possessed his influence, and none whose general reputation stood so high with the public at large. Foreigners were sometimes puzzled to account for the preëminence which was granted him, as if by common consent. But, in the first place, no bishop combined so many of the elements of greatness as he did. In the second, he possessed in a remarkable degree the faculty of impressing everybody that saw him with a sense of his intellectual superiority. It was an almost universal belief that there was more power within him than circumstances had ever called forth. Another element of success which entered largely into his character was an unbounded confidence in his own powers. It was not a vain confidence. It sprang from a consciousness of the purity of his intentions and the justice of his cause. He never fought for private ends or party purposes. He was an ambitious man, it is true, but he was above scheming for his own aggrandizement, and in his battles he had no end in view but the good of the Church or the advantage of his flock. No thought of possible benefit to himself, or his relatives, or his friends, ever influenced his conduct. Confident that he was doing the right thing from the right motives, he went boldly ahead, and never considered the possibility of failure.

In addition to all this, he excelled in those qualities of courage and promptness which are so especially valuable to a public man in America. His indomitable pluck gained him a vast deal of popular respect. We cannot help admiring a man who never falters before an antagonist, and never hesitates when he has once started on a course of action. It cost him little trouble to distinguish right from wrong. He decided with quickness, and neither hesitated in his decision nor feared to carry it out to its proper consequences, though every man's hand should be against him. Archbishop Bedini once asked an American priest how it happened that Dr. Hughes enjoyed so much higher popular consideration than any other prelate in the United States. "I think," was the reply, "that it is because he is always *game*."

Lastly, there was never even a suspicion against the purity of his personal character. However much his conduct may have been at times misrepresented, and his efforts for the mental and moral improvement of his people attributed to political trickery, no man questioned the spotless morality of his private life.

"We have this to say in conclusion," remarks Archbishop McCloskey in his funeral discourse, "that if ever there was a man who, in the whole history and character of his life, impressed upon us the sense and the conviction that he had been raised up by God, was chosen as His instrument to do an appointed work, and was strengthened by His grace and supported by His wisdom for the accomplishment of the work for which he had been chosen and appointed, that man was Archbishop Hughes. He was, from the beginning until the end, clearly and plainly an instrument in the hands of God."

APPENDIX.

WILL OF ARCHBISHOP HUGHES.

In the name of the Most Holy Trinity, I, John Hughes, Archbishop of New York, being of sound disposing mind and memory, but mindful of the uncertainty of human life, do hereby make, publish, and declare my last will and testament.

First—I direct my executors, hereinafter named, to pay all my just debts as soon as conveniently may be, after my decease.

Second—I hereby give and bequeath to my two brothers, Michael Hughes, of Chambersburg, in the State of Pennsylvania, and Patrick Hughes, now of Lafargeville, in the State of New York, and to their heirs and assigns forever, all that certain piece or parcel of land situate on lots forty-five and forty-six of Tenet Square, in the town of Orleans, in the county of Jefferson and State of New York, being the same premises conveyed by John Lafarge and wife to the Right Reverend Dr. Dubois, now deceased, late Bishop of New York, by indenture bearing date the 1st day of March, in the year of our Lord 1838, to have and to hold the said lands and premises, together with the tenements, hereditaments, and appurtenances thereunto belonging, to the said Michael and Patrick, their heirs and assigns, for their own use and behalf forever; subject, nevertheless, to certain mortgage on said land and premises, and upon the condition that the said Michael and Patrick shall assume, satisfy, and discharge the said mortgage; but it is my will that in case the said mortgage should be foreclosed, and upon the sale of said lands and premises on such foreclosure, the proceeds thereof should not be sufficient to pay the amount due on said mortgage, together with the expenses thereon, that such deficiency shall be paid and satisfied out of my estate, and shall not be a personal charge against the said Michael and Patrick.

Third—All the rest, residue, and remainder of my estate, real and personal, of whatsoever kind, and wheresoever situated, I give, devise, and bequeath unto the Right Rev. John McCloskey, Bishop of Albany; the Right Rev. Francis Patrick Kenrick, Bishop of Philadelphia; and the Right Rev. John Fitzpatrick, Bishop of Boston, to have and to hold the same to them, their heirs, executors, administrators and assigns forever, as joint tenants, and not as tenants in common.

Fourth—I appoint the said Right Rev. John McCloskey, the Right Rev. Francis Patrick Kenrick, and the Right Rev. John Fitzpatrick, executors of this my last will, and I revoke all other wills heretofore by me at any time made.

In witness whereof, I have hereunto set my hand, this 13th day of November, 1850.

JOHN HUGHES.

Subscribed and acknowledged by the testator in our presence, and at the time of such acknowledgment and subscription declared by him to be his last will and testament; whereupon we, at his request, and in his presence, and in presence of each other, have hereunto subscribed our names as witnesses.

J. R. BAYLEY, 263 Mulberry Street.
J. MCMAHON, 263 Mulberry Street.
T. JAMES GLOVER, No. 3 Varick Place.

CODICIL TO THE WILL.

I, John Hughes, Archbishop of New York, do make this codicil, to be taken as part of my last will and testament, that is to say:—

Whereas, since the making of my said last will, I have become seized of, and entitled to, certain real estate situated in the State of New Jersey; and whereas, doubts have been expressed whether the said real estate would pass and be disposed of by said last will; now, therefore, I do hereby give and devise all my real estate, wheresoever situate and of whatsoever kind, whether in possession, reversion, remainder, or otherwise, and whether acquired before or since the making of my said last will, and also all such real estate wheresoever situate, and of whatsoever kind, and whether in possession, reversion, remainder, or otherwise, that I may hereafter in any manner acquire, unto the Right Rev. John McCloskey, Bishop of Albany; the Right Rev. Francis Patrick Kenrick, late Bishop of Philadelphia, and now Archbishop of Baltimore; and the Right Rev. John Fitzpatrick, Bishop of Boston, to have and to hold the same to them, their heirs and assigns for ever, as joint tenants, and not as tenants in common. I hereby ratify and confirm all and singular the matters and things in my said last will contained.

In witness whereof, I have hereunto set my hand and seal, this 23d day of December, in the year of our Lord 1851.

JOHN HUGHES.

Signed, sealed, published, and declared by the said John Hughes, the testator, as and for a codicil to be annexed to his last will and testament in the presence of us, who, in his sight and presence, and at his request, and in the presence of each other, have subscribed our names as witnesses hereto.

J. R. BAYLEY, 263 Mulberry Street.
EDWARD W. TIERS, 23 Clinton Place.
T. JAMES GLOVER, 47 Clinton Place.

INDEX.

A.

Accounts, Bishop Hughes without any idea of, 335.
Adams Centinel, early poetry of John Hughes published in, 39.
Address from Irish Nationalists, 482.
Advice, religious, letters of, 320, 321.
Advice to government on the conduct of the war, 440.
Albany, the Rt. Rev. John McCloskey appointed bishop of, 286.
American college in Rome, foundation of the, 400.
American people and Catholicism, 350.
"An Answer to Nine Objections," 49.
Ancestry of Archbishop Hughes, 9.
"Andrew Dunn," notice of and extracts from, 77–84.
Anecdote of John Hughes's college life, 34; of a journey of Mr. Hughes with Bishop Kenrick, 111; showing why Father Hughes was not appointed bishop of Cincinnati, 147; showing his excessive confidence in the effect of logic, 158; told by Thurlow Weed of Bishop Hughes, 269; of a Maryland priest, 488.
Annaloghan, the birthplace of John Hughes, 14.
Antwerp, Bishop Hughes at, 270.
Appearance, personal, of Bishop Hughes, 327, 430.
Archbishop, Bishop Hughes appointed, 337.
Archbishoprics, the erection of three new, recommended, 337.
Assassination, Bishop Hughes threatened with, 279.
Astor House, banquet given in honor of Archbishop Hughes at, 341.
Astronomy, Archbishop Hughes's taste for, 496.
Atlantic telegraph, Archbishop Hughes on the, 405; celebration, 407.
Auchnacloy, John Hughes transferred to a grammar-school at, 15.
Augher, John Hughes attends school at, 15.
"Auxiliary Church Building Association," 352.

B.

Baltimore and New York, alleged rivalship between the sees of, 395.
Baltimore, John Hughes lands at and works there as a gardener, 20; unpopularity of Archbishop Hughes in, 488.
Basileopolis, Father Hughes appointed bishop of, *in partibus infidelium*, 184.
Baxter, Rev. Mr., death of, 75.
Bayley, Rev. Mr., conversation of Bishop Hughes with, 305.
Bedell, Dr. Gregory T., controversy with, 73.
Bedford, Pa., Father Hughes at, 50.
Bedini, Monsignore, arrival of, in the United States, 356; secret departure of, through fear of a mob, 361.
"Belligerents," remarks on, 453.
Bennett, James Gordon, private character of, assailed by Bishop Hughes, 279.
Bible as a school-book, remarks of Father Hughes on, 177.
Bible in the public schools question, 280.
Biddle, Mr. Clement C., an intimate friend of Bishop Hughes, 329; letter of, of March 11, 1852, 346.

Billiard-table, Archbishop Hughes's, 496.
Biographical sketches of—
  Bruté, Bp. Simon William Gabriel, 29.
  Cooper, Mr. Samuel, 22.
  Dubois, Bishop, 26.
  Gallitzin, Madame Elizabeth, 253.
  Gallitzin, Prince Demetrius Augustine, 110.
  Kenrick, Rev. F. P., 100.
Birth of John Hughes, 14.
Birthplace, visit of Bishop Hughes to his, 284.
Bonaparte, Joseph, a "Flagellation of Christ" presented by, 128.
Breckinridge, Rev. John, first controversy with, 134; oral discussion with, 153; letter of, of Jan. 21, 1835, 155.
Bright, Mr., proposed letter to, 401.
Brooks, Hon. Erastus, controversy with, 374.
Brownson, Dr., opinions of, controverted by Archbishop Hughes, 383; opinions of on emancipation reviewed, 437.
Bruté, Bp. Simon William Gabriel, biographical sketch of, 29; early letter of John Hughes to, 35; intimate relations of Mr. Hughes with, 72; letters of, to Mr. Hughes, of Sept. 18 and Oct. 8, 1827, 73; of March 12, 1828, 83; of Feb. 1, 1829, 86; of March 12, 1832, 128; letter of, to Bishop Kenrick, of March 31, 1833, 142; death of, 202.
Buchanan, Mr., on the proposal to send Bishop Hughes to Mexico, 286.
Buffalo, difficulties with the trustees of St. Louis' Church at, 261-263; Rev. John Timon appointed Bishop of, 286.

C.

Calls, number of, upon Bishop Hughes's time, 318.
Candidates for the legislature pledged against change in the school-system, 244.
Canonization of the Japanese Martyrs, 473, 477, 478.
Cardinal, project for making Archbishop Hughes, 340, 486.
Carey, Matthew, a special associate of Father Hughes, 329.
Carroll Hall, enthusiastic meeting of Catholics at, 245.

Cass, General, reply to a speech of, 363.
Cathedral, New York, trouble with the trustees of, 192-196. (See St. Patk's).
Catholic Annual, proposal to publish, 163.
Catholic Church in New York, property of, 375; remarks on the condition of, 389.
Catholic Emancipation, sermon of Mr. Hughes on 91.
Catholicism and the American people, 350.
Catholic Press, essay on the, 382.
Catholics, disabilities of the Irish, 17; efforts of, to obtain a portion of the New York school fund, 227; services of, in the Revolutionary War, 346; native and foreign, 351; Northern and Southern, 438.
Catholic University in Ireland, project to establish, 341.
"Catholic vote" solicited by Cassius M. Clay for the Republicans, 378.
Chambersburg, Pa., Patrick Hughes settles at, 19; John Hughes at, 20.
Chaplains, request of President Lincoln for, 445.
Charleston, Archbishop Hughes at, 421.
Children, fondness of Bishop Hughes for, 335.
Church Debt Association of New York, 254.
Church, early predilection of John Hughes for the, 15.
Churches destroyed by a "Native American" mob in Philadelphia, 275; protected in New York by armed men, 276.
Church in New York, remarks on the condition of the, 889.
Church-property bill, 374.
Cincinnati, Father Hughes nominated for the bishopric of, 146.
Circular of Bishop Hughes to the Sisters of Charity, 300.
City Inspector and Archbishop Hughes, 429.
Clay, Cassius M., on political alliances, 378.
Clay, Henry, and Bishop Hughes, 288.
Clergy, Bishop Hughes's government of his, 324.
Coadjutor, Archbishop Hughes applies for a, 400.
Coat of arms of the Hugheses, 11.

Collection for the Pope, 428.
College, American, foundation of in Rome, 400.
College at Nyack destroyed by fire, 186.
College established by Bishop Hughes at Fordham, 203.
College life of John Hughes, 33; anecdote of, 34.
Colony, Irish, in Nebraska, project of, condemned, 393.
Common Council of New York, debate before, in relation to the school fund, 234–238.
Congress, sermon preached before, 316.
"Connaught men," societies of denounced, 258.
Consecration of Bishop Kenrick, 100.
Consecration of Father Hughes as coadjutor to the Bishop of New York, 184; Archbishop McCloskey's recollections of the, 185.
Consecration of the Bishops of Charleston and Hartford, 394.
Controversy, John Hughes's first published, 84; with Dr. Delancey, 93; with "Fergus McAlpin," 108; with Breckinridge, 134; preliminaries of, 137; second with Breckinridge, 153–160; with David Hale, 260; with "Kirwan," 317; with Gen. Cass, 363; with Senator Brooks, 374; with *The Ca'holic Mirror*, 487.
Conversation with the Emperor and Empress of the French, 465.
Conwell, Bishop, journey of John Hughes with, 48; departs for Rome, 69; returns to America, 71, 94; recommends Mr. Hughes to the Holy See for the bishopric of Philadelphia, 94.
Cooper, Mr. Samuel, biographical sketch of, 22.
Cork, dinner given to Archbishop Hughes by the citizens of, 485.
"Corkonians," societies of denounced, 258.
Council, first provincial of New York, 366; decrees of, 367.
Council of Baltimore, the fifth, 266; the sixth, 286; erection of three archbishoprics recommended by the seventh, 337.
"Cranmer," letters to *The Protestant* over the signature of, 105.

D.

Daily life of Archbishop Hughes, 332, 496.
Dayton, Mr., Archbishop Hughes's reception by, 456.
Death of Archbishop Hughes, 502.
Debate before the New York Common Council in relation to the school fund, 234–238.
Debts of the New York churches, plan for paying off, 267.
Decline of Protestantism, lecture on the, 338.
Definition of the dogma of the Immaculate Conception, 370.
Delancey, Rev. Dr. W. H., controversy with, 93.
Deluol, Very Rev., letters of to Bishop Hughes, of June 17, 1846, 292; of June 26, 1846, 297.
De Smet, Father, accompanies Bishop Hughes on his second voyage to Europe, 268.
Dignity of manner of Bishop Hughes, 327.
Diocese of New York, Bishop Hughes appointed administrator of, in place of Bishop Dubois, 199; condition of, 186; letter to the Leopoldine Society relating the history and wants of, 212; division of, 286.
Disabilities of the Irish Catholics, 17.
Distress, Bishop Hughes easily moved by a tale of, 335.
Drafting, remarks on, 487.
Draft riots in New York, 499.
Dublin *Freeman's Journal*, letter to, of Dec. 11, 1861, 17.
Dublin, letters from, 218–222; reception of Archbishop Hughes in, in 1862, 481.
Dublin Rotundo, remarks at a meeting in the, 481.
Dubois, Rt. Rev. John, biographical sketch of, 26; Mr. Hughes chosen coadjutor to, 178; letter of, to Mr. Hughes, of Nov. 6, 1837, 179; struck with paralysis, 187; faculties of, become impaired, 198; letter of Bishop Hughes respecting the condition of, 199; Bishop Hughes appointed administrator in his place, 199; resignation of, 205.
D——, Col., account of the conversion of, 201.

E.

Education, ecclesiastical, letter on, 402.
Education of John Hughes, 15, 25.
Egan, Rev. Mr., death of, 90.
Emancipation, Catholic, 91.
Emancipation, negro, 216; Archbishop Hughes's views on, 435; his review of Dr. Brownson on, 487.
Emigration of Patrick Hughes, 18.
Emmitsburg, Md., John Hughes goes to, in quest of work, 21.
Emperor and Empress of the French, conversation of Archbishop Hughes with, 465.
Emprunt Catholique de New York, 270.
Enactments of a synod convoked by Bishop Hughes, 257-260.
England, Bishop, letters of, to Mr. Hughes, of Jan. 24, 1837, 170; of Dec. 21, 1837, 183.
"Equitas," attack of, upon Archbishop Hughes, in the *Times*, 386.
Essay on the Catholic Press, 382.
Étienne, Mother, letter of, to Bishop Hughes, of Aug. 8, 1846, 298.
Europe, voyages of Bishop Hughes to, 206, 268, 281, 337, 370, 448; his remarks on the state of society in, 283; his special mission to, 448; sermon after his return from, 487.

F.

Family of Patrick Hughes, 13.
Famine in Ireland of 1847, 303; Bishop Hughes on the causes of, 304.
"Far-downs" and "Far-ups," societies of, denounced by Bishop Hughes, 258.
Favor Royal, early lessons in gardening at, 16.
"Fergus McAlpin," controversy with, 108.
Fillmore, President, Archbishop Hughes dines with, 337.
Fire in the woods near Mount St. Mary's College, 37.
Fishing, Archbishop Hughes's, on the St. Lawrence, 413.
"Flagellation of Christ" presented by Joseph Bonaparte, 128.
Fondness of Bishop Hughes for children, 335.
Forbes, Dr., apostasy of, 424.
Fordham, a new college established, at, 203.
Frenaye, Mr. M. A., important aid rendered by, in the foundation of St. John's Church, Philadelphia, 116.
Friends, intimate, of Bishop Hughes, 329.
Funeral of Archbishop Hughes, 502.

G.

Gallitzin, Madame Elizabeth, biographical sketch of, 253.
Gallitzin, Prince Demetrius Augustine, biographical sketch of, 110.
Gardening, lessons of John Hughes in, 16.
Geography, Archbishop Hughes's taste for, 496.
Gettysburg *Adams Centinel*, early poetry published in, 39.
Girard, Stephen, sharp remarks on the will of, 126.
Government of his clergy, Bishop Hughes's, 324.

H.

Hale, David, controversy with, 360.
Hargous, Mr. Peter A., an intimate friend, 329.
Harley, Rev. John, accompanies Bishop Hughes on his third voyage to Europe, 281.
Harold, Rev. William Vincent, called to St. Mary's Church, Philadelphia, 52.
Harvey, Mr. Jacob, an intimate friend, 329.
Havana, Archbishop Hughes sails for, 361; letter from, 361.
Health, way of life unfavorable to, 331; decline of, 381, 400, 494, 501.
History of the United States, Catholic chapter in the, 344.
Hogan, Mr., connection of, with St. Mary's Church, Philadelphia, 51; turns Protestant and marries, 53.
Holy Father, letter on the reëstablishment of, at Rome, 312; collection taken up for, 313; Bishop Hughes on the temporal power of, 315; pastoral letter in relation to, 418; mass meeting proposed to express sympathy with, 420, 426; money sent to, 428; Archbishop Hughes on the situation of, 339; confers the pallium on Archbishop Hughes, 341.
House of Bishop Hughes attacked by a mob, 250.

Houses, purchase of for Archbishop Hughes, 382.
Hugheses, origin and coat of arms of the, 11.
Hughes, Patrick, father of John, notice of, 13; emigration of, 18; settles at Chambersburg, 19; removes to Youngstown, 20; death of, 21, 173.
Hurley, Rev. Michael, letter of, to John Hughes, of Nov. 1825, 46; death of, 175.

I.

Immaculate Conception, definition of, as an article of faith, 370.
Income of Bishop Hughes, 336.
Institutions, republican, the Church not hostile to, 349.
Insurrection in Ireland, of 1848, 304; aid given to, by Bishop Hughes, 306; his mortification at the failure of, 307.
Interview with the Emperor and Empress of the French, 465.
Ireland, letters of Bishop Hughes from, 218–222; improved condition of the people in, 283; famine of 1847 in, 303; insurrection of 1848 in, 304; project to establish a Catholic University in, 341; speech at a meeting for the relief of, 497.
Irish Emigrant Society, lecture for the benefit of the, 271.
Irish population, great influence of Bishop Hughes over the, 246.

J

Jesuits brought to New York from Kentucky, 285.
Journal of Commerce, calumnies against the Catholic faith published in, 242.
Journey of John Hughes with Bishop Conwell, 48; with Bishop Kenrick, 110, 149.
"Jubilee of American Freedom," an early poem, 44.

K.

Keating, John, Mr. Biddle's reminiscences of, 347.
Kenrick, Rev. F. P., appointed Bishop of Philadelphia, 100; letters of, to Mr. Hughes, of April 21, 1830, 99; of Jan. 19, 1837, 168; project for translating to Pittsburg, 166; letter of, to Bishop Dubois, of Oct. 4, 1837, 179; appointed Archbishop of Baltimore, 101; death of, 101, 498.
"Kirwan Unmasked," 317.
"Know-Nothing" excitement, 365.
Kossuth, arrival of, in New York, 342; letter to the Chevalier Hulsemann about, 343.

L.

Ladies of the Sacred Heart, schools founded by, 252.
Lafargeville, foundation of a seminary at, 189; seminary at removed to Fordham, 252.
Lecture on the "Catholic Chapter" in American history, 344.
Lecture on the Decline of Protestantism, 338.
Lectures in New York, 271, 272; at Baltimore and Pittsburg, 381.
Lessons of John Hughes in gardening, 16.
Letter to Angela, Sister, of June 23, 1830, 103; of Aug. 24, 1830, 104; of Sept. 30, 1831, 120; of Dec. 15, 1831, 123; of Sept., 1832, 132; of Nov. 28, 1832, 132; Jan. 20, 1834, 147; of April 19, 1837, 173; of Dec. 3, 1845, 282; of Feb. 24, 1846, 285; of June 21, 1846, 296; of Jan. 23, 1854, 361; of May 10, 1862, 478. See Letter to Hughes, Ellen.
" Baltimore, Archbishop of, of May 9, 1861, 441.
" Barnabo, Cardinal, explaining his mission to France, 449.
" Bayley, Rev. J. R., of June 6, 1848, 317.
" Bruté, Mr., without date, 35; of Jan. 31, 1828, 64; of May 2, 1828, 66; of May 14, 1828, 68; of March 3, 1828, 83; of Oct. 21, 1828, 84; of Nov. 18, 1828, 85; of Feb. 21, 1832, 126; July 28, 1832, 130; of Dec. 14, 1832, 136; of March 8, 1833, 140; of April 5, 1833, 142; of June 10, 1834, 149; Aug. 14, 1834, 151.

Letter to Camerou, Secretary, of Oct., 1861, 437.
" Clay, Cassius M., of Feb. 6, 1856, 378.
" Clogher, Bishop of, on the origin of the Hugheses, 12.
" Connolly, Bishop, of Sept. 3, 1858, 408.
" Coskery, Rev. Henry B., of July 9, 1863, 498.
" Cullen, Archbishop, of Dec. 5, 1862, 483.
" C——, Miss., of Sept., 1859, 412.
" Deluol, Very Rev. Mr., of June, 1846, 290, 294; of July 7, 1846, 297; of midnight, 1846–'47, 301.
" De Smet, Rev., when about to sail for Europe, 267.
" Donaghoe, Rev. T. J., of Oct. 1, 1831, 122.
" Donnelly, Mr. Terence, of Oct. 29, 1855, 376.
" Dublin *Freeman's Journal*, of Dec. 11, 1861, 17.
" Dupanloup, Mgr., of April 13, 1860, 427.
" Emmet, Robert, of Nov., 1848, 308.
" Frenaye, Mr. M. A., of Jan. 3, 1838, 183; of Feb., 1838, 187; of March 18, 1838, 187; of March 22, 1838, 188; of May 3, 1838, 190; of March 20, 1839, 196; of April 22, 1839, 197; of Sept. 19, 1839, 204; of Nov. 16, 1839, 210; of June 1, 1840, 218; of May 17, 1841, 256; of Oct. 12, 1842, 266; of June 4, 1843, 268; of June 21, 1844, 280; of Feb. 13, 1857, 394; of May 18, 1858, 403.
" Friend in America, of July, 1843, 269.
" Friend in Rome, without date, 384, 386; of March 30, 1858, 388; in relation to his European mission, 489.
" Gentleman in Paris, of March 29, 1849, 312.
" Greeley, Horace, of Nov. 21, 1851, 342.
" Harper, Mayor, 274, 279.
" Heyden, Mr. Thomas, Sr., of Feb. 2, 1829, 86.

Letter to Heyden, Rev. Thomas, of May 19, 1827, 60; of July 3, 1827, 61; of July 22, 1827, 63; of Oct. 21, 1828, 69; of May 23, 1827, 75; of Sept. 24, 1827, 76; of May 25, 1837, 175.
" Hughes, Ellen, of Sept. 17, 1829, 94; of Nov. 11, 1829, 95; on the eve of departure for Europe, 281. See Letter to Angela, Sister.
" Hulsemann, Chevalier, of Dec. 11, 1851, 343.
" Kirby, Very Rev. Dr., of Aug. 10, 1854, 359; of March 27, 1860, 423.
" Leopoldine Society at Vienna, 212.
" Lynch, Bishop, of Aug., 1861, 488.
" McCloskey, Very Rev. Dr., of Dec. 4, 1861, 460; of July 22, 1863, 500.
" McNally, Bishop, of May 26, 1858, 396; of March 20, 1863, 484.
" Maguire, Mr., of Nov. 24, 1862, 483.
" Mullock, Bishop, of June 16, 1860, 429.
" Nuncio, Papal, of July 3, 1854, 364.
" O'Callaghan, Rev. J., of Dec. 1843, 271; of March 8, 1859, 411.
" O'Conor, Mr. Charles, of April 4, 1860, 426.
" O'Donovan, Dr. John, of April 10, 1860, 10.
" Pax, Rev. Mr., of Jan. 28, 1843, 261; of Feb. 23, 1843, 262.
" Purcell, Rev. Mr., of April 23, 1829, 90; of Dec. 21, 1829, 96; of March 24, 1830, 97; of June 3, 1830, 101; of Sept. 27, 1830, 108; of Jan. 12, 1831, 112; of May 24, 1831, 115; of Feb. 14, 1831, 118; of June 8, 1831, 119; of September, 1831, 120; of Feb. 21, 1832, 123; of Feb. 14, 1833, 139; of April 16, 1834, 148; of May 8, 1834, 149; of Feb. 6, 1835, 162; of Jan. 2, 1837, 171; of June 27, 1837, 176; of Nov. 23, 1837, 180

Letter to Rodrigue, Mr., of Nov. 20, 1861, 455.
" Rodrigue, Mrs., of Nov. 6, 1839, 206; of April 4 and 25 and May 9, 1862, 477; of June 25, 1862, 480.
" Rome, of April, 1858, 395.
" Rosalia, Sister, of Aug. 24, 1846, 299.
" Seward, Wm. H., of Oct. 10, 1861, 437; of June 18, 1861, 441; of July 21, 1861, 442; of Aug. 13 and Sept. 12, 1861, 443; of Oct. 12, 1861, 444; of Oct. 15, 1861, 445; of Nov. 13, 1861, 452; of Nov. 20, 1861, 453; of Nov. 28, 1861, 455; of Dec. 5, 1861, 458; of Dec. 1861, 462; of Dec. 12, 1861, 462; of Dec. 27, 1861, 463; of Jan. 3, 1862, 468; of Jan. 11, 1862, 469; of Feb. 1, 1862, 470; of Feb. 11, 1862, 472; of Feb. 21, 1862, 473; of March 1 and March 29, 1862, 474; of April 18, 1862, 476; of June 12, 1862, 479.
" Sisters of Charity, of Dec. 6, 1846, 300.
" Smith, Rev. Bernard, of March 30, 1858, 394; of Feb. 21, 1859, 402; of Aug. 12, 1858, 405; of Sept. 10, 1858, 407; of Feb., 1859, 410; of Sept. 24, 1859, 415; of Dec. 11, 1859, 416; of Jan. 20, 1860, 418; of Jan. 30, 1860, 419; of March 26, 1860, 422; of Sept. 9, 1860, 431; of Oct. 16, 1862, 490; of Dec. 15, 1862, 491.
" Southern bishop, of May 7, 1861, 438.
" Stone, Col. Wm. L., of May 27, 1844, 279.
" Stonestreet, Rev. Charles, of Sept. 3, 1859, 411.
" Unworthy priest, 324.
" Varela, Rev. Felix, from Rome, 211; from Dublin, of June 1, 1840, 420.
" Weed, Mr. Thurlow, of Oct. 29, 1861, 451; of Dec. 10, 1861, 461.
" ——, Miss, of Oct. 4, 1848, 321.
" ——, Mr., of May 15, 1848, 320.

Levins, Rev. Thomas C., his personal controversy with Mr. Hughes, 108.
Library of Bishop Hughes, always in disorder, 334; extent and character of, 495.
Lincoln, President, letter of, to Archbishop Hughes, 445.
Logic, Mr. Hughes's excessive confidence in the effect of, 158.
London, Bishop Hughes in, 215.
Louis Philippe, Bishop Hughes presented to, 210.
Lynch, Dr., consecrated Bishop of Charleston, 394.
Lynch, Rev. Mr., death of, 85.

M.

McCloskey, Rev. John, recommended as coadjutor to Bishop Hughes, 267; consecrated coadjutor, 272; appointed Bishop of Albany, 286.
McFarland, Dr., consecrated Bishop of Hartford, 394.
McGee, Thomas Darcy, sharp replies to his attacks on the Irish clergy, 310.
McKenna, Margaret, becomes wife of Patrick Hughes, 13.
Maclay's school bill passed, 250.
Madiai family, 364.
Manhattanville, house purchased for Archbishop Hughes at, 382.
Manner, Bishop Hughes's dignity of, 327.
Marriage, registry of, 429.
Martin, Rev. Mr., accompanies Archbishop Hughes to Havana, 361; letter of, to Sister Angela, 362.
Martyrs, Japanese, canonization of the, 473, 477, 478.
Mason and Slidell, capture of, 457-459.
Mason, Rev. Henry M., letters addressed to, on the Rule of Faith, 152.
Matrimony, synodical action in relation to, 257.
Mayne, Mr., death of, 162; Archbishop Hughes visits the grave of, 422.
Memorial Church, erection of, 397.
Memorial to the New York legislature in relation to public schools, 240.
Methodist university at Troy purchased, 492.
Metternich, Bishop Hughes introduced to, 215.
Mexico, Bishop Hughes declines a mission to, 286.

Mission to France and England, 448.
Mitchell, Jno. his abuse of Archbishop Hughes, 365.
Mob, house of Bishop Hughes attacked by a, 250.
Morris, Mayor, interview of Bishop Hughes with, 278.
Mother of Archbishop Hughes, 13; her amiable character, 14; death of, 21, 121.
Moylan, General, Mr. Biddle's reminiscences of, 347.
Mount St. Mary's College, John Hughes engaged to superintend the garden of, 23; admitted as a regular student at, 25; history of the foundation of, 27; new building for, destroyed by fire, 88; money collected for the rebuilding of, 39.
Mulberry Street, residence of Bishop Hughes in, 336.
Multitude of calls upon Bishop Hughes's time, 318.
Murray, Rev. Nicholas, author of the "Kirwan" letters, 317.

N.

Nancrede, Dr., letter on the death of, 394.
"Nationalists of Ireland," deputation of the, 482.
Native American movement, 273–281.
Nebraska, project of an Irish colony in, 392.
Newfoundland, visit to, 380.
"New school" Catholics, essay against, 383.
Newspaper poetry of John Hughes, 40.
New York and Baltimore, alleged rivalship between the sees of, 395.
New York, removal of Father Hughes to, as coadjutor of Bishop Dubois, 183; condition of the diocese in 1838, 186; trouble with the trustees of the cathedral at, 192–196; remarks of Archbishop Hughes on the condition of the Church in, 389.
Nunciature, permanent, at Washington, project of, 358; views of Archbishop Hughes on, 359.
Nuncio, Papal, arrival of, in the United States, 356; secret departure of, from New York, through fear of a mob, 361; mortification of Archbishop Hughes at the treatment of, 361, 391.
Nyack, college at, destroyed by fire, 186.

O.

Occupations, daily, of Bishop Hughes, 332, 496.
O'Connell, Daniel, Bishop Hughes's account of his interview with, 216–218.
O'Connor, Thomas, nominated by the Catholics for mayor of New York, 250.
"Ode to Death," selection from, 41.
O'Donovan, Dr. John, letter of Archbishop Hughes to, of April 10, 1860, 10.
Onderdonk, Bishop, Mr. Hughes's review of, on the Rule of Faith, 144.
Onondaga county, colony of converts in, 201.
Ordination of John Hughes as deacon, 46; as priest, 49.
Origin, humble, Bishop Hughes not ashamed of his, 328.

P.

Paintings, Archbishop Hughes a collector of, 496.
Parentage of Archbishop Hughes, 13.
Paris, Bishop Hughes at, 210, 455.
Pastoral Letters, of Sept. 8, 1842, 360; in relation to the position of the Holy Father, 418; reception of, in Italy, 421.
Pax, Rev. Mr., ill treated by the trustees of St. Louis' church, Buffalo, 262.
Peace-maker, Bishop Hughes as a, 323.
Periodicals, Catholic, Archb'p Hughes's opinions of, 382.
Personal appearance of Bishop Hughes, 327, 430.
Petitions of the New York Catholics for a share of the school fund, 228, 232.
Philadelphia, Father Hughes recalled to, by Bishop Conwell in 1827, 50, 55; Rev. F. P. Kenrick appointed bishop of, 100; Mr. Hughes nominated to succeed Bishop Kenrick at, 166; riot provoked in, by the "Native Americans," 275.
"Philo-Veritas" letters to the *Times*, 365.
Pittsburg, project for translating Bishop Kenrick to, 166.
Poetry, early, of John Hughes, 40.

Politics, Irish, familiarity of Bishop Hughes with, 304.
Preaching, characteristics of Bishop Hughes's, 325.
Press, Catholic, essay on the, 382.
Prison discipline, Bishop Hughes on, 330.
Promotion of Archbishop Hughes suggested to the Holy See, 448.
Propaganda, report of Archbishop Hughes to the, 387.
Protestanism, lecture on the decline of, 338.
Public Schools, reasons for the opposition of Catholics to, 230; question of the Bible in, 280.
Public School Society of New York, contest with, 223–251.
Purcell, Bishop, accompanies Bishop Hughes on his second voyage to Europe, 268.

R.

Red Republicans, condemnation of, by Bishop Hughes, 312.
Registry of marriages, 429.
Reminiscences, revolutionary, of Clement C. Biddle, 346.
Report of Archbishop Hughes to the Propaganda, 387; favorable impression produced by, 391; quotations from, 389–391.
Republican institutions, the Church not hostile to, 349.
Residence in Mulberry street, 336.
Resignation, Archbishop Hughes talks about, 398.
Revolutions, political, Abp. Hughes's views of, 345.
Riot provoked by the "Native Americans" in Philadelphia, 275.
River Head, Newfoundland, corner-stone laid at, 381.
Roman question, letters on the, 415–428.
Rome, Bishop Hughes at, 210, 211, 338, 370; his remarks on, 211; letter from, with regard to the Papal Nuncio, 357; foundation of the American college in, 400; reception of Archbishop Hughes in, in 1862, 473.
Rule of Faith, Father Hughes on the, 138, 144, 152.

"Rules for the administration of Churches without trustees," 264.

S.

St. Augustine, Florida, Archbishop Hughes at, 421.
St. Augustine's Church, Philadelphia, Father Hughes at, 49; destroyed by rioters, 275.
St. John's Church, Philadelphia, foundation of, 117; corner-stone of, laid by Bishop Kenrick, 118; dedication of, 129; Fourth of July celebration at, 130; financial difficulties of, 129, 164.
St. John's College at Fordham, foundation of, 203; opened, 252; names of the officers of, 252.
St. John's, Newfoundland, reception of Archbishop Hughes at, 380.
St. John's Orphan Asylum, Philadelphia, account of the origin of, 88.
St. Joseph's Church, Philadelphia, Father Hughes called to, by Bishop Conwell, 55; leaves it for St. John's, 129.
St. Joseph's Seminary established at Fordham, 252.
St. Louis' Church, Buffalo, difficulties with the trustees of, 261–263.
St. Mary's Church, Philadelphia, history of the troubles of, 50–71; decision of the Holy See respecting, 62; revival of the troubles of, 114.
St. Michael's Church, Philadelphia, destroyed by rioters, 275.
St. Patrick's Cathedral, preparations for the commencement of, 403; money collected for, by Archbishop Hughes, 406; laying of the corner-stone of, 407; erection of, suspended, 408.
St. Patrick's Day, how celebrated by Bishop Hughes, 331.
St. Peter's Church, settlement of the affairs of, 352.
St. Vincent of Paul's Seminary, opening of, 191.
School days of John Hughes, 15.
School fund, efforts of the Catholics to obtain a portion of the, 227.
School question, 223–251.
School reform, independent ticket in favor of, 245.
Schools without Christian instruction,

remarks of Archbishop Hughes on, 338.
Scorn, Bishop Hughes's power of expressing, 325.
Scott, Gen., his return to America, 461.
Secret societies, action of Bishop Hughes in relation to, 258.
Seminary at Lafargeville, foundation of, 189; removed to Fordham, 252.
Seminary at Troy, building and grounds purchased for, 492, 494.
Senate, New York, the school question in, 242.
Sermon preached before Congress, 316; giving an account of the definition of the dogma of the Immaculate Conception, 370; preached at the University of North Carolina, 430; of Archbishop Hughes after his return from, 487; his last, 498.
Sermons, begins to preach extempore, 119; the characteristics of Bishop Hughes's, 325; controversial, preached at Rome, 388.
Seward, William H., intimacy of Bishop Hughes with, 241; extract of a letter from, 248; urges the school question on the attention of the legislature, 249; a Friday dinner with, 485.
Shield for Ireland, 306.
Shiffler, George, shot in the "Native American riot" in Philadelphia, 275.
Sickness, last, of Archbishop Hughes, 487.
Sir Roger de Coverley's chaplain, 125.
Sisterhood of Charity, division of the, 289; correspondence with Mr. Deluol in relation to the, 290-301.
Sister of Gen. B——, visit of, to Archbishop Hughes, 445.
Sisters of Charity, house of, in Philadelphia, destroyed by rioters, 275.
Sisters of Mercy brought to New York, 285; Bishop Hughes requests that his contribution for a *shield* may be transferred to, 309.
Slavery question, sentiments of Archbishop Hughes on the, 42, 216, 434.
Slave trade, Archbishop Hughes on the, 436.
Society, Bishop Hughes in, 330, 497.
Society, Protestant, Father Hughes much in, 160.
Speech at Carroll Hall, 245.
Speech at Vauxhall Garden, 306.
Spencer, Hon. John C., change in the New York school system recommended by, 240; plan of, supported by Bishop Hughes, 244.
Storm at sea, 208.
Synod convoked by Bishop Hughes, 257; enactments of, 257-260.
Synod, diocesan, of Philadelphia, Mr. Hughes appointed promotor in the, 130.

T.

Tabernacle, curious scene at the, 392.
Tuileries, Archbishop Hughes at the, 465.
Temperance in Ireland, 221.
The Catholic Herald, establishment of, 138.
The Catholic Mirror, Abp. Hughes attacked by, 489.
"The Cuckoo Sermon," 48.
The Freeman's Journal controlled by Bishop Hughes, 275.
The Metropolitan Record, establishment of, 495.
The Nation, severely handled by Bishop Hughes, 310.
The New York Herald, Bishop Hughes violently attacked by, 247, 279.
The Protestant, letters to, over the signature of "Cranmer," 105.
"The Slave," an early poem, 42.
Timon, Rev. John, appointed bishop of Buffalo, 286; accompanies Archbishop Hughes to Rome, 370.
Toleration, religious, Abp. Hughes on, 342.
"To the Home of my Fathers," an early poem, 40.
Tract Society, attempt to establish in Philadelphia, 77.
Trent affair, 457-459.
Troy Seminary, building and grounds purchased for, 492, 494.
Trustees, Rules for the administration of Churches without, 264.
Trustee system, troubles arising from, in Philadelphia, 51; synodical action in relation to the, 259; end of, in New York, 355.

U.

Umilta, ancient convent of the, purchased by the Pope for the American College, 401.

University of North Carolina, Archbishop Hughes preaches at the, 450.

V.

Vauxhall Garden, Bishop Hughes's speech at, 306.
Vienna, Bishop Hughes at, 211, 215, 341.
Visitation, Bishop Hughes's, of his diocese, 265.
Voyages to Europe, 206, 268, 281, 337, 370; last, 448.

W.

Wales, early ancestors from, 11.
Walsh, Bishop, letter of, of April, 1848, 331; death of, 408; letter of Archbishop Hughes in relation to, 408.
War, suggestions on the conduct of the, 440.

Washington Hall, meeting of Catholics at, to sustain Bishop Hughes on the school question, 248.
Weed, Mr. Thurlow, intimacy of Bishop Hughes with, 241; accompanies Bishop Hughes on his second voyage to Europe, 268; his mission to England, 448.
Will of Archbishop Hughes, 506; codicil to, 507.
Will of Stephen Girard, sharp remarks of Mr. Hughes on, 126.

Y.

"Young Ireland" party, contempt of Bishop Hughes for, 304, 307; his strong language in reference to the journalists of, 311.
Youngstown, Pa., Patrick Hughes removes to, 20.

THE END.

www.ingramcontent.com/pod-product-compliance
Lightning Source LLC
Chambersburg PA
CBHW051157300426
44116CB00006B/347